The Dividends of Dissent

The Dividends of Dissent

*How Conflict and Culture Work in
Lesbian and Gay Marches on Washington*

AMIN GHAZIANI

THE UNIVERSITY OF CHICAGO PRESS   CHICAGO AND LONDON

AMIN GHAZIANI is a postdoctoral fellow in the Society of Fellows and lecturer in sociology at Princeton University.

The University of Chicago Press, Chicago 60637
The University of Chicago Press, Ltd., London
© 2008 by The University of Chicago
All rights reserved. Published 2008
Printed in the United States of America
17 16 15 14 13 12 11 10 09 08   1 2 3 4 5

ISBN-13: 978-0-226-28995-3 (cloth)
ISBN-13: 978-0-226-28996-0 (paper)
ISBN-10: 0-226-28995-8 (cloth)
ISBN-10: 0-226-28996-6 (paper)

Library of Congress Cataloging-in-Publication Data
Ghaziani, Amin.
   The dividends of dissent : how conflict and culture work in lesbian and gay marches on Washington / Amin Ghaziani.
      p. cm.
   Includes bibliographical references and index.
   ISBN-13: 978-0-226-28995-3 (cloth : alk. paper)
   ISBN-10: 0-226-28995-8 (cloth : alk. paper)
   ISBN-13: 978-0-226-28996-0 (pbk. : alk. paper)
   ISBN-10: 0-226-28996-6 (pbk. : alk. paper)
      1. Gay liberation movement—Washington (D.C.)—History. 2. Civil rights demonstra-
tions—Washington (D.C.)—History. 3. Gays—United States—Washington (D.C.)—Political
activity. I. Title.
   HQ76.8.U5G53 2008
   306.76'60975309045—dc22

                                                        2007045305

TO MAHEMAHEL, FOR THE POSSIBILITY
AND MY FAMILY AND FRIENDS, FOR ITS NURTURANCE

Contents

Figures

Tables

Preface

This is the first book that offers a descriptive, historical, and socio-logical account of all four national lesbian and gay (and later bisex-ual and transgender) marches on Washington (in 1979, 1987, 1993, and 2000). When I first told Doug Mitchell, executive editor at the Univer-sity of Chicago Press, that no prior comprehensive record existed of these four marches, he replied with the perfect exclamation: "Unthinkable!" My thoughts exactly—especially since both the 1987 and 1993 demon-strations were the largest Washington marches organized during their respective times. The second march, in 1987 (which activists to this day remember as "the Great March"), also assembled a massive civil dis-obedience action that remains the second-largest in our country's history, after a similar one protesting the Vietnam War. Lesbian and gay marches on Washington deserve to have their histories told. They have waited far too long to claim their place in the venerable pages of human history.

A Roadmap for How to Approach This Book

What drove and sustained this project was a personal commitment to pre-serving what I believe are historically critical and neglected events. To do this, I offer a journalistic account of activist organizing and disputation, a previously untold history, and a sociological engagement of these marches with an eye toward the role of infighting in the formation of movement culture, solidarity, strategy, and identity. To some this may seem three distinct enterprises. I tell my story by blending these approaches, as I see one complementing and enhancing the others.

I am a sociologist by training and engage two disciplinary dialogues. The first pertains to an ongoing debate in the field of social movements over the following questions: Are internal conflicts purely detrimental or can they have some positive repercussions for mobilization? Under what conditions might one outcome prevail over the other? My first theoretical objective, therefore, is to elevate the status of infighting as a central category in the analysis of social change. Rethinking infighting allows me to engage a second theoretical ambition as well: to propose a novel conceptual framework for how culture works, that is, how expressive systems of meaning influence what people think and how they act. Here I'm driven by a methodological directive Gary Alan Fine articulated thirty years ago, namely, for scholars to prevent the treatment of culture as "an amorphous, indescribable mist which swirls around society members." I seek to find new ways of precisely measuring the culture concept. Yet I have not written this sociological enterprise in a way that is out of reach for nonspecialist readers, as I am deeply committed to advancing scholarship *and* engaging those who may have organized, attended, or simply heard of one or more of the Washington marches featured in these pages.

I imagine this book will appeal to march participants, activists who cut their teeth in assorted contexts, community organizers, and academics from sociology (especially in culture, social movements, political sociology, sexualities, and organizations), political science, history, gender/women's studies, and LGBT/queer studies. Chapter 1 opens with vignettes about infighting across political situations. I then outline guiding research questions, theoretical objectives, and an argument overview, after which I proceed to build a sociology of infighting. Academics will likely find more interest in this first chapter. They will find the conclusion of equal appeal, since it is here that I flesh out theoretical implications for how we think about conflict and culture in political organizing, the conditions of generalizability, and what all this might suggest about democratic politics. Those who are drawn to this book primarily for its four Washington march cases may want to skim the theory sections of chapter 1 ("Building a Sociology of Infighting") and chapter 10 ("Democracy and the Dividends of Dissent: Implications across Contexts" and "Theoretical Implications: A Resinous Culture Framework").

I devote two chapters to each march. The first outlines the sociopolitical context within which the respective event was organized, followed by an organizational history with an emphasis on infighting. These two chapters for each event, eight in total, comprise the core of the book that I hope will be of broad interest. In addition to reviewing material that may be familiar to some readers, I use context chapters to stake a perspective and spin an interpretive point of view in a way that links developments in gay life to the respective march. However, and to be perfectly clear, this is not a generalist book on lesbian and gay history. *The Dividends of Dissent* is a history specifically of the Washington marches, which I use to make theoretical progress on distinctly sociological questions of conflict and culture.

After each context chapter, readers will encounter a companion march chapter. These provide a detailed accounting of the key players assembling the demonstrations; the organizational structure of the marches; various meetings (or "national conferences") activists held throughout the country and what they discussed at each; the major debates and dividing points around six key logistical tasks (whether to march and if so when, how to organize it, what to title it, what to include in the demands, and who to invite as speakers); and sources of disputation around the overall messages each march distilled from start to long after its finish. I use introductory and concluding comments to assess the significance of the events for the movement as a whole. These companion chapters thus provide a perspective that goes beyond a historical blow-by-blow of the making of the marches. For academics, my objective is to provide fresh insight into theoretical questions of conflict and culture. For activists and attendees, I hope the story I tell "rings true," teaches something new about each march (how they were organized, the disputes that surrounded each, and their overall messages), and leaves a lasting impression about the changing meanings of gay life across thirty years of political organizing.

A Comment on Terminology

This book is organized around the concept of infighting. Whenever I speak with others about my research, they inevitably ask, "Why *infighting*?"

Some of this concern stems from the charged connotations and negative imagery the word can sometimes evoke. There are alternatives, including arguments, battles, conflict, contests, debates, differences, disagreements, disputes, dissent, disunity, factionalism, fragmentation, resistance, and strife, among many others. Given my interest in culture, I turned to prominent cultural sociologists for advice. Wendy Griswold, who was my dissertation chair, counsels that analytic categories should derive from original texts (such as the newspaper articles and archival documents I use) instead of being superimposed by scholars. "Infighting" was the word the gay media used; it was the word activists transcribed in meeting minutes; and it was the word they used in our interviews. This logic from cultural sociology is redolent of an anthropological perspective that stresses "member meanings" (sometimes called "indigenous voice") rather than researcher-derived categories that do not originate or resonate with the people and situations under investigation (sometimes called "authorial voice"). In accord with this advice, the words in this book come from those whose lives I sought to document and preserve. In the end, it remains an empirical question (outside the scope of this book) what different words activists used, who used which, under what circumstances, and to what effect.

Other terms also require comment, especially those related to sexual identity. In *Forging Gay Identities*, Elizabeth Armstrong does a fantastic job discussing the variable use of "gay," "lesbian and gay," "lesbigay," "lesbian, gay, bisexual," "lesbian, gay, bisexual, transgender," "LGBT," and "queer." She notes that these terms are "highly political," "continually evolving," and "highly contested." There is no single term that can fairly or accurately describe the thirty years I chronicle in this book (1970–2000). I approach this dilemma in two ways. First, I use terms in a way that is historically situated. Thus, in the 1970s activists generally used "gay" or "lesbian and gay" in the later part of the decade (evidenced by the title of the first march). Bisexuals found linguistic representation in the late 1980s and especially in the 1990s (evidenced by changing titles from "lesbian and gay" in the 1979 and 1987 events to "lesbian, gay, and bi" for the third march in 1993). Transindividuals became increasingly visible and understood in the mid- to late 1990s and found representation in the title of the fourth march in 2000. Thus, as we move forward in time, my rhetorical characterizations expand to reflect activists' language. Second, when I refer to the overall time period or make claims that cut across time, I follow Armstrong and use the convention of "gay" or "lesbian and gay" because,

as she notes, "These terms dominated between the years 1970 and 1990."
Even in the later years and later marches, as sexual-identity labels expanded, activists retained the use of "lesbian and gay." I remain critical in
my investigation, always asking why leaders constructed identity the way
they did and how different audiences reacted to these decisions.

Acknowledgments

It has taken a village to raise this book. My largest debt is to the countless activists who helped construct or who participated in one or more of the marches. I am particularly grateful to the forty-four individuals who agreed to be interviewed. I remain touched by their stories, awed by their sharp understanding of political and cultural dynamics, and obliged for their assistance in getting me in touch with others. I thank Wayne Barbin of the National Lesbian and Gay Journalists Association (NLGJA) for brokering contact with all the national cochairs from the 1993 march and for arranging an introduction with Elizabeth Birch. I also thank Donna Redwing for the memorable offer to create a "gay witness protection program" after the book is released. Of the activists I interviewed, I especially acknowledge Michael Armentrout, Steve Ault, Joan E. Biren, Paul Boneberg, Ann DeGroot, Bill Dobbs, Jeff Graubart, Billy Hileman, Joyce Hunter, David Lamble, the late Eric Rofes (who will be sorely missed), Nicole Murray-Ramirez, Reverend Troy Perry, and Robin Tyler. Each not only provided considerable time but also entrusted me with their personal papers. I communicated repeatedly with Steve Ault and Billy Hileman, neither of whom tired of me, my requests, or questions. They kept my historical facts in check; any missteps are solely my fault.

I also relied heavily on archival documents. I thank the many individuals who volunteer to ensure these vital information storehouses remain open and accessible. I extend my heartiest thanks to Gerber Hart Library in Chicago, a veritable treasure chest of LGBT history. Archivist Karen Sendziak was tireless in assisting me, entertaining a flurry of questions, pointing me in the right direction, and sharing her stories. Her celebration and preservation of our history is inspiring. Dave Howser and the rest of the volunteer staff at Gerber Hart made manageable the daunting task of collecting nearly 1,200 newspaper articles and several hundred primary source materials. I also warmly thank Mark Meinke of the Rainbow History Project in Washington, D.C., for his professional and networking efforts and friendship; Stuart Timmons for helping me navigate the voluminous collections at the ONE Institute in Los Angeles; Martin Meeker and Lea Salem for their assistance in combing through the impressive collections at the Gay, Lesbian, Bisexual, and Transgender (GLBT) Historical Society of Northern California in San Francisco; the Lesbian, Gay, Bisexual, and Transgender Community Center of New York; and Brian DeShazor, director of the Pacifica Radio Archives in North Hollywood, California.

I am lucky to have met many talented photographers who granted permission to use their images. My gratitude to 1979 march co-coordinator Steve Ault for permission to reprint images from the program; Amy Bartell and the Syracuse Cultural Workers; Joan E. Biren; Kevin Naff at the *Washington Blade* for putting me in touch with David Brady, who gave me permission to use his editorial cartoon; Cynthia Laird at the *Bay Area Reporter* for permission to use Ben Carlson's editorial cartoon; JD Doyle; Bettye Lane; Patsy Lynch for her photographs of the march banners; James Decker and Janice Hughes at the Human Rights Campaign for securing and granting permission to use Richard Renaldi's photo of the Millennium March banner; and Josef Molnar for putting me in touch with Wallace Merritt, who put me in touch with Kevin Sloan, who then put me in touch with Rich Williams, who gave me permission to use his late brother's editorial cartoons. I also thank Rich for sharing his personal stories about his brother which, for me, breathed life into Ron's art.

In a past life this book was my dissertation, and so I thank my advisors at Northwestern University (in alphabetical order): Wendy Espeland (in proposal days), Josh Gamson, Wendy Griswold, Aldon Morris, Hayagreeva Rao, and Brian Uzzi. Wendy Griswold was my chair and helped give birth to this project in our conversations, her shrewd and incisive (not to mention quickly turned-around) comments on fledgling drafts, and especially her leadership in seminars I attended, including Cultural

Methods and the Culture Workshop. Periodic discussions with the rest of the committee helped give smooth shape to rough edges.

Josh Gamson merits pause. No amount of praise is enough, nor can it adequately capture his influence on my intellectual journey. I met Josh at the first ASA meetings I ever attended during the summer of 1998 in San Francisco. I was twenty-one, had just earned my undergraduate degree from Michigan, and was considering graduate school. I was chatting with a woman at a social event the Sexualities section and LGBT caucus had jointly organized when I mentioned that I wanted to meet "Dr. Gamson." She was clearly a friend, endeared by the phrasing of my request, and introduced me to him. And the rest, as they rightfully say, was history. In my tenure as a grad student, Josh has been an influential mentor and a beloved friend. When it came time to do the dissertation, Josh offered sage words: "Don't write the dissertation; write the book." Like the entire experience of graduate school, this project would never have happened without his counsel, rigorous yet embracing comments, hours of patient phone chats, and network supports. Anyone who knows Josh's work will hear his voice in these pages—and not just in those places where I cite him. Josh sees the world in ways that resonate with me. His orientation to scholarship and especially LGBT culture and politics is deeply stitched in my own thinking and writing. I can only hope that what I have done here is half as interesting and smart as the numerous projects he has shared with the world. You're amazing, Josh.

Verta Taylor and an anonymous reviewer at the University of Chicago Press provided a nice balance of complimentary and critical comments. Tim McGovern and Carol Saller have been strongholds for technical advice, while Alex Lubertozzi provided expert copyediting. Executive editor Doug Mitchell has been a soundboard, friend, and fellow drummer. He was able to see clearly the soul of this project, even while it was buried under a cloudy prospectus. Doug is a charmed man whose inner lights have forever brightened my life. His editorial brilliance is surpassed only by his rhythmic talents as a percussionist (who commands a fierce cadence behind emerald green Gretsch drums).

I have benefited from smart conversations with colleagues around the country who pushed me out of slumps and carried me over obstacles. Thanks to John D'Emilio for coffee chats and gentle nudges on the first chapter I ever wrote about the 1979 march. Meeting and befriending him has been a blessing. Thanks to Ellen Berrey, another gift in my life, for brunches and beers and style and substance along the way. Other colleagues have lent me their ears, challenged me in conversations, engaged me in written correspondences, and guided me through written and oral presentations. Standouts include (in alphabetical order) Elizabeth Armstrong, Amy Binder, Japonica Brown-Saracino, John Evans, Corey Fields, Kathleen Hull, Brian Donovan, Steve Epstein, Gary Fine, Jeff Goodwin, Rebecca Klatch, Ryon Lancaster, Ray Maietta, Dick Madsen, Doug McAdam, John Mohr, Keith Murnighan, Joane Nagel, Monica Prasad, Vinnie Roscigno, Richard Schneider Jr., John Skrentny, Brett Stockdill, Marc Ventresca, Klaus Weber, participants of the Spring 2002 Cultural Methods seminar, and participants of the Culture Workshop at Northwestern University from spring 2003 onward.

Instructional support and technical advice comprise only half the battle. I have also benefited from developmental encouragement, emotional support, and morale boosts from colleagues without whose friendship this project would have surely faltered. Tom Cook radiates in this already stellar crowd. Whenever I was in danger of losing hope, conviction, stamina, strength, or belief in myself, he wielded his magic and reenergized me to keep pressing forward. Because of him, I have always felt that someone was watching over me. Other colleagues who bestowed upon me their love and friendship include Barry Adam, Dan Brouwer, Denise Lewin Loyd, Matt Mutchler, and the ever-sassy Wenona Rymond-Richmond.

I also benefited from friendships outside the academy, people who believed in me, were excited by what I was doing, treated me to lunches, dinners, and drinks, and provided balance to an otherwise highly cerebral academic life. I thank the following for their gift of joy and laughter: Kevin Babb, Larry Bell, Billy Brown, Mark Canuel, Barry Coleman, Scott Conway, Roger Cummings, Warren Davis, Roger Evans, Steve Fontana, Aaron Franks, Dave Frech, David Getsy, Tony Ghidorzi, Rob Gray, Valerie Harder, Matthew Harvat, Rick Hayhurst, Barry Jacobs, Jon David, Paul Langevin, Logan Massey, Cindy Mathys, Dwight McBride, Carolyn Mildner, Keith Molter, John Mullican, Patrick O'Brien, John Peasley, Jeff Pool, Mark Reese, Marcos Ryle, Dennis Schultz, Dave Siembal, Peter Simpson, Scott Slavin, John Squatritto, Perry Smrz, Kim Star, Paul Steinke, Scot Thompson, Stu Zirin, Joe Zuniga, and the legions of friends and acquaintances I made at circuit parties. I have never felt freer than I did on the dance floor surrounded by my tribe; that freedom and inspiration found its way into these pages as well.

A project is only as good as the resources that sustain it. My deepest appreciation goes to the Dispute Resolution and Research Center (DRRC) at the Kellogg School of Management (and especially to Jeanne Brett and Keith Murnighan). Thanks also to the Department of Sociology at Northwestern for its MacArthur Research Support and the university's Research Grants Committee for its Graduate Research Grant. Coordinating and compiling all the information that went into this project was a daunting task. I extend my appreciation to the unflinching administrative support I received. Nancy McLaughlin at the Dispute Resolution and Research Center at the Kellogg School of Management was incredible every step of the way. Thanks also to Erik L. Kjeldgaar, IRB coordinator at Northwestern's Office for the Protection of Research Subjects, for assistance in getting the project off the ground in an ethically responsible manner; David Hull and Michael Green at the Office for Sponsored Programs and Research and Northwestern University for reviewing fellowship applications; and Transcription Professionals for their efficient support in transcribing so many interview tapes.

And finally, a profound thanks to my family. I dedicate this book to my aunt Mahemahel, who put me through college. She carved the possibility for me to become who I wanted to be. I also owe so much to my beautiful mom, Zeenat, all her fabulous Ghaziani sisters, my supportive brother, Aziz, and his cool wife, Wendy, all of whom nurtured me through the long years of graduate school. I love you all very much.

The Problem of Infighting in Political Organizing

People fight. This is a simple fact of social life. Consider the following illustrations. As early as 1895, Booker T. Washington and W. E. B. DuBois disagreed on strategies of black political and economic progress. Washington advocated accommodation to white oppression, advising blacks to trust the paternalism of southern whites and accept of white supremacy. To conciliate the radical elements in the slavery South, he articulated the "Atlanta Compromise": "In all things purely social we can be as separate as the five fingers, and yet one as the hand in all things essential to mutual progress."

Despite cooperative gestures, DuBois found Washington's "cult" with "unquestioning followers" intolerable. He believed that persistent agitation, political action, and academic education were the means to achieving full citizenship for black Americans, a principle he developed in his influential *Crisis* magazine. DuBois encouraged the airing of dissent: "The black men of America have a duty to perform, a duty stern and delicate,—a forward movement to oppose a part of the work of their greatest leader. . . . So far as Mr. Washington apologizes for injustice . . . and opposes the higher training and ambition of our brighter minds . . . we must unceasingly and firmly oppose [him]." DuBois took umbrage with Washington's muting of dissent, declaring, "The hushing of the criticism of honest opponents is a dangerous thing."[1]

Fast-forward some years. Originally composed by suffragist Alice Paul in 1921, the National Woman's Party unveiled in Congress for the first time in 1923 a constitutional amendment for women's rights—the Equal Rights Amendment, or ERA. The ERA was reintroduced in every congressional session until its ultimate defeat in 1982. Its failure to ratify has been partly credited to an organized counterforce of women working against the feminists. Spearheaded by Phyllis Schlafly and called STOP ERA, this conservative women's group felt the ERA would blur gender distinctions and women's unique sense of self and place in society. Schlafly charged that the ERA would force women into the military, promote unisex restrooms, advocate for same-sex marriage, and remove labor laws that protected women. When she became involved in the anti-ERA movement in 1972, the amendment had been ratified by thirty of the required thirty-eight states. Schlafly's tireless organizing helped finally defeat the amendment in 1982. Her crusade of conservatism against women's progressive organizing compelled feminist Betty Friedan to snap, "I'd like to burn you at the stake!"[2]

Friedan herself would later become the object of scorn. The second wave of the women's movement was internally fractured by the homophobic rhetoric of the "lavender menace," a colorful phrase Friedan coined in 1969 that defined lesbians as a public relations threat to the emerging movement. As president of the National Organization for Women, Friedan launched rhetorical warfare to protect the cultural boundaries of the movement, which she felt were being threatened by a growing lesbian presence. For her, lesbianism and feminism were incompatible.[3]

Friedan's divisive rhetoric made explicit taken-for-granted assumptions of what it meant to be a woman. The resulting ruckus gestated the Radicalesbians in 1970 in New York. The group appropriated Friedan's "Lavender Menace" as their name. Their manifesto, "The Woman-Identified Woman," opened with the question, "What is a lesbian?" to which it provided an answer that augmented the definition of a woman: "A lesbian is the rage of all women condensed to the point of explosion." Dissent between Friedan and the Radicalesbians prompted a sense of "women creating a new consciousness of and with each other," a process that was "at the heart of women's liberation, and the basis for the cultural revolution." Accordingly, women's "authentic selves" could only be discovered in dissentious dialogues: "For to confront another woman is finally to confront one's self—the self we have gone to such lengths to avoid."[4]

These currents converged around contested meanings of strategy and identity: What is a woman? What are female values? What is a lesbian? Answers facilitated "the recognition of differences among women."[5] This generated the "erosion of . . . [the] fantasy of female . . . solidarity" and a "frustrating fragmentation of the women's movement" into the distinct branches of cultural, radical, and lesbian feminism.[6] Cultural feminists came under additional attack for their perceived prohibitions against the airing of dissent. Some believed they "have not only characterized criticism as 'unsisterly' or a carryover from the 'trashing style' of the male left, but as 'male-identified.'"[7] Lost was the idea that disunity was a healthy artifact of diversity that motivated "the creative function of differences among women."[8]

The modern civil rights movement was also burdened by infighting. In one explosive incident, a group of sixteen young, militant black members of the Revolutionary Action Movement were arrested during the summer of 1967 on charges of conspiring to murder Whitney Young, Roy Wilkins, and other black leaders who were deemed "too moderate."[9] Another milder situation split the Seattle chapter of the Congress of Racial Equality (CORE) into conservative and dissident wings. Seattle's original CORE chapter charged radical members, congealed in the Ad Hoc Committee, with circulating "divisive and derogatory allegations" of chapter leaders. Ad Hoc members attacked CORE's black chairman and vice-chairman as "too respectable" and "too fearful of losing their jobs and homes by participating in militant tactics."[10] Such disputes littered the landscape of the civil rights movement, for example, in classic debates between Martin Luther King Jr. and Malcolm X and between the Student Nonviolent Coordinating Committee (SNCC) and the Southern Christian Leadership Conference (SCLC) on the effectiveness of violence.[11]

We would expect challenging groups to work together in solidarity to oppose a common external enemy. But rather than unite, subgroups incessantly snipe.[12] Examples of such "horizontal hostility," a term coined by feminist Florynce Kennedy in 1970 to describe infighting within minority groups, are not limited to social movements.[13] Instances in contemporary politics also abound, most deliciously captured by the late President Ronald Reagan's "Eleventh Commandment": "Thou Shalt Not Speak Ill of a Fellow Republican." Another memorable moment occurred when Harry Belafonte dubbed former Secretary of State Colin Powell a "house slave" who only served his "master" (read: President

George W. Bush) and was therefore selling out the black community. CNN quoted Belafonte, "There's an old saying. In the days of slavery, there were those slaves that lived on the plantation, and there were those slaves that lived in the house. You got the privilege of living in the house if you served the master . . . exactly the way the master intended to have you serve him."[14] This argument contends that if you are a conservative black person, like Powell, you are against the black community and damage the movement. Malcolm X argued similarly against King, that by wanting to be part of the white man's world, he was doing more harm than good. This is the same argument that DuBois launched against Washington and that, one hundred years later, Richard Goldstein, executive editor of the *Village Voice,* articulated against "Homocons," or conservative, especially Republican, lesbians and gay men.[15]

There are less media-sensationalized examples, as well. As Judith White and Ellen Langer detailed, "Consider what happened to a law professor who happens to be a light-skinned Black woman. Her appointment at a prestigious university was opposed by the Black Students Association, whose spokesperson said the professor wasn't 'black enough.' Similarly, when Heather Whitestone was heralded as the first Deaf Miss America, Deaf activists protested. Since Ms. Whitestone uses oral English, and not American Sign Language, Deaf activists didn't consider her Deaf enough. Even a proposal to broaden The Society for the Psychological Study of Lesbian and Gay Issues (Division 44 of the American Psychological Association) to include the word 'bisexual' met resistance from lesbian and gay members, despite the position of the Society's president, Robin Buhrke, that inclusiveness would strengthen the division."[16]

Infighting is deeply stitched in the American political and cultural fabric. It, like other forms of conflict, is inevitable, necessary, and of great sociological relevance in its capacity to distill contested meanings of group life. In this book, I grapple with this problem in the national-level political organizing of lesbian and gay people. The story I narrate in the pages that follow is motivated by three sets of questions. First, how prevalent is infighting in lesbian and gay political organizing, specifically, in assembling a march on Washington? And how much of the movement's resources do activists invest in this problem? Second, what does infighting do—that is, what is its role? And under what conditions might it corrode, versus contribute to, political organizing? Third, if assessed longitudinally, do activists fight over the same or varying issues? And how can we account for either or both? These questions converge on the following broader concern: under what conditions do groups either hold together or fall apart in light of currents (such as infighting) that threaten to tear them apart? To seek answers, I investigate four previously unstudied marches on Washington (staged in 1979, 1987, 1993, and 2000) that span thirty years of organizing efforts (in the 1970s, 1980s, and 1990s). No prior sociological account exists of these demonstrations.

There will always be competing visions for why and how to organize an event like a Washington march, along with contestation over what it means to be and who is counted as part of the group. These tensions of strategy and identity, respectively, can remain unarticulated and hover just beneath activist radars for many reasons. Certain questions, like what should be done, who speaks for us, and who do we think we are, may be too abstract to meaningfully engage. There may be too few institutional arenas within which to voice them, too few opportunities for activists from across the country to convene and brainstorm. The realities of discriminatory legislation and rights-stripping referenda may make such questions seem self-indulgent and wasteful. As a result, there may be too few or even negative stakes attached to the conversations. Things can quickly change in light of a proposal for activists to channel their resources toward Washington. There are now consequences. Such a decision can influence how and where resources are invested. It can bolster or drain local organizing. It can create or exhaust leadership. It can influence how Americans think about the organizing constituency by attaching to them a public face and demands. Depending on the turnout, it can give the movement a black eye or situate it as a formidable force and voting bloc. It can even shape how marchers think about themselves.

I use this notion of a Washington march as the site where politics and culture collide to springboard two theoretical objectives. I first argue against popular perceptions of dissent as damaging or indicative of the decline of political potency. Instead of being responsible for social disorganization, as most scholarship and lay wisdom predict, I assert that infighting can be generative by allowing activists to muse on what I call the *state of the movement*. Activists articulate dissent to engage in another conversation, a cultural, or meaning-centered, meaning-enhanced, communiqué to their imagined national community that specifies vital questions of what can and should be done, what they want and how to secure it, who has the power to decide and speak for the collective, who belongs in this struggle, and how various contenders are connected. Infighting, in other words, carries meaning-rich conversations that give voice to strategy and identity that together provide a glimpse into the state of the movement.

I tell my story about infighting by chronicling four lesbian and gay Washington marches. These national protest events provide a catalyst that can bring to the surface rumblings of division that previously may have remained dormant or were discreetly managed in local pockets. A march on Washington can provide a much-needed space for activists from across the country to collectively hash out ideologies of political organizing.[17] But these are often painfully abstract matters. My foray into these four marches uncovered a mechanism that can help make this process more concrete and tangible. In each case, activists fight over a handful of organizing tasks (for example, how to construct the platform or who to invite as speakers). This coupling allows for a more precise calibration of cultural concerns by imbuing logistical decisions with symbolic carrying capacity. Simply put, major strategic visions and cultural identities emerge from hashing out tasks that must get done.

I use this measurement mechanism to elaborate my second theoretical objective pertaining to the question of how culture works, that is, how symbolic-expressive, meaning-making processes influence what people think and how they act. It is unlikely that activists of any political stripe will sit around a table and muse, "Who do we think we are?" Rather, activists link dissent with practical tasks to enable cultural exchanges to transpire. I develop implications for this *resinous culture framework* later in this chapter and in detail in the conclusion.

I introduce supporting conceptual characters along the way. Besides producing the march, activists also codified dissent into what I call a *cultural template* that consolidated lessons learned. Infighting, in other words, does more than just give voice to abstract, cultural concerns; it also serves as a guide for future organizing. Through infighting, a cluster of assumptions, agreements, and meanings are developed that structure future conventions of argumentation, disputation, and decision-making. The cultural template exerts considerable influence in these matters, and there are very real consequences for rupturing it.

During each demonstration, activists stumbled over the same exact six debates: whether to march; if yes, then when to march; what to title the march and what theme to give it; how to assemble the demands; who to invite as speakers; and what organizing structure to use. Given this regularity, why were activists not able to anticipate their debates in hopes of mitigating weekends full of acrimonious fights? Why does freedom become a series of endless meetings, to allude to Francesca Polletta's work,[18] despite the predictability of conversations and conflict? As we will see, debates that deceptively looked the same on the surface actually inflected very different meanings. Four factors account for this, including the nature of external threat that confronted the movement, the changing cultural and political status of gay people, organizational development within the movement, and the consciousness or "subjective roots"[19] of the rank and file. These dimensions inflected *structurally similar debates* (over the same six tasks) with *culturally varying scripts* (or different meanings) that capture the state of the movement.

The remainder of this chapter is organized as follows: I begin with a rationale for the study of lesbian and gay social movements in general and marches on Washington in particular. I then build a sociology of infighting in an effort to open up new ways of thinking about how conflict and culture work in political organizing. Finally, I elaborate the parameters of infighting as a concept and explain how I use it to develop a resinous culture theoretical framework.

Lesbian and Gay Marches on Washington

The Movement

The American lesbian and gay movement has "received relatively little notice from scholars who emphasize the sociological literature on social movements."[20] Those who have examined it have documented its rich internal diversity and competing visions for a collective project. While some suggest the movement developed "unity through diversity," in the words of sociologist Elizabeth Armstrong, others have shown that diversity drives dissent.[21] Some activists on the ground challenged, "What the heck was that ['unity through diversity'] supposed to mean? Does it mean anything at all? . . . How does that diversity constitute or lead to some sort of unity? . . . All that diversity would seem to constitute a problem rather than a solution . . . 'Unity Through Diversity' offers an unsubstantiated claim to unity instead of offering any evidence . . . that any unity actually exists."[22] Activists might be able to smooth over diversity during local events (such as a gay pride parade) that utilize an organizational structure that does not force confrontation. This does not explain diversity-induced dissent in national demonstrations such as a march on Washington. A lowest-common-denominator, shared gay identity might allow "real political differences" to be "finessed" and "integrated" in a parade where participants are "simply accepting [of] the diversity of goals and identities expressed by others."[23] Evidence from marches on Washington, however, suggests that activists were not always satisfied with this approach. Armstrong appears to be right about the gay movement ultimately holding together, but we have an incomplete accounting of the involved mechanisms and what happens when activists work on the ground to organize a massive, national protest event amid a flurry of infighting.

Although this "tricky infighting" is a staple of American politics, it is particularly pronounced within an "increasingly fragmented" lesbian and gay movement.[24] This was evident in a cover story produced by the *Advocate,* a leading national lesbian and gay newsmagazine, which featured infighting on its cover as cannibalistic (see fig. 1.1). Titled "Eating Our Own," the cover asks, "Is the gay movement eating itself alive?" The movement's internal diversity therefore makes it ripe for a focused study of dissent.

I leverage infighting to understand changes in identity and strategy.[25] Steve Epstein underscores the importance of both in any historical analysis of lesbian and gay political organizing.[26] Since 1950s homophile activity, infighting has illuminated "the very question of the movement's collective identity: who is the 'we' on behalf of whom activists speak?" Indeed, the movement is often considered the "quintessential identity movement" due to its concerns with the cultural transformation of societal attitudes, the modification of members' identities, and the acquisition of legislative rights.[27] In their articulation of identity, lesbians and gay men have generally oscillated between two claims. On the one hand, activists embraced a liberal, quasi-ethnic, minority model of identity as a fixed group with discrete demands. Alternately, radical groups advocated a "'nonidentitarian' politics of difference" that called attention to internal differences and questioned the stability of essentialist identity claims. The latter group criticized the former for promoting a "false universalism."[28] The issue of identity, therefore, "seems particularly problematic for gay and lesbian movements."[29]

The movement has also experienced regular cleavages around strategy, or where the movement was headed, and how to accomplish its desired goals. Strategy battles similarly shook along liberal-radical fault lines. Liberals advocated "single-issue pragmatic politics," whereas their sidekicks promoted a "multi-issue radical politics" of social justice. Here,

FIGURE I.I. "Eating Our Own." *Advocate*, August 13, 1992.

infighting addressed questions such as: What are our issues? How should
decisions be made? And who controls the movement?

Epstein's treatise informs my story in three ways. His ambitious review of more than fifty years of gay political organizing reveals the centrality of dissent. Leaders often cite "community infighting" as the most
pressing concern for gay political organizing.[30] Epstein notes that the gay
struggle is characterized as a contest between groups who "have competed to lay claim to 'the movement' and say what it 'really is.'" These
"difference troubles"[31] have arisen over issues of identity and strategy
that together provide a photograph of the state of the movement—or
"our fractal subculture," as some gay journalists have called it.[32]

Epstein's review also makes an observation I develop in further detail: certain debates resurface again and again. I agree with Epstein that
"these debates . . . are at the heart of the struggle to define what sort of
politics gay people should promote" and who gay people believe themselves to be. I analytically reconstruct the face of gay America by focusing on these debates. Lastly, Epstein acknowledges that his "essay . . . is
not based on my own primary research. Instead, I have strived to synthe-
size the existing scholarly research." His statements can benefit from additional empirical support.

The Marches

Beginning in 1894 with Jacob Coxey and his army's "petition in boots"
and for more than one hundred years since, numerous groups have used
Washington as a national public space to "project their plans and demands on national government, where they can build support for their
causes, and where they can act out their own visions of national politics."[33] Marches on Washington are a firmly established tradition in the
American political repertoire. They comprise the heartbeat of American politics.

The conventionality of the tactic compels some scholars, activists, and
laypeople to dismiss it as unremarkable. However, and as Lucy Barber
identifies, the historical record makes clear that these events still affect
American politics by marshalling "the power of collective displays of citizenship" while serving as vehicles for "personal affirmation and movement building."[34] As I have already suggested, marches on Washington
are places where politics and culture collide. They raise participants'
consciousness, affect their belief structures, and are often life-altering.

Washington marches also mobilize and create consensus by linking local communities in a concentrated physical and symbolic space.[35] Gay activists concede that national marches delineate the public face of gay America amid rampant infighting: "I believe we grow as a community when we engage in such a public conversation [of march debates]. . . . Marches are a good place to have political conversations with the rest of our collective community."[36] To better understand this process, we must first build a sociology of infighting.

Building a Sociology of Infighting

The Study of Conflict in Early American Sociology

No analysis of social change can neglect the role of conflict. One influential thinker after the next commented on its ubiquity. In *The Methodology of Social Science,* for instance, Max Weber asserted that "conflict cannot be excluded from social life." Robert Park later recognized that "only where there is conflict is behavior conscious and self-conscious." Park and others in the early Chicago School centralized the role of conflict in solidifying social structure and community boundaries. Others, such as Georg Simmel and Lewis Coser, asserted a fundamental interdependence between conflict and unity. Simmel said it most directly: "Conflict . . . is a way of achieving some kind of unity"; Coser added that "conflict sew[s] the social system together." In *The Principles of Sociology,* Edward Alsworth Ross additionally suggested that "society is sewn together by its inner conflicts."[37] Theorists in this first camp asserted that conflict was productive.

Not everyone agreed. Talcott Parsons shunned conflict as pathological, as a "form of sickness in the body social." In *The Structure of Social Action,* he likened conflict to a "disease," an "illness" that undermined normative structures of societal health. He and other structural functionalists repeatedly "disregard[ed] its positive function" due to an orientation toward the conservation of social order, whereas their contemporaries concerned themselves with social change and development.[38] In this second dissenting camp, conflict was pernicious.

Regardless of whether they sang its praises or heard it as a requiem for social health, conflict theorists did not neglect the particular problem of infighting. "People who have many common features," noted Simmel, "often do one another worse or 'worser' wrong than complete strangers."

He defined infighting as a subtype of conflict that does "not lead to the proper break-up of the group. For once the group is dissolved, there is a certain release of the conflict." Simmel recognized the need for "treating this type [of conflict] separately" due to its capacity to articulate and preserve group boundaries. "A weakening of the group is not a necessary result of such struggles," Coser added. Infighting paradoxically "ties the members more closely to each other and promotes group integration" by materializing "the basis of the relation itself" and increasing their "awareness of the issues at stake." It does this by articulating strategy ("the issues at stake") and identity ("the basis of the relation").[39] Early conflict theory reveals that infighting is a prevalent phenomenon and one that is analytically distinct from general conflict. It *precedes* the proper break-up of the group, that is, organizational defection or dissolution. By connecting these theories of conflict with scholarship in social movements and cultural sociology, I provide a situated understanding of infighting in Washington marches.

Contemporary Social Movement Approaches to Infighting

Similar to conflict theory, there is to the present day an ongoing debate in the field of social movements over whether infighting is purely detrimental or if instead it might have some positive repercussions. Although unsettled, the dialogue overwhelmingly favors dissent as symptomatic of a fragmented movement in decline. Much of this research emphasizes factions, factionalism, factional splits, schisms, defections, and countermovements. These phenomena are important to study in their own right, but they are analytically distinct from infighting, which as we saw in the prior section, merits separate consideration.[40] Factions, splits, splinters, schisms, and defections are a common class of phenomena in which groups fail at conflict resolution, that is, phenomena in which there is "the proper break-up of the group."[41]

While extensive, the dialogue on infighting has not proceeded in an organized fashion. To correct for this, I construct a genealogy of infighting in social movements that I divide into three ideal-typical traditions I refer to as classical, conditional, and causal (see table 1.1). We set the stage with Karl Marx. In *The Communist Manifesto,* he observed that proletariat organizing was "being upset" and "broken up . . . by the competition between the workers themselves." Internal warfare within proletariat ranks was indicative of its early stage of organizing. Over time

TABLE I.I. **Classical, Conditional, and Causal Traditions in the Study of Infighting**

	Tradition Type		
	Classical	Conditional	Causal
Dimensions of Infighting:			
Why study it?	To predict occurrence	To determine impact	Epiphenomenal
Distinct from defection?	No	Sometimes	Yes
Why does it matter?	Spews forth defection	Prompts defection, decline or growth	Highlights diversity
Why does it occur?	Organizational form	Organizational form	Host of variables
How can it be resolved?	Change organizational form	Allow articulation of dissent	Remedy causal variable(s)
Positive or negative?	Negative	Positive or negative or both	Negative, but rectifiable
Relationship to defection?	Inevitable—always causes defection, decline	Unclear—may or may not cause defection, decline	Unspecified—emphasis of research is elsewhere
Examples:	W. Gamson (1975); Zald and Ash (1966)	Balser (1997); Benford (1993); Mushaben (1989)	Cohen (1999); Polletta (2002)

and as they formed into a class, internal competition would cede to revolutionary potential. Marx anticipated infighting to subside and be transferred to antagonism against those who owned the means of production. He saw intra-proletariat conflict as an antecedent to inter-group conflict, from which revolutions spring forth.[42]

The Classical Tradition

During the 1960s and 1970s, movement scholars followed Marx and emphasized organizations. Situated within then dominant rational, economic, and resource mobilization paradigms, classical studies—spearheaded by John McCarthy, Mayer Zald, Sidney Tarrow, Frances Fox Piven, Richard Cloward, and others—predicted the occurrence of infighting by isolating factors such as degree of heterogeneity within the support base and adherents (i.e., diversity of participants and the need for doctrinal purity, or ideological similarity); the choice of organizational form (i.e., were

social movement organizations [SMOs] inclusive, permitting multiple
member affiliations, or were members subjected to strict regulations as
part of an exclusive organization that was highly demanding of time and
allegiance?); and an artifact of competition between SMOs (e.g., competition between different civil rights or lesbian and gay organizations).[43]

Classical research was dominant from the 1960s to the early 1980s.
Scholars working in it often conflated infighting with splits and defections. This obscured insight from conflict theory that sought to make the
two distinct. Classical researchers also favored predicting the occurrence
of infighting and therefore remained silent on whether it was a resource
or detriment once it did arise. There is one notable exception. Former
president of the American Sociological Association (in 1994), William
Gamson wrote a pathbreaking book that examined fifty-three American protest groups operating from 1800 to 1945. His research marshaled
such appeal that it almost single-handedly represents how movement
scholars still think about infighting today. Replete with provocative language, Gamson argues that internal divisions are a cause of movement
failure. He begins by conceding to the ubiquity of infighting:

> Internal division is a misery that few challenging groups escape
> completely—it is the nature of the beast. Men and women of the best inten-
> tions, sharing common goals, will disagree on strategy and tactics. . . . And
> they may compete for control of the organizational apparatus with power as
> an end in itself, using particular ideological postures as means of gaining sup-
> port over rivals. . . . All groups experience internal disagreement.[44]

Gamson then delivers his punch: "*The sorry reputation of factionalism is a deserved one.* . . . Factional splits, I am arguing, are the primary
manifestation of the failure of the group to solve the problem of internal conflict. . . . That factional splits are a concomitant of failure is clear
enough" (emphasis added). Gamson declares that dissenting groups will
be "capriciously struck down by this malady." Their fate is inevitable: infighting "*may hasten their collapse*" (emphasis added).[45] There is little
room for ambiguity here: infighting is malignant for mobilization.

The Conditional Tradition

Throughout the 1980s and 1990s and as Gamson's work increased in
prominence, some scholars wondered whether infighting was always

maladjustive. Leila Rupp and Verta Taylor's study of the early American women's movement in its organizational doldrums, for instance, challenged Gamson's assertion that internal division is always the death knell of a movement.[46] The signature in this conditional tradition was the specification of parameters. The focus shifted from predicting infighting to considering its impact. Using the example of the West German peace movement, Joyce Mushaben argued that conflict can be "a mobilization resource in its own right" and did not necessarily result in group decline or defection.[47] Similar to classical scholars, conditional researchers also isolated organizational problems, often texturing them by considering funding, goals, and tactics. Infighting's value lay in its potential to generate creative strategic possibilities and promote closer monitoring and pressures for accountability.

Conditional scholars approached the problem of infighting more critically than their predecessors, although they too often confounded dissent with defection. Luther Gerlach and Virginia Hine's work on the Pentecostal and Black Power movements, for example, took issue with classical research that pungently dismissed infighting as "internecine dog fighting," although they conflated "fissiparous tendencies" with "intramural bickering" and "organizational segmentation," or schisms. Unlike classical theorists, however, Gerlach and Hine concluded that organizational fragmentation, fission, and lack of cohesion can be adaptive in facilitating a redefinition of goals by creating "additional thorns in the flesh of the establishment." Movement survival and success may occur because of, rather than in spite of, infighting.[48]

Captivated by this possibility yet aware of the tendency to frown upon infighting, Robert Benford diplomatically offered that "infighting is detrimental and facilitative of movements" in four ways. It can prompt the demobilization of some SMOs while encouraging others. Infighting can deplete resources for some while increasing it—and thus overall political efficacy—for others. Although it could provoke splits, it could also encourage cohesiveness. And finally, infighting could stimulate what he calls "a division of interpretive labor," a type of culture work that helps movement members wrestle with questions of strategy and identity. Benford, like many in this tradition, theoretically sits on the fence separating the two sides of the debate.[49]

One study after another elaborated this middle ground. Deborah Balser offers a tour de force of infighting. She compares it across four SMOs: Students for a Democratic Society (SDS), the Student Nonvio-

lent Coordinating Committee (SNCC), the American Federation of Labor (AFL), and Earth First! (EF!).[50] Balser aptly distinguishes infighting
from schisms and splits. Redolent of insights from early conflict theory,
she observes that group defection is a variable outcome that requires explanation, cannot be assumed, and cannot be conflated with infighting.
She also observes strategy and identity battles recurring across her four
cases, although the meaning-making mechanisms remain unspecified.

The intellectual climate shifted dramatically in 1982 with Doug Mc-
Adam's groundbreaking *Political Process and the Development of
Black Insurgency*. Similar to Gamson, McAdam was also inexorable in
his treatment of infighting, which he explicitly connected to the decline
of the civil rights movement: "Once effective insurgent organizations
were *rendered impotent by factional disputes that drained them* of the
unity, energy, and resolve needed to sustain protest activity" (emphasis added). He continued, "The growing divisions within the movement
not only reduced the possibility of cooperative action between movement groups but further diminished the organizational strength of insurgent forces by stimulating disputes within these groups that reduced
their effectiveness."[51]

McAdam's research quickly became a leading voice in social movement scholarship. His position on infighting situated it as invariably producing social disorganization. Emerging studies followed suit. Joyce
Mushaben provides a sweeping summary of how most scholars conceptualized the problem: "Intramovement or group conflict is viewed as
a disruptive, destructive force, with few exceptions." She then offers a
more provocative assessment: "Factionalization is engraved all too often
as the *'cause of death' upon the tombstones of protests past in the grave-
yard of SMOs*"[52] (emphasis added). Gamson and McAdam's influence
continues unabated. "Death by Infighting" is all too often the epitaph on
political tombstones.

The Causal Tradition

The popularity of Gamson and McAdam's study spawned a tradition
from the 1980s to the present that sought specific variables to explain
infighting. In the background was an accepted wisdom that likened infighting's "sorry reputation" to "internecine dog fighting," something
that "hastened movement collapse" by rendering insurgent groups "im-

potent." Infighting was more or less accepted as the cause of death of political organizing. It therefore behooved scholars to identify causal factors to prevent inflaming this mobilization malady, although they now did so as part of an omnibus design to understand other dynamics (e.g., recruitment, leadership, framing, etc.). Developing within the cultural turn, many writers in this tradition shifted their attention to nonorganizational factors such as ideologies, identities, and consciousness, among others. Thus the 1980s and 1990s comprise what I call a causal tradition that isolated single variable explanations for the origins of infighting.[53]

A non-exhaustive list of answers to the question, "Why does infighting occur?" includes: members' racist, sexist, and classist attitudes and beliefs; coordination and reconciliation problems activists confront when they are situated at the intersection of multiple oppressions; the changing generational and cohort profile of activists; an inadequate economic aggregation of individual choices and interests; failure to mobilize consensus; disagreements over tactics and strategies; and challenges associated with participatory, democratic decision-making.[54] Queries specifically within the cultural turn isolated contradictions in movement culture; pressures for ideological purity; and framing disputes over diagnosis (identifying and defining the problem), prognosis (what to do about it), and motivation (how to inspire people to act). Framing disputes provided competing answers to questions such as: Who are we (the protagonists)? Who are they (the antagonists and audience)? What are we doing? And why are we doing it?[55]

Table 1.1 reveals an ongoing debate over how infighting affects political organizing. Across traditions, scholars generally fall on one of three sides. At one end, Gamson and McAdam represent the majority of scholars who view infighting as sapping political potency. It is likened to "internecine dog fighting" that deserves its "sorry reputation." Scholars frown upon it for "hastening movement collapse," for rendering insurgent groups "impotent," and for being the "cause of death upon the tombstones of protests past." The imagery here is powerful and unambiguous. In the middle is a small but diplomatic group that is open to infighting being beneficial or burdensome. And at the other end is a group of scholars who, by far in the minority, assert unequivocally that infighting can be a movement resource in its own right.

Infighting as a Culture Carrier

The preceding conversation begs the question of the analytical parameters of infighting. I define it as the expression of a difference of opinion or the offering of a discrepant view that does not produce or occurs prior to an organizational defection or dissolution. Infighting involves both a recognition of divergent courses of action rooted in competing world views and an awareness that relatively stable subgroups or alliances are urging the collective embrace of these actions through whatever explicit or implicit decision-making mechanisms that might be available. It is a subtype of conflict that specifically carries concerns of strategy and identity. Strategies "specify a course of action as desirable" by enumerating objectives and goals (e.g., reform versus revolutionary). Relevant concerns include the issues on which activists should focus, how decisions should be made, where the movement is headed, how to get there, and what this suggests about who controls the movement. Strategies therefore specify the end goals of collective action along with the means for obtaining them.[56] Identity is "the agreed upon definition of group membership, [and] boundaries." To make systematic this slippery concept, I focus on how the category *gay* is elaborated (its "catness," "categoryness," or groupness) and on how different types of gay people are connected (its "netness," "network-ness," or connectedness). Identity is therefore a feeling of "we-ness" that specifies "categorical commonality and relational connectedness," or shared attributes and networks. This emphasis has the advantage of blending cultural and social structural perspectives and correcting for widespread conceptual and explanatory confusion.[57]

Infighting assumes a strategic and identity battle that draws attention to contrasts and polarities in which people seek advantageous positioning to advance a particular ethos. As a type of conflict, it provides an opportunity to explore how group cultures can diverge, despite seeming commonality, in light of currents that threaten to divide participants in terms of their instrumental and expressive goals. The concept of infighting therefore treats divergent meaning systems as centers of local contention between rival cliques in a challenge for power, limited resources, and public image. Infighting directs attention away from consensus (and unity) and toward contestation (and diversity). This definition excludes personality conflicts, finger-pointing, name-calling, and other sociologically less productive activities. Activists also identify such distinctions:

"Can we not reason together without engaging in name-calling and mean-spirited comments? . . . Let us not attack each other's integrity, but confine our comments to the debate at hand."[58] Said another, "When disagreement escalates to such an extent that the personal attacks are relentless, it becomes a form of abuse."[59] I agree and therefore emphasize task conflicts, that is, disputes over the content of the work in which activists engage (including "differences in viewpoints, ideas, and opinions"), rather than relationship conflicts, that is, interpersonal friction (including "tension, animosity, and annoyance among members within a group").[60]

The state of the movement, built from strategy and identity disputes, matters. How the movement frames its issues can impact whether Americans define sexuality as a moral or civil rights issue, which can then affect their overall attitudes toward gay people. Americans are more comfortable with the idea of equal protection and freedom from discrimination than they are with the idea of sex between men or between women. Thus, how the movement configures its calculus of politics versus sex can confer advantages or disadvantages. Political scientist Cathy Cohen similarly emphasizes that cultural battles have material consequences: "Contestation . . . has tangible effects, influencing the distribution of resources, services, access, and legitimacy."[61] Infighting captures what went well and what did not in the organizing process, while permitting an evaluation of lessons learned. These can range from political (e.g., Was marching effective? Did legislators hear our demands?); organizational (e.g., Did our infrastructure adequately represent our own diversity? Did we provide sufficient opportunities for all people to have a voice?); and cultural (e.g., Do we have a better sense of who we are as a people and movement? Did we transform societal attitudes?).

Gay political commentators suggest that infighting is "a natural result of our diversity" and that it "signals that discussion is required."[62] It is through the expression of a difference of opinion or the offering of a discrepant view that organizers can speak to the rank and file and where they in turn can assess, by way of the media, what it means to be a part of the movement. To isolate these under-theorized, meaning-making processes, I use infighting as a case of cultural skepticism. According to Ann Swidler, scholars cannot study cultural concerns without also acknowledging dissent: "Our ability to describe a cultural perspective, or to see it at all, comes only from our skepticism about it."[63] This insight was identified years earlier by Dick Hebdige: "If we emphasize integration and coherence at the expense of dissonance and discontinuity, we are in danger of denying the very manner in which the subcultural form is made to crystallize, objectify, and communicate group experience."[64] The idea is the same: infighting is a key site for culture and political work. This type of conflict brings to the fore cultural assumptions that may otherwise remain implicit.[65]

The dividends of dissent lie in activists' use of infighting to engage in another conversation, an abstract one that allows activists to converge on shared meanings of political organizing. This, in other words, is a story about how infighting carries and concretizes cultural conversations. Activists make material abstract ideas such as who we are and what we want by fighting over discrete organizing tasks. In this manner, infighting operates as a vehicle or *culture carrier* that transports meta-meanings fashioned from the assemblages of logistical decisions. I say meta-meanings deliberately because at one level, the debates described in the pages that follow are ostensibly about six recurring, practical questions. Is there a collective wisdom to march? If so, then when? How should we organize it to best represent the internal diversity of our movement? What should we title and select as a theme for the march? What should we include in our platform? Who should we invite to speak? At another level, however, infighting captures activists engaged in a process of culture work, actively debating the meaning of the state of their own movement.

Rethinking infighting in this way allows me to propose a novel framework for the question of how culture works in political organizing. *How culture works.* These three deceivingly simple words have long captured the sociological imagination. For decades scholars have labored over how to prevent culture from being "an amorphous, indescribable mist which swirls around society members," in Gary Alan Fine's provocative words.[66] But how does one make culture concrete? How does one measure something that by various definitions defies materiality? For example, how can one sketch boundaries around classic definitions as "the best that has been thought and known" and "that complex whole which includes knowledge, belief, art, morals, law, custom, and any other capabilities and habits acquired by man as a member of society"?[67] The concept has become so ubiquitous yet elusive that some suggest, "There is no such thing as 'culture' . . . out there in the real world."[68] Here we encounter a paradox: if culture is that complex whole, then it is everywhere and is everything—"an amorphous, indescribable mist"—at which point its analytic utility dissipates.

It is today common wisdom that the culture concept means different things and that scholars may do better to measure those more specific things than aim to study that complex whole. Culture is now more narrowly conceived as discourse, symbols, boundaries, frames, cognitive schema, narratives and stories, identities, values, works of art, ways of life, and institutional codes, among others. Each term enables scholars to ask more specific questions about culture and how it works. Sociologists Roger Friedland and John Mohr note that investigating these "matters of culture" continues to be blocked by a persisting duality between what they notably term "material, objective 'social' things that are separate, and fundamentally different, from more subjective, interpretive, cultural artifacts." Despite moving toward specificity, "the social [remains] the domain of materiality, of hardness, thingness." Culture, in consequence, remains deprived of concreteness, of tangibility.

Although culture has found a "new prestige" within sociology in part through efforts to isolate its autonomy from social structure, measurement concerns—what I call *cultural concretization*—require further consideration. Depending on how one chooses to study culture, sociologist Ann Swidler suggests that it remains even today "extremely hard to grasp concretely...a diffused mist within which social action occurs." Redirecting the study of culture toward concerns of operational rigor may help sociologists distinguish culture from that which is not and to see from a fresh perspective how it might matter in social life.[69]

I move this dialogue forward by offering a *resinous culture framework*. In the story I tell, infighting is linked with a series of recurring organizing tasks. This coupling concretizes, that is, makes more material, cultural concerns by imbuing logistical decisions with symbolic carrying capacity that gives form to otherwise abstract conversations of strategy and identity. In other words, dissentious dialogues concerning nuts-and-bolts decisions provide a metaphorical resin onto which cultural exchanges attach and more effectively transpire. As I will show in the pages that follow, this measurement mechanism permits a rethinking of how culture works by releasing it from its status as "an amorphous mist."

Organization of the Book

This book compares infighting across four lesbian and gay marches on Washington staged in 1979, 1987, 1993, and 2000, respectively. My

TABLE I.2. **Dimensions Influencing March Organizing**

	1979	1987	1993	2000
Internal Dimensions				
Community Consciousness	Gay neighborhoods; "We Are Everywhere"; rainbow flag	National consciousness set; continuity of New Left organizers	Queer theory and politics	Gay market niche; gay celebrities
Organizational Development	Stonewall; lesbians vs. gay men; whites vs. people of color	AIDS organizations; racially-specific organizations	Bisexual groups; transgender groups	Diversification: queers, bisexuals, and transgenders; homogenization: national organizations
External Dimensions				
Threat	Anita Bryant; John Briggs; Harvey Milk	AIDS; *Bowers v. Hardwick*; U.S. intervention in Central America	AIDS; Don't Ask, Don't Tell; special rights	AIDS; Dr. Laura; ex-gays; hate crimes
Political/ Cultural Status	APA; federal gay rights bill; Hollywood	Pariahs at the periphery	Media and legislation explosion	Gay celebrities, sitcoms, and movies; ENDA; Don't Ask, Don't Tell; *Romer v. Evans*; gay marriage

objective is to inquire into the prevalence of infighting (i.e., How much of the movement's communication resources do activists devote to this problem?); to identify its sources (i.e., Why does it happen?); operations (i.e., What role does it play?); and patterns (i.e., Does it take regular form?). This case-controlled longitudinal design facilitates identification and explanation of commonalities and differences across thirty years of one movement (1970s, 1980s, and 1990s). Methodologically, I illustrate two ways of studying historical cases. Scholars can compare them analytically as semi-distinct, stand-alone episodes and can also tell a story that locates each in relation to the others.

The book is organized chronologically, moving from the first march in 1979 to the fourth in 2000. I devote two chapters to each march. The first outlines the context in which the respective march was organized. Lesbian and gay life in any epoch is infinitely complex, and so I focus only on currents that directly inspired march organizing. In other words, I use the national demonstrations as a lens for narrating a more focused history. Context chapters (2, 4, 6, and 8) serve as a steel frame of generalist material upon which, in the follow-up companion chapters, I construct a previously untold and specific history of the Washington marches. Forerunner chapters lay out a skeletal structure and provide descriptive support, rather than formal sociological analysis, which is developed in subsequent chapters. Context chapters are entrusted with capturing changes along four specific dimensions (see table 1.2).

I pair each context chapter with another that traces the development of infighting, again chronologically, in each march (chapters 3, 5, 7, and 9). I track each of the four demonstrations, from initial deliberations on whether the movement should consider marching, to the formal announcement that the march will indeed happen, and through the organizing process. I focus on events that transpired at a half-dozen national conferences where activists convened to deliberate and vote on all the major decisions pertaining to the march. I isolate debates over six key tasks: whether to march, when to march, what the title and theme should be, who should be invited to speak, what the march's platform ought to be, and what kind of organizing structure to use. Dissent over these tasks provides an empirical focal point and theoretical resin to better understand how conflict and culture work in political organizing. Figure 1.2 summarizes this argument.

I do not limit my analysis to a historical blow-by-blow of the making of the marches. I do this but go beyond and evaluate significance. Across the four demonstrations, we will also see in detail how activists managed a shifting calculus of emphasizing distinction (we are an organizable minority, different from you and others, and therefore are hardening our

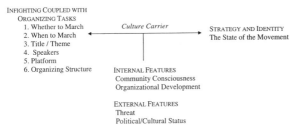

FIGURE I.2. Infighting as a Culture Carrier.

boundaries) versus de-emphasizing it (we are no different from you or others, want to be treated like everyone else, and therefore are blurring our boundaries). I consider these matters, along with the resinous culture theoretical framework, throughout the book and especially in the conclusion.

CHAPTER TWO

The Stonewall Spark:
Lesbian and Gay Life in the 1970s

In the 1970s, gay people widely internalized medical, moral, and legal views of homosexuality as a sickness, sin, and crime.[1] Despite a long history of activism and the rapid development of extensive and increasingly public, local pockets of community infrastructures, American gays generally feared to speak out about their sexual orientation. This stunted political organizing, left unimpeded cultural stereotyping, and exacerbated individual feelings of isolation. How could there be a coordinated, national effort for social change when acts as basic as sex and love were deemed morally abominable, a punishable felony, and a psychiatric disorder?

It was within a contradictory mix of opportunities and constraints that lesbians and gay men imagined the scaffolding upon which they built their first national march. Early visions for this project were considered radical, given that many people were struggling with whether being gay was a strong enough cultural thread to weave together a community against competing allegiances. It was a time when consciousness strained to stretch nationally, threats were overwhelmingly local in nature, and gays were generally relegated to the periphery of American life. This configuration set the stage for the first march. Organizing efforts and eruptions of infighting converged on a common theme: the quest of gay people to imagine themselves as part of a national movement.

Stonewall, Coming Out, and Organizational Development

The 1960s and 1970s were a special time in American history, a time
when a critical mass of people across a wide spectrum of humanity felt
the need to be seen and heard and to build a better world.[2] Lesbians and
gay men, many of whom still lived under a cloak of invisibility and silence, also felt the need to matter. Although American gays had a long
and impressive history of cultural development and political resistance
that traced back to at least the nineteenth century, historians regard
1969 as a turning point.[3]

   That year the country heard the Stonewall Riots. On June 28 the
Stonewall Inn, a gay bar located at 53 Christopher Street in New York
City's Greenwich Village, was raided. Compliance during these raids
was as routine as the raids themselves. But this time, the patrons and a
growing crowd outside fought back, resulting in five days of violent riot-
ing that forever changed the face of gay America. Bar owners and patrons had defended themselves at other raids. Nonetheless, activists and
academics often lift the Stonewall Riots of 1969 onto a venerable ped-
estal, under which they inscribe: "sparked the beginning of the gay liberation movement," "*the* emblematic event in modern lesbian and gay
history" that "resonates with images of insurgency and self-realization,"
"that moment in time when gays and lesbians recognized all at once
their mistreatment and their solidarity," the moment when lesbians and
gay men found "the courage to declare themselves for the first time," and
a "symbol of a new era of gay politics" best captured by the phrase "gay
power."[4]

   As an iconographic event that has made its way into the folklore of
gay imagination, Stonewall, especially in light of radical currents of the
New Left, motivated gay people to come out, that is, to self-identify as
gay—even more so than they had already. As a strategy, coming out was
premised on a logic of identity politics that equated the potential for social change with individual authenticity. Coming out also compelled
gay people to organize in droves across the country. A new philosophy
of gay identity fueled by interest-group politics and policy change began competing with the 1960s-inspired and still-operative gay liberation
movement that emphasized structural inequality and societal transformation.[5] When it came time to organize the first march, activists would
be burdened by the resulting strategic clash. What do we want? How do

we best secure what we want? Are we a single-issue gay-identity movement or are we instead a social justice and liberation movement?

As gay identity smoldered with the Stonewall spark, activists rejected
the notion of a "uniform and monolithic movement"—indeed, they dis-
credited uniformity altogether since it supported "one of society's favor-
ite myths about gay people," namely, "that we are all alike."[6] In this confrontation of coming out and cultural mythmaking, activists embraced a
diversity initiative that defined its expression as a political resource. They
embraced the expression of diversity for its ability to counter stereotypes about gay people. This was evident at the Eastern Regional Conference of Homophile Organizations in the fall of 1969, where activist
Craig Rodwell proposed to annually commemorate the Stonewall Riots.
Attending activists agreed to organize the first gay pride parade in New
York City during the last weekend of June in 1970. Originally called the
"March on Stonewall," activists intended this first demonstration to be a
protest against discrimination, police bar raids, and anti-gay violence.[7]

Dissent immediately emerged around the most effective form for the
event. Some argued that a march would display the community's political power and confront repressive politicians and public officials. Others
championed cultural concerns of "celebrating [the] gay community." Although initially a demonstration, founders discarded all political references and changed its form to a parade to be "held annually on the last
Saturday in June in New York City to commemorate the 1969 spontaneous demonstrations on Christopher Street." Conference attendees proposed and passed a second resolution that gay organizations across the
country should hold parallel demonstrations on the same day to make
visible the sprouting movement's networked and national organizational
infrastructure.[8]

The next several years proved activists had discovered a form of collective gathering that blended unity and diversity. The language of *celebration* and *pride* emerged at this historical moment, with leaders "committed to unifying the community," feeling a parade would be broadly
palatable. "A non-political Gay Pride celebration," activists argued,
"would be able to unite all spectrums of the community." According to
Elizabeth Armstrong:

> The fit between the parade as a form and the message displayed was perfect. . . .
> The parade demanded the display of both shared gay identities and second-

ary, modifying identities. That everyone needed a contingent, a secondary identity, constructed diversity as a point of commonality.[9]

Slowly, and in part through the strategies of coming out and com-memoration, lesbians and gay men began to see themselves as compris-ing a distinct identity movement, national in scope.

A major effect of the diversity initiative was to challenge activists to be accountable for representing the many segments of their tribe. This materialized around specific challenges with gender and race. Gay liber-ation, for example, accumulated momentum in the 1960s and early 1970s while many white women developed a separate, lesbian feminist project. This program "argued that directing energies toward men was counter-productive" and that shared gender ought to be the basis for solidarity. Whereas the gay identity movement was congealing around notions of "pride, rights, and sexual expression" embodied in the aphorism "unity through diversity," lesbian feminism focused on social justice embodied in the statement "the personal is political."[10]

Gay liberation and lesbian feminism collided around the cultural politics of the meaning of sexual-identity labels. Armstrong notes that the word *gay* was often used in a reductionist way to refer to men and women. The problem, however, was that "organizations composed of gay men could and did represent themselves as including both gay men and lesbians even when lesbian participation was minimal or nonexistent."[11] Consciously or not, gay men took advantage of ambiguities in the word *gay*. This often rendered women invisible and incorrectly suggested they had identical concerns.

Women eventually rejoined the ranks of the gay movement as lesbian feminism wilted in the late 1970s. Many decided that "gay men had to be forced to see the gendered nature of homosexual experience" that as-sumed "the typical homosexual person was male and viewed gay men's problems as generic to gay life while viewing lesbian issues as particular-istic." As a corrective response, women demanded for all existing orga-nizations to rename from gay to gay *and* lesbian. This linguistic strategy had profound cultural consequences:

Simply by demanding that "lesbian" be included in organization names, les-bians asserted that: 1) women's experience of being gay was different; 2) it was both as universal and as specific as men's experience; 3) lesbian is-sues were of equal importance; 4) one could not claim to represent lesbians without including "lesbian" in the organization's name; and 5) organizations that claimed to represent lesbians had to have lesbians as members and leaders.[12]

As a label, *gay* insufficiently represented the internal diversity of the movement by neglecting women. The rhetorical stretching from *gay* to *gay and lesbian* symbolized a corollary expansion of the boundaries of gay identity.

Gay people of color also challenged the gay liberation and lesbian feminism projects, although with comparatively less success. "Unlike women . . ." notes Armstrong, "in the 1970s people of color were not able to retreat into a world in which both their racial and sexual identities were recognized." Gays of color were trapped: they felt the stings of racism from within the predominately white gay community and homophobia from communities of color. Gay men and women of color often felt they had to subordinate their racial to their sexual identity to find a place within urban gay communities. As Audre Lorde expressed, "I find I am constantly being encouraged to pluck out some one aspect of myself and present this as the meaningful whole, eclipsing or denying the other parts of self. But this is a destructive and fragmenting way to live."[13] This problem would haunt the movement across its four national marches. But the articulation of dissent by such challenging groups prompted identity augmentation: from *gay* in the 1950s and 1960s, to *gay and lesbian* in the 1970s and 1980s (and for the first two marches), to *gay, lesbian, and bi* in the 1990s (and for the third march), and finally to *gay, lesbian, bisexual, and transgender* at the turn of the century (and for the fourth march).

In addition to prompting a reconfiguration of identity, the challenge presented by people of color also generated healthy debate on issues of strategy. Should gay people define themselves as politically sui generis or as a social justice movement seeking solidarity with other groups? This question reinvigorated liberationist ideologies through the language of coalition politics that suggested real change would only arise when different movements linked together. This perspective cast a shadow over the effectiveness of identity politics with its essentialist, single-issue focus that purported to operate in the service of some fixed community. A single-issue approach, according to the critique, assumed that gay identity existed as a natural, independent fact. This contrasted with a multi-issue, multiracial, social justice politics. The challenge gay people

of color presented, in other words, questioned the validity of the movement's claims to be at once universal and embracing of diversity. "Unity
through diversity," these activists argued, was "quite particular and homogenous." Although gay people of color were successful in raising their
voices, their "challenges [were] met with limited success,"[14] at least during the 1970s. It would not be until the second and third national marches
that their visions for racial representation and coalition politics would
touch actual organizing, inciting a corresponding reconfiguration of the
state of the movement.

We Are Everywhere: Developing a National Consciousness

Although gay life was still radical in many ways, liberationist ideologies
were disappearing in the mid-1970s, replaced by the drive to create organizations. As previously mentioned, "the building of gay identity became the central task" of this project, with ancillary objectives for "the
pursuit of gay rights and the elaboration of a sexual subculture" so far as
"they contributed to the expansion of possible ways to be gay."[15] As the
sun was setting on the heyday of gay liberation, the horizon was shifting
instead toward coming out, authenticity, and pride, along with a continued quest to build gay culture, community, and identity. The Stonewall
generation experienced pressures for political involvement and, through
this, to come out of the closet of compulsory heterosexuality and self-
identify as gay.[16] Some versions of this project appealed to women and
men, while others were specific, for example, with women's music festival organizing for lesbians and the radical faeries for gay men.

Whether general or specific, one should not mistake organizational
proliferation as evidence of a national movement. Gay life during the
1970s was mostly decentralized and local, lacking national fiber. Major
urban areas had well-established though secluded gay ghettos that provided freedom to be gay, however one might choose. One could build
organizations or engage in sexual experimentation or both. Although
there were competing ways to construct gay life, many did so within self-
contained, delimited spaces, which rapidly developed after World War II.
Such "eroticized topographies" were physically concentrated sites in
which sexual acts and identities were enacted and connected to a political paradigm.[17] Visible gay life blossomed in urban gay neighborhoods,
where a national imagination incubated.

Geographic (and oftentimes interactional) insularity had positive repercussions. Variously referred to as *abeyance structures, cultural labo-
ratories, free spaces, free territories, protected spaces, safe spaces, seques-
tered social sites,* and *submerged networks,* urban gay neighborhoods
promoted group insularity, which facilitated autonomy from the dominant group and the development of an oppositional consciousness. The
1970s gay ghettos established an infrastructure for public debate on what
it meant to be gay, for the formation of a self-affirming group culture,
and the development of indigenous institutions, resources, networks, and
political strategies. The Castro in San Francisco and the Village in New
York City were particularly prominent, serving as magnets where activists met and exchanged ideas.[18]

People flocked to urban gay centers, from which was born the wildly
popular mantra, "We Are Everywhere." Some attribute its origins to
1960s radical hippie activist Jerry Rubin of the Youth International
Party, or "yippies," who published a manifesto with this title in 1971.
Gay liberationists traveled in similar circles with other New Left activists. It therefore did not take long before "the slogan was picked up by
gay activists in the early '70s who printed up stickers so that a gay person who saw one, say in a conference room in the Pentagon, or a soror-
ity house, would know that another proud gay person had been there."[19]
Appropriating "We Are Everywhere" articulated something many knew
but could not see: although lesbians and gay men still struggled for visibility, they were in fact omnipresent: "We are in every city and town, in
every occupation, in every community."[20] The slogan made a proud appearance at the first Washington march (see fig. 2.1).

"We Are Everywhere" had additional resonance in light of Kinsey's
1948 volume *Sexual Behavior in the Human Male.* The study made a
splash in gay circles around its conclusion that "10 percent of males are
more or less exclusively homosexual for at least three years between
the ages of sixteen and fifty-five." Kinsey's findings catapulted early homophile organizing. Pioneering activists like Harry Hay, who went on
to found the Mattachine Society in Los Angeles in 1950, interpreted the
figure to suggest that gays were an organizable minority. The report, its
implications for how gays understood themselves, the appropriation of
"We Are Everywhere," and the increasing concentration of gays in urban locales were all seismic precursors to the development of a national
consciousness and movement.[21]

Political organizing developed rapidly through the 1970s as gays

FIGURE 2.1. "We Are Everywhere" Banner at the 1979 March. Photo by JD Doyle, Queer Music Heritage.

became more and more visible—collectively, through their annual free-dom day parades and, individually, by coming out. This physical pres-ence, along with an effervescing feeling of being everywhere, created a demand for a community symbol. In 1978, San Francisco native Gil-bert Baker embraced the challenge. Responding to the request of the San Francisco Gay and Lesbian Freedom Day Committee, Baker and thirty volunteers hand-dyed and hand-stitched two flags for the June 25, 1978, San Francisco Freedom Day Parade, when it first flew. The flag contained eight horizontal stripes, each a different color, producing an effect that resembled a rainbow.[22] Baker's design earned him the affec-tionate nickname, "the gay Betsy Ross."

Baker's blueprint was aesthetic and deliberate; each color was it-self a symbol. Hot pink represented sex, red stood for life, orange for healing, yellow the sun, green serenity with nature, turquoise symbol-ized art, indigo harmony, and violet represented spirit. The colors com-bined to affirm community diversity, united under a single symbol. Prac-tical factors such as costs and production constraints (e.g., hot pink was not then commercially available) resulted in the dropping of hot pink and turquoise—and royal blue replaced indigo. Thus, 1979 witnessed the birth of what we recognize today as the primary symbol of gay pride: a six-striped (red, orange, yellow, green, blue, and violet) rainbow flag, sometimes referred to as "the freedom flag."[23] Especially after the assas-sination of San Francisco city supervisor Harvey Milk, the rainbow flag diffused rapidly across the country—indeed, across the globe. The ac-

celerated pace by which it was internationally embraced helped crystallize a national consciousness for American lesbians and gay men. It soon
became *the* symbol for gay pride (as opposed to the pink triangle which
symbolized gay liberation and was appropriated from Nazi Germany)
and has since been flown in pride parades around the world.

Bryant, Briggs, and Milk: Local Conflict, National Impact

As American gays were relishing the fruits of visibility, organizational
development, and a budding national consciousness, a state-centered
backlash gained momentum. Three events provide a context for the conservatism that affected the first and second marches: Anita Bryant's Save
Our Children campaign in Florida; Senator John Briggs's Proposition 6
in California; and the election and assassination of the first openly gay
San Francisco city supervisor, Harvey Milk.

Bryant's Save Our Children Campaign

The local gay rights battle that drew the most media attention was Dade
County (Miami), Florida's anti-discrimination measure adopted in January 1977. Following its passage, former beauty queen (Miss Okla-
homa, 1958, and second runner-up for Miss America, 1959) and record-
ing artist–turned–born-again Christian evangelist mother Anita Bryant
spearheaded what she called a "Save Our Children" campaign. Bryant
claimed that "the recruitment of our children is absolutely necessary
for the survival and growth of homosexuality" and that "no one has the
human right to corrupt our children."[24] Bryant argued that gay people
were wicked, godless, and out to recruit America's innocent children.
She personalized her message: "As a mother, I know that homosexuals cannot biologically reproduce children; therefore, they must recruit
our children."[25] Bryant selectively displayed images from San Francisco's gay freedom day parades and argued that the city was "a cesspool of
sexual perversion gone rampant." She cautioned, "Don't let Miami become another San Francisco." In the name of God and with the aid of
fundamentalist churches and conservative Roman Catholic groups, Bryant helped repeal Florida's gay rights ordinance by a two-to-one margin
(69 to 31 percent) on June 7, 1977, unleashing a domino effect of anti-gay
violence nationally.

The Florida fight was a watershed in light of the regional (i.e., state and local) organizing it sparked. Ethan Geto, then a resident of Dade County, prophesied: "I thought it was the first great opportunity nationally to mobilize the gay community with a political consciousness. I hoped that gay rights would mature into a major civil rights issue on the national agenda." Protests broke out epidemically across the country—such as the 3,000 who turned out in San Francisco—as word of the Florida repeal spread. Bryant's local campaign had a national impact, evidenced by placards Washington marchers carried that pungently declared, "Piss on Anita."[26]

Bryant's campaign self-fulfilled gay identity. According to Armstrong, "By defining gay life as a threat worthy of attack, anti-gay activists acknowledged that the gay movement could no longer be dismissed as a joke." Although Save Our Children was psychically lacerating, it placed gay issues on the table of national media and public opinion. Bryant inadvertently "participated in creating her enemy" by affirming "the reality and solidity of gay identity."[27]

Briggs's Proposition 6

Soon after Miami's Bryant came archconservative Republican State Senator John Briggs of Orange County, California. Briggs proposed a statewide ballot initiative—Proposition 6—to prevent lesbians and gay men from teaching in public schools. To him, gay people symbolized a "precipitous decline in morals sweeping the nation." The Briggs Initiative, a feverish campaign driven by the desire to "defend your children from homosexual teachers," called for the firing of any public school educator who was "advocating, imposing, encouraging, or promoting" homosexuality. Similar to Bryant, Briggs also used the rhetoric of children's wellbeing to suggest that "a coalition of homosexual teachers and their allies are trying to use the vast power of our school system to impose their own brand of non-morality on your children."[28] Briggs broadened the tactical attack (from Bryant's mostly media-based platform) by marshalling 500,000 signatures of registered voters needed to place his initiative on the November 1978 election ballot.

Although pollsters predicted a victory for gay rights, it was expected to be narrow. California voters, however, rejected Brigg's Proposition 6 in an overwhelming 58 to 42 percent margin. This sent the initiative "down in flames" and made it one of the first statewide electoral victories for gay rights. It also provided "much-needed inspiration" for a developing "national movement," as quoted in the gay press.[29] Similar to Bryant, anti-Briggs references also appeared at the first march.

"Saint" Harvey Milk

Perceptions of belonging to a national movement accelerated with the electoral victory of the first openly gay politician in California.[30] Despite being told that "no openly gay man could win political office," Harvey Milk joined San Francisco's board of supervisors and became a part of the city's history as the first openly gay elected official. Milk was flooded with mail from inspired people across the country, who wrote, "I thank God. I have lived long enough to see my kind emerge from the shadows and join the human race."[31] Harvey Milk campaigned tirelessly to debate and defeat anti-gay propositions such as the Briggs Initiative. He became a national symbol of gay oppression, activism, freedom, and the struggle for human rights. Milk believed that injustices toward gay people were driven by invisibility. This inspired his mantra and familiar refrain: "Come out! Come out! Come out!"[32]

Anti-gay forces were not prepared to accept a gay political presence. On November 27, 1978, supervisor Dan White, feeling betrayed by the emerging "liberal bloc on the council," climbed into a side window of City Hall to avoid metal detectors at the main door. Carrying his .38-caliber police revolver, White walked into Mayor George Moscone's office and shot him twice in his chest and twice in his head. White then proceeded to Milk's office, where he shot him five times in total, twice in the head, at point-blank range.[33]

San Francisco locals responded with one of the largest candlelight vigils and processions the city had ever seen. Some months later on May 21, 1979, the jury trying Dan White announced an innocuous verdict of five years with parole for voluntary manslaughter based on the much-derided "Twinkie Defense": "Psychiatrists pronounced him 'depressed' and suffering from 'diminished capacity' owing to a junk food diet"—that is, White had eaten too many Twinkies, which exacerbated his depression and drove him to kill. Gays were outraged. After this verdict was announced, thousands marched on City Hall, declaring that White had "got away with murder" and that the court's decision meant that it was "open season on faggots." San Francisco erupted in what have since been remembered as the White Night Riots. Protestors set ablaze

eleven police cars and smashed the windows of City Hall, holding up
placards that read, "Did Harvey Milk Die for Nothing?"[34]

On January 6, 1984, Dan White was secretly paroled from Soledad
Prison, where he had served five years. Fearing the local reaction to what
he had done, White was transported to Los Angeles, where he agreed
to carry out his probation. After he completed the terms, White still desired to move back to his home city by the bay. His fears, however, were
true; White would not be able to escape the thick stigma associated with
his actions and the city's outrage. On October 21, 1985, less than two
years after his release, White committed suicide in his car garage by connecting a garden hose to the exhaust pipe of his 1970 Buick LeSabre.[35] In
the years since, Harvey Milk has been mythologized as a saint and martyr for gay rights, evidenced by a 2003 exhibit at the Museum of GLBT
History in San Francisco titled, "Saint Harvey: The Life and Afterlife of
a Modern Gay Martyr."[36]

These and other local fights precipitated a national consciousness.
A June 1979 editorial in the *Gay Community News* linked them and
Stonewall to an imperative to build a national movement: "Stonewall
means fighting back. In the past ten years, gay people have begun fighting back: in cities and in small towns, in the courts and legislatures, and
in the streets. The fights have been local, the leaders unconnected, the
movements disparate. Slowly, we have begun to develop a national consciousness, a sense of our own common identity. We made contact with
each other in the Dade County fight and in raising money to defeat the
Briggs Initiative. Now we are creating a national grassroots organizing and mobilization structure to plan the March on Washington."[37]
Four months later, another editorial observed, "In the ten years which
have passed since the Stonewall Rebellion, gay people have organized
into local movements in communities across America. Slowly, a national
mass movement has evolved out of necessity, to respond to the crises in
Dade County, in California, and elsewhere."[38] The time had come: from
the seeds of local gay rights battles, a national consciousness and movement were taking root.

Life on the Periphery

Organizational struggles of gay people, their nascent sense of belonging
to a national movement, and the recurring episodes of local conflict that

confronted them illuminate different angles of their same peripheral positioning. Although cast off to the margins, lesbians and gay men did feel
bursts of optimism and political efficacy—the "necessary cognitions,"
according to sociologist Doug McAdam, that provided a "will to act."[39]
Advances on the medical and legislative fronts—with the American Psychiatric Association's revised stance on homosexuality and the first-time
introduction of a federal gay rights bill in Congress—spurred these cognitions. These political steps forward, however, were tempered by Hollywood's harmful cultural depictions. The net result was a sense of hope
amid persisting horrors for a group of people who, despite their most
earnest efforts, still felt marooned on the peripheries of American life.

Cured: The APA's (De-)Classification of Homosexuality

The notion of homosexuality as either an acceptable "lifestyle" or a genetically determined "orientation" is exceedingly modern. Prior to 1973,
homosexuality was largely considered a mental illness. Gay people have
long fought the scientific community's definition of non-heterosexuality
as a disease or disorder. Such definitions hurt individual self-esteem and
impeded collective organizing. Veteran activist Frank Kameny commented on the impact of medical classifications: "An attribution of
mental illness in our culture is devastating," and that classification has
served as "one of the major stumbling blocks" for gay rights advocacy.
Kameny dedicated himself to this fight. In the summer of 1968, he was
watching Stokely Carmichael on television orchestrating a group of civil
rights protestors in a collective chant of, "Black is beautiful!" Kameny
was inspired: "I understood the psychodynamic at work here in a context in which *black* is universally equated with everything that is bad."
Gay people needed to engage in a similar inversion. In July of that same
year, Kameny coined the cultural catchphrase "gay is good" as an in-
spirational equivalent to "black is beautiful." He was forever changed
by this: "If I had to specify the one thing in my life of which I am most
proud, it is that."[40]

Psychodynamic struggles came to a climax on December 15, 1973, in
Washington, D.C. Ten days before Christmas, an era ended when the
board of trustees of the American Psychiatric Association voted 13–0
(with two members abstaining) to remove homosexuality from its list of
disorders in the *Diagnostic and Statistical Manual* (*DSM*). This removal
ended a battle that had begun with the publication of the *DSM* in 1952,

in which homosexuals were defined as "ill primarily in terms of society and of conformity with the prevailing social milieu." Since then, the APA had remained "one of the key targets of gay activists in the early 1970s," with activists engaged in a "politics of diagnosis."[41]

The APA endorsed painful psychiatric treatments, such as shock, aversion, and reparative therapy, to cure the homosexual pathology. Lesbians and gay men often attended APA meetings to protest readings of so-called "research" in favor of such therapies. At one convention in 1962, one inflamed audience protester shouted, "Where did you take your residency—*Auschwitz*?" This type of direct action continued until the reversal in 1973. Activist Kay Lahusen reminisced, "You don't realize what it was like back then. They were the experts. They said we were sick, and that's what most people believed."[42]

Kameny and others participated in this battle since the 1960s. In a spring 1964 television interview, Kameny radically declared, "I see nothing wrong with homosexuality, nothing to be ashamed of. . . . It is not a disease, a pathology, a sickness, a malfunction, or a disorder of any sort. . . . Psychiatrists are a biased group."[43] Nine years later, the APA finally listened. Although homosexuality remained a sin in most denominations and a crime in most states, the December 15 vote dissolved its scientific stronghold. For too long, gay people had endured their own "tripartite system of domination," to allude to Aldon Morris's characterization of civil-rights-era oppression, in which homosexuality was culturally imprisoned as a sin (religious domination), sickness (scientific domination), and crime (legal domination).[44] As activist Barbara Gittings recalled, "Besides being sick, we were sinful and criminal." One of the obstructions had finally lifted. Homosexuals were suddenly cured of their "illness" in what was one of "the most hopeful sign[s] of change." No longer could Americans justify discrimination on the grounds of it being officially classified as a "sexual perversion."[45]

The Federal Gay Rights Bill

Another moment of optimism arrived on May 14, 1974, five short months after the APA reversal. Representative Bella Abzug (D-N.Y.) introduced the first federal gay rights bill in the House of Representatives. Illustriously titled the "Equality Act of 1974," the bill would have augmented the 1964 Civil Rights Act to outlaw discrimination based on sexual orientation in the areas of "public accommodations, federally assisted programs, public facilities, the sale and rental of private housing, private employment, and education."[46] Abzug's endorsement reveals that 1970s activists directed their efforts in part at promoting non-discrimination legislation. The first such state-level law succeeded in 1972, when the city of East Lansing, Michigan, passed a resolution prohibiting sexual-orientation-based discrimination. Abzug's 1974 proposal was the first national equivalent. Unfortunately, it did not pass. With activist encouragement, some congressperson has introduced a similar piece of legislation ever since, though, at the time of this writing, none has yet achieved passage.

That the bill did not pass in its first introduction is not surprising. Historians suggest its passage was out of the question; proposing it was more symbolic: "The introduction of legislation was the kind of symbolic moment the Task Force [a prominent gay rights organization] was looking for, an affirmation of its leaders and their mainstream sensibilities."[47] Its passage was less important than its signaling of gay people's resolve to march out of the periphery. Although they would not occupy this desired mainstream status at the time of either their first or second march, growing forces would thrust them there during the third march—and even more so at the turn of the century. Activists did not anticipate, however, that this dangling carrot would bring them more internal warfare than its illusory promises.

Cruising

The transformation of cultural attitudes lagged behind political change. This is exemplified in the 1979 film *Cruising*, considered by some to be "the most notorious film from the late 1970s . . . assault of Hollywood-inflamed homophobia." Directed by William Friedkin and starring Al Pacino, the film's plot unravels in Greenwich Village gay leather bars and other "cruising" areas—that is, places where gay men meet for casual and sometimes anonymous sex. Heterosexual cop Pacino goes undercover to capture a psychotic serial killer of gay men. In addition to the troubling violence, the film also shows Pacino, with his apartment in the "heart of darkness" (read: a gay neighborhood), becoming so caught up as to question his own sexuality, implying that "contact with gays could lure a man into their web." This was one of Hollywood's first acknowledgments of the burgeoning gay scene. And its depiction was loathsome.[48]

The film's graphic images of victimized gay men and its message—that "homosexuality is contagious as well as lethal"—set ablaze national protests and boycotts. Lesbians and gay men took to the streets, chanting, "Stop the movie *Cruising*! Stop the movie *Cruising*!" New York activist Arthur Bell described the film as a cultural commentary that "promised to be the most oppressive, bigoted look at homosexuality ever presented on the screen." Protestor-distributed leaflets portended that the film "will encourage more violence against homosexuals." Their warnings proved correct. The documentary *Celluloid Closet,* for example, interviews a man who recounts an experience when his partner and he were gay-bashed. Their perpetrator cursed, "If you saw the movie *Cruising,* you know what you deserve." Given Hollywood's role in teaching America about itself, the film revealed that favorable cultural attitudes lagged behind forward-running legislative strides.[49]

The Stonewall Spark

Gay life in the 1970s was saturated with contradictory activity. Sparked by the Stonewall Riots, gay organizational development burst onto the scene with the annual, commemorative, freedom day parades. The decline of New Left radicalism forced the mostly white and male gay liberation movement to dialogue with the lesbian separatism and people of color communities. This revealed that the reductionist category *gay* strained to represent the spectrum of specific identities that nonetheless desired a place at the table. The simple act of including lesbians in all titles—that is, changing the nomenclature from *gay* to *gay and lesbian*—had the consequence of augmenting the boundaries of gay life to denotatively include women. A similar battle would erupt around bisexual inclusion during the second march, although they would not achieve representational success until the third march.

Expansion occurred with the rise of identifiably gay neighborhoods in major urban hubs of the country. Gays became increasingly organized, developed the rainbow flag as their primary symbol, and were able to believe in the veracity of their self-appropriated slogan, "We Are Everywhere." Visibility came with advances in science and the law. The APA removed homosexuality from its list of mental illnesses in 1973, and a federal gay rights bill was introduced for the first time in Congress in 1974. Strides danced with setbacks, most notably with the release of the homophobic film *Cruising,* Anita Bryant's "Save Our Children" campaign, California State Senator John Brigg's Proposition 6, and the cold-blooded murder of gay-friendly San Francisco Mayor George Moscone and openly gay supervisor Harvey Milk.

The events narrated in this chapter speak to the three major facets of gay life in the 1970s. First, they reveal a movement situated on the margins. But the historical record also identifies a desire to travel inward toward the center of citizenship. This mainstream momentum would steadily accumulate over the course of the four marches and would yield what was for 1970s activists wildly unanticipated controversies. Second, political activity was generally local in character. Coast to coast, from New York City, where the Stonewall Riots took place and the film *Cruising* was shot, to California with Harvey Milk and John Briggs, to Dade County with Anita Bryant—gay life had a distinctively regional feeling. Third, some of this activity acquired national resonance. This local-national tension was personified in the annual freedom day parades celebrated in gay neighborhoods across the country. Collectively, the episodes chronicled in this chapter motivated the movement to begin imagining itself as a national player on the American political and cultural landscape. As we will see in the next chapter, the first national march on Washington solidified this entrée, while its associated infighting captured the experiential reality of the transition.

The Birth of a National Movement: The 1979 National March on Washington for Lesbian and Gay Rights

A publicly identifiable national lesbian and gay movement was effete in the 1970s. American gays were active in this time period, as discussed in the previous chapter, although most of their energies were concentrated at the local and state levels. Precocious activists who had begun to imagine a national movement felt it was only "a loose confederation of local organizations that rarely interact with one another."[1] They stumbled onto the insight that "up until now, our struggle has been centered around local and state issues. We are realizing that these local issues are part of a national pattern, and that we need to unite nationally to ultimately win these local battles." A march on Washington would be the magic bullet. "[The] Lesbian and Gay movement . . . is about to take a giant leap forward, to go national, and the March on Washington is the focus that will make it possible."[2] This event could gestate a national movement by producing "tangible new organizing resources" as simple as "a massive national mailing list," a communications network, and other less tangible reserves, such as providing "a national focus for a movement which has worked mostly at the local level."[3]

But how do you build a national movement when no prior visible artifact or consciousness of it is yet in place? Add to this already formidable task the movement's long history of being riddled with internal strife. How did the movement accomplish the difficult task of developing a national self-understanding, especially amid raucous infighting? Did infighting hurt or help? And what did it reveal along the way? Just as Armstrong suggested that "the creation of a public organization [such as Mattachine and the Daughters of Bilitis] contributed to identity building [in the 1950s] by asserting the public existence of a group and making it possible for interested individuals to find it,"[4] I argue in this chapter that the first march gave birth to a national movement. Activists aired dissent along the way to give voice to and thus make incarnate who they felt they were, what they wanted, and how to go about securing it.

The Urbana-Champaign Meeting

From where did the idea for the very first march originate? Some trace it to a remark by lesbian comic Robin Tyler at a benefit for the St. Paul Citizens for Human Rights on Friday, April 21, 1978. After her performance, Tyler said, "We must fight back! It's time to forget about being 'nice.' How long will lesbians and gay men tolerate not having rights in this country? We must organize for a national march on Washington, D.C."[5]

Most, including recent scholarship, link the idea to Harvey Milk, who urged the community to march on Washington in an address he gave at the June 1978 gay freedom day parade in San Francisco.[6] Its origins aside, the idea of marching on Washington was an established element in the New Left repertoire and was often connected to the civil rights movement's 1963 March on Washington for Jobs and Freedom. The sentiment that "it's our turn" was captured in a letter Steve Ault sent to gay organizations across the country:

> On August 28, 1963, there was the first mass Civil Rights March on Washington. Lesbians and gay men were there, hidden in that crowd that cheered Martin Luther King Jr.'s dream. There have been many marches since then — anti-war, Earth Day, ERA — and slowly lesbians and gay men began to raise our own banners and march behind them. Now, on October 14, 1979, lesbians and gay men, and our supporters will march for our own dream: the dream of justice, equality and freedom . . .[7]

Contrary to every published historical account, the earliest paper trail dates the first organizing efforts to a 1973 Thanksgiving weekend meeting convened by the National Gay Mobilizing Committee for a March on Washington (NGMC), the first organization ever created to consider

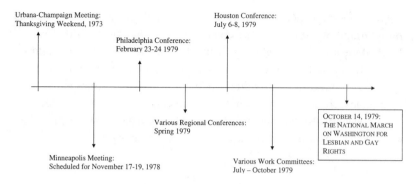

FIGURE 3.1. An Organizational Timeline of the 1979 March.

the possibility of lesbians and gay men marching on their nation's capitol. The NGMC held a meeting in the student union at the University of Illinois's Urbana-Champaign campus.[8] A timeline of the major organizational events that transpired from this point forward and that served as the architecture for the 1979 march appears in figure 3.1.

Spearheaded by University of Illinois undergraduate Jeff Graubart, the NGMC launched the first Washington march campaign. Activists envisioned a "peaceful, massive march on Washington, D.C., calling for the repeal of all sodomy and solicitation laws and full civil and human rights for Gays."[9] Early organizers intended to use the Champaign convention to iron out three critical organizing tasks: to set the date (benchmarked for the spring of 1974), lay out the demands, and establish a coordination and communication system. Graubart acknowledged that the idea for "some kind of march on Washington" had been floating around in progressive circles—inspired, in part, by Anita Bryant's vitriolic crusade in Dade County.[10] Coming four short years after Stonewall, when activists were still laboring to procure local liberties, this first organizing effort did not flower. However, reviewing why pioneering activists felt a march was necessary, as well as the fault lines along which they debated, provides a snapshot of the state of the movement during the 1970s.

Graubart was nothing short of a visionary in imagining an autonomous, national movement with palpable political power. On behalf of the NGMC, which operated out of a meek financial budget, Graubart mailed letters to all known gay organizations that he and his friends could find

by pillaging through the pages of local gay newspapers. In one portion of
his letter, he pleaded:

> Dear Brothers and Sisters in Gay Liberation,
>   . . . . Such a convention [to brainstorm a march on Washington] is impera-
> tive, as we witness isolated Gay groups around the nation forming multi-issue
> alignments with either the Democrats or various socialist formations. . . . Be-
> cause they are isolated, they feel too insecure to engage in independent polit-
> ical action. . . . Gay people can feel solidarity . . . as it is realized that we are
> a political force on our own. . . . It will be our Gay Pride and our Gay Power
> that will raise our consciousness. . . . The structured organization must be
> prepared to defend Gay people throughout the nation.[11]

The rumblings of a unified national movement were in the air.

Graubart was a savvy organizer cognizant of the subtle representational politics involved in constructing a national demonstration. He was
aware that conservative currents in the movement "must be assured that
no crazy will seize the podium and call for some 'stop the government'
nonsense. Women must be assured of an equal number of speakers at
the demonstration. This will insure male/female unity at the demonstration. Black Gays must be given ample representation on the speakers list, along with other Third World Gays. Only they can tell the people of the United States how Black Pride and Gay Pride are both rooted
in self pride and human decency. This is essential for our movement and
solidarity."[12]

Despite such inclusive gestures, the idea to march was immediately
criticized. Don Goodwin, then president of the Mattachine Society of
New York, argued that to gain nationwide support for such an event,
"you have to have goals to go after, such as national legislation, or something in the Supreme Court. You've got to have a bill. We're nowhere
near having a nationwide bill. We're having enough trouble in New York
City just passing something through the city council." This sentiment
was expressed by other representatives as well, who voiced that most gay
organizations were still trying to deal with local and state sodomy laws
and other forms of oppression at the local level. A paradox emerged: how
could there be a national march when activists could not even conceptu-
alize that they were part of a national movement?

In reply, Graubart, who coordinated the meeting, said one of the
goals of the proposed march is "to gain 'solidarity' for the gay movement

in the country, which . . . is now 'isolated' and fragmented." As a national movement, lesbians and gay men were ineffective. The dialogue between Goodwin and Graubart underscores that lesbians and gay men did not envision themselves as stretching across the nation. Indeed, that was an explicit intention of marching in the first place, namely, to "raise the national consciousness."[13] Both the motivation and the infighting over the proposed march were enmeshed in this line of thinking.

Gay people had no way of believing (or verifying) that their movement existed on a national scale. Despite early studies by Alfred Kinsey, which suggested that gays comprised about 10 percent of the population, and despite the modicum of organizational momentum this precipitated, lesbians and gay men still did not have faith that there were enough of their own kind to sizably gather in Washington. For example, D.C. representatives objected to the march because they felt organizers would not be able to attract a large enough crowd. A poor turnout would embarrass gay people everywhere, at best, or sign the movement's obituary, at worst. Larry Maccubin, then chairperson of the Washington Area Gay Community Council, an umbrella coalition of over twenty D.C. gay organizations, articulated this concern in a personal letter:

> I can safely say that, unless you can guarantee a minimum of 50,000 gays marching down Pennsylvania Avenue this spring, the march will be a political disaster. The numbers game is a political fact of life here. If less than 50,000 gays march, it won't rate a two-inch write-up on the obituary pages, much less any serious consideration of the issues by the Congress. A small march will hurt, not help, the movement for justice and equality. A march of 50,000 gays, on the other hand, is not a very likely event in Washington. The largest gay marches to date drew less than 20,000 and that was in New York, where the vast majority of gays are privately employed and have little need to stay in the closet. There are about a quarter of a million gays in this area, but the majority . . . cannot or will not risk exposure at this time.[14]

Longtime activist Franklin Kameny, then affiliated with the Mattachine Society of Washington (D.C.), expressed similar reservations: "We are concerned as to how realistic it is to expect that large numbers of Gays will actually participate in such a march. *IF* there could be any reasonable, realistic assurance of the participation of significantly large numbers of people, we would enthusiastically support the march, but a much-publicized effort attended, in actuality, by a pathetically small handful of people would do us far more harm than good."[15]

D.C.'s local gay community's impedance of the march made the pages of the budding national gay press. An article written in the *Advocate* declared, "Most of the people who will represent Washington-area organizations at the Champaign convention will bring the message: Don't come!" Why? "Their objections center mainly on deep skepticism that a large enough crowd can be attracted to such a march to avoid embarrassment."[16] These debates indicate a newly hatching consciousness with activists burdened by the invisibility effects of the closet. Even those who were optimistic squeezed the notion of a "sizable" turnout through narrow parameters. Graubart replied to concerns about attracting enough participants by suggesting a crowd of five to ten thousand "would not be bad" since he had "never seen a march of five to ten thousand be looked down upon for being too small." Thus, even those who were visualizing a national movement did so on a small scale.

The Urbana meeting did not blossom into an organizational infrastructure. The dividends of dissent were obscured in this particular case for a variety of reasons. Concerns such as having tangible goals to pursue suggest that many did not perceive an adequate trigger to justify march organizing. This, in connection with a lack of precedence (after all, gays had never marched on Washington before), paralyzed consensus and forward motion. Lack of precedence also meant that there was a fuzzy (and untested) vision for how to organize the event. As I will continue to demonstrate across the four marches, an organizing structure, in whatever form, is critical since it holds conversion potential for dissent to translate into solidarity. Without this, and for Urbana activists, dissent remained diffuse and its dividends unactualized. These reasons may also explain why so few even remember Urbana happened.

The Minneapolis Committee

The next deliberative effort occurred one month before the defeat of Briggs in October 1978. At that point, a group calling itself the Committee for the March on Washington based in Minneapolis also tossed around the idea of a national demonstration. They organized an Interim Steering Committee (ISC), consisting of members of the National Gay

Task Force (NGTF), Metropolitan Community Church (MCC), and elected gay officials like San Francisco Supervisor Harvey Milk. The ISC projected the march for Sunday May 6, 1979, and envisioned two intentions: to demonstrate to the nation that gay rights were part of the larger issue of human rights; and to unify what at the time were local, disconnected, and scattered organizations around a focus that could possibly interest everyone.[17]

The ISC sent out a questionnaire to known gay organizations across the country, soliciting viewpoints on the proposed march and intending to use responses to facilitate discussion during its first meeting the weekend of November 17–19, 1978, in Minneapolis. The ISC used returned replies to draft a six-page statement memorably titled "An Idea Whose Time Has Come: A March on the Nation's Capitol," in which activists explained their reasons for organizing a march. The passage of gay rights ordinances—or even general human rights ordinances—at the local level was no longer a viable strategy.[18] According to Joyce Hunter, who would become one of the national co-coordinators, "There was no precedent for reliance on a localities strategy in the United States." No minority group had gained rights by concentrating exclusively at the state or local level. To ensure equality for lesbian and gay citizens, efforts would have to be channeled toward the passage of national legislation. Although this possibility seemed remote, the groundwork needed to be laid without delay.

Bracing for national entrée required five strategic preparations. These included: 1) the transformation of fragmented and local activity into a reasonably unified, national movement; 2) the creation of a coalition in support of gay rights composed of people from feminist, civil rights, civil liberties, religious, and progressive organizations to bear witness that the movement for gay rights was in the same tradition as earlier civil rights and human rights struggles; 3) organizing lobbying campaigns; 4) sustaining a high level of visibility in the media; and 5) the organizational capability to mobilize thousands of people in Washington.[19]

Many were not convinced that working for the passage of national legislation was feasible. If this was not the strategic direction the movement should take, then the rationale for holding a Washington march itself fell apart. The committee, however, anticipated these objections. Even if pressing for national legislation was not the ultimate objective, organizing the march would still have value. The committee equated demanding national legislation with weaving together a national movement out of the disparate threads of local activity. The march's strategic value would be to reflect both the size and strength of this patchwork.

The committee then articulated four additional strategic rewards, all of which had implications for nationalizing an otherwise decentralized, local movement. These included the march's capacity to: 1) provide a national focus and goal that all lesbian and gay activists and organizations could work toward and, in the process, develop a communication network; 2) stimulate new organizing, similar to the impact of Stonewall, but also coalition building with other national interest groups; 3) generate new political organizing in localities where none existed prior, while also identifying existing local organizations and individual activists that could be assembled into a national entity; and 4) develop a new line of communication that could link local pockets of political activity into a national network.[20]

The first march would provide a national focus for a movement that had heretofore been local. It would do this by what it symbolized: it would demonstrate to the nation the size and power of the gay community and draw connections between its demands and the issue of human rights. Activists realized "the symbolic value of thousands of Americans marching on the nation's capital to demand human rights protection for gays would be an effective way to dramatize the idea that gay rights should be viewed within the broader context of human rights."[21] Drawing this link was savvy since the Carter administration had been outspoken about human rights abroad. In 1977, President Jimmy Carter pronounced "human rights" (his phrase) an American foreign policy objective.[22] Similar to strategies employed by the civil rights movement, which used the cold war and the Truman administration's foreign policy that denounced international racism to mobilize anti-segregation advocates at home, lesbians and gay men exploited the Carter administration's rhetoric of human rights abroad to identify hypocritical treatment at home.[23]

Human rights fared prominently in march literature. Minneapolis activists envisioned the coupling of gay and human rights as part of the march's value. The march on Washington would "provide a highly visible challenge to the Carter Administration and the Democratic congressional establishment on the issue of . . . human rights" as it would "have considerable symbolic value in driving home the point that human rights for gays is part of the larger historic movement for equal rights for all people." Minneapolis activists also incorporated the theme of human rights into their brainstorms for the title of the march, which included suggestions such as a "Human Rights March" and a "Lesbian/Gay Human Rights March."[24] Delegates later circulated a press release after the Philadelphia conference that stated, "President Carter has said, 'Human Rights are absolute.' With one stroke of the pen the president could end discrimination."[25] The state of the movement was linked with the rhetoric of human rights to establish legitimacy and mobilize protest. Here we see the earliest evidence for an identity and strategy that diminished the uniqueness of gay sexuality. In other words, the quest for gay rights was not driven by the particular plight of gays in the United States, per se, but instead as equal rights for *all people*. This was an example of boundary-blurring that emphasized porousness ("we deserve the same as everyone else"), as opposed to boundary-hardening that emphasized distinction.

The committee proposed for a representative group of leaders from across the U.S. to issue the formal call to action. To ensure this, the ISC planned to bring together more than twenty nationally recognized activists to participate in the first organizing phase. On October 31, 1978, a little over two weeks prior to the scheduled weekend meeting of lesbian and gay leaders, the Minneapolis-based ISC dissolved after deciding that problems of internal dissension would keep it from effectively planning the proposed march. Brian McNaught, a Boston gay activist invited to the Minneapolis meetings, told the *Gay Community News* that he received word from the committee that it had disbanded due to problems of "classism and racism" within its membership.[26] The differences boiled down to gender disputes between gay men and lesbians regarding the type of audience for whom fund-raising efforts ought to be directed. According to Barbara Metzger, co-chairperson of the ISC, "The differences between gay men and women play a role in everything we do." Metzger noted, "The problem was that our fund-raising was directed at one particular type of audience; it was an issue of whom we were appealing to. . . . My own personal opinion is that the fund-raising was being directed to middle- and upper-class men." Thus, infighting in the early organizing process revealed that gender differences sometimes trumped perceptions of sexual commonality.

Regionalism was another area of dispute. Washington, D.C.'s community expressed reluctance to have the march in their backyard, citing concerns that it might jeopardize local efforts and accomplishments.

According to Harvey Milk, "The people in Washington don't want [the march because] it might upset the balance they have achieved, but they must take responsibility for being in the nation's capital, at the center of things." When *Gay Community News* reporters asked Milk if he thought the proposed demonstration would be detrimental to Washington's local community, Milk replied, "That's a tenuous position they have, and if it gets pushed to a vote, they lose . . . so many gay people are afraid of upsetting the apple cart." Graubart encountered similar reservations from D.C.'s community in his 1973 attempts. At that time, Larry Maccubin expressed his skepticism about a Washington march and, in so doing, alluded earlier to what Milk later meant by "upsetting the apple cart":

> Most D.C. gay organizations have spent the past several years developing a community program that includes services to the community (such as the new Gay Health Clinic) and strengthening our position with the political forces which govern us (in our case the District City Council and the Congress). That effort has begun to yield significant gains. . . . We do not want to risk any set-backs at this time due to a poorly conceived, hastily planned, and shabbily supported demonstration.[27]

As activists fought over regionalism, they were therefore speaking to broader concerns associated with transitioning from many local programs to one national program.

For reasons similar to those that account for the demise of the Urbana conference, infighting dissolved, rather than productively propelled forward, the Minneapolis committee. This prompted Harvey Milk to assume responsibility for continuing efforts. With him, the organizational epicenter shifted to San Francisco. Milk maintained the march's unifying, symbolic impact while recognizing that infighting was intimately woven into the fabric of gay culture and politics: "You won't ever be able to get everyone to agree," he astutely observed. "I hope that the gathering will take place on the weekend following the Fourth of July. That would have great symbolic impact, reminding people of the Declaration of Independence, in which gay people were left out." In addition to the strategy of drawing on Carter's rhetoric of human rights, Milk's invocation of the Declaration of Independence was an additional effort at boundary-blurring—that is, gay people being among the many *left out.*

On November 27, 1978, less than a month after Milk assumed organizing responsibilities and won over D.C.'s local groups, he and mayor George Moscone were assassinated by Dan White in City Hall. In addition to the resulting local White Night Riots, the tragedy triggered a national response with memorial services held throughout the country. After a San Francisco service, an aide and personal friend commented, "We are all dedicating ourselves to carry on the work that Harvey held so dear."[28] Milk's connection to the first march on Washington was memorialized in the official program and by rally speakers, as well. In the article, "Long, Long Road to Washington," published in the march program, activist Jim Kepner linked the 1979 march to Harvey Milk and Stonewall: "The Milk-Moscone shootings . . . did so much to bring us here. The Dan White verdict and riots last November were an echo of Stonewall—but with what a difference!"[29] Similarly, Ray Hill told the crowd assembled on the mall during the march itself, "Let's tell Harvey that we're here."[30] These remarks may explain why so many link the idea of the first march to Harvey Milk. Although the movement's consciousness was still firmly local, his death provided a nationally resonating catalyst to launch the transition.

Milk believed that a Washington march "made up of all people—lesbians, gay men, heterosexual supporters, young people, the elderly, people of all races, all ethnic backgrounds, all walks of life—would show the president and Congress that our movement is a force to be reckoned with." Invoking Milk's memory, the individuals who would spearhead the first march wrote to gay leaders all across the country, "This project must be carried out as a tribute to Harvey Milk and to the countless others who have suffered and perished at the hands of bigots. We must fulfill Harvey's dream for those who are still alive and for those yet unborn who shall love a person of their own sex."[31] This was, after all, a movement fighting for the right to love. The sentiment also reverberated in the lyrics of a popular gay-themed tune at the time: "Tell your sister. Tell your brother. It's okay to love one another. Sing it loud. I'm gay, and I'm proud."[32] At the demonstration, a group of marchers held a sign that declared, "The Time Is Come: Lovers of Your Own Sex, ARISE!"[33] This cultural sensibility was poignantly printed in the official march program, as well, which included a photograph taken outside New York's city hall at a protest for the passage of a gay civil rights bill (see fig. 3.2).

FIGURE 3.2. The Right to Love. Photo © Bettye Lane.

The Philadelphia Conference

Milk's death sealed the deal on the march. Soon after, three hundred people in San Francisco organized an ad hoc National Outreach Committee (NOC) to ensure Harvey's dream would come true. The San Francisco–based NOC, in conjunction with an ad hoc committee in Philadelphia and the New York Coalition for Lesbian and Gay Rights, put out a call for a conference in Philadelphia the weekend of February 23–25, 1979, at the historic Quaker Friends Meeting House. Known lesbian and gay organizations across the country were invited to send two delegates—one man and one woman—to the conference. Racial minority participation (i.e., "Third World" delegates, in the argot of times) was also strongly encouraged.

Included with the invitation was a cover letter that explained that Philadelphia delegates would establish an agenda and make decisions regarding the date and focus of the march.[34] Attached to the letter was a questionnaire that solicited feedback on the date, focus, demands, theme, and entertainment: "Several dates have been proposed for the march. Please rank them in the order of your preference: May 6, 1979; July 8, 1979; early fall 1979; July 4, 1980; other." Regarding the focus: "Please rank the following numerically according to the importance you feel they should portray in the march/rally, assuming that all elements will be represented to some degree: political; educational; cultural/entertainment; other." The demands: "What should be our central political demands?" The theme: "What should be the educational theme?" And entertainment: "What should the cultural/entertainment segments consist of?"[35] This was very much a grassroots effort.

Unlike Minneapolis, the San Francisco group, variously referring to itself as the National Outreach Committee and the National Conference for the March on Washington, did not dissolve. More than three hundred lesbians and gay men from across the country met in Philadelphia on February 23–25 to discuss the proposal of organizing a national march. The conference made progress in three areas: 1) whether and when to march, 2) the organizing structure, and 3) the march's platform.

Should We March?

The first agenda items were the questions of whether and when to march. Results from a nationwide survey supported the idea of a march in the early fall of 1979. But some disagreement still lingered. The dissent once again centered on whether the march would attract enough people. Longtime activist Frank Kameny expressed skepticism: "If I was assured that there would be enough people at the march, I'd support it. But I'm not sure that would happen."[36] Much of this skepticism was fueled by fear that people would not risk being visible under a national spotlight where "you either win big or lose big—there is very little middle ground."[37] Also similar to before, local D.C. groups did not support the march. Bob Davis, representing D.C.'s Gay Activist Alliance, told Philadelphia delegates

that "Washington groups are not exactly happy" with the idea of lesbians
and gay men demonstrating in the nation's capital. Davis did not go so
far as to reject the proposal. Instead, he said delegates needed to come
up with concrete objectives, ensure broad representation of women and
Third World group members, and secure a strong financial backing.[38]

Philadelphia delegates struggled most with issues of representation.
The second morning of the conference convened with a motion from
the newly formed Hinterlands Caucus, a group composed of people who
were "non-urban, from non-coastal states" who vociferously argued that
delegates should vote to "delete the word 'national' from the march title
until adequate representation of all regions is obtained." Capturing the
national-local tensions prevalent in the 1970s, the Hinterlands Caucus
accused delegates of "cultural and regional imperialism" and "blatant
disregard of regional delegates." Attendees, however, voted down their
motion 74–24. They then deliberated on the basic questions of whether a
Washington march was advisable and when would be the best time for it.
Delegates passed a resolution to postpone the march from the Fourth of
July (July 8 was the closest weekend), as Milk had envisioned, to sometime in September or October of that same year. July 8 was voted down
for three reasons: both the president and Congress would be out of town,
hotels would be filled with tourists, and college student organizations
would be inactive.[39] During the Philadelphia weekend, Kameny's concerns of a political black eye, the D.C. activists' reluctance, and the Hinterlands' discontent all contributed to raising questions over whether to
march and thus the viability of a national movement.

Disagreement persisted about whether the march should take place
in 1979 or 1980. Those who favored 1980 responded that there was not
enough time to plan, organize, and finance a 1979 march. The majority, however, favored 1979, arguing that it marked the tenth anniversary
of the Stonewall Riots. The 1979/1980 split captured a tension between
symbolic impact and practical planning. Stonewall was a factor even before Philadelphia. David Thorstand, of the New York–based Coalition
for Lesbian and Gay Rights, wrote a letter to the Minneapolis Committee in late 1978, remarking, "Next year is the tenth anniversary of the
Stonewall Riots. . . . What better way to commemorate it than by organizing hundreds of thousands of people to march on Washington in
1979?"[40] Other activists also drew bridges to Stonewall: "A march on
Washington will be an event so important that it will propel our cause
forward like no event has done since the birth of our movement ten

years ago when, at the Stonewall Inn in NY's Greenwich Village, gay people united to fight back."[41] Even the mainstream press picked up on the Stonewall connection. The *Washington Post* ran an article between the Philadelphia and Houston Conferences (over Stonewall weekend) with the headline, "Gays Mark Riot That Sparked Movement," which framed the march as "the tenth anniversary of an incident many say was the start of the nationwide gay rights movement. . . . The marchers commemorated the Stonewall Riot."[42] Activists etched early on the notion of commemoration into their cultural template, something they would continue to develop over the course of the four marches.

Many national organizations were absent or underrepresented in Philadelphia. Although there were only a few such organizations of consequence in the late 1970s, those that did exist did not endorse the march.[43] The National Gay Task Force, for example, expressed feeling "troubled by the process used in planning and organizing the march" and, as a result, said that it was "not now in a position to endorse the march."[44] The NGTF had questions about lesbian and Third World visibility (i.e., wanting them to be in the front of the march and in large numbers).[45] After being chided by the rank and file for its lack of support, in September 1979 (only one month before the event), the NGTF gave in and endorsed the march.

Despite sentiments by Chicago delegate William Kelley that Philadelphia was "one of the most chaotic conferences I have ever attended,"[46] the group did finally vote on whether and when to have a march. Maria Hernandez, who chaired the conference's Saturday plenary session, counted the votes and exuberantly announced that, by a two-to-one margin, "We have a march on Washington in 1979!"[47] Figure 3.3 is a photograph of this historic vote.

How Do We Organize It?

Philadelphia delegates also decided the march's organizing structure. The All-Night Caucus, a group of delegates who stayed up until dawn to draw a working structure, presented a draft of their three-tiered structure on the second morning. At the top was a national board comprised of representatives from every supporting group. This board would be primarily a communications network. Underneath was a steering committee made up of an equal number of delegates from each of the seven regions into which the country was then divided. This was the organizational nucleus responsible for energizing local efforts and establishing march pol-

FIGURE 3.3. Philadelphia Delegates Vote Yes on the First Washington March. Photo ©
Eric Rofes.

icies and demands. Then there was the coordinating committee, made
up of the gender-equal cochairs of six committees (fund-raising, media,
outreach, cultural events, constituent lobbying, and logistics) plus two
office coordinators from the National and Logistic Offices. The coordinating committee was responsible for making the quick decisions on the
march.[48] Local and regional committees (in sixty-four cities across the
country) would do the everyday work, including outreach, fund-raising,
media attention, and generating enthusiasm.[49] After a heated discussion,
delegates accepted the proposal.

Delegates also accepted a proposal to form an advisory committee
for groups experiencing "special oppression within the gay community—
Third World people, gay youth, the disabled, [and] older gays."[50] At
some point after Philadelphia, Steve Ault and Joyce Hunter were elected
co-coordinators (as they were officially titled) of the march, overseeing
and organizing operations of all the committees and march planning as
a whole. Finally, the Women's and Third World Caucuses proposed that
all elements of the organizing structure reflect 50 percent female representation (i.e., gender parity) and 20 percent Third World representation. The proposal was seamlessly accepted. The later election of Steve
Ault (a Caucasian gay man) and Joyce Hunter (a biracial lesbian) as co-
coordinators fell within these parameters.

The gender parity and racial representation proposals redressed historical legacies of racism and sexism that date at least as far back as homophile organizing in the 1950s. Early gay identity was built around the experiences of white men. White, male, gay leaders were often charged with being "oblivious to the concerns expressed by women," while people of color felt that making a place for themselves at the table was "too painful," requiring them to subordinate their racial identity to their sexual identity.[51] Gender parity and racial representation would ensure solidarity across lines of diversity. In a flier headlined, "Sisters . . . We Need You in Washington," a group of lesbian activists wrote, "Not only have we been invisible in the women's movement, but for years lesbians have been invisible in the gay movement. The National March on Washington wants to change this and place women at the head of the struggle for our rights. In all march planning—an effort is being made to ensure that women make up at least 50 percent of all march committees."[52] A movement committed to redressing racism and sexism was emerging. This was perhaps most evident when the Salsa Soul Sisters, a lesbian-of-color organization, carried the march banner (see fig. 3.5).

After this proposal was accepted, there was some discussion about whether the march should coincide with the Third World Conference, already being planned over the weekend of October 5–7, 1979. This proposal was rejected because the date conflicted with a National Organization for Women conference planned for the same weekend in Los Angeles. A follow-up motion was made by a member of the Third World Caucus to hold the Third World Lesbian and Gay Conference over the same weekend as the national march on the following weekend. This proposal was accepted, moving the Third World Conference and the march to the following weekend.[53] These debates illustrate that activists used the organizing task of when to march to carry on a cultural conversation over how to forge a unified identity across lines of gender and racial divisions. By coordinating the march with the Third World Conference and avoiding conflicts with a women's conference, organizers displayed their commitment to racial and gender equality.

What Will We Demand?

Discussion about the organizing structure was fairly uncontroversial. The heat rose once the committee discussed demands. Two debates surfaced early on: Should we demand the passage of the Equal Rights

TABLE 3.1. **Demands, 1979 March**

Pass a comprehensive lesbian/gay rights bill in Congress

Issue a presidential executive order banning discrimination based on sexual orientation in the federal government, the military, and federally contracted private employment

Repeal all anti-lesbian/gay laws

End discrimination in lesbian-mother and gay-father custody cases

Protect lesbian and gay youth from any laws which are used to discriminate against, oppress, and/or harass them in their homes, schools, jobs, and social environments

---

Source: Official Program of the 1979 National March on Washington for Lesbian and Gay Rights. Primary source materials: Rainbow History Project.

Amendment (ERA)? And should the demands include issues not focused exclusively on lesbian and gay rights?

Joe Smenyak of New York City proposed the first draft of the demands, which included five single-issue items: 1) repeal all anti-lesbian/gay laws; 2) pass a comprehensive lesbian/gay rights bill in Congress; 3) issue a presidential executive order banning sexual discrimination based on sexual orientation in the federal government and in federally contracted public employment; 4) non-discrimination in lesbian mother and gay father custody cases; and 5) full rights for gay youth, including revision of the age-of-consent laws. He also suggested a statement of purpose: "An end to all social, economic, judicial, and legislative oppression of lesbian and gay people."[54] The committee agreed that "whatever our basic demands, it is important to keep their number down to a minimum."[55] After some revisions, "the Five Demands," as they came to be known, were simple, punchy, single-issue demands (see table 3.1). The fact that they were *not* multi-issue in focus reveals the implausibility of forging links across movements when a group is still struggling to grow into its own skin.

Although the statement of purpose was easily accepted, there was controversy over the demands (before reaching the final version in table 3.1). The Women's Caucus dissented over the fifth item, moving to "strike reference to age-of-consent laws." There was a difference between protecting gay youth and protecting young women from harassment and the possibility of rape. The age-of-consent laws, they reasoned, were a protective measure that prevented rape of young girls. Although this opinion was applauded, the motion was defeated. The discussion that fol-

lowed urged the Women's Caucus to present a minority position against
including the age-of-consent laws with the demands.[56] The Women's
Caucus and members of Gay Youth worked together to draft an alternate fifth demand that read: "Protect lesbian and gay youth from any
laws which are used to discriminate against, oppress, and/or harass them
in their homes, schools, jobs, and social environment." This revision was
accepted, and the fifth demand revised accordingly. In later marches, the
platform would be considerably more burdensome as the movement became more internally complex.

The Women's Caucus also dissented over excluding support for the
ERA from the demands. Some delegates felt that associating with the
ERA would be the march's death kiss in the conservative South, where
most of the unratified states were located. Others argued that including
any non-gay demands into the platform would deflect focus from the
main reason why lesbians and gay men were marching in the first place.
The caucus eventually voted and agreed to make ERA ratification an
ancillary demand and to support a boycott of unratified states.[57] This
would not be the last time delegates would struggle with the question of
whether to pursue single-issue, gay-rights-only or multi-issue, coalition
politics in assembling the march.

The conference ended on a high note with an amiable discussion of
possible march logos. Delegates debated the two logos in figure 3.4. Scott
Alpert was the creative mind behind the "Liberty Logo" (see fig. 3.4,
left). He drew inspiration from Harvey Milk's address to San Francisco's Gay Freedom Day Rally in 1978.[58] In the end, delegates adopted the
logo on the right in figure 3.4 to represent the national march, whereas
Alpert's creation became San Francisco's galvanizing local logo, further
commemorating Harvey Milk.

Philadelphia marked the beginning of consistent organizing for the
1979 march. From that point forward, it continued in two ways: one more
national conference in Houston and several regional and local meetings. The latter proved an effective way to network and mobilize local
gay communities across the country. Philadelphia delegates did not believe their conference was "as inclusive as it might have been desired.
Therefore, a second National Planning Conference has been set . . . in
Houston, Texas. . . . This conference will be an historical event—the first
nationwide gathering of regionally distributed delegates of lesbians and
gay persons and their supporting friends for the cause of their rights. . . .
'There is no power as great as an idea whose time has come!'"[59]

FIGURE 3.4. 1979 March Logos. Source: GLBT Historical Society of Northern California.

The Houston Conference

Delegates organized their next major conference the weekend of July 6–8 at the University of Houston in Texas to finalize plans for the march. Consistent with the drive to birth a national movement, they envisioned the weekend as an "an important step in forming a national network of lesbians and gay men working for the march." The weekend was designed to weave together a nationally networked community from the fibers of local activists. The *Advocate* echoed this sensibility: "Here we are knitting a whole new identity out of the once-scattered threads of our community."[60] More than two hundred lesbians and gay men, representing thirty-eight states, gathered in Houston, comprising "the first regionally, sexually, racially, and ethnically representative body in the history of the lesbian and gay movement."[61] Philadelphia attendees were mandated to have at least 50 percent lesbian and 20 percent Third World representation, which is in part why Houston was the most diverse organizing body to have assembled to date.

The conference successfully won the support of delegates who had from the beginning been skeptical. Some reticence remained on questions of leadership, with dissenting delegates taking issue with the untraditional structure of the march. To this Joyce Hunter responded, "The leadership of the march has not been the traditional gay rights leadership, but rather, has come from the grassroots level. The leadership is drawn from seven regions around the country . . . is representative of men, women, and Third World groups. Leadership is decentralized and democratic, and it reflects a more progressive segment of the gay movement than is usually reflected in gay leadership."[62] These and other concerns were quickly resolved by the weekend's end. Championed by Paul Boneberg and consistent with an identity political logic simmering in the 1970s, delegates also established the first Lobby Day for gays to meet and talk with their local representatives.[63]

Several other progressive decisions were made in Houston. Delegates recommended that rally speakers should "address only lesbian and gay issues,"[64] flagging the movement's choice to stand firmly with single-issue politics. The conference also incorporated signers for the hearing-impaired, bilingual speakers, and an immigration speaker. Delegates agreed that "the demonstration be peaceful and nonviolent." Finally, they voted that all "aspects of the march and all literature and speakers be non-sexist, non-racist, and non-ageist." The Women's Caucus moved "that a minimum of 10 percent of the funds raised by each region be set aside for providing free seating for more oppressed third world and white sisters" and that "there be strong third world and lesbian participation in the rally and that third world lesbian speakers will be chosen with the approval of third world lesbians and that these speakers do not appear at the bottom of the agenda." To this, activist Chuck Jones replied, "Now is the time for gay men to accept and embrace the challenge made by our lesbian sisters. We not only have to embrace our lesbian sisters, but we must now begin to take on a feminist perspective." Through a familial rhetoric, lesbian sisters and gay brothers discovered solidarity.

The most feverish identity issue in Houston concerned transpeople. The Transpeople Caucus moved that the "inclusive term 'Gay Transpeople' be included in all statements. . . concerning the October march." They were not asking for separate demands but rather a cultural reworking. Categorical references ought to be augmented to say "Lesbians, Gay Males, and Gay Transpeople." The caucus explained that the term *transpeople* included "transsexuals, female impersonators, transvestites, the drag society, and transgenderists who identify with gay issues." They recognized that not all transpeople were lesbian or gay—a fact that would plague trans inclusion in all later marches: "Some Transpeople are not homosexual. The people who oppress us do not recognize that distinction. . . . Some Transpeople do not wish to be represented as a Gay issue; therefore, we wish to ask for inclusion of the term 'Gay Transpeole.'"[65]

The caucus recognized that sexual orientation was in some ways distinct from transpeople's concerns, although the differences remained un-clear. There is no evidence that the caucus had the necessary language to contrast sexual orientation from gender identity, a rhetorical distinction activists would use in later marches. In 1979, the boundaries of sexual identity could not accommodate transpeople due to pervasive ignorance about gender identity and its relationship to sexual orientation. Activists had their hands too full with gender parity and racial inclusion to deal with this particular issue.

This conversation catapulted the biggest conflict at Houston, namely, "whether to have a transperson (transvestite or transsexual) speak." This issue was voted down on the Saturday of the conference amid a bois-terous argument. The Transpeople Caucus informally lobbied delegates later that night and moved to reopen the discussion. In a revote, dele-gates decided to have one speaker representing the interests of trans-people at the post-march rally.[66] Transpeople made claims for represen-tation, and activists responded by slightly stretching their conception of gay identity. Infighting over practical tasks (should we include transpeo-ple in the demands and speakers?) therefore enabled activists to engage in identity work (are they part of the lesbian and gay movement?).

A closer look at dissent within the Women's Caucus reveals why trans issues were so heated in Houston. Some women admitted they were not sure what the term even meant. Lucia Valeska, the new co–executive di-rector of the National Gay Task Force, argued that supporting transpeo-ple would divide the women's community, and if delegates agreed to the motion, then lesbians would not support the march at all. Betty Santoro of New York told the delegates that the march embraced all lesbians and gay men, including lesbian and gay transpeople. Accepting the Trans-people Caucus's proposal, however, might create unmanageable burdens of representation. Said Santoro, "We would then have to include 'lesbian and gay youth' and 'lesbian and gay third world people'" in all march literature. Other delegates argued that "transgender, transvestite, and transsexual people are not necessarily lesbian and gay."[67] After some de-bate, the motion was defeated. An integrative motion was later accepted to include transpersons whenever a list was given of members of the gay community.

Lack of precedence partly explains inconsistent trans inclusion (i.e., including them in the literature and granting them one speaker, but not including them in the demands or the title). Transpeople's relationship with the movement and with future marches would change as knowledge circulated. Although the boundaries of gay identity proved permeable in its inclusion of women and semi-permeable with people of color, debates over trans inclusion evinced boundary reticence. This was evident in a *Gay Community News* letter to the editor titled "Nomenclature." Massachusetts resident Bunny LaRue mocked the category *transperson*:

> Since the March on D.C. Committee lent its imprimatur at its Houston Confab to the new gay category of "transperson," several questions have since arisen to which I hope I can provide answers:
> Q: What do you call an individual whose offspring is a "transperson"?
> A: A trans-parent.
> Q: What do you call a nun who is cross-gender identified?
> A: A trans-sister.
> I thought I'd pass along this new nomenclature so that many of your readers will now not have to write Dear Abbie [*sic*].[68]

In the end, delegates fabricated a "tenuous unity" across lines of "intransigence and ignorance," in the words of delegate Lee Stone.[69] Stone articulated a principle for how conflict works in political organizing: "We found that on some issues, *the broader and more generalized ones,* agreement was reached with more ease" (emphasis added). Here, Stone is alluding to what has since become a well-established edict of intergroup relations: "The more narrowly defined . . . groups are, the more competitive and self-serving their behavior is. Conversely, when they focus on the larger collective, they are more cooperative. The challenge . . . is to know how to focus on higher-order group affiliations."[70] Broader issues, such as including a statement of purpose, or ensuring gender parity and racial representation, were less contentious. Discussions of more refined issues, often related to the management of specific identities such as transpeople and gay youth, were more contested.

The 1979 National March on Washington for Lesbian and Gay Rights

On October 14, 1979, an estimated 75,000 to 125,000 lesbians and gay men from across America marched on Washington. Activists and critics

FIGURE 3.5. 1979 March Banner. Photo © 2004 Patsy Lynch.

saw reflected in the event a unified patchwork of the diverse face of gay America, animating the mantra "We Are Everywhere":

> Today in the capital of America, we are all here, the almost liberated, and the slightly repressed; the butch, the femme, and everything in-between; the androgynous; the monogamous and the promiscuous; the masturbators and the fellators and the tribadists; men in dresses and women in neckties; those who bite and those who cuddle; celibates and pederasts; diesel dykes and nelly queens; amazons and size queens, Yellow, Black, Brown, White, and Red; the shorthaired and the long, the fat and the thin; the nude and the prude; the beauties and the beasts; the studs and the duds; the communes, the couples, and the singles; pubescents and the octogenarians. Yes, we are all here! We are everywhere! Welcome to the March on Washington for Lesbian and Gay Rights![71]

The Salsa Soul Sisters, the oldest lesbian-of-color organization, carried the march banner into the pages of history and sealed organizers' commitment to racial inclusion (see fig. 3.5).

This was the first Washington march staged by American gays, rending it in collective memory as the symbolic "birth of a national gay movement," in the words of Lucia Valeska.[72] Keynote speaker Betty Santoro of the Lesbian Feminist Liberation echoed, "This historical event has laid the foundation for a national mass movement for lesbian and gay rights." The gay media picked up the idea as well: "This was our day, this was our Declaration of Independence. We were in the capital of *our* country. We were suddenly, as a mass of humanity, not as isolated indi-

viduals, free. . . . We are no longer a movement of isolated individuals . . .
dealing solely with local problems. We are a national movement."[73] Many
years and marches later, Joyce Hunter remembered: "It [the march] put
us on the map as a national movement."[74]

It is instructive to recall that coming out was still a novel political
strategy, a sentiment activist Jim Kepner captured in the march program:
"The new frontier is inside us. . . . It is time to look inside ourselves, individually and collectively, to explore the gay spirit, the roots and nature of
our uniqueness. . . . We have only begun this exploration."[75] The movement then existed more simply than it does today, reflected in a photograph by Joan E. Biren (see fig. 3.6).

"Gay" is the answer—short and sweet—to every statement expressed
in the image. The 1979 march was for *gay people*. One can hardly imagine a similar placard at a modern demonstration.

This was the first time lesbians and gay men assembled in their nation's capital as a movement. Gay people increasingly understood themselves as part of an "organizable minority," in Harry Hay's words, and
a normal social group rather than a series of disconnected and pathological individuals, as the APA's long-standing classification had labeled
them prior. One march attendee commented, "Were these the 'homosexuals' who were condemned as 'sick' or 'evil' by the outside world? Not
by a long shot. . . . We are a people."[76]

Activists used infighting over six organizing tasks to engage in and
make tangible otherwise abstract concerns of strategy and identity. Infighting over whether to march, when to march, what to title it, how to
organize it, how to construct its platform, and who to invite as speakers, operated as a vehicle or *culture carrier* for questions of how activists
defined who they were and what they desired. For example, recall that
none of the national organizations initially supported the march. This
lack of support stemmed from fear that not enough gay people would
show up—that there were simply not enough of them or, in the event that
there were, they would not risk exposure. A poor turnout would give the
movement a black eye. Going to Washington—to publicly bear witness
in the nation's capital—was bold. Debates over whether to march were
thus a proxy for strategic concerns about the viability of moving from
many local programs to one national program. This is why, more than
twenty years later, the *San Francisco Chronicle* points to the social and
political significance of the first march as the "coming out of the movement on the national political agenda."[77]

FIGURE 3.6. The Simplicity of "Gay." Photo © 2007 JEB (Joan E. Biren).

The strategy and identity articulations infighting captured suggest a nuanced struggle with how to define gay sexuality. If gays were an organizable minority, then were they just like any other? Or somehow distinct? Activists responded differently based on their audience. In a maneuver that mimicked the women's movement, national conference delegates opted for ideological purity, or boundary-hardening, vis-à-vis *internal* audiences. Evidence for this comes from activists' systematic exclusion of transpeople from the title and platform while they displayed heightened receptivity toward the Women's Caucus's concerns over the fifth demand.[78] On the other hand, an attraction to Carter's rhetoric and policy of human rights indicates activists erring on the side of boundary porousness vis-à-vis *external* audiences, that is, softening the demarcation between gays and others in a way that would allow for the inclusion of gay rights with everyone else. This made sense given Carter's claim that human rights were "absolute," which activists may have interpreted as "universal." By adding the second march as an over-time comparison case, we will see in the next two chapters how the viability of this approach during the first march—but not the second—is comprehensible in light of three factors: changes in consciousness (from imagining a nascent national consciousness to aggressively elaborating it); organizational development (a more prominent people-of-color presence); and threat (the rise of discrete, national, and life-threatening conflict situations).

To celebrate the twenty-fifth anniversary of the first march, the National Gay and Lesbian Task Force (NGLTF) asked everyday people for personal reflections. A sampling of remembrances highlights the reception of the march, capturing the unforgettable sense that this was, in fact, the birth of a national movement.[79]

> When I think of the March I think of it as one of the first (the first?) times our separate gay communities around the country ever really worked on anything together. I remember it as the beginning of a real national lesbian and gay movement. (Richard D. Burns, executive director of the New York LGBT Center)

> I had only just recently graduated from the idea that I was the only man in the world who felt like I did for other men. I now thought maybe there might be a couple hundred guys like me. Then I went to Washington, and I was blown away to realize that I was really part of a worldwide brother and sisterhood. (Mike Dittmer)

I KNEW we were not alone, but that was the first time that I felt it to the very core of my being! (Beverly Brubaker, Ohio)

It was the largest gathering of gay and lesbian people I had ever seen or could even imagine. (Lorri L. Jean, former NGLTF executive director, currently CEO of the Los Angeles Gay and Lesbian Center)

It was the beginning of the age of empowerment. Over the years, in good times and bad, we have developed a most significant sense of community that has attained worldwide recognition. (Anonymous)

There were my people. There was my tribe! I've never been alone again thanks to those, the bravest queers among us! (Don Davis, former NGLTF board member, Virginia)

The mainstream press also remembers the 1979 march as the "coming out of the movement on the national political agenda," while scholars suggest it produced "an increasingly national sense of gay solidarity."[80] The march forged feelings of belonging to a national movement via the symbolic power of gay people gathering for the first time en masse in their country's capital. History, however, also forces us to reckon with the centrality of infighting in the organizing process. As expressed by Lee Stone, a delegate at the Houston Conference: "We who wished to create the most kind of times, could not ourselves be kind."[81] What does infighting reveal about political organizing? What role did it play in the 1979 march?

As this chapter has shown, infighting captured three facets of the state of the movement in the 1970s. First and most important, the 1979 march stitched a national movement out of the scattered fabrics of local activity and skepticism. Activists debated the basic question of whether to march in order to reconfigure the boundaries of strategy from local to national. Tensions in this process were evident in several ways, including: the lack of endorsements from national organizations; concerns that not enough people would turn out for the march (due either to a smaller-than-estimated gay population or people staying away out of fear of exposure), resulting in a black eye for the movement; criticisms of geographic imperialism (e.g., the Hinterlands Caucus's challenging the validity of national representation); insecurities of not having federal gay rights legislation; and the contentious decision to construct a single-issue platform.

In the course of this debate and by the act of braving an appearance that chilly October weekend, lesbians and gay men reemphasized the need to come out and made tangible their slogan "We Are Everywhere."

Dissent also enabled gay people to build bridges across lines of race and gender. One attendee proclaimed, "We have finally fused all the disparate elements of ourselves. We are whole and healed."[82] Activists used infighting to expand gay identity, that is, to define how different types of gay people were connected to each other as part of the same movement. This was reflected symbolically by organizations changing their name from just *gay* to *gay and lesbian*. It was also exemplified by coinciding the march with the Third World Conference, the first-ever weekend of workshops specifically for lesbians and gay men of color. There were, however, limits, evidenced by Houston delegates' reticence to fully include transpeople. The boundaries of gay identity could not fully stretch amid confusion over what the term *gay* meant, that is, over definitional roadblocks. Were transpeople gay? What was the relationship between gender and sexual orientation? Given a lack of information, delegates internally hardened identity boundaries and excluded those they did not understand. In effect, Houston delegates defined *gay* as distinct and different from trans.

Infighting also carried the language of *gay brothers* and *lesbian sisters,* suggesting a familial model for early categorical commonality. One organizer asserted, "We'll be 'coming out' nationally and greeting our sisters and brothers in a unified demonstration of our pride, our spirit, and our determination to have our rights."[83] The gay media used similar language: "It was quite possible, on Sunday, to say in absolute honesty that we were members of one, loving family, that we looked on each other as brothers and sisters with the care and concern that family members should . . . have for each other."[84] These were indeed gay brothers and lesbian sisters.

The 1979 march was successfully staged despite, or perhaps because of, rampant infighting. The gay media commented, "What love, what courage, and what a magic trick it was to pull the March together despite all the infighting."[85] Dissent had its dividends. One Houston delegate observed, "It is healthy to revisit some of the conflict involved in reaching the final unity necessary to mobilize our community on a national basis."[86] This was not easy. The gay media commented on the philosophy of black lesbian feminist Barbara Smith: "It's really important that we don't use differences as a reason to put each other down. [Smith] said that we sometimes have a jugular vein psychology which [compels us] to kill and to annihilate the differences . . . that can actually be enriching and enlivening." Similarly, representatives from the Salsa Soul Sisters said, "It's good for us to have a place where we can fight our differences out."[87] Although sometimes painful, infighting did not inhibit the arrival of the first-ever national march. On the contrary, it triumphantly carried gays onto the national scene.

CHAPTER FOUR

War and Protest:
Lesbian and Gay Life in the 1980s

Despite setbacks at the local level that had national resonance, lesbian and gay activists in the late 1970s maintained their optimism. The general feeling was that the community was moving forward—that equality and acceptance were on the horizon. Indeed, the movement in the early 1970s is sometimes described has having "an effervescent quality" in which being politically involved was "a way of life, for others life itself." This sensibility generated "collections of movement writings that still quicken the pulse."[1]

Then came AIDS. And everything changed.

"I don't know anybody who doesn't know somebody who has died of AIDS," one activist asserted. "We're watching the leadership of our community being devastated by it, and we're watching our community's resources being used for it because the federal government has failed to respond in any sort of appropriate way." Steve Ault, who cochaired the first two marches, framed AIDS as the biggest difference between the events, remarking that it was "the least abstract issue that any of us have ever worked on."[2] AIDS single-handedly reconfigured gay life in an era that longtime activist Urvashi Vaid characterized as "the worst years of our lives."[3] This is the story of those years.

The lesbian and gay movement staged its second march on Washington on October 11, 1987, immersed in a time dramatically different than the one in which it was situated for its first. The 1980s were "a resistant cultural and political climate" that created a sense of political urgency.[4] According to the *Advocate,* "Compared with the 1979 march, the 1987 gathering almost *has* to be more impressive, if only because of the greater sense of urgency with which it is being staged." In 1979, the movement was not experiencing any disastrous setbacks and was, indeed, enjoying some strides forward. This had consequences for their articulations of strategy and identity. Vis-à-vis external agents, activists emphasized boundary permeability, seeking inclusion under, and domestic applications for, Carter's pronouncements of human rights as an American foreign policy objective. With respect to contending insiders, however, activists were generally inclined toward boundary-hardening, for example, by excluding transpeople from the first march's title and demands. But by the time of the second march in 1987, lesbians and gay men found themselves badly shaken by AIDS and stung by the most devastating blow to their rights yet—the Supreme Court's *Bowers* decision: "Both the anti-gay ruling and, more manifestly, the government's poor response to the AIDS crisis have raised the level of anger among gays to such a high level that more people will feel compelled to travel to Washington."[5] The shifting sociopolitical context altered the state of the movement.

In the 1980s, the movement was entrenched in a war with AIDS, against the backdrop of a presidential administration too arrogant and too effete to publicly mention the word. Engulfed by loss and death, the Supreme Court dealt another blow in 1986 with the ignominious *Bowers v. Hardwick* case that criminalized consensual sodomy. By holding that gay men did not have a constitutional right to engage in sodomy even in the privacy of their own bedrooms, the Supreme Court effectively negated the existence of gays as a people. According to activist Susan Cavin, a local organizer of the civil disobedience action held over the march weekend, "They took away gay people's right to even be in the closet in the privacy of their own bedrooms. When they took away our closet, they really took away our right to exist at all."[6]

Federal repression was asphyxiating the movement at every turn, providing a vigorous sense of urgency to the "(still) unfinished project of building a gay and lesbian movement."[7] Cochair Steve Ault observed, "People are saying, 'We have no other recourse, we have to turn to the streets.' . . . There just doesn't seem to be a response coming otherwise. It's a matter of necessity, really. It's a matter of survival."[8] *Bowers* made "people feel up against the wall" and "created a more militant stance among people who never had any intention of becoming militant. It was the last straw for many of us."[9] This was the context in which progressive lesbians and gay men rose with fervent indignation to organize their second march. These times of war brought no promise of peace but only protest, culminating in what, decades later and despite two other marches still yet to come, would be singly and simply remembered as "the Great March."

This chapter will emphasize three dimensions of difference between the first two marches. In 1979, the movement was stitching scattered fragments of local fibers into a national political patchwork. Gay people had not yet established a national self-consciousness, the organizational landscape was nascent, and situations of threat were local. Although gay people remained on the periphery of American politics and culture across the first two marches, the first demonstration congealed a sense of national consciousness, catapulted a program of self-affirmation, and inspired locally based, though nationally networked, organizational development. This all affected how activists defined and debated the state of their movement. During the first march, activists deemphasized the uniqueness of gay sexuality to external agents in the hopes of securing legitimacy under the broad rubric of human rights. Second march activists, in contrast, found their sexual orientation to be an isolated and inescapable source of injustice, while various subgroups became increasingly organized and visible. Times no longer afforded a strategy of diminishment but now called for distinction, a crystalline clarity on who gay people were, what they wanted, and how they were *not* so similar to other groups.

Life During Wartime: The Anathema of AIDS

Pariahs at the Periphery

In the late 1970s and especially through the first couple years of the 1980s, doctors in New York, Los Angeles, and San Francisco saw an alarming number of cases of the rare cancer Kaposi's sarcoma (KS) among young, otherwise-healthy, self-identified gay and bisexual men. KS is a malignant skin tumor that was found with low overall prevalence and generally among elderly men with impaired immune systems. During the first couple years of the 1980s, coastal hospitals were flooded with patients who displayed a particularly severe form of KS, with dark blue and/or violet lesions forming on internal organs as well as on the surface of the skin. The growing tensions generated by KS were compounded by the simultaneous outbreak of *pneumocystis carinii* pneumonia (PCP), a rare form of pneumonia, again in Los Angeles and other coastal cities. Doctors were baffled.[10]

KS and PCP were not unfamiliar to American doctors. What was enigmatic was their sudden concentration in self-identified gay and bisexual men, which prompted the media and some medical circles to call it "the gay disease," or, more virulently, "the gay cancer" and "the gay plague" by 1980.[11] This motivated the Centers for Disease Control (CDC) to give it its first name: Gay-Related Immune Deficiency, or GRID, an acronym that mistakenly connected the syndrome with homosexuality and affirmed gay people's occupancy as pariahs on the American periphery.[12] Gay men across the country, especially in urban areas, were stamped with a scarlet letter. No one knew anything about this "gay cancer," especially since the causal agent, the human immunodeficiency virus (HIV), was not isolated until 1984, and the U.S. Food and Drug Administration did not license the first clinical tests to detect antibodies until 1985, four years after its public recognition.[13] The mystery was compounded by the fact that visible manifestations of KS could remain dormant for up to ten years. Did you have *it*? How did you get *it*? Was *it* contagious? No one could explain what was happening, as friends and lovers died one after another, and the flames of fear spread like a conflagration.

On July 3, 1981, the *New York Times* ran a headline reporting, "Rare Cancer Seen in 41 Homosexuals," noting that the "outbreak occurs among men in New York and California" and that "eight died inside two years."[14] This was the first public, mainstream mention of the "rather devastating" disease. The hysteria grew as the *New York Times* stated that "the cause of the outbreak is unknown" and that "doctors investigating the outbreak believe that many cases have gone undetected because of the rarity of the condition and the difficulty even dermatologists may have in diagnosing it." The stains of stigma against gay men were deepened as the article concluded, "No cases have been reported to date outside the homosexual community."

The outbreaks of KS and PCP, along with the burgeoning public scare, prompted the CDC to release a medical alert on July 4, 1981.[15] The report confirmed that KS and PCP were "an uncommonly reported malignancy in the United States," adding that the occurrence of KS among twenty-six young, homosexual men (twenty in New York and six in California) "during the past thirty months" is "considered highly unusual." The sobering CDC report amplified gay men's panic when it concluded that "it is not clear if or how the clustering of KS, pneumocystis, and other serious diseases in homosexual men is related." The CDC report and the *New York Times* article exacerbated the stigma against gay men while confirming for the medical community and American public that this "rare cancer" was in fact a "gay disease," if not a "gay plague."

The lack of information about the disease catalyzed "a dizzying array of acronyms . . . as possible monikers for an epidemic that, though ten months old, remained unnamed."[16] Besides GRID, some in the medical community called the disease ACIDS, for Acquired Community Immune Deficiency Syndrome, an acronym that conjured up horrific images of the disease's impact. Others preferred CAIDS, for Community Acquired Immune Deficiency Syndrome. As Randy Shilts notes, "The 'community' . . . of course, was a polite way of saying gay; the doctors couldn't let go of the notion that one identified this disease by whom it hit rather than what it did. . . . By now, somebody was dying almost every day in America from an epidemic that still did not have a name."[17] Even the CDC categorized cases by "risk groups" rather than "risk behavior," which "increased the pariah status of gay and bisexual men while failing to offer critical information that could prevent additional transmissions."[18] It wasn't until July 27, 1982, a year after the initial report, that the CDC linked the disease to blood as new cases were reported outside gay and bisexual men. The CDC then formally renamed the disease to what we know it as today: Acquired Immune Deficiency Syndrome, or AIDS. AIDS was defined as "a disease, at least moderately predictive of a defect in cell-mediated immunity, occurring in a person with no known cause for diminished resistance to that disease."[19] The CDC explicated four identified risk factors: male homosexuality, intravenous drug abuse, Haitian origin, and hemophilia A.[20]

The increase of new diagnoses and deaths aggravated a phobia of gay people. According to the Gay Men's Health Crisis (GMHC), by 1985, polls showed that 72 percent of Americans favored mandatory testing and 51 percent supported the quarantining of people with AIDS.[21] These attitudes sealed gay people's fate as pariahs at the periphery. Not only were they generally deplored for their sexuality, gay men were now also specifically stereotyped as all having AIDS. Some conservative zealots proclaimed AIDS was "God's punishment for gays" due to their "sinful" sexuality.[22] In 1983, Pat Buchanan championed this sentiment: "The poor homosexuals; they have declared war upon nature, and now nature is exacting an awful retribution."[23]

The moral hysteria associated with AIDS must be viewed against a backdrop of national homophobia.[24] This explains why, in a 1986 *New York Times* article, William F. Buckley, the most respected of moderate conservatives, publicly supported mandatory HIV testing and the forcible tattooing of HIV-positive gay men "on the buttocks, to prevent the victimization of other homosexuals."[25] Homophobia and AIDS-phobia also account for Patrick Buchanan's call to cancel all gay political marches to avoid the spread of AIDS.[26] Buckley and Buchanan supported the logic that homosexuality breeds illness. Many measures suggested to deal with people with AIDS (PWA) in the 1980s were consistent with a definition of gay men as outsiders.[27] The desire to stamp a scarlet letter on the buttocks, the sweeping mania of forced HIV testing and quarantining of the seropositive (for example, with the LaRouche Initiative on the ballot in California during the fall of 1986),[28] and persecution of PWA continued unabated throughout the 1980s and early 1990s. Indeed, through at least the beginning of 1983, it was "virtually an article of faith among homosexuals that they would somehow end up in concentration camps."[29]

The early cultural coupling of AIDS with gay male sexuality allowed the federal government to ignore the disease and not fund prevention or research programs.[30] Federal neglect was compounded by internal sarcasm, as congressional staffers joked that NIH really stood for "Not Interested in Homosexuals."[31] It was not until June of 1987—an astonishing six years into the epidemic—that President Ronald Reagan used the word *AIDS* for the first time in a public address, though he did not honor those who were disproportionately dying—never did the president use the word *gay*.[32]

Reagan's neglect fueled gay rage from an already ravaged community. At a National AIDS Network event, Representative Gerry Studds (D-Mass.), playing off Nancy Reagan's "Just Say No" antidrug message, issued a plea to Reagan to "just say something [about AIDS]." In an address given at the 1987 march, actress Whoopi Goldberg implored, "Mr. Reagan, did you explain . . . that sometimes ignorant people act in such a way [toward people with AIDS] that it is frightening? . . . How long is it gonna take before people get smart? . . . We're not talking about illiterate people, we're talking about senators and congressmen and the fucking president."[33] Gay history books have immortalized

Reagan as an unresponsive president who "did nothing during his eight years," a time frame circumscribed by angry activist chants of, "History will recall, Reagan did least of all." Reagan's ignorance and homophobia blinded him to the reality that AIDS was not a gay disease and could never be. "Viruses," notes sociologist Elizabeth Armstrong, "do not respect social identity boundaries."[34]

Prejudice and discrimination against lesbians and gay men "became terrifyingly concrete with the advent of AIDS." Reagan's blanket refusal to speak publicly about AIDS for the first six years of the epidemic, widespread lack of information about the disease and its transmission, inimical stereotypes, and the advocacy of vitriolic public policies against gay men come into focus in the context of neoconservatism. Historians argue that the most formidable challenge to gay cultural acceptance and political progress was "the resurgence of overall hostility to civil rights claims in general." According to this perspective, the Reagan administration's politics of gross neglect—what some historians term "an official conspiracy of silence"—was inspired by the ascendancy of the New Right, which viewed lesbians and gay men as a blemish upon family values and thus a stable social order. Conservatism and anti-gay attitudes saturated American culture. The *New York Times,* for example, prohibited printing the word *gay* unless it was in the official name of an organization or part of a direct quote.[35] It was not until June 15, 1987, that the *New York Times* declared the words *gay* and *lesbian* were "fit to print." The *Wall Street Journal* maintained a similar policy which it did not reverse until 1984.

Reagan's landslide election victory on November 4, 1984, was viewed as an expansion of the political power of Evangelical Christians. Robert J. Billings and Jerry Falwell's Moral Majority, founded in 1979, along with fundamental Christians generally, were credited for the Republican sweep. *Moral Majority* became a household phrase, as analysts heralded Falwell and his fundamentalist followers as "the most important new political force to emerge in America in decades." The Moral Majority exerted influence on matters of politics and policy through 1989, when the organization disbanded, only to be replaced in the same year by Pat Robertson's Christian Coalition, a more venomous countermovement that has jousted alongside the lesbian and gay movement ever since.[36]

Despite the devastation, there was "renaissance and renewal in the midst of the holocaust," in the words of political consultant David Mixner. The AIDS crisis compelled the coming out of lesbians and gay men

FIGURE 4.1. Poster for the 1987 March. Photo by Amy Bartell/SCW Design © 1987, www
.SyracuseCulturalWorkers.com.

across the country, including Congressman Barney Frank (D-Mass.) in
the late 1980s, who came out after fellow Representative Stewart McK-
inney (R-Conn.) died of AIDS. Organizers of the 1987 march capitalized on these currents in a popular march poster which set the headline,
"Come out . . . Come Out," in the foreground against a pink triangle,

invoking the persecution of gays in the Holocaust (see fig. 4.1). By "refocusing the cultural content" of the Holocaust, organizers compared
American oppression of gays with German oppression of Jews, emphasized their distinctiveness, and thus steered away from seeking indistinguishable human rights.[37]

Organizational Development

AIDS inspired a new wave of political mobilization that promoted a program of self-affirmation and distinction. Some of this was stimulated by
the first march, an outcome organizer Rita Goldberger predicted: "This
effort [of the 1979 march] is a quantum leap forward for the gay rights
movement. . . . Organizations will be springing up in the remotest cor-
ners of the country."[38] The 1979 demonstration brought "into being a
real national network of gay groups, a network which . . . surviv[ed] the
March itself." This network was one of its many lasting legacies. Although unwitting, the gay media described the impact of the 1979 march
using words that resonated against the backdrop of AIDS: "Through the
creation of this march, we [will] develop a national organizing structure,
one which can generate funds and mobilize people to action *when we are
alone, isolated, in crisis* in our home communities" (emphasis added).[39]
Due in part to the success of the first march, when AIDS hit, local gay
communities had accumulated the vision and resources required to
respond.

The tight coupling of AIDS with gay identity compelled activists to
forge "a strong link between 'ownership' of the disease and responsibility to 'deal with it.'" Lesbians and gay men began developing their own
organizations to raise awareness and funds to combat AIDS. If the government was not going to respond, then they would take care of their
own. As such, the 1980s witnessed a massive growth in AIDS organizations (see fig. 4.2).[40]

Founded in New York City in 1982, the Gay Men's Health Crisis
(GMHC) was the first community-based AIDS service provider in the
U.S. It was created by gay men who were mostly unknown and uninter-
ested in gay politics in the 1970s, but who were thrust into it as a result
of AIDS. Notables included Larry Kramer, Nathan Fair, Paul Popham,
Paul Rapoport, Dr. Larry Mass, and Edmund White. Early executive director Robert McFarlane recalled, "For a white man with a graduate de-

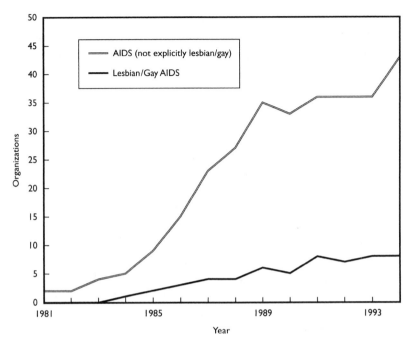

FIGURE 4.2. AIDS Organizations in San Francisco. Source: Armstrong (2002:163).

gree and a good job who can pass [for straight, discrimination was] not
an issue. Never was. Until [AIDS] really got down to it and you realized they want you to die. . . . You are literally left to die." AIDS incited
to action so many who, under different circumstances, might have been
complacent.[41]

AIDS catalyzed the formation of an entire industry and gave rise to
a distinct social movement that mobilized through a novel set of tactics.
The AIDS Coalition to Unleash Power (ACT UP), a militant and confrontational group, is an exemplary case of AIDS activism. Inspired in
part by organizing for the 1987 march on Washington, the founding of
ACT UP on Tuesday, March 10, 1987, in New York City marked the beginning of a distinct AIDS-based political movement that demanded adequate health care for all Americans.[42] ACT UP combined demonstrations, street theater, and other acts of civil disobedience to bring into
focus issues related to the AIDS crisis that the authorities (defined as
"government officials, researchers, politicians, the church, and the law")

were thought to ignore. ACT UP sought to empower people with AIDS and their communities. The New York chapter, which many considered the national headquarters, was "a diverse, non-partisan group of individuals united in anger and committed to direct action to end the AIDS crisis." The organization's purpose was to meet "the challenge of the AIDS epidemic and its crisis of conscience with vigilant acts of political and cultural provocation—thereby giving voice to the essential creative will of our humanity."[43] A new style of in-your-face activism was born.

One of ACT UP's signatures—and legacies—has been the production of powerful artistic images to ensure that the history of the disease will not be forgotten. ACT UP used art to shape cultural understandings of the disease, to document societal responses, and to motivate people to act.[44] Two examples are particularly famous. The first, what would become the official logo, is a poster against a solid black background with the phrase "SILENCE = DEATH" scrolled in striking white capital letters beneath a pink triangle. Another memorable image depicts Reagan's face in yellow-green, his eyes fuchsia, with the word "AIDSGATE" also in fuchsia scrolled in capital letters underneath.

Although ACT UP succeeded in pressuring the federal government and insurance providers to lower the price of AZT, the only available medication at the time, people were still dying of complications. In February of 1987, Cleve Jones and Joseph Durant made the first two fabric panels of what has since become known as the AIDS Memorial Quilt. Approximately the dimensions of a human grave (three feet by six feet), each panel commemorates a person who has died of the disease. Cleve Jones first came up with the idea in November of 1985 "when the number of San Franciscans dead from AIDS reached one thousand."

> So many had died, and there'd been no memorial. . . . If there was an obituary, and often there was not, it would describe the cause of death as cancer. The slate was wiped clean, as if this person had never been. Close friends were erased; lovers were never identified. Every one of us, whether friend or family, felt the empty echo of loss and grief and saw no way to express it. We were on the wrong side of a cultural canyon. I wanted to change all that, and believed that when we unfolded thousands of quilts on the National Mall, the stony walls of Congress would come tumbling down and the nation would awaken—that our quilt, my quilt, would crash through the fear and indifference.[45]

The AIDS Memorial Quilt had its inaugural display on the Mall at the 1987 march amid an eerie silence interrupted frequently by the sobs of grief-stricken persons remembering someone they had lost to AIDS.

Unity, Division, and AIDS

Conflict can compel group integration by making members conscious of their common bonds and need for cooperation.[46] As such an instance, AIDS gave birth to a "new spirit of cooperation and solidarity between lesbians and gay men." Some lesbians were motivated by personal ties of friendship while others were driven by feelings of political solidarity with the movement. Regardless of why, many lesbians devoted generous amounts of personal time to help fight AIDS.[47]

Although AIDS facilitated cooperation between lesbians and gay men, it also exposed "long-simmering internal differences."[48] AIDS precipitated infighting around bathhouses and sex clubs, a debate that centered on the sexual practices of gay men. Three years prior to the *New York Times* article that brought the "rare cancer" to American living rooms, gay activist Larry Kramer published *Faggots,* an acerbic, yet sobering, account of upper-middle-class white gay life in Manhattan. In his treatise, Kramer portended the crisis to come: "Why do faggots have to fuck so fucking much? It's as if we don't have anything else to do. . . . I'm tired of using my body as a faceless thing to lure another faceless thing." Things had to change, suggested the narrator in the ostensibly fictional novel, "before you fuck yourself to death."[49]

From a medical standpoint, bathhouses were a breeding ground for transmitting the virus. However, because of federal neglect and conspiracy theories that framed AIDS as biological warfare against gays, there was rampant distrust of medical reports, especially those that impinged on elements of gay culture.[50] Some (rightfully) argued that there was a lack of scientific evidence that patronizing bathhouses was a risk factor for AIDS.[51] Others less rationally equated science with chicanery, a sentiment stitched into gay culture since at least the days when the APA classified homosexuality as a mental disorder.

The bathhouse debates heated up in 1983, a year *before* science identified HIV as the culprit for AIDS, leading many owners to charge those who argued for bathhouse closure as "sexual fascists" who would "stifle sexuality."[52] New York City's Office of Gay and Lesbian Health refused to close the baths because "there is no science to support the closing of the bathhouses." Nobody really knew, the rationale went, how AIDS was spread. In the words of Randy Shilts, "You were as likely to get this from somebody you picked up in a bar as at the baths." Even if they closed, there was no assurance that people would not go elsewhere in pursuit of casual sex. "Out of the tubs, into the shrubs," went the party line. That HIV was an infectious viral agent spread through sexual activity was speculative, at best, even though it was becoming clearer that there was a relationship between sex and AIDS. A *New York Times Magazine* article reported what was generally believed even if not scientifically validated: AIDS was a virus or some other sort of infectious agent transmitted through bodily fluids, especially semen and blood. Thus, some of the infighting that erupted over what to do with the bathhouses can be explained by the dearth of scientific information, particularly concerns over infection. Sex remained a speculative perpetrator. And so to use that as a defense to close a lucrative industry central to gay men's culture met with much resistance and rancor.[53]

Sex has always been vitally important to gay men. Bathhouses were "a cornerstone of gay men's public sexual culture" that defined sex as a revolutionary act, "part and parcel of political liberation." Some thought that easy access to casual and/or anonymous sex was evidence of gay political success. Others felt it ironic that a movement fighting for the right to love was defending an institution "so entirely devoid of intimacy." The net effect was a gay community ideologically divided over whether public health warranted the closing of the baths or if keeping them open was an indicator of freedom. As Larry Kramer explained, "Oh God, the battle over whether or not to close the baths became such a red herring because of this issue of sexual freedom." In the end, some bathhouses closed and later reopened. Despite this non-uniform outcome, the debates pitted gay men against each other, marking the early 1980s as a rupturing time when "gay trust broke apart, one tribe willing to sell the other back."[54]

Bathhouse debates were also linked to economics. The hundreds of such establishments comprised a $100 million industry across the U.S. and Canada. Shilts recounts one sobering exchange between a bathhouse owner and Paul Volberding, then AIDS clinic director of the San Francisco General Hospital: "'We're both in it for the same thing,' the bathhouse owner told Volberding. 'Money. We make money at one end when they come to the baths. You make money from them on the other end when they come here.' Volberding was too horrified to reply."[55]

Uncertainty circulated fear against the specter of death. This blended with cultural currents that equated sex with freedom and economics to produce a climate ripe for mutiny. Bathhouse supporters lined up on one side and argued that sex was revolutionary and a fundamental right. Those on the other side framed bathhouses as little more than "officially condoned homicide" where the community was "let[ting] gay business-men murder gay people." Opposers turned the rhetoric of rights upside down by suggesting that gays had a "right to commit suicide in bath-houses." The fight was protracted and left many with the impression that "gays would flout . . . public health for their own interests." The right to love, a gay rights mantra that was often equated with sex, scarred many who were politically active at the time.[56]

The Toll of AIDS

By the end of the 1980s, more than 150,000 AIDS cases had been diag-nosed, and the disease had claimed more than 90,000 American lives (see fig. 4.3).

AIDS decimated a generation of gay men. The movement lost count-less individuals with activist experience and know-how, individuals who were early homophile architects and who may have gone on to orches-trate more activism. These were times of war. As historian Charles Kai-ser recounts:

> If you are a sexually active gay man in America, being alive at the begin-ning of this epidemic feels like standing without a helmet at the front line of a shooting war. Friends are falling all around you but no one even knows where the bullets are coming from. There are no weapons to defend yourself, no medicine for the wounded, and if you want to flee, when you start running you won't know whether your own wounds are fatal—or nonexistent. Three years into this war, the battlefield is just as lethal, but now it feels more like a huge tunnel filled with fire, strewn with bodies and booby traps. If you're still standing—one of the "lucky" ones—you keep running faster and faster, but you can never outpace the inferno. . . . At the beginning, there was nothing but terror and mystery.[57]

Consumed by devastating loss and death, gay men, with the help of lesbians, emerged as a matured movement, evidenced in "their willing-ness to take on onerous burdens of caring for others." Recounts one

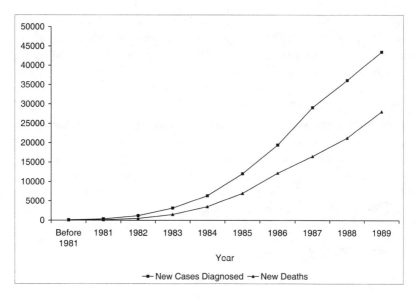

FIGURE 4.3. New AIDS Cases and Deaths, 1980–1989. Source: Centers for Disease Control and Prevention. *HIV/AIDS Surveillance Report,* 2001; 13(2):30.

historian, "Homosexual leaders agreed the community has developed a new maturity in coping with the AIDS crisis." These are indicators of what sociologists call "a real community" to the extent that lesbians and gay men used their past to shape their future.[58] Death brought lesbians and gay men together in a way that infighting could not so simply unravel.

Bowers v. Hardwick

The second march was in large part a reaction against AIDS and federal negligence. Reagan's blind eye, rising neoconservatism, and rampant homophobia produced perceptions of asphyxiating political opportunities, prompting activists to turn toward non-institutionalized means of expressing their grievances. Although AIDS was one of the largest blips pulsating on the radar, it was certainly not the only one. On March 31, 1986, the Supreme Court—"a crucial engine of the movement for . . . equality"—heard arguments in *Bowers v. Hardwick,* a case that blurred the separation between church and state, conflated religion and politics, and promoted institutionalized homophobia. The case pushed gay people further into the periphery by serving as a "badge of second-class citizenship painfully stitched into the psyches of gay Americans."[59]

On August 3, 1982, with the inadvertent assistance of a friend sleeping off a hangover on the couch, patrolman Keith Torrick entered the home of gay, then twenty-nine-year-old Atlanta bartender Michael Hardwick. The officer had a warrant for Hardwick to appear in court. Rewind one month to the early morning hours of July 5, 1982: after having spent all night at work, Hardwick grabbed a beer as he headed out of the bar. Torrick spotted him throwing his bottle in the trash and gave him a ticket for drinking in public. Torrick admonished Hardwick that he would be arrested if he missed his court date. Hardwick dutifully went to court, paid a $50 fine, and mistakenly assumed that he had wiped his hands clean of the matter. One month later, Torrick entered Harwick's home with an arrest warrant for a ticket Hardwick had already paid—hence one of the greatest ironies that affected gay life for the next seventeen years.[60]

Once inside, Patrolman Torrick searched for Hardwick. Torrick stopped outside his bedroom, whose door had been left slightly ajar. The officer pushed the door and walked—"uninvited and unannounced— into the candle-lit bedroom. There he was 'shocked' and 'grossed . . . out' . . . to discover that Hardwick and his male guest were engaging in mutual fellatio." The officer announced that Hardwick was under arrest, to which the latter retorted, "What are you doing in my bedroom?" Torrick handcuffed Hardwick and his guest and took them both to the station, where the officer "made sure everyone . . . knew I was there for cocksucking," Hardwick recalled. He was charged with violating the State of Georgia's sodomy law, which stated:

> (a) A person commits the offense of sodomy when he performs or submits to any sexual act involving the sex organs of one person and the mouth or anus of another . . . [and] (b) A person convicted of the offense of sodomy shall be punished by imprisonment for not less than one nor more than 20 years.[61]

Realizing the legal complexities involved with the case, the politically savvy district attorney dropped the charges. With the assistance of ACLU attorneys Kathleen Wilde and John Sweet, Hardwick filed a suit in a federal district court, arguing that the Fourteenth Amendment of the United States Constitution, which guarantees due process of the law, had been violated. Hardwick pressed the case with the intention of hav-

ing the sodomy law declared unconstitutional, feeling that the right to
engage in consensual sexual activity in the privacy of one's own home
comprised a guarantee of life and liberty under the law. Hardwick, who
had never been politically active before, recalled:

> I realized that if there was anything I could do, even if it was just laying the
> foundation to change this horrendous law, that I would feel pretty bad about
> myself if I just walked away from it. . . . They'd been trying for five years to
> get a perfect case. . . . I was fortunate enough to have a supportive family who
> knew I was gay. I'm a bartender, so I can always work in gay bar. And I was
> arrested in my own house. So I was the perfect case.

The federal court dismissed the suit, while the Eleventh Circuit Court
of Appeals overturned the previous ruling. Judge Frank J. Johnson Jr.
concluded in Hardwick's favor: "The Georgia sodomy statute infringes
upon the fundamental constitutional rights of Michael Hardwick. On remand [back to the district court], the state must demonstrate a compelling interest in restricting this right and must show that the sodomy law
is a properly restrained method of safeguarding its interests." The stage
was set for a Supreme Court battle.

Georgia attorney general Michael Bowers argued against Michael
Hardwick on March 31, 1986. A bitterly divided Court upheld the statute in a 5–4 vote and decided that the state's sodomy statute did not violate any fundamental right under the Constitution for homosexuals to
engage in sodomy.[62] The majority opinion and accompanying dissent illustrate a fractured Court struggling to define *Bowers* as a case. Was it
about the right to privacy? Or a constitutional right to engage in sodomy? In delivering the opinion of the Court, Justice White defined the
issue as the latter: "Respondent would have us announce . . . a fundamental right to engage in homosexual sodomy. This we are quite unwilling to do. . . . In Constitutional terms there is no such thing as a fundamental right to commit homosexual sodomy."[63]

White's rhetorically charged opinion used punching analogies and
blurred the line between church and state. Using the deep roots of Western civilization's traditions, Chief Justice Burger concurred: "'The infamous *crime against nature*' [is] an offense of 'deeper malignity' than
rape, a heinous act 'the very mention of which is a disgrace to human
nature,' as it is an 'abominable crime not fit to be named among Christians.'" Accordingly, "to hold that the act of homosexual sodomy is

somehow protected as a fundamental right would be to cast aside mil-
lennia of moral teaching." Burger justified religion as a principle for law.
Hardwick tried preemptively to refute this as an inadequate rationale,
arguing that there is no basis for sodomy laws other than "the presumed
belief of a majority of the electorate in Georgia that homosexual sodomy
is immoral and unacceptable." To this, White responded, "The law . . . is
constantly based on notions of morality" and effectively blurred the line
between politics and religion. This further sealed gay people's fate as pariahs on the American periphery.

Justice Blackmun, who wrote the majority decision in *Roe v. Wade,*
along with Brennan, Marshall, and Stevens joining, filed a fierce dissenting opinion: "This case is . . . [not] about 'a fundamental right to engage
in homosexual sodomy.'" According to the dissenters, the case exemplified principles of privacy. Blackmun began with the observation that
"the statute at issue . . . denies individuals the right to decide for themselves whether to engage in particular forms of private, consensual sexual activity." To avoid ambiguity while marshalling morality arguments
as did the majority, Blackmun defined privacy: "The concept of privacy
embodies the 'moral fact that a person belongs to himself and not others
nor to society as a whole.'" *Bowers* was therefore about "the most comprehensive of rights and the right most valued by civilized men," namely
"the right to be let alone."[64]

Blackmun then turned his attention to sexual intimacy. He noted,
"What the Court really has refused to recognize is the fundamental interest all individuals have in controlling the nature of their intimate as-
sociations with others" and that "depriving individuals of the right to
choose for themselves how to conduct their intimate relationships poses
a far greater threat to the values most deeply in our Nation's history than
tolerance of nonconformity could ever do." Blackmun recognized that
there was "no basis for the Court's decision to treat this case . . . solely
on the grounds that it prohibits homosexual activity," since the actions
of the police and the state involved "an unconstitutional intrusion into
his [Hardwick's] privacy and his right of intimate association." Blackmun understood that sexuality was profoundly connected to how people defined themselves and, as such, was tightly stitched into the fabric of
human existence:

> Only the most willful blindness could obscure the fact that sexual intimacy is
> "a sensitive, key relationship of human existence." . . . The fact that individu-

als define themselves in a significant way through their intimate sexual relationships with others suggests, in a Nation as diverse as ours, that there may
be many "right" ways of conducting those relationships, and that much of the
richness of a relationship will come from the freedom an individual has to
choose the form and nature of these intensely personal bonds. . . . A way of
life that is odd or even erratic but interferes with no rights or interests of others is not to be condemned because it is different.

Citing Justice Robert Houghwout Jackson (in *West Virginia Board of
Education v. Barnette,* 319 U.S. 624, 641–42, 1943), Blackmun continued
to emphasize the value of diversity and difference. He pleaded that the
Court ought to "apply the limitations of the Constitution with no fear
that freedom to be intellectually and spiritually diverse or even contrary
will disintegrate the social organization. . . . Freedom to differ is not limited to things that do not matter much. That would be a mere shadow of
freedom. The test of its substance is the right to differ as to things that
touch the heart of the existing order." Jackson found it abhorrent that xe-
nophobia was writing the law and delimiting human diversity. *Bowers* allowed the government to barge into the privacy of people's homes. And
once inside, America's puritanical government decided that gay people did not have the right to conduct their own adult, consensual, intimate relationships, even in the privacy of their own homes. The Supreme
Court negated the very existence of lesbians and gay men as people and
with one broad rhetorical sweep smothered their lives under the oppressive papers of the U.S. Constitution.

War and Protest

AIDS and *Bowers* symbolized a bitter rejection of gay people's aspira-
tions for equality. *Bowers* in particular became "our *Dred Scott* case,"
said one activist in reference to the 1857 Supreme Court case that ruled
Negroes were property, not citizens. Pat Norman, who would become
one of the national cochairs of the 1987 march, told *Newsweek,* "We believed in the Constitution. Guess what? It doesn't mean us." Because
of *Bowers,* noted the *Advocate,* "gays and lesbians are legal ghosts, essentially in the same predicament that blacks and women were in the
19th Century. We just have no constitutional standing right now."[65]
These times of war and protest forced activists to recalibrate their

self-definitions. Organizers of the first march, agents situated in the sociopolitical climate of the 1970s, deemphasized the uniqueness of gay
sexuality. They defined gay rights as part of human rights. The shifting
context of the 1980s, however, prompted an analytic shift about the nature of lesbian and gay life. Second-march activists made more distinct,
rather than dissolved, the boundaries of their sexuality. The strategy was
no longer to sneak gay rights as if it were a rider clause in through the
broader rhetoric of human rights. Government neglect of gay people as
they became infected and died of AIDS along with a trial over the very
souls of gay people in the halls of the Supreme Court made the second
march fundamentally, inescapably, and irreducibly *about gay people.* In
these times of war and protest and against an increasingly solidified national consciousness and subgroup development, activists could not afford to loosen or blur their boundaries as they had done before.

All this imprinted onto the Great March. One newsletter observed,
"The AIDS crisis has grown to potentially devastating proportions,
and our local, state, and federal governments are still acting as though
it is someone else's problem. The AIDS issue and the related erosion
of gains made toward our civil rights is no doubt the catalyst for this
national march."[66] The ink of such emotions spilled onto the pages of
the *Advocate*: "With so many gay men dying . . . the urgency of winning
some sort of decent treatment in this society has become apparent."[67]
Like the others, the 1987 march would also have to manage infighting.
Unlike the other three, however, the second march was fueled by an unprecedented rage. People were dying. And the government was preoccu-
pied with gay sex.

Gay people were ignited into activism. Fund-raising for national organizations spiked as it did after Bryant's vituperative rhetoric in Dade
County and Briggs's homophobic legislation in California. Protests
erupted in nearly every major American city. New York's Greenwich
Village witnessed the largest spontaneous gay political gathering since
Stonewall, with more than three thousand people congregating to disrupt the flow of traffic around Sheridan Square. Joyce Hunter addressed
the crowd: "Nobody's going to tell me what I can do in the privacy of my
own home or hotel room."[68] One could no longer even seek solace in the
closet.

In the wake of *Bowers,* two dozen activists began planning the second
march to protest federal inaction around AIDS and "a government in
the bedroom," according to a *Newsweek* headline. Echoing what would

become the official theme—"For Love and For Life, We're Not Going Back"—Steve Ault emoted, "We need to say that we're not going back into the closet." Foreshadowing what would become the theme for one of the largest civil disobedience actions organized in this country—"Out and Outraged"—the *Advocate* declared in a headline: "The Time for Gay Rage Is Now!" The editorial asserted, "Just as white society would never have voluntarily torn down the evil system of segregation without being pushed back by militancy, so too the [heterosexual] world will never give gays a fair shake unless it learns that there's a high price to pay for anti-gay violence and discrimination"[69]

And so began the organizing for the second national march. As stated on a flier: "In 1969 there was Stonewall. In 1979 there was the first Lesbian and Gay March on Washington. In 1987 we return to Washington, stronger and more determined, to proclaim FOR LOVE AND FOR LIFE, WE'RE NOT GOING BACK! Now, more than ever before, we need to . . . show the world that we cannot be ignored."[70] Despite an onslaught of federal repression that closed political opportunities, the movement declared it would not allow for the repeal of its civil rights, that it would not be forced back into the closet of invisibility and silence.

For Love and For Life, We're Not Going Back! The 1987 National March on Washington for Lesbian and Gay Rights

Many 1979 organizers kept in touch years after the demonstration. Over the next couple of decades, they would form a leadership nucleus, or core group, serving as the stalwarts of the three subsequent marches. The rise of a conservative backlash served as an "originating spark," "triggering event," or "precipitating factor" for 1987 march organizing.[1] Steve Ault and Joyce Hunter, 1979 march co-coordinators, drafted a document proposing another march. They first circulated it at a leadership conference in Los Angeles and later mailed it to select national organizations for endorsements. Unlike the first march, however, interest this time was "almost . . . phenomenal," with letters and calls flooding in before any formal outreach was initiated. Organizing committees sprouted from Atlanta to Los Angeles before the march decided its politics or even a name, underscoring the restlessness that characterized the second event.[2] This made receptiveness to the demonstration no longer a concern, especially since activists had established a precedent by successfully executing their first march and were in the midst of suffocating episodes of national threat.

After the endorsements came in, Ault and Hunter organized an initiating meeting for July 16, 1986, in New York City. The meeting was drenched with a sense of urgency, given it was sixteen days after the *Bowers* ruling. "If you have any self-respect," argued one activist, "you can't just leave this situation unchallenged. You have to stand up for

yourself at some point in your life without running from yourself and the
people who hate you."[3] Attendees agreed that the time was right to return to Washington, although they disagreed on whether to do so in the
fall of 1986 or 1987. Nineteen eighty-six would require immediate action
and require a discussion on the strategy of marching during a congressional election year, whereas 1987 would allow more time and might produce a larger turnout.[4] To decide this and the other key organizing tasks,
attendees disseminated a further-reaching call for a national conference
that could better represent the spectrum of the movement, again in New
York City, in November 1986. Representatives from all known lesbian
and gay organizations were invited to hash out the politics, logistics, and
organizing structure for the demonstration.

Organizing for the second march utilized the cultural template, or
precedential guidelines, established by the first in 1979. Activists again
assembled a series of national conferences where they deliberated six
major questions: Should we march? If so, when should we march? What
should we title the demonstration? How should we organize it? What
should we include in its platform? And who should we invite to speak
at the post-march rally? Activists again made use of infighting over these
practical tasks as a culture carrier to give voice to and make material
abstract concerns of identity and strategy. Although the debates were
structurally similar—that is, they arose over the same exact six tasks—I
will show that they inflected culturally varying scripts, or very different
meanings, as a result of changes in the sociopolitical context and developments within the movement.

The Call to Action

Between the initial meeting in July and the first national planning conference in November, activists mailed a call to action with a deliberately political focus to all major gay organizations in the country.[5] The
call drew attention to the repressive political context and formalized the
theme: "For love and for life, we're not going back." This suggests a refusal by lesbians and gay men to return to the closet, despite symbolic
Supreme Court shoves and material ones by the Reagan administration
in its proposals to quarantine, in concentration camp–like fashion, HIV-
positive people. Activists organized the 1979 march in response to a variety of local triggers that took on national resonance. That first march

congealed a consciousness and movement, as suggested by the forward motion in the theme of the second march. Lesbians and gay men were not going back into their closets now. Or ever.[6] The 1987 march provides evidence of the momentum that comes from an awareness of belonging to a national movement.

In reading the two-page call to action, one cannot escape the energy of injustice and anger that effervesces through pages drenched with emotion. The architects of the call used loaded language to entice to action those who might otherwise opt for apathy and inaction—the classic free rider problem in political organizing.[7] The call opened with a boxed excerpt of Justice Harry Blackmun's dissenting opinion in *Bowers*: "Depriving individuals of the right to choose for themselves how to conduct their intimate relationships poses a far greater threat to the values most deeply rooted in our nation's history than tolerance of nonconformity could ever do." It then urged response to this "agenda of hatred, of fear, and of bigotry—against us, against freedom, and against love," underscoring the 1980s political climate that denied lesbians and gay men "the right to make love, even in the privacy of our own homes."

The call did not stop at *Bowers;* AIDS was also central to the text: "The AIDS crisis is manipulated to advance this agenda. . . . The federal government plunders already-underfinanced social programs, pitting victim against victim, as it offers too little too late to combat AIDS. . . . The Justice Department sanctions discrimination against people with AIDS and people with ARC [AIDS-related complex]."[8] The 1987 march had a discrete and angry purpose. It was not a diffuse attempt to generate consciousness or establish the much-needed veracity of a national movement, as was its predecessor. This march was about AIDS. And the right to love.

The acuteness of external threat prompted some activists to consider coalition-building, that is, "to stand in solidarity with the lesbian and gay movement at this time of crisis."[9] This theme came up repeatedly, sometimes with fierce debate, sometimes with an air of self-evidence, beginning with the call itself: "The United States is in danger of becoming a place where everyone's privacy and freedom yield before the prying eyes of a fearful, lunatic fringe." The call concluded that "the escalating attacks on our community are part of a pattern of assaults on human rights." Organizers drew comparisons between gay rights and those of people of color and women: "As the rights of lesbians and gays are threatened, racist attacks increase; the hard-won civil rights of People of Color are dismantled. . . . As lesbians and gay men are denied the right to make love, the right of women to control their own bodies is in jeopardy."

Coalition-building could potentially augment the appeal of the march, amplify attendance, and use the politics of numbers to signal the cause as worthy.[10] But why was it not as central in 1979? And why did it manifest differently in 1993 and 2000? Coalition-building is a very New Left strategy, the training ground for many gay activists. They brought to their movement experiences with women and antiwar organizing, in particular. Because many 1979 organizers assisted in the 1987 effort, as well, New Left training is a necessary but insufficient explanation. A more complete account must consider changes in the sociopolitical context and developmental features within the movement.

The first notable difference between 1979 and 1987 was that a national consciousness was now in place. Bolstered by the success of the first march, organizers no longer wondered: if we build it, will they come? In the forward-moving theme of the 1987 event, there is additional evidence that the first march influenced how activists approached their second go-around. In 1979, there was bitter disagreement over whether the march should be organized at all. Activists in 1979 feared that a poor presence on the Mall would give the movement a black eye. Because the event did happen and because it was deemed a success, no such concerns resurfaced in 1987. Steve Ault remarked, "The real difference here is that we do not have to convince people that they have to go to the demonstration. . . . We just have to tell them it's happening."[11] With AIDS and *Bowers* looming large, and emboldened by their conviction that people would support the march in a way they had not before, organizers were now able to frame coalition-building as a key component in a social justice program. They were now able to stretch beyond their formerly single-issue vision.

A second difference was the international political context. Scholars have recently identified the impact of international politics on domestic organizing. In the civil rights movement, for example, international events "provided leverage and new political opportunities that were successfully mobilized by civil rights advocates at home."[12] With the end of American isolationism and the advent of the cold war, activists identified the hypocrisy between America's rhetorical stance of justice abroad with the realities of racism at home. Organizing for the 1987 march proceeded against the backdrop of U.S. intervention in Central American countries during President Reagan's term of office.[13] Activists of all stripes interpreted U.S. intervention as evidence of American racism (especially against third-world countries). This catalyzed conversations around the importance of coalition-building among progressives who saw racism as intricately connected to all domestic and international affairs. Lesbian and gay rights, too, could not be understood independently of American racism (and sexism).

The international political context still required "resonance"[14] to affect organizing, drawing attention to a third difference between the 1979 and 1987 marches. Racially specific gay organizations grew sizably during the 1980s, before which there were only a tiny number. Gay people of color developed a recognizable presence during the 1980s, thereby catapulting an identity-building program. They argued that gay life was "premised on the assumption of whiteness."[15] Coalition-building therefore resonated with U.S. intervention efforts, internationally, and within the movement with the rise of these organizations.

These three factors—consciousness (continuity of New Left–trained organizers, a national consciousness in place, and a program of self-affirmation and distinction in progress), threat (domestic and international activity in the sociopolitical context), and organizational development (resonance of this context within the movement)—account for why coalition-building was a central and viable strategy for the 1987 march whereas it was not for the first march in 1979. The fourth variable—lesbian and gay men's political/cultural status—remained constant across the first two demonstrations. Viability of coalition-building, however, should not be equated with inevitability. Although the gay imagination expanded onto a new horizon, activists still heavily debated whether a single-issue march might not still be more effective.

The call to action concluded by evoking the ever-popular iconography of Stonewall: "In 1969, the Stonewall Rebellion released the pent-up yearnings that had been stilled through eons of oppression. And today, after all the suffering and all the struggling, we issue this Call for a March on Washington as we proclaim to friend and foe alike, FOR LOVE AND FOR LIFE, WE'RE NOT GOING BACK!" Sixty-five prominent activists, leaders, and politicians signed the call. They invited organizations to send representatives to attend the first national planning conference in New York, urging delegations to be of gender parity

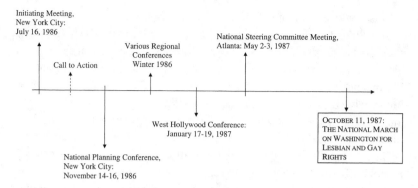

FIGURE 5.1. An Organizational Timeline of the 1987 March.

and inclusive of people of color. Delegates were asked to consider in advance four questions: 1) What will a March on Washington accomplish?; 2) How should we proceed?; 3) What should be the focus?; and 4) When should we have the march?[16] In assembling a grassroots planning conference in New York, organizers replicated the 1979 march structure, and thus affirmed their cultural template, by incorporating a series of national conferences, as depicted in figure 5.1.

The grassroots structure activists used in 1979 was valuable for at least two reasons. First, they used national conferences and local meetings to develop an insurgent, or oppositional, consciousness critical for the success of any political organizing. That this was possible was confirmed in organizing the first march.[17] The national conferences were places where leaders communicated about the problems their movement needed to address; developed a sense of optimism and political efficacy; committed themselves to the movement; and, with the help of the media, created a public forum for the rank and file to provide feedback.[18]

The national, regional, and local conferences also stretched a fabric of organizations across the country. Activists frequently defined a march on Washington as a "movement-building exercise." This is evinced in the fact that many local organizing committees stayed in place after the respective march was over, and each march inspired the formation of new organizations, as well.[19] March planning facilitated organizational expansion and the creation of an infrastructure that stayed firmly in place, propelling growth at the local and national levels long after the weekend of any given march. Each march therefore reconfigured the organizational landscape the movement used to assemble its next demonstration.

The National Planning Conference, New York City

The first national planning conference—attended by more than four hundred delegates representing 180 lesbian and gay organizations from across the country—was held in New York City over the weekend of November 14–16, 1986, under the now widely circulated slogan, "For love and for life, we're not going back!"[20] Along with invoking the directive to continue building a national movement, an introductory flier distributed to all attendees made use of external threats to unify the delegates: "We're here to do no less than make history—to build an event and a national movement to fight the rising tide of anti-gay and anti-lesbian bigotry and to make our community . . . valued."[21]

History was indeed made. Recall that the first national conference of the 1979 march (the Minneapolis meeting) dissolved due to irreconcilable infighting. Although dissent was also part and parcel of the New York conference, the delegation did not disband. None of the meetings and conferences, for that matter, dissolved. Although there were regular disputes, they were generally framed as cathartic. One representative, for example, commented that dissent was "natural" and that "it's good to get everything that's on your mind out in the open."[22] This comment is redolent of a "political public sphere" argument that sees the airing of controversial opinions as a healthy part of the process of democratization, in which the exercise of power and political domination is held up for scrutiny. Infighting, in other words, motivated organizing by facilitating a cultural audit of decisions, thereby enhancing group performance.[23]

The productive outcomes of infighting—its ability to culturally carry and make concrete otherwise ineffable expressions of strategy and identity—were ensured at all the national conferences for the second march due to the confluence of five factors: 1) a national consciousness was by now firmly in place; 2) a nationally resonating trigger (AIDS and *Bowers*) justified organizing; 3) activists remained allegiant to the cultural template they themselves drafted during their first march; 4) in particular, activists honored a participatory-democratic decision-making structure in which dissent was perceived as welcome through "opennness norms"[24]; and 5) they linked these with a discussion of practical tasks to ensure the dividends of dissent would be harnessed.

The New York conference was a weekend full of workshops and plenary sessions organized around the themes of AIDS, celebrating lesbian and gay relationships, demanding civil rights and equality, and specific

concerns for people of color. The conference accomplished three objectives: 1) it set the date and established the physical structure of the
march; 2) it developed the organizing and leadership structure; and 3) it
drafted the demands.[25]

Date and Physical Structure

Due to the timing of the conference (in November of 1986), the question of when to stage the march resolved itself. The upcoming march was
set for Sunday, October 11, 1987. Delegates chose this particular weekend for its symbolic continuity with the first march (which was held on
Sunday, October 14, 1979, to commemorate the ten-year anniversary
of Stonewall) and because it overlapped with a Columbus Day holiday
weekend. Similar to 1979, organizers decided to maintain the spirit of
a march instead of a parade.[26] And finally, with regard to the physical
structure, delegates agreed that people with AIDS (PWA) and AIDS-
related complex (ARC) would commence the march, underscoring its
centrality.[27]

Organizing and Leadership Structure[28]

Delegates adopted the same structure from 1979 with little to no debate.
Organizing would be participatory-democratic and assembled into three
national committees and several local ones across the country. In comparing the first two marches, this provides evidence that infighting does
more than just transport competing meanings. Activists use it to accomplish this but also do more. In the back-and-forth between dissenting and
decision-making in the first march, activists generated a cultural template that also prescribed material, organizational guidelines.

With regard to the national committees, at the base was the largest
decision-making structure, the steering committee (SC), which was composed of four types of representatives. First were representatives from
each of the eleven regions into which the country was divided. The fact
that the country was now divided into eleven regions, instead of seven as
it had been in 1979, suggests that the movement had developed a more
nuanced sense of itself. Each regional delegation was required to bring
at least two women and one person of color to be seated on the SC. Nine
seats went to constituency representatives, who provided voice for traditionally underrepresented groups such as PWAs, seniors, S&M, and

transsexuals/transvestites. Seventeen seats went to representatives of national organizations. The last group on the SC comprised national committee chairs not already represented from one of the other groups. Delegates mandated that the SC be 25 percent people of color and 50 percent women to ensure representation across lines of demographic diversity.[29] At the next level was the coordinating committee (CC), which contained all national committees and chairs of official events. Then came the seven-member executive committee (EC), composed of three elected national cochairs (Steve Ault of New York, Pat Norman of San Francisco, and Kay Ostberg of Washington, D.C.), the national secretary, and three at-large seats. Members of the SC elected the cochairs at the West Hollywood Conference (see fig. 5.1).[30]

Although the two marches shared this cultural template, the demonstrations differed in the role played by national organizations. Organizers of the first march struggled until the very end with obtaining endorsements from the National Gay Task Force and the Gay Rights National Lobby. "The mainstream organizations opposed us last time," remembered the late 1979 media cochair Eric Rofes.[31] In 1987, the national organizations, which had developed substantially in the seven intermediary years, were now eager to support the march, perhaps because they too deemed the 1979 demonstration a success. Thus, the first march affected how national organizations perceived the second march, which influenced the timing and enthusiasm of their support.

The notably renamed National Gay *and Lesbian* Task Force (NGLTF, formerly National Gay Task Force, or NGTF) supported the 1987 march so aggressively that some delegates accused it of trying to co-opt the event. Then spokesperson Urvashi Vaid said they pledged $2,000 "no strings attached" to help get the march underway.[32] The difference in the role played by national groups suggests a complex relationship between organizations and protest events. Although some suggest synergy, it is not absolute. Organizational endorsements are often conditional and variable.[33] In 1979, the skepticism of the national organizations hurt perceptions of the march's need and efficacy. This relationship was reversed by 1987. The reason why national organizations withheld endorsing the first march until the last minute—and even then with reluctance—was because of bitter disagreement over whether a march should even be staged. According to 1979 and 1987 march cochair Steve Ault, "The real difference here is that we do not have to convince people that they have to go to the demonstration. We just have to tell them it is happening."[34]

Ault's testimony illustrates that the success of the first march affected the meanings of marches along with how to organize them.

AIDS and *Bowers* muted similar debates on whether to march. This muting had two consequences. First, it crushed what was in 1979 a serious source of internal division. Second, it created an initial unifying effect that was absent in 1979 when similar episodes of discrete, national conflict were absent, providing evidence that external threat can reduce infighting. I say reduce, not eliminate, because the second march was not without disunity. This time, dissent did not focus on the question of whether to march, as it had in 1979, but instead on how gays should situate themselves vis-à-vis other movements. This suggests a more refined understanding of who comprises the external audience. In the first march, activists emphasized Carter and the government. In 1987, activists again targeted the government (and Reagan), but now also included other protest movements in their "protagonist identity field."[35] Should lesbians and gay men proceed autonomously with their own grievances? Or should they build coalitions with other groups? The demands became a lightning rod for this particular debate.

Demands and Title

Although conference organizers desired delegates to work through the agenda "in a spirit of cooperation and mutual respect,"[36] many participants described the meeting as "a hard birthing," using descriptors such as "contentious," "disruptive," and "confusing." It was a conference that resurfaced "chaos and old animosities between different ideologies," at times almost eclipsing the grave external threats to which the movement was trying to desperately respond.[37] The biggest source of controversy concerned the demands.

Delegates compiled a laundry list far longer than 1979's. Prominent among these were the repeal of all sodomy laws, the passage of a federal lesbian and gay rights bill, the extending of heterosexual benefits and rights to lesbian and gay couples, the end of discrimination against people with AIDS, the end to discussions of mandatory HIV testing and quarantine, and a massive increase of funds for AIDS research, treatment, and education.[38] These single-issue demands for lesbian and gay rights met with little resistance. One particular demand the Lesbian and Gay Network of Mobilization for Survival (MOBE) proposed—"money for AIDS, not for war"—was unanimously adopted and, until the time of the march, became a galvanizing slogan. Again we witness the unifying properties of external conflict.

The most rancorous debate of the conference developed over whether the march should be exclusively single-issue in focus (i.e., identify only traditionally gay demands), as the 1979 march had been, or whether it should embrace a multi-issue approach (i.e., include other traditionally non-gay demands). Votes to formally make the march a single-issue demonstration were defeated twice, each time by a 3–2 margin. Those favoring a single-issue march argued that introducing racism, sexism, and U.S. intervention in third world countries would divert the focus from gay concerns and alienate conservative supporters of the march. Multi-issue supporters responded that all oppressions were interconnected, that homophobia and discrimination against gays was part of a larger system that subjugated women and people of color. A multi-issue march would broaden its appeal, both within the movement and among allies outside, especially third world people, women, and antiwar activists.[39]

After much debate, Steve Ault proposed an enthusiastically endorsed middle ground. Ault advised using march literature to create bridges with other groups, but avoiding non–gay demands in the platform itself. "There's a place for single-issue demonstrations by many movements, not just ours," he argued. "Lesbians and gays are always the constituency left out—it's always a real battle to get our issues raised."[40] Given the reality of exclusion within other movements—what civil rights scholars describe as "the principle of silent acceptance" or "inclusion without empowerment"[41]—Ault proposed for the movement to center itself in its own concerns (in the platform) while building bridges in an ancillary statement on racism and sexism. Conceived by Gwendolyn Rogers of the National Coalition of Black Lesbians and Gays, the text read:

> As members of the lesbian and gay movement, we too are affected by the rising racism and sexism which oppresses people of color and women; thereby the liberation of lesbians and gays is intricately linked to the struggle against racism, sexism, and anti-Semitism. We realize that none of us are free until we are all free. We therefore call upon all of our sisters and brothers to actively confront racism and sexism on all levels, both within our movement and in the larger society. We demand an end to all social, economic, judicial, and legal oppression of lesbians and gays, and people of every race, gender, ability, class, ethnicity, faith, political ideology, transgenderal orientation and sexual orientation.[42]

After the New York conference, the People of Color (POC) Caucus circulated a memo expressing their reactions to the meeting, focusing in particular on debates related to this statement. The caucus observed, "There was general agreement that most of us were outraged by the enormous amount of racism, sexism, and insensitivity expressed by many whites present [at the New York conference], especially gay white men. We also agreed that the demands to be incorporated in all of our literature were the most progressive statement on racism and sexism ever overwhelmingly approved by such a diverse group from the gay and lesbian community." Ault's integrative solution, it appears, was effective in conciliating some tensions.

Lest the toils of debate be forgotten, the caucus pushed further: "The march cannot be a single issue march if People of Color are to be vocally and critically involved. . . . Racism inside and outside the gay and lesbian community must become a serious agenda item for white gays and lesbians if this community is to become a viable entity in which we actively participate at all levels. . . . Spread the word—this is our march, too! And no one, or anything, not even racism, will stop us from fully sharing our role."[43] The caucus used the platform to debate a larger issue, namely, how different types of gay people (whites and people of color, in this case) were connected as part of the same movement. Did gay whites and gay people of color share something—anything—other than their sexual orientation?

The POC Caucus pressed to include more resolutions than were ultimately approved. A consideration of what was *not* passed reveals boundary limits within which the movement was willing to situate itself vis-à-vis other causes. For example, a demand to "end U.S. intervention throughout the Third World" was voted down 90–70 the first night and by a similar margin the second day when delegates tried again. Some also demanded "an end to U.S. corporate and government support for South African apartheid and the freedom of South African political prisoners." The newly formed DAFFODIL (Dykes and Fags Fighting in Our Own Defense and for International Liberation), who cosponsored the intervention resolution, voiced dismay at its defeat: "While it's 'safe' to be against apartheid, denouncing intervention—particularly CIA backing for the Nicaraguan contras—is a little too challenging. We have to work hard to counter the rightward move in the gay community, which only reflects the general trend in this society."[44]

Delegates were quick to identify the hypocrisy between the call to action, which stated that "the escalating attacks on our community are part of a pattern of assaults on human rights," and the desire of many delegates to push a single-issue platform. What kind of movement was this? In one memorable position paper, MOBE responded with an astute observation: "One of the keys to the success of the right wing has been its ability to pull together all segments of the right wing agenda. . . . If the lesbian/gay movement . . . [is] to succeed, we must gain strength from a unified effort against the right in its many manifestations."[45] MOBE pressed for forging links with progressive movements to fight the rise of organized conservatism. These and other debates capture a movement questioning its boundaries: can gay rights be separated from concerns of racism and sexism? That delegates voted to include the statement on racism and sexism suggests an augmenting of the boundaries of gay identity beyond the narrow confines of sexuality to include an expansive understanding of social justice. But within certain limits.

Delegates agreed that any march literature released by any committee was required to print the statement. In one revealing case that garnered national media attention, Southern California organizers refused, citing concerns that the "potentially inflammatory references to sexism, racism, and apartheid in South Africa" would adversely affect fund-raising and outreach efforts in conservative Orange and San Diego Counties. After "nearly two days of acrimonious debate . . . the national steering committee voted 35–15 to condemn [local organizers] for deliberately omitting" the statement. Although the censure amounted to "little more than a slap on the wrist,"[46] it had a strong symbolic impact: this march was committed to coalition politics and thus broad social justice.

The SoCal debates illustrate that the march did not have an anti-organizational ethic common to the Old and New Left.[47] The lesbian and gay movement struck a balance between organization and decentralization through a loosely structured, participatory-democratic national organization that functioned as a centralized core. Although local groups remained autonomous, the national organization simulated a centralized structure (by having the power to censure, for example). This facilitated monitoring and imposed discipline, which controlled factional splits.

Activists and the rank and file alike used the tangibility of the demands to reflect on the abstract state of their movement. An exemplary letter to the *Washington Blade,* titled "List of March Demands Is a Lam-

poon of Itself," argued that "the central importance of our sexual orientation . . . is obscured in a barrage of liberal propaganda. . . . The whole
tone of the document, with its 'demands' and cries of 'oppression,' is na-
ïve and pretentious." The writer, Rick Rosendall of Washington, D.C.,
was keenly aware of the platform's capacity to concretize cultural concerns: "Of course, these demands that bear no conceivable relation to
Gay and Lesbian rights represent an effort to build coalitions." Yet
this should not proceed uncritically. Rosendall asked, "But how effective is this?" To which he himself responded, "Whenever I hear the lit-
any of oppressed minorities recited, I listen in vain for any mention of
Gays. We adopt other groups' agendas without their adopting ours. Assembling questionable coalitions serves only to destroy the focus of the
march and alienate those who disagree on the other issues." For him,
some of the proposed demands were simply outrageous: "And why, for
God's sake, must apartheid and the contras be dragged into everything?
We have to pass every liberal litmus test or we are out of step. . . . Forgive
me if I seem hard, but polite murmurings would hardly be noticed amid
the inflated clamorings of reflexive, indiscriminate liberalism. . . . Surely
as a community in the 1980s we can do better than this."[48] Although
it is difficult to assess whether Rosendall is representative of a broader
sensibility, platform critiques were neither isolated within particular circles nor regionally bound. Many perceived the demands as having "an
unabashedly leftist tilt," a description printed in the *Advocate,* the largest national gay newsmagazine.[49] This may be an indicator of its wider
reach.

A multi-issue march is historically most effective when a variety of
groups, however burdened by their disparate cultural and political commitments, can come together around a shared, *material,* goal. For example, a crowd of 750,000 people—students from diverse college campuses,
middle-class suburban residents, labor unions, war veterans, civil rights
activists, feminists, and housewives—all came together under a concrete
and attainable vision of ending the Vietnam War. In what was the largest
rally against the war, this mass marched on Washington in 1971, an event
that marked a turning point in the antiwar movement. The march's effectiveness has been attributed in part to the impressive coalition of groups
united around this common cause.[50] Gay activists approached the coalition question in ways impossible to resolve. Demands for "an end to sexist oppression" and "an end to racism" are too abstract. Without tangibility, the motivation to build coalitions becomes unclear, as groups

wonder why they are working together, to what demonstrable effect, and what they have in common.

In addition to the platform, activists also debated the title, especially with respect to bisexual inclusion. Activists used title debates as a vehicle to engage in a meta-conversation over what it meant to be gay (i.e., categorical commonality) and how different contenders were connected as part of the same movement (i.e., relational connectedness). One bisexual supporter argued in the *Washington Blade*, "Gay liberation is our liberation, so we have to work for Gay causes at every opportunity. The list of demands drawn up by the March organizers expresses many of our concerns. However, bisexual and Gay issues aren't identical. We can't let Gays represent us in D.C. . . . Once we publicly claim our bisexual identities, we will no longer go unacknowledged or left out. The very fact that the March isn't called 'The Lesbian, Gay, Bisexual March on Washington' is symptomatic of the fact that we haven't been visible enough, as bi's, within the Gay community."[51]

For whom was this march? Did bisexuals count? Title debates resembled those had between lesbians and gay men in the late 1970s over inclusion of the term *lesbian* in organization names. Previously, the term *gay* connoted the experiences of men *and* women. In the late 1970s, women demanded inclusion of the word *lesbian* in all titles because: 1) women's experiences of being gay were not identical to those of men; 2) women's experiences were equally universal and specific as those of men; 3) lesbian issues mattered just as much as men's issues; 4) an organization could not claim to adequately represent lesbians without including the word *lesbian* in its name; and 5) organizations that purported to represent lesbian interests had to have them as members and leaders.[52] The idea is the same: rhetorical representation was required for bisexuals, in the later days, and lesbians, in the earlier days, to feel that they shared in a collective identity. Infighting over the title carried this identity work.

The title has been hotly debated in each march. Representational struggles were part and parcel of the movement's growing pains. Although AIDS and *Bowers* had an initial unifying effect, organizers were still burdened by inclusion battles that reconfigured the us-versus-them dichotomy to what sociologist Joshua Gamson calls "us versus thems inside," that is, "particular subgroups battle[d] to gain or retain legitimate us standing."[53] Although bisexuals were ultimately not included in the demands or title, the 1987 march was the first in which they had a distinct and recognizable contingent present on the mall.[54] These visibility debates raised enough awareness for the genesis of an identifiable group and helped foster the blossoming of a bisexual culture, community, and politics in the late 1980s and 1990s. Although it is difficult to attribute causality to the march itself, one thing is clear. Dissent brought into focus bisexuals as a distinct subgroup within what had until then been just the lesbian and gay movement. The most direct evidence for this would come from the title of the third march, which was for lesbian, gay, *and bi* rights. Dissent over practical tasks carried and concretized this culture work. It augmented identity boundaries, rather than prompting a bisexual defection.

The West Hollywood Conference

After New York, activists convened in West Hollywood, California, the weekend of January 17–19, 1987, at which point the sixty-four-member steering committee finalized the organizing structure and politics by solidifying the demands and beginning a discussion on the speakers.[55] Wishing to not reproduce the raucousness of New York, delegates agreed to "ensure unity, bonding at all times," and that in the event of severe infighting, "task forces will be formed to work out a compromise that everyone can live with." Delegates realized that internal disputes were not effectively managed in large, steering committee sessions with diverse and firm opinions. Compartmentalization of conflict within focus groups could defuse emotion and provide an organizational mechanism to resolve dissent.

Organizing Structure

Delegates approved without controversy New York's three-tiered structure, which contained a steering committee (SC), coordinating committee (CC), and executive committee (EC). The sixty-four-person SC represented eleven U.S. regions and was the empowering group that directed the CC and EC.[56] Delegates then introduced a motion to have three cochairs, with at least one man, one woman, and one person of color. The motion carried, and the discussion concluded with nominations and by outlining eight primary responsibilities as follows: to coordinate committee outreach and referral; to pinpoint trouble spots and fix them as appropriate; to serve as a resource person for regional media tasks; to serve as a resource person for regional fund-raising tasks; to coordinate miscellaneous logistics; to supervise personnel; to assist in national fund-raising; and to assist in national media endeavors. Nominated individuals spent that evening lobbying on their own behalf before the morning vote.

Delegates reconvened at 10:00 a.m. the following Sunday. At the start of the meeting, they decided at least one cochair must be from Washington, D.C., to manage local concerns (such as permit acquisition). After this discussion, Kay Ostberg was automatically elected as the D.C. cochair since no one else from the region was nominated. The rest of the nominees spoke for three minutes on why they would make an effective cochair. After hearing everyone speak, delegates voted and elected Steve Ault and Pat Norman with thirty-three and eighteen votes, respectively.

Delegates next affirmed the goals for representation in all levels of march organizing, which they operationalized as gender parity and 25 percent people of color representation. This upheld "the spirit of inclusion and not exclusion" established in New York, which "ensure[d] that all persons in our community have an opportunity to be represented." Such requirements—established as a minimum, not maximum—were another organizational mechanism to ensure unity across lines of internal diversity.

Demands and Speakers

The platform discussion was smoother in West Hollywood than it had been in New York. Although disputes lingered, delegates discovered another integrative solution. New York participants generated a lengthy list that West Hollywood attendees condensed into major planks. There would be seven demands, five of which would be single-issue, bulleted by ancillary supporting statements. The genius of this integrative solution was twofold: 1) it utilized both/and framing, that is, the platform would include both single- *and* multi-issue demands—rather than an either/or positioning; and 2) it used ancillary statements that allowed activists to compile a laundry list without the appearance of being overburdened.

Here we discover a striking similarity between 1979's single-issue Five Demands and the 1987 delegates' decision to denote the first five of their demands as single-issue, as well. Using planks to subsume supporting statements drew on a principle of parsimony established by the first march. Although the total list was long (see table 5.1), activists used

TABLE 5.1. **Demands, 1987 March**

THE LEGAL RECOGNITION OF LESBIAN AND GAY RELATIONSHIPS

Lesbian and gay male domestic partners are entitled to the same rights as married heterosexual couples; social services for lesbian and gay youth should be greatly augmented.

Outside of rarely tested contract law, no option exists to provide lesbian and gay partners equal opportunity to form legally recognized relationships. What do exist are laws and opinions that clearly discriminate in favor of heterosexual marital relationships.

Changes must be made in the courts and the legislatures to provide homosexual couples the same privileges and benefits as heterosexuals who commit themselves to similar relationships. Changes must also be made in public opinion so that society recognizes and celebrates the diversity in family relationships.

These changes include but are not limited to:

- rights of inheritance
- extended medical benefits
- visitation and custody rights
- insurance rights
- parenting rights
- foster care opportunities
- adoption opportunities
- immigration rights for a citizen's spouse

Since lesbian and gay youth are often without societal and familial support, funding for a broad range of social services is needed and must be targeted to them, including, but not limited to:

- alternative housing
- foster care
- counseling services, including legal aid

Also at issue is the availability of safe sex information and health-care services for lesbian and gay youth, sexuality and anti-homophobic curriculum in the schools, access to lesbian and gay publications in public and school libraries and freedom to participate in related school activities.

THE REPEAL OF ALL LAWS THAT MAKE SODOMY BETWEEN CONSENTING ADULTS A CRIME

All state and federal laws criminalizing consensual sex should be repealed as they violate the constitutional right to privacy.

Sodomy laws form the cornerstone of discrimination against lesbian and gay people.

Since 1961, 25 states have decriminalized private consensual adult sexual activity. Lawmakers in those states have broadened personal freedoms, reduced governmental intrusion, expanded protection of privacy and relieved their states' criminal justice systems of a vague and discriminatory law. All citizens benefit when sodomy laws are reformed.

Like Jim Crow laws of the American South, which sanctioned and promoted racism, sodomy laws give the government's stamp of approval to the hatred of lesbian and gay people. To single out lesbian and gay people for special prosecutorial attention stigmatizes all who are gay and lesbian whether or not they are ever arrested or charged with sodomy.

Sodomy laws bolster the application of other laws used to restrict gay and lesbian people's freedom of association and movement. Gay bars are raided and customers charged with "lewd and lascivious behavior," "gross indecency," or "disorderly conduct." Police and prosecutors claim they were foiling the more heinous crime of sodomy by bar patrons since gay bars are meeting places for unconvicted criminals.

Sodomy laws are used against lesbian and gay people in a variety of noncriminal contexts. Most commonly, sodomy laws are cited in custody cases to discredit lesbian and gay parents by characterizing them as immoral as evidenced by laws making their conduct illegal regardless of

TABLE 5.1. *(continued)*

their abilities to provide a loving home for their children. Sodomy laws are used in similar ways against lesbian and gay people seeking security clearances or applying for professional licenses or attempting to remain in the military.

A PRESIDENTIAL ORDER BANNING DISCRIMINATION BY THE FEDERAL GOVERNMENT

That the President ban by Executive Order all discrimination based on sexual orientation in the federal government particularly in the military and in immigration; that the President end exclusion of people with AIDS or HIV-antibody positivity from government employment. Eliminating employment discrimination based solely on sexual orientation in the government sector would send a signal to the rest of the country that this discrimination is immoral and should be illegal.

A strong response to redress present discriminatory policies and practices is the use of full presidential authority to eliminate all discrimination based on sexual orientation in all aspects of executive branch employment, programs and policies.

More specifically:

·   A Presidential Executive Order should be issued to ban discrimination based on sexual orientation in federal employment, the military, federally contracted private employment, granting security clearances, and all federally funded programs.
·   Since excluding lesbian and gay people from this country has no valid medical or scientific basis, the public health exclusion policy should be eliminated.
·   All military regulations discriminating against lesbian and gay people should be eliminated, including sodomy regulations. Upgrades of all less-than-honorable military discharges based on homosexuality should be granted with fully restored benefits.
·   A Presidential Order should be issued guaranteeing uncensored access to information for lesbian and gay prisoners, equal visitation rights, and protection from discrimination based on AIDS and/or sexual orientation.
·   The Justice Department shall stop interpreting laws to deny civil rights of lesbian and gay people as well as other people, including repeal of their interpretation of discriminating against workers associated with AIDS.

PASSAGE OF THE CONGRESSIONAL LESBIAN AND GAY CIVIL RIGHTS BILL

That a federal bill banning discrimination on the basis of sexual orientation be passed. Twenty million Americans can lose their jobs regardless of performance if their private sexual orientation becomes known. Thousands more can lose their shelter if their sexual orientation becomes known to their landlords or to a housing authority. Still thousands more can lose their right to participate in federally assisted programs.

A Congressional civil rights bill would give lesbian and gay people the same basic civil rights that other citizens take for granted.

In addition:

·   The government should provide protection from discrimination based on sexual orientation in education just as protection is provided regardless of race, creed, color, sex, or national origin.
·   The government must also pass, strengthen, and enforce civil rights and criminal laws making violence and harassment against lesbian and gay people illegal.
·   The government should ensure all public education programs include programs designed to combat lesbian/gay prejudice.
·   The government should allocate federal funds to identify and eliminate violence and harassment of lesbian and gay people.
·   Institutions that discriminate against lesbian and gay people should be denied tax-exempt status and federal funding.

(continued)

TABLE 5.1. *(continued)*

AN END TO DISCRIMINATION AGAINST PEOPLE WITH AIDS, ARC, HIV-POSITIVE STATUS OR THOSE PERCEIVED TO HAVE AIDS. MASSIVE INCREASES IN FUNDING FOR AIDS EDUCATION, RESEARCH, AND PATIENT CARE. MONEY FOR AIDS, NOT FOR WAR.

Discrimination based on real or perceived AIDS, ARC, or HIV antibody–positivity must be ended in the public and private sectors; funding for AIDS education (including safe sex information), research, and patient care be massively increased; those monies must come from the military budget, not existing social services.
Right wing extremists have seized upon the AIDS epidemic as an excuse to promulgate ordinances and legislation which attack lesbian and gay people.
Elected representatives at the county, city, state, and federal levels must oppose any bills or ordinances whose effects would be to limit the civil rights of persons with AIDS or ARC, persons with HIV antibodies, or persons in groups thought to be at high risk to HIV infection. In addition:

- There must be an end to discrimination in the delivery of health care, insurance, social services, housing, employment, public accommodations, and education.
- There must be no federal funding or tax advantages for organizations or businesses that discriminate.
- Compassionate, comprehensive health-care services must be available for patients without regard to ability to pay. Special attention must be given to health care services for people of color and those in economically disadvantaged areas.
- Federal, state, and local governments must protect the absolute confidentiality of anyone tested for the HIV virus.
- The government must provide safe sex education to all youth.

Short of a cure, the only means available to break the chain of HIV infection and transmission is a comprehensive, well-funded public education program. Additional government appropriations are needed to continue and expand prevention efforts along with research and patient services. Funding for these programs must come from the military budget, not already existing appropriations in the social service budget. Social service programs, which are already underfunded, cannot be pitted against one another to provide funding.
More specifically:

- There must be complete federal funding of all health and social services for all people with AIDS/ARC.
- The federal government must underwrite and insure all research for a cure and a vaccine.
- The federal government must fund a massive AIDS education and prevention program that is explicit, culturally sensitive, lesbian- and gay-affirming, and sex positive.

REPRODUCTIVE FREEDOM, THE RIGHT TO CONTROL OUR OWN BODIES, AND AN END TO SEXIST OPPRESSION

A person's right to control his/her own body is basic to controlling his/her life economically, socially, and spiritually. The lesbian and gay civil rights movement recognizes that limiting control of reproductive rights has been used to control women over the centuries. This sexist oppression is promoted and practiced by the same people who deny lesbians and gay people the right to practice our sexuality freely. In order for all of us to be free, sexist oppression must be stopped.
More specifically:

- All people must have access to birth control, with the recognition that birth control is the responsibility of both sexes.

TABLE 5.1. (*continued*)

· Those who wish must have the right to artificial insemination by donor.
· Public and private institutions should support parenting by lesbian or gay couples.
· There must be an end to sterilization abuse.
· All people must have access to free abortions and contraceptives on demand regardless of age.
· Congress must enact the Equal Rights Amendment.

AN END TO RACISM IN THIS COUNTRY AND APARTHEID IN SOUTH AFRICA

Any form of discrimination is unacceptable. Discrimination against any group in society affects
all people living in that society. Racism both denies basic human rights to sizeable minorities of
the population and robs society of the talents and resources of productive and useful members.
In order to secure the rights of all people, we must rid society of the fears, prejudices, and laws
that prevent any person from realizing her/his potential. In order for lesbian and gay people to
be free, racist oppression must be stopped.
In addition:

· Apartheid is racism in its ugliest and most blatant form. It violates all human rights, and it
  must end.
· Freedom must be secured for South African black gay activist Simon Nkodi who is facing
  treason charges.
· Freedom must also be secured for all South African political prisoners.
· The lesbian and gay civil rights movement supports the South African freedom struggle, and
  we demand an end to U.S. governmental and corporate support of South African apartheid.

*As members of the lesbian and gay movement, we too are affected by rising racism and sexism
which oppresses people of color and women; thereby, the liberation of lesbians and gays is
intricately linked to the struggle against racism, sexism and anti-Semitism. We realize that none
of us are free until we are all free. We therefore call upon all of our sisters and brothers to actively
confront racism and sexism on all levels both within our movement and in the larger society.
We demand an end to all social, economic, judicial, and legal oppression of lesbians and gays,
and people of every race, gender, ability, class, ethnicity, faith, political ideology, transgenderal
orientation, and sexual orientation.*

Source: Official Program of the 1987 National March on Washington for Lesbian and Gay
Rights. Primary source materials: Gerber/Hart Library.

planks to lump together seven demands. Similar to the organizing structure, this is additional evidence that activists do not simply fight over
tasks to concretize strategy and identity. In addition to such culture work,
1979 activists also etched platform concerns into their cultural template
to prescribe for future generations how to assemble the demands and the
meanings associated with different decision options.

   The 1987 demands were "the most progressive statement on racism
and sexism ever overwhelmingly approved by such a diverse group from
the gay and lesbian community."[57] That said, it is notable how infighting
managed to sneak inside. The concluding statement on racism and sexism declares, "We . . . call upon all of our sisters and brothers to actively
confront racism and sexism on all levels both *within our movement* and

in the larger society" (emphasis added). Recall that the single-versus-multi-issue debate was most heated in New York. Those who favored a coalition march experienced their opposition as being unconcerned, at best, if not blinded to the realities of racism within the movement and in the larger society (and here it is instructive to additionally recall U.S. intervention efforts in Central American countries). This discussion attracted a related conversation surrounding racism and sexism *within* the movement. A POC press release captured this by admonishing those who opposed a multi-issue march: "The march cannot be a single issue march if People of Color are to be vocally and critically involved from its organization to it implementation."[58] This warning was so pronounced that activists added to the demands. Lesbians and gay people of color used the platform to assert their rights of inclusion.

Activists also used the organizing task of speaker selection to debate strategy and identity boundaries. Speaker selection had stakes for several reasons. It was one of the most visible manifestations to straights of gay America's public face. Speakers also symbolized nodes of representation into which traditionally marginalized groups could plug. Having a gay black speaker or a gay Latino speaker, for instance, were meaningful to the black and Latino gay communities, respectively, who felt invisible and silenced in the movement. There were other concerns, as well. Should non-gay individuals speak? What about celebrities? Or should delegates assemble grassroots activists who may be less flashy but more invested in the movement?

West Hollywood attendees did not finalize speaker decisions. Instead, they charged Robin Tyler, chair of the rally committee, to compile a potential list. Tyler would submit this to the executive committee for discussion and final approval at the Atlanta meeting in May. For checks and balances, the executive committee also asked the sixty-four-person steering committee to submit names for speakers right then and there. Everyone was advised that speakers must address at least one of the demands and maintain racial and gender parity.

Atlanta and Beyond[59]

On Saturday and Sunday, May 2 and 3, the sixty-four-member steering committee met for the last time before the march. After Atlanta, organizing continued at the regional and local levels, where activists planned activities and finalized speakers. If they encountered obstacles, they called the national office, where secretary and march coordinator, thirty-four-year old, Los Angeles native Lee Bush, would assist. Bush was responsible for networking and organizing disparate local groups for a unified national effort.[60]

The Atlanta meeting was a nuts-and-bolts gathering where delegates heard updates from fund-raising, outreach, media, rally, transportation and housing, people of color, and march committees. By the end of the weekend, delegates had encountered two major stumbling blocks: debating who would speak (a carryover from West Hollywood) and what events to officially sponsor. Infighting, however, was less caustic than before. As reported in the *Gay Community News,* "Despite the optimism of almost everyone associated with the march, considerable controversy continues to surround the platform, civil disobedience, plans for a mock wedding, and speakers. However, the acrimony that marked earlier national meetings receded in favor of compromises reached at a May 1 national steering committee meeting in Atlanta."[61]

Who Will Speak For Us?

Determining who would speak was the most difficult dialogue of the weekend. Indeed, from Atlanta onward, "the most contentious debate [revolved around] the process of selecting speakers . . . and the politics of speakers invited."[62] In West Hollywood, Robin Tyler was charged with compiling a list of suggested speakers and bringing it to Atlanta. Tyler was a mastermind of planning and emceeing rallies, drawing on her extensive experiences in the women's movement from the 1970s. She knew that choosing speakers always generated controversy. To diffuse dissent, she suggested having two rallies, one in the morning before the march and one in the late afternoon afterward. According to Tyler, this strategy would "help increase the diversity of speakers and serve as a good welcome to those arriving in the morning." She added that "the people of color caucus will help sponsor [both rallies]" and that "we will have a Native American speaker first at the morning rally." Tyler was clearly aware of the politics of representation. Although Atlanta delegates accepted her proposal, they expressed reservation during the months leading up to the march. Over time, it became clear that the afternoon rally would be better attended and more prominent. There were concerns over which speakers were slotted at which rally. Steering committee members also expressed concern over Tyler's selection of celebrity speakers over grassroots activists, along with her inclusion of straight speakers whom the steering committee felt displayed little understanding of gay issues or had troubling stands on various march demands.

Months after Atlanta, organizers received word that the Reverend Jesse Jackson, who at the time was the leading Democratic presidential hopeful, agreed to speak. Organizers announced that actress Whoopi Goldberg had also agreed to speak. March cochair Kay Ostberg explained the delegates' rationale for these speakers: "We never intended to invite presidential candidates. Our intention was to invite a civil rights leader, a labor leader, and a women's rights leader."[63] Gil Gerald, former executive director of the National Coalition of Black Lesbians and Gays and an SC member, chimed in on the importance of Jackson specifically as a civil rights leader: "We consider the march an important civil rights event. . . . The Rev. Jackson's involvement in the civil rights movement provides an important link between the movement of Martin Luther King Jr. and the movement for Gay and Lesbian rights." Ostberg and Gerald's comments capture how activists used speaker selection to define the movement. In addition to Jackson and Goldberg, and to continue outlining a coalition-based, social-justice movement, organizers reported that farm labor organizer Cesar Chavez and former National Organization for Women president Eleanor Smeal had also accepted invitations to speak.

Lesbians and gay men across the country did not hesitate to offer their input. As a "cultural form," observes Joshua Gamson, celebrities are seldom received neutrally.[64] Any individual history of personal action perceived as incompatible with any goals of political organizing is intensely scrutinized and caustically criticized. Given that all actions have multiple meanings, their interpretation, that is, cultural reception, is never fixed and thus always capable of generating dissent based on the receiver's "horizon of expectations," or a person's prior social and cultural experiences.[65] Rank and file dissent over their leaders' organizational decisions, in other words, is almost inevitable.

Jesse Jackson was soon embroiled in this politics of perception. Jackson was invited for several reasons, as evidenced in Ault's initial invitation: "Dear Rev. Jackson: Your statements in support of lesbian and gay issues made during the 1984 presidential campaign, and your more recent statements of compassion and reason on the AIDS crisis are very much remembered and appreciated by our community. By speaking at this rally you would help forge an important link between the struggle against racism and the movement for civil rights for lesbians and gays. As you have so eloquently stated . . . it is through these types of links that we will develop the strength to build a better society for all."[66] Leaders defined Jackson's invitation as valuable because of his perceived support of gay issues and the potential that inhered in linking the gay and black movements. In other words, activists used speaker decision as a means to concretely redefine the lesbian and gay movement as progressive and concerned with social justice (via the faces of Jesse Jackson, Eleanor Smeal, and Cesar Chavez).

Some glossed over Jackson's stature as a civil rights leader, emphasizing instead his traces of homophobia. A *Gay Community News* report quoted one local organizer objecting to Jackson's reluctance to include gays in his Rainbow Coalition[67]: "To have someone not 100 percent behind our goals is not good enough." Terry Ortiz of the POC Caucus disagreed, claiming that Jackson's coalition-building potential outweighed his homophobia: "This is a great opportunity to educate him on these issues and, given the other candidates, he is certainly the best we could have."[68] As this interchange suggests, the cultural reception of having Jackson speak varied based on the personal experiences and social location of the person interpreting. Nonetheless, activists once again used dissent over practical tasks such as speaker selection as a vehicle to culturally outline competing strategic visions.

Activists also questioned non-gay invitees, creating a double-whammy for Jackson, Goldberg, Chavez, Smeal, and others who were interrogated for being part of some A-list despite a potentially soiled record on gay issues. Pat Norman observed, "As progressives, we look for somebody who embodies the purest of the pure—that's not going to happen." Name speakers could validate the movement and forge alliances with other causes. Experienced organizers such as Ault recognized that "you won't have total agreement on all issues. . . . People will have flaws from somebody's perspective." Cochair Pat Norman conceded, "There's every kind of ideology going on here. We're making every accommodation to make certain no one is left out."[69]

Some used dissent to define and assert gay autonomy. Virginia Apuzzo, New York Governor Mario Cuomo's liaison to the lesbian and gay community, argued that the community must learn to speak for itself. Non-gay speakers, while nice, asphyxiated gay visibility, a critical objective of the march. Apuzzo asked, "What does it say about us that our own community wishes to make us invisible? We need to develop our own strength. We need our own Martin Luther King, Jr. and Malcolm X. We can and do speak for ourselves all around the country."[70]

Speaker debates never resolved, resurfacing in conversations up to the day of the march. Their resolution matters less than what they suggest about how conflict and culture work in political organizing. Dialogues of dissent clarified the contours of the movement. The speaker debate, like those of whether to march, when to march, what to title the march, how to organize it, and how to construct the platform, highlighted tensions between being politically sui generis and building coalitions. As one organizer succinctly asserted, "This is *our* stage."[71] But who would that include? By dissenting over whether the march would be single- or multi-issue, activists wrestled with how best to draw the face of gay America. What would this face look like if its representatives selected someone with a tainted record on gay issues? What does it say about lesbians and gay men if they selected someone to speak on their behalf who, in other circumstances, does *not* support them or their cause? These abstract questions materialized in light of dissent over practical organizing tasks.

What Events Will We Sponsor?[72]

Attendees recognized the need to assemble a weekend of diverse events for the march to have appeal to those traveling from distant places. National secretary Lee Bush opened the conference with this advice: "We need to stress that the March is a five-day event. People from the West Coast are more likely to attend if there is a week's worth of events."[73] Recognizing this value, delegates sponsored an array of events, some of which proved quite controversial.

Several events were planned in recognition of AIDS. In June 1987, the National Association of People with AIDS and the National March on Washington jointly announced *A Time to Shine,* a project designed to ensure representation of PWAs at the march. The event's slogan captured its objective: "Send a person with AIDS to Washington for the March!"[74] The project subsidized the trip for a PWA since many could not afford the associated costs due to medication and hospital expenses. Many PWAs felt it was critical for them to be there as a personal testimony to the tragedy.[75]

The AIDS Memorial Quilt was one of the largest and most poignant events of the weekend. On Sunday, October 11, the Names Project, an organization founded by Cleve Jones, had its inaugural display of the AIDS Memorial, a quilt composed of thousands of individual three-by-six-foot fabric panels, each inscribed with the name of someone who had died of AIDS. The panels were assembled into one massive expanse of names displayed across the Mall. The quilt was a breathtaking memorial of the loss of human life. Some described it as the "quilt of tears," others a "patch-quilt of love." Founder Cleve Jones desired to document the lives he feared history would forget. Volunteers were overwhelmed with emotion as they assembled the quilt in a makeshift factory in San Francisco. "We cry every day when we receive panels in the mail," said one volunteer. Recalled another, "One, made by the mother of a Gay man who died of AIDS last year [in 1986], consists of fabric from the shirts of the dead man and his surviving lover. Since the man who died was deaf, his mother sewed onto the panel a drawing of a hand giving the sign-language symbol of love. . . . That one had us in tears for most of the day."[76] The quilt covered an area larger than a football field, included 1,920 panels, and drew over half a million visitors.[77] Cleve Jones's AIDS Memorial Quilt is nothing short of a stroke of genius, standing even today as a powerful visual reminder of the AIDS crisis.

For Tuesday, October 13, organizers planned a nonviolent civil disobedience (CD) action at the Supreme Court—with intentions to get arrested—to demand full civil rights for lesbians and gay men.[78] The CD action was a symbolic protest against the Supreme Court's *Bowers* decision which upheld Georgia's sodomy law.[79] According to Michelle Crone, chairperson of the CD committee, "This promises to be a watershed for the lesbian and gay political movement. . . . This will be the first time a large national direct action tactic has been used to fight exclusively for lesbian and gay civil rights." The theme for the action was "Out and Outraged: Love, Life, and Liberation."[80]

The CD action was not inconsequential. As the national gay press noted, "Never before have gay activists undertaken such an urgent, ambitious, and publicly visible act of civil disobedience. And while civil disobedience is hardly new to gay politics, the upcoming Supreme Court action underscores a deepening recognition within the gay community that a more dramatic form of moral and legal resistance is needed." The CD action drew on civil rights strategies as another mechanism to link the two movements. The action symbolized "a certain coming of age for the gay rights movement" and forging of links "with other great civil rights movements of this century." One organizer explicitly drew such connections: "If blacks had mainstreamed all their issues, this country would still be trying to pass a civil rights act."

Similar to blacks in the 1950s and 1960s, lesbians and gay men felt moral outrage against a government that denied them basic human dignity and civil rights. At the action itself, organizers continued to draw connections to the civil rights movement as they told the crowd of more than three thousand supporters, "Today we are sitting in at the lunch counters of the lesbian and gay civil rights movement. We act with the knowledge that the [Bowers v.] Hardwick decision, like the decision before it upholding slavery, can and must be overturned."[81] Between 650 and 850 individuals were arrested during the six-hour action on the steps of the Supreme Court, making it the largest number to participate since the anti–Vietnam War demonstrations of the 1960s and 1970s. To this day, the CD action remains the second largest demonstration of its kind ever executed.

The quilt and CD were fairly uncontroversial. One particular event, however, remained cacophonous all the way through. For Saturday, October 10, organizers sponsored the Wedding, a non-sectarian union ceremony celebrating gay relationships and demanding gay partnerships be entitled to the same rights as married heterosexuals. The slogan— "Love Makes a Family, Nothing Else, Nothing Less"—spoke to the invisibility of gay families.

The Wedding was at once a celebration for participating couples and a political demonstration to demand recognition for what organizers believed were an invisible group of people. This political aspect of the demonstration was critical. According to Carey Junkin of Couples Inc., a Los Angeles–based organization coordinating the event, "The wedding is just a media handle. . . . It's going to be a political demonstration for equal rights."[82] Walter L. Wheeler, president of Couples Inc., concurred that the Wedding "is a demonstration for equal rights to demand recognition of our existing ongoing relationships. . . . The reception following the demonstration will be a celebration of our relationships where we and our supporters can share the love commitment we have in our families."[83] To drive home the politics of the event, the Wedding was held in front of the IRS building. This symbolic setting focused on the fact that gay couples, deprived of legal married status, were ineligible for tax benefits reaped by married heterosexual couples. The Wedding therefore emphasized the march's demand for legal recognition of lesbian and gay relationships (see table 5.1).

In sponsoring the Wedding, march organizers embraced gay couples as an identifiable constituency and granted a seat on the coordinating committee to Couples Inc., a national organization working for the advancement of lesbian and gay couples.[84] This consolidated a distinct identity for gay couples. Wheeler expressed this in a letter he wrote to the steering committee: "We believe that Lesbian and Gay couples are an important part of our community. Contrary to the 'Cinderella Concept,' we cannot just go off together and live happily ever after. We have real issues and concerns that affect us because we are Lesbian and Gay couples. . . . Please include a discussion of a National Representative for Lesbian and Gay Couples as a member of the Steering Committee. . . . This way we can be properly represented."[85]

The Wedding screamed with dissent. The gay press dubbed it "the most controversial of the officially sanctioned march-related events"[86] for four reasons. One group, composed of gay pastors and other religious persons, expressed concern that the demonstration would "turn into a mockery of a ceremony that has deep roots and sacred meaning to those of us who are in the religious community." This group threatened "to publicly disavow any support for or connection with this activity" should their concerns not be addressed.[87] Carey Junkin and Walter Wheeler's framing of the event as political assuaged much of these concerns.

A second group, largely in the minority, felt the event would be frivolous and devoid of meaning and impact. This conservative group felt that an inevitably campy event would cast a negative light over the entire march. The third, politically progressive group, felt the Wedding would reproduce a repressive heterosexual institution.[88] Similar to progressives, the fourth and final group was concerned that the Wedding would affirm only one type of relationship and erase what they perceived to be one of the gay community's most valuable contributions to society, namely, its support of alternative relationship structures. Individuals in this group were concerned about reducing the diversity of lesbian and gay relationships into something monolithic that "look[ed] like heterosexual families." These critics argued that "the wedding validates only traditional relationships. It's opposed to a gay lifestyle which means community."[89]

In a *Gay Community News* editorial, a Boston-area group called Positively Revolting complained, "While the history of marriage . . . makes
us want to pull our hair out, the idea of fitting lesbian and gay relationships into the context of marriage makes us want to burn buildings." The
group also addressed the value of dissent: "If we want our relationships
to be just like 'theirs,' what have we gained? It doesn't get us real valida-
tion for our lives, our lovers, our friends."[90]

Movement scholars suggest tactical innovation quickens the pace of
insurgency.[91] As a novel tactic, the Wedding spurred mobilization *and*
engendered dissent. One group of rank-and-file activists declared, "We
were going to stand outside of the ceremony carrying larger-than-life
toaster ovens and blenders 'congratulating' the newlyweds. But we decided our limited energy was better spent elsewhere. And going to a
massive, exciting lesbian and gay event and protesting other lesbians and
gay men is a real bummer."[92] This calls into question a straightforward
relationship between innovation and insurgency.

In the end, more than seven thousand people, including nearly two
thousand couples, attended "an exuberant public acknowledgment of
both the existence and legitimacy of [lesbian and gay] relationships."[93]
Speakers took time to respond to criticisms. Robin Tyler asked the
crowd, "How can we support a patriarchal institution?" To this she replied, "We are not here to parrot heterosexual marriage, an unequal
bond of unequal partners—that is sick. We believe in the right to love,
the right to bond, the right to commit forever." Carey Junkin of Couples Inc. was more aggressive when he voiced opposition "not only to the
Moral Majority, but to the self-appointed guardians of political correctness in our movement."[94]

The event, its criticisms, and its responses all implicitly drew comparisons between gay and straight couples. Were these different relationships identical? Do gays have anything unique to contribute toward
societal conceptions of love, marriage, and family? In asking these questions, the Wedding chimed into an ongoing tension between boundary-
tightening and -loosening. Under what conditions should gays emphasize
that which makes them distinct from others? And under what other conditions might they consider diminishing those distinctions? The Wedding represented early seeds that, by the third march, would sprout into
a more explicitly articulated desire to mainstream the movement. Finally
and unbeknownst to many, the Wedding also signified the early roots of
contemporary same-sex marriage and family battles.

The 1987 National March on Washington for Lesbian and Gay Rights

On October 11, 1987, amid tears and laughter in a spirit of love and life, an estimated 200,000 to 650,000 lesbians and gay men, fully embracing their now-axiomatic national consciousness, demanded justice from a hostile American government. The situating of the march symbolized an epoch of war and protest, as it was "sandwiched between the display of the Names Project quilt on the Mall and an unprecedented mass civil disobedience action outside the Supreme Court."[95] AIDS and *Bowers* unleashed an incensed movement that refused to go back in the closet, exemplified in the themes of the march and the CD action: "For Love and For Life, We're Not Going Back" and "Out and Outraged," respectively. The movement born in 1979 had roared into its own by 1987.

The mammoth, emotionally saturated march was the largest gay rights demonstration ever assembled, dwarfing the 1979 march, and it ushered in a new milieu in the movement. Gay activists and non-gay supporters such as Cesar Chavez and Eleanor Smeal commenced the march, carrying a boldly lettered sign that read, "National March on Washington for Lesbian and Gay Rights." Behind them was a contingent of people with AIDS, some marching, some wheeled by friends. Actress Whoopi Goldberg was one such somber-looking marcher in the front line, wheeling her old friend Jim Manness for the duration of the march (see fig. 5.2).

The 1987 event is the only one of the four that is remembered to this day as "the Great March." The confluence of volcanic and visceral anger generated by the unconscionable loss of life due to AIDS, the erasing of gay people with a single judicial stroke of the pen, and the profound inspiration catalyzed by the march itself contributed to its greatness. Although there would always be something to fight for and some backlash to resist, the emotions would be different. Gay rage would not rise in quite the same way for the two marches yet to come.

The longest lasting legacy of the 1987 march was the formation of National Coming Out Day. Sponsored by the National Gay Rights Advocates and the Experience Weekend, National Coming Out Day (NCOD) was designed to commemorate annually the anniversary of the 1987 March on Washington. Celebrated every year on October 11, the event was a mechanism to bring the spirit of the march home to local communities and touch the lives of millions of lesbian and gay Americans. The goal of NCOD was "to increase the visibility and political clout

FIGURE 5.2. 1987 March Banner. Photo © 2004 Patsy Lynch.

of the more than 20 million gay men and lesbians in this country." Drawing explicit links with the 1987 march, organizers declared, "No matter how far in the closet or out of the closet you are, you have a next step. . . . On October 11, 1988, the anniversary of the historic March on Washington for Lesbian and Gay Rights, thousands of people will be bringing the spirit of the March *home* to their local communities." National Coming Out Day is still celebrated to this day in cities and small towns across the United States.[96]

Despite its greatness, the 1987 demonstration, like its predecessors and the two that would follow it, had to wrestle with chronic infighting. "Unity is not the same thing as unanimity," cautioned Urvashi Vaid.[97] The event shows that infighting develops along a curve, suggesting that divisive processes are best understood as a matter of degree and as a continuum rather than static or fixed. Dissent progresses over a range and period of time, mediated by the shifting sociopolitical context and developmental features within the movement.[98] The 1987 march witnessed a delayed onset of infighting due to a sense of urgency established by external threat. AIDS and *Bowers* made the need to return to Washington compelling and thus muted most of the initial quibbling, evidenced in the amicable atmosphere of the initiating meeting.

Recall that there were failed organizing attempts during the first march in 1979. The 1973 Urbana-Champaign meeting, for example, dissolved and has been all but forgotten.[99] Five years later in 1978 when the idea returned, the first organizing committee in Minneapolis also crumbled due to irreconcilable infighting. No such dissolution occurred during the second march, lending additional evidence to the unifying effects of external threat. But this is not absolute. Although no committees disbanded, and although the initiating meeting displayed remarkable unity across diverse activists, the volume of discord was raised at the first and second national conferences (in New York and West Hollywood, respectively). With the march date approaching, activists once again united around the premises that ignited their initial efforts, concentrating on the potential impact of the march while setting ablaze the fury fermenting within their movement.

Infighting was often perceived as necessary en route to October 11. One activist expressed that he was "delighted to see the *Advocate* article [that reported extensively on dissent in the organizing process], not for what it said about the March, but rather for what it evidences about the Gay press becoming willing to engage in self-criticism. I wish I heard more critical reviews of why we are marching again." Another *Advocate* editorial also asked, "Are we going forward?" It recognized that "yes, there are plenty of good reasons to go to Washington" and that the march "could not come at a more compelling moment in our history." Seemingly unwilling to abandon an acerbic angle, the editorial chided, "The march is emerging as the political equivalent of a one-night stand. It may feel good while we're doing it, but what will we be left with the day after?"[100] A letter to the editor in D.C.'s local gay press wondered the same. Titled, "The March: What will we get for the investment?" the writer wondered whether the march addressed "the deeper reality of the state of the Gay rights movement in the U.S. today."[101] Although these questions of political efficacy were never definitively resolved, they encouraged leaders and the rank and file to use dissent to muse on the state of their movement. One writer poetically captured this by asking, "Where are our visionaries, our prophets, our voices of leadership?" In the ensuing public debate, one could hear answers: "Dare to look with me, deeper into the spirit of ourselves. Question with me,"[102] the writer pleaded.

Changes in infighting across the first two marches correspond to adjustments in strategy, or activists' desired goals and the means for obtaining them. Nineteen seventy-nine was the coming out of the movement on a national scale, and infighting spoke to the deep skepticisms this process entailed. Things had changed by the time of the second march in 1987. The movement was now remarkably self-aware of its national scope. Specific organizations for women, people of color, and

bisexuals had become stronger and more visible. These strengths, however, were burdened by *Bowers* and emaciated by AIDS at the height of
the epidemic. In this mix the movement re-confronted the strategic question of whether to proceed autonomously or vis-à-vis others in social justice. The decision to augment the platform to a multi-issue framework,
however, did not imply boundary permeability (i.e., incorporating other
groups as part of the movement) in a manner comparable to the decision to subsume gay rights under human rights in 1979. The diminishment strategies of the first march made sense in light of an underdeveloped national consciousness. This time activists were keenly self-aware,
proceeded through an additive constellation of progressive groups, situated themselves as a distinct social justice bloc, and thus hardened their
boundaries vis-à-vis external agents.

This decision to build coalitions in the second but not in the first can
be explained by the configuration of movement consciousness (continuity of New Left–trained organizers, a national consciousness in place,
and a program of self-affirmation and distinction in progress), threat
(domestic and international activity in the political context), and organizational development (resonance of this context within the movement).
The fourth variable I chronicle in this story—lesbian and gay men's po-
litical/cultural status—remained constant across the first two marches.
The 1987 march's decidedly leftist agenda, however, was not inevitable.
Although the gay imagination expanded to a new horizon of possibility, activists repeatedly debated the tradeoffs between gay autonomy and
coalition-building.

In addition to strategy concerns, infighting in 1987 also had implications for identity, or what attributes and relationships activists felt they
shared. National conference delegates reconfigured the term *gay* to
reach beyond just sexuality and sexual freedom. This self-redefinition
resonated with developments within the movement, most notably, with
the growth of people of color organizations. One might mistakenly read
this as evidence of unqualified boundary plasticity and thus another reversal from 1979 when internal boundaries were hardened (e.g., by excluding transpeople). In fact, 1987 was riddled by a duality over the
groups with whom activists drew connections. On the one hand, a social justice positioning suggests augmentation by linking gay and other
progressive causes. Willingness to engage in bisexual inclusion debates
suggests a similar receptiveness to boundary expansion, but the decision to ultimately exclude them, on the other hand, indicates a carryover

boundary-tightening from the first march. It is instructive that both the 1979 and 1987 marches were titled "for lesbian and gay rights" despite (failed) identity work by transpeople and bisexuals.[103] Boundaries vis-à-vis internal agents were therefore only semi-permeable, expanding to include some yet refusing others. It would not be until the third march in 1993 that the title would expand to include bisexuals and not until the fourth in 2000 that transgenders would be embraced. Finally, although the first two marches were undeniably progressive, the officially sponsored Wedding event and its accompanied debates serve as a reminder that other forces were also in play that sought to redirect the movement down a more mainstream path that, as we will see for the third and fourth marches, successfully overpowered this initial leftist course.

CHAPTER SIX

The People Next Door: Lesbian and Gay Life in the Late 1980s and Early 1990s

"Something happened in the 1990s, something dramatic and irreversible," mused historian John D'Emilio. "A group of people long considered a moral menace and an issue previously deemed unmentionable in public discourse were transformed into a matter of human rights, discussed in every institution of American society. . . . During the 1990s, the world seemed finally to turn and take notice of the gay people in its midst."[1] Recognizing the gaze of American society on them, gay people worked hard to return a palatable and selective image. The *New York Times* picked up on this impression management during the 1993 march: "This march was Ozzie and Harriet compared with the Stonewall days. . . . They [lesbians and gay men] wanted to show America that they were 'regular' people, the kind that live next door, go to work every day and pay their taxes. . . . 'Ordinary' and 'The People Next Door' were mantras of the weekend."[2] This is the story of when the world turned to look upon the gay people next door.

The lesbian and gay movement held its third national march on Washington on April 25, 1993, situated in an era distinct from the prior two. The Center for Lesbian and Gay Studies (CLAGS), a lighthouse for scholarship on gay issues, reflected on the puzzling cultural currents in the 1990s:

> The 1990s find lesbians and gays in a paradoxical situation. On the one hand, we are experiencing greater visibility and greater tolerance than ever before.

On the other hand, we continue to find ourselves at the center of a national debate where our adversaries depict us as the epitome of all that is morally wrong with America. . . . People coming out in the 1990s must sort through a maelstrom of conflicting information about lesbians, gays, bisexuals, and transgendered people. As we seek to define ourselves, we must face loud, often cantankerous, frequently pernicious public debate about the meaning of lesbian and gay lives.[3]

The third march differed from the prior two along four dimensions: gay people's political and cultural status; the nature of external threat confronting the movement; members' consciousness; and internal developmental features. Where the 1980s were a derisive decade, the 1990s were an era of pronounced visibility. Lesbians and gay men found themselves moving from the periphery to near the center of national attention. Politically, the 1990s were a veritable battleground in which legislative houses on the state and federal levels entertained bills for and against gay rights. Culturally, gay visibility exploded with the public coming out of celebrities such as k. d. lang and Melissa Etheridge. Gay themes proliferated in film and theater with *The Crying Game* and Tony Kushner's award-winning *Angels in America*. The media was quick to sensationalize the trend, with *Entertainment Weekly* running a cover story that tagged the era "The Gay '90s." In February of 1993, NBC produced a television documentary titled *The Gay 90's: Sex, Power, and Influence*. The production proclaimed that "gays and lesbians say they just want what most of the rest of us want—health and happiness, a good job, a loving spouse, and more and more to be moms and dads, raising kids, going to the Little League games and the PTA."[4] The people next door had moved in. And suddenly the love that once dared not speak its name was on everyone's lips.

In the 1980s, the movement was burdened with AIDS. People were dying. And enemies were readily identifiable. Although AIDS was omnipresent in the 1990s as well, the primary foe was an intangible and diffuse cultural backlash championed by an increasingly influential Religious Right, which had successfully framed gay rights as a case of special rights, or preferential treatment. This argument gained traction in a societal context where Americans were heavily debating the origins of sexual orientation: was it born or bred?

The movement also confronted a discrete villain in the "Don't Ask, Don't Tell" policy that prohibited openly gay men and women from serving in the United States Armed Forces. This, however, would not enter activists' radar until a short four months before the march. During his 1992 presidential campaign (which occurred during the peak of march organizing), Bill Clinton courted lesbian and gay voters by promising to lift the blanket ban on gay service members. Upon entering office in January 1993, President Clinton announced the possibility for a compromise. After revisions and negotiations between the White House, the Department of Defense, and Congress, in July—three months *after* the march— President Clinton presented his proposal, which, four months later on November 30, 1993, was codified into the "Don't Ask, Don't Tell" policy. Thus, although the military was a discrete adversary targeted on the march's rally stage, it was not confirmed until after the march.

Finally, the 1993 march also differed in terms of movement development. In the six years between the second and third marches, gay organizations continued to blossom, with a notable rise in racially specific organizations. The early 1990s also witnessed the emergence of "queer politics," an anti-identity ethos that implicitly celebrated the proliferation of identities—especially bisexual and transgender identities—while explicitly questioning the utility of all identity categories themselves. Queer politics emerged in part as a critique to identity politics, which, through the 1990s, was thought to fragment social change efforts. Although the building and affirming of identities was necessary, there were now questions as to whether it was the most politically effective approach. Thus, in terms of community development, lesbians and gay men in the early 1990s witnessed conflicting logics of identity-blurring (deemphasis) and identity-building (distinction).[5]

In this chapter and to set the stage for how the third march was organized, I elaborate activity across these four dimensions: cultural and political status (from periphery to near center), conflict (from discrete to diffuse), organizational development (growth of gay organizations), and consciousness (new identity-blurring impulse). The particular changes in the sociopolitical context and features within the movement that became operative by the 1993 march inspired activists to take a step outside the deemphasis (1979) *or* distinctiveness (1987) dichotomy within which they had conceptualized their strategy and identity across the first two events. Something had indeed happened in the 1990s. The advent of cultural buzzwords such as *people next door, ordinary, mainstream, regular,* and *tolerance* in a context of persisting legislative threats generated a program of simultaneity: selective deemphasis *and* selective distinctiveness.

Although *visibility* was the mantra of the times, it was highly focused. New questions arose: What does visibility even mean? Which lesbians and gay men are visible? In what manner and contexts are they made visible? And what does this suggest about who we have become and what it is we now want? Cultural skepticism provided a deliberative system of checks and balances to leaders' efforts to occupy the mainstream. Thus, during the years in between the second and third marches, the movement managed to maintain a tenuous yet productive tension between leftist and centrist impulses.

Out of the Closets, Into the Living Rooms: The Gay '90s

Lesbians and Gay Men in Culture

Scholars have long professed the powers of the mass media. Broadcasting, for example, can be biblical in its impact:

> [It] wields a power once reserved for religion: the power to tell people what is real. The social norms embedded in television shows have the capacity to shape public thought as much as any preacher, politician, or journalist. . . . Regardless of whether the messages are explicit or implicit, many viewers come to accept them as common knowledge after hearing them repeated night after night.

This influence extends to print and film as well. Film historian Vito Russo argued, "We go to the movies to see ourselves. Motion pictures in America have been a reflection of the way we see our country and our people. So when you go to the movies and you don't find yourself up there, it really comes home to you in a double sense that you're an alien in your own culture."[6] How gay people are depicted can speak to their cultural standing in a particular society.

On September 8, 1995, *Entertainment Weekly* ran the headline, "The Gay '90s," centered in large block letters against a collage of photographs (see fig. 6.1) that collectively captured the *Geist*, or spirit, of the times.[7]

One can see a sickly Tom Hanks who played a gay lawyer with AIDS in *Philadelphia;* homoerotic Mark Wahlberg half-naked in his iconographic Calvin Kleins; a sinewy Batman and Robin; a fabulous Ru-Paul; a smiling Melissa Etheridge; a not-very-masculine Patrick Swayze in drag; bisexual Michael Stipe from R.E.M.; k. d. lang, handsome as

FIGURE 6.1. The Gay '90s.

ever; a Marilyn Monroe–esque Madonna: and Elton John. The cover story, "America Sees Shades of Gay," chronicled how "the gay stream flows freely into the mainstream" while "the voices opposing this cultural shift are being drowned out." Welcome to the Gay '90s, a time of "revolution" when "pop culture loosen[ed] its straight jacket" on its sexual sensibilities.

Once upon a time, the *New York Times*'s well-known motto "all the news that's fit to print" deemed stories pertaining to lesbians and gay men unfit for the American public. The *Times* hardly noticed the Stonewall Riots of 1969 that gave birth to gay liberation. More severely, the newspaper had an official policy that forbade the use of the word *gay* in any of its articles. The *Times* was not alone in this rhetorical homophobia; smaller presses across the country had similar policies. In the 1980s, the word *gay* was overwhelming for some. In 1982, for example, an Illinois state senator emoted: "It galls me that sexual deviates are called 'gays.' . . . Wouldn't you join me in an effort to retrieve the word *gay* from ignominy?" Before the late 1980s and early 1990s, the mainstream media's lack of attention to gay issues was ubiquitous. The first national march in 1979 was the largest gay rights demonstration of its time, yet the *New York Times* looked the other way, printing only a brief account on page 14. Nor did magazines and television networks notice. Both *Time* and *Newsweek* ignored the march entirely. It was not until 1987 that the *New York Times* finally allowed use of the word *gay*. This policy change "signaled the start of a new era in the *Times*'s coverage of gay issues." Once they gave the green light, smaller outlets followed suit. The stage was set for a lavender media explosion.[8]

From 1987 and through the 1990s, the mainstream media heralded gay visibility, carrying *certain* lesbians and gay men out from the closeted fringes into living rooms across the country. Images of "respectable looking" gay people erupted onto the pages of local and national newspapers, specialty and news magazines, television, and film. This development came with a corollary rise of the gay press in which a broader cross-section of lesbians and gay men explored issues that touched their own lives.[9]

Gay visibility educated straights generally about those gay people who looked and talked as they did, and also inspired healthy debates among gays about the images themselves and what they suggested about gay identity (who we are) and strategy (our plans for social change). Many journalists turned to what would be the monstrous 1993 march as confirmation that "gay was in." The effect was a crystallization for America that gays comprised their own, distinct community. According to historian John Loughery, "Rarely had the words *gay community* been spoken or used in print as frequently—by allies, enemies, and gay men themselves. . . . Everyone knew, or thought they knew, what they meant when they referred to 'the gay community.'" The gay community became the quintessential "imagined community," in which large groups incapable of knowing each other personally lived "in the image of their communion."[10]

One measure for the imagined community moving from the periphery toward the center (but not quite in it) is the outpouring of cover stories on them. The 1990s witnessed a veritable explosion in prominent magazines as *Time, Newsweek,* and others. From 1989 to 1993, headlines captured the public coming out of Congressman Barney Frank (D-Mass.) (*Newsweek,* September 25, 1989), debates on whether homosexuality was born or bred (*Time,* September 9, 1991; *Newsweek,* February 24, 1992), gays in the military (*Newsweek,* February 1, 1993), and general interest covers titled, "The Future of Gay America" and "Gays Under Fire" that endeavored to "uncover the limits of tolerance" and to get to the bottom of "what America thinks," respectively (*Newsweek,* March 12, 1990; *Newsweek,* September 14, 1992). According to communication scholar Larry Gross, this journalistic mainstreaming "signifies a major shift in societal definitions. On the one hand, the media are paying more attention to issues of primary concern to gay people. . . . On the other hand, gay people are becoming a part of the landscape that does not require special justification to be included in news stories that do not directly concern homosexuality."[11] The media, in other words, helped culturally define gays as the people next door.

Lesbians and Gay Men in Politics

Gay visibility was not confined to the mass media. "State legislatures joined the parade, too," noted John D'Emilio, "as several of them extended legal protections based on sexual orientation, and many more enacted statutes punishing hate crimes against lesbians and gay men." By 1990, the movement had gained two national legislative victories: the Hate Crimes Statistics Act, which required the FBI to collect statistics on hate-motivated crimes, including those against lesbians and gay men, and the augmentation of the Americans with Disabilities Act to include discrimination against people with AIDS. A birds-eye view finds more than one hundred cities and counties and four states with laws protecting gay rights. A handful of municipalities had gone as far as passing domestic partnerships that, despite only conferring limited benefits, bestowed a much grander symbolic sense of equal footing.[12]

Political visibility was animated by the coming out of prominent politicians as hysteria about sex seeped into Congress. It began with the censuring of Representative Gerry Studds (D-Mass.) for his sexual relationship with a seventeen-year-old male congressional Page. Soon after, Studds announced he was gay, becoming the first member of Congress to acknowledge his homosexuality. Then, in the spring of 1987 while in his late forties, Representative Barney Frank announced that he too was gay. *Newsweek* took to the front page and quoted Frank, "Yes. So What? . . . I don't think my sex life is relevant to my job." Frank's coming out had national significance. Lobbyist Hilary Rosen asserted, "His coming out was very important. . . . So much in Congress happens in those cloak rooms. You really can't discount the importance of having openly gay people in those meetings." By 1992, there were sixty-one openly gay elected officials nationwide, including congressmen, judges, mayors, and city councilors.[13]

Joining forces with the National Association for the Advancement of Colored People (NAACP), arguably the nation's most prominent (not to mention conservative) civil rights organization, also pushed the lesbian and gay movement out of the periphery of American politics. The NAACP endorsed the 1993 march, marking the first time the organization has officially supported laws that ban discrimination against gays. Torie Osborn, then executive director of the National Gay and Lesbian Task Force, remarked that the endorsement "really launched us into the more broad-based civil rights movement. That gave us a tremendous amount of credibility, and it heralded a powerful new coalition."[14] News commentators agreed, arguing that the joining of forces flagged that "gay rights finally has become a major political issue, not the fringe topic it was only a few years ago." This more convincingly situated lesbians and gay men as "a major civil rights movement."[15]

Activists used the NAACP coalition to redefine themselves as a mainstream civil rights movement. Cochair Nadine Smith called it "historic" and argued that gays had "moved from being viewed as a special interest fringe group to being in the mainstream of America. . . . We're now seen as part of the broader civil rights movement."[16] News analysts, activists, and march participants all used "mainstream" as sound bytes.

An editorial in Chicago's *Windy City Times* declared, "Certainly, no one can argue anymore that the gay-rights movement is a fringe political element."[17] The title of a news story from the same newspaper plainly declared in large, bold letters, "The March's Legacy: Mainstreaming the Movement."[18] This language marked a major shift from the 1987 march when activists used similar efforts to strategically define themselves as a social justice movement seeking to build solidarity with others. Although sexuality boundaries were becoming clearer over the course of the first three marches, they did so within parameters that deemphasized differences between gay and straight people. Yes, we are a distinct people, went the party line, but we are still not that different from you—we are mainstream. Lesbians and gay men moved out of the periphery into the near center by way of this highly controlled process.

The 1992 Democratic National Convention towered as another significant sociopolitical marker that the movement was marching steadily into the mainstream. Inside Madison Square Garden in New York City, one could see a sprinkling of attendees holding up posters declaring, "Lesbian and Gay Rights NOW," among a smaller crowd of jubilantly waving rainbow pride flags. There were 133 lesbian and gay delegates and alternates at the convention supporting their "savior." During his election campaign, Bill Clinton openly courted lesbians and gay men for their votes, marking the first time that a U.S. presidential candidate connected with the gay community. In his speech, Clinton proclaimed, "Them, the liberals. Them, the gays. We've gotten to where we've nearly themed ourselves to death. Them, and them, and them." The crowd cheered enthusiastically to Clinton's drive for unification. "This is America," Clinton enunciated slowly and emotively. "There is no them. There is only us." Clinton's convention speech ushered in an era of hope for gay people as they had never known, leading some to mark it as "the gay moment."[19] An ambassador for gay rights had presumably arrived.

Activists believed the Clinton administration was "going to offer our movement and our community an alternative to outsider status." Clinton was unafraid to approach the gay community, offering promises of inclusion and citizenship. In an address to the Los Angeles–based organization ANGLE (Access Now for Gay and Lesbian Equality) on May 18, 1992, Clinton declared in a style reminiscent of Martin Luther King Jr.:

> Let me say again, this is not an election, or should not be, about race or gender or being gay or straight or religion or age or region or income. What kills

this country is not the problems it faces. . . . What kills the country is to proceed day in and day out with no vision, with no sense that tomorrow can be better than today, with no sense of shared community. What I came here today to tell you in simple terms is: I have a vision and you are part of it.[20]

Clinton vowed to recognize lesbians and gay men "in ways unheard of during previous presidencies," promising them greater access to the political system. He also promised increased funding for AIDS research, to hire an AIDS czar, to overturn the military ban, to support a gay civil rights bill, and to issue an executive order to ban discrimination on the basis of sexual orientation in all federal agencies. There was finally a "friend in the White House."[21]

President William Jefferson Clinton was elected to office with an overwhelming majority of the gay vote, estimated by pollsters at 75 percent. There was a palpable sense that the lesbian and gay movement had turned a corner onto the streets of equality. Urvashi Vaid declared, "This is a rite of passage for the gay and lesbian movement. . . . For the first time in our history, we're going to be full and open partners in the government." Although this jubilance would be tempered by the cold realities of American politics (with the military debacle, for example), even those who were most doubtful had a reason to be "cautiously optimistic."[22]

Gays played prominently in the 1992 election season—so prominently, in fact, that even the Republican Party was forced to recognize them. In stark contrast to Clinton's rosy rhetoric, presidential candidate George Bush, along with his ultraconservative cadre, lit fire to the anti-gay vitriol of the conservative and Religious Right wings of their party. The Republican stance reveals the intensity of the emerging backlash against gay visibility.

Republicans used Clinton's courtship with the gay community to divide the Democratic Party and circulate fear among conservative Americans. In March 1992, Bush's senior campaign advisor suggested using gay rights as "a major dividing line in the election." This promoted gay-bashing by a major party speaker. A vituperative Patrick J. Buchanan—described as "a political pit bull"—addressed the Republican National Convention in August 1992. Back in the 1980s, Buchanan declared, "The poor homosexuals—they have declared war upon nature and now nature is extracting an awful retribution." Buchanan revisited his repugnance toward homosexuality at the convention by launching what he called a "culture war" against lesbians and gay men:

There is a culture war going on in our country for the soul of America. . . . A militant leader of the homosexual rights movement could rise at the [Democratic] convention. . . . Like many of you last month, I watched that giant masquerade ball at Madison Square Garden, where twenty thousand radicals and liberals came dressed up as moderates and centrists in the greatest single exhibition of cross-dressing in American political history.[23]

From once attacking gays for leading a sinful life, Buchanan now defined any promotion of those unholy gays as a culture war over America's soul. Indeed, sociologist Paul DiMaggio attributes Buchanan's call to arms as largely responsible for the phrase *culture war* becoming a household expression. Buchanan launched one homophobic epithet after another, telling Houston Convention delegates that gay rights have no place "in a nation we still call God's country." Delegates held placards proclaiming, "Family Rights Forever. 'Gay' Rights Never!" Other conservative figures followed suit. In publicly defending Buchanan, Newt Gingrich denounced Democrats as promoting "a multicultural, nihilistic hedonism that is inherently destructive of a healthy society." In the fall of 1992, Pat Robertson's Christian Coalition—with 2.2 million names on its list at the time—convened in Virginia Beach to discuss "the homosexual-rights agenda and how to defeat it."[24]

Gay activists were livid. Urvashi Vaid described the Republican convention as "the most explicitly anti-gay campaign we've ever seen. . . . It's hateful." The *New York Times* commented as well, reporting that "behind the scenes, Republican strategists . . . unapologetically proclaimed their intention to follow Patrick J. Buchanan's declaration of a religious and cultural war with the Democrats." The next day, the *Times* ran a story reporting that "privately, top Bush campaign officials said they would hit the issue [of gay rights] hard in the campaign, portraying Mr. Clinton as a promoter of homosexuals."[25]

According to *Newsweek,* the homophobic rhetoric of the Republican National Convention "turned off most Americans."[26] That the Republican strategy was potentially unsuccessful is telling of the prominence lesbians and gay men were enjoying in the early 1990s. The American public, however, was torn between an impulse to be tolerant and what was still a visceral discomfort with homosexuality. When they thought about lesbians and gay men, their imaginations stumbled onto images of gay sex, which elicited the proverbial "ick factor." Gay politics were more palatable than gay culture (which was equated with gay sex).

Washington political analyst William Schneider noted that "upper-middle-class suburban voters are not wildly pro-gay, but they do not want to be associated with a party that is overtly bigoted." A 1989 *Newsweek* poll titled "Homosexuality and Politics" showed that 45 percent of Americans would vote against a public official who disclosed that he or she was homosexual. This number was far below the 77 percent who would vote against a public official for accepting money from a special-interest group, 64 percent who would vote against a public official for failing to pay income taxes, and 63 percent for having a drinking problem. When asked whether being homosexual should keep someone from holding various public positions, Americans responded that it should *not* keep someone from the holding these positions by the following percentages: 50 percent for president; 48 percent for member of the clergy, 50 percent for teacher, 57 percent for cabinet member; 59 percent for judge, 60 percent for member of Congress, 60 percent for city government official, and 61 percent for policeman. Americans were clearly divided about gays. Although 54 percent did not consider homosexuality an acceptable lifestyle, most believed that being gay should not keep someone from holding public positions.[27] It was at once okay and not okay to be gay.

A New York Times/CBS poll taken ten days after the 1992 Republican convention (three years after the *Newsweek* poll) found 80 percent agreed that gays should have equal job opportunities, and over 50 percent favored gays serving in the military. Only 38 percent, however, described homosexuality as an "acceptable alternative lifestyle" (down 8 points from 1989's 46 percent). In a separate study, sociologists found a pattern of increasing conservatism throughout the 1980s and liberalism in the 1990s, when Americans distinguished between morality and civil rights. While the American public still viewed homosexuality as morally wrong, they were unwilling to restrict civil liberties based on sexual orientation.[28] The lines of the culture war were becoming etched into the American imagination.

The Changing Face of Threat

As the preceding discussion indicates, gays were not only increasingly distinct as a group, but distinctively the enemy as well. Having been identified as such, and in addition to the persisting threat of AIDS, the late

1980s and early 1990s also witnessed the development of a culturally diffuse backlash as the Religious Right framed gay rights as a case of what
they called "special rights." This argument was successful within a societal debate on whether gay people were born or chose to be that way.
Questioning the origins of homosexuality, defining a group as a lifestyle,
and debating whether they were entitled to special rights unleashed a
domino effect of anti-gay referenda in state legislatures.

AIDS, 1987–1993

AIDS taught lesbians and gay men that they were capable of rapid and
productive activism.[29] A critical difference between the second and third
marches was federal acknowledgment and response to the disease, even
if activists still deemed it inadequate. On March 19, 1987, the year of
the second Washington march, the U.S. FDA approved and released the
highly toxic AZT (azidothymidine or zidovudine), the first drug discovered to control the progression of HIV and the onset of AIDS. AZT
was very expensive, costing several thousand dollars per individual per
year. The most effective drugs, such as protease inhibitors, were not released until 1996, well after the third march. As a result, the death toll
from AIDS continued to climb. From 1987 to 1993 (between marches
two and three), a staggering 222,310 individuals died from AIDS, and
378,385 new cases of HIV were diagnosed (see fig. 6.2).

Although AZT slowed AIDS-related deaths, more medical intervention was desperately needed. The rising number of new diagnoses suggested that education was also required to inform the public how to reduce their risks of infection. AIDS education and prevention was a sore
spot for the Reagan Administration. In 1987, the U.S. Congress adopted
the Helms Amendment—known colloquially as the "no promo homo"
policy—that banned use of federal funds for AIDS education materials
that "promote or encourage, directly or indirectly, homosexual activities." It was not until 1988 with the passing of the Health Omnibus Programs Extension (HOPE) Act that federal funds for AIDS prevention,
education, and testing were finally authorized.[30]

AIDS was a prominent part of gay life between the second and third
marches. President Ronald Reagan made his first public speech about
AIDS in 1987 and established a Presidential Commission on HIV (the
Watkins Commission) that same year. In his speech, he described AIDS
as "public health enemy number one."[31] In the same year (on April 29),

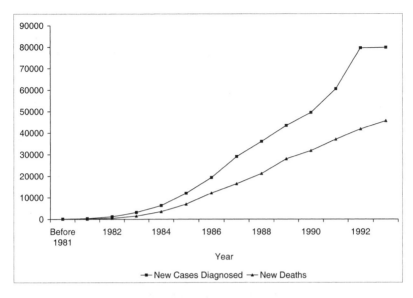

FIGURE 6.2. New AIDS Cases and Deaths, 1980–1993. Source: Centers for Disease Control and Prevention. *HIV/AIDS Surveillance Report,* 2001; 13(2):30.

the FDA approved the first Western blot blood test to detect HIV antibodies—the second such test (in addition to the ELISA test approved in 1985). Also in 1987, Congress approved $30 million in emergency funding to all fifty states for AZT. Other notable events during this year included: the World Health Organization (WHO) launched a global program on AIDS called "World AIDS Day"; the CDC initiated its first AIDS-related public service announcements called "America Responds to AIDS" and held its first National Conference on HIV within communities of color; Randy Shilts's groundbreaking account of the AIDS epidemic, *And the Band Played On,* was published; and the AIDS Coalition to Unleash Power (ACT UP) formed.

The trend toward response continued into the late 1980s and early 1990s as follows: Congress created the National Commission on AIDS (1989); with the death of Ryan White at the age of eighteen, Congress enacted the Ryan White Comprehensive AIDS Resource Emergency (CARE) Act that provided federal funds for community-based care and treatment services (1990); the HIV infection rate among non-white individuals exceeded for the first time the rate for whites (1990); NBA superstar Earvin "Magic" Johnson announced that he was HIV-positive and retired from basketball (1991); Broadway Cares/Equity Fight AIDS and Visual AIDS introduce the red ribbon as the international symbol of AIDS awareness at the Tony Awards (1991); AIDS became the number-one cause of death for U.S. men ages twenty-five to forty-four (1992); President Clinton established the White House Office of National AIDS Policy (1993); the CDC broadened the definition of AIDS to capture a greater range of the disease, including adding a condition specific to women and those more prevalent among injection drug users (1993); the FDA approved the first Reality Female Condom (1993); and Tony Kushner's *Angels in America,* a play about AIDS, won the Tony Award and the Pulitzer Prize (1993).[32]

The prominence of AIDS also gave birth to a "new field, the AIDS field," characterized by organizations designed specifically to fight the disease and that did not have an explicitly lesbian and gay focus. AIDS organizations grew quickly—indeed, quicker than most mainline gay organizations, with whom they competed for resources such as volunteers and funding. AIDS also helped communities of color get organized. The late 1980s and early 1990s witnessed a "dramatic increase in the level of organization and visibility of gays of color" who assumed leadership positions in AIDS organizations. At the dawn of the new decade, the fight against AIDS had become institutionalized, which "allowed for new and existing gay rights groups to begin turning their attention to classic issues, including . . . anti-gay violence, and the status of gay people in the military," in the words of Elizabeth Armstrong.[33]

These political developments (e.g., federal and international response to the epidemic), cultural developments (e.g., the introduction of the red ribbon to raise awareness, the coming out of celebrities as having AIDS), medical developments (e.g., AZT and the Western blot test), and organizational developments (e.g., the institutionalization of an AIDS response) explain why the third march focused less on AIDS than the second. Much had productively transpired in the ten-plus years since the 1981 *New York Times* article identified the "rare cancer," affording activists an opportunity to respond to other concerns, especially the military and the Religious Right.

Don't Ask, Don't Tell: Gays in the Military

Clinton was not the originator of the military debate. The military had prevented gays from serving since at least 1943, arguing from the beginning that they would compromise unit cohesion, promote violence against gay service members, hurt morale, threaten straight people's privacy, and lead to problems incited by illegal sex acts. In 1947, *Newsweek* ran a story titled "Homosexuals in Uniform" that detailed Army regulations that "strictly forbade the drafting of homosexuals" and various procedures used to "screen out this undesirable soldier-material [of] inverts." In 1975, *Time* magazine ran a feature story with a cover photograph of Leonard Matlovich, an openly gay Air Force sergeant, accompanied by large black letters, proclaiming, "I Am a Homosexual."[34] The issue had been around for a while.

After his election, Clinton issued a memorandum that would have lifted entirely the ban against gay service members. At that moment, organizers tasted what would prove to be a fleeting moment of optimism. Clinton's proposal fueled fear in Congress, as the issue of gays in the military became hotly debated across the country. It paralleled President Harry Truman's campaign to integrate black and white battalions after World War II. Arguments against racial integration mirrored those against gays: "The idea that if blacks and whites—or gays and straights—served together it would 'weaken unit cohesion.'"[35]

The military issue gained prominence in October 1992 when petty officer Allen R. Schindler was brutally murdered in Japan by his own shipmates for being gay. In his personal diary, a tortured Schindler wrote, "More people are finding out about me. It scares me a little. You never know who would want to injure me or cease my existence." The high visibility of this case is evidenced by Schindler's mother speaking on the main stage of the 1993 march. Clinton continued to encounter considerable opposition, especially from within the military and conservative lobbying groups, while Defense Secretary Les Aspin would not move an inch in negotiations with the Joint Chiefs of Staff to devise a policy to reflect the president's wishes. A pressured Clinton called his friend and political advisor David Mixner and asked for a six-month respite. Replied Mixner, "I said, 'what I need to know is at the end of that six months that you will definitely say there will be an executive order. That we will not back down from that now that we're in the middle of the battle.' And he said, 'I promise you.'"[36]

Clinton broke his promise. Once elected and in January 1993, he announced a compromise.[37] The issue continued to heat up in public debate, making the cover of *Newsweek* in February 1993 with a headline: "Gays in the Military: How Far Will Clinton Go?" After many revisions and negotiations between the White House, the Department of Defense, and Congress, in July—three months after the march—President Clinton presented his proposal which, four months later on November 30, 1993, was codified into the "Don't Ask, Don't Tell" policy.[38] Accordingly, the Pentagon would not ask soldiers and recruits if they were gay, and those who self-identified would have to remain silent (read: closeted) about their sexual orientation, both on and off base. If they dared to disclose, they risked an almost-certain discharge. Although the compromise intended to better serve gays, in the years following codification, discharge rates rose every year from 617 in 1994 to 1,241 in 2000.[39] Gay supporters of Clinton were disgusted. President Clinton himself declared the policy a failure in his second term.[40] Although the military was a discrete adversary targeted on the rally stage of the march weekend, it is important to note that its "Don't Ask, Don't Tell" incarnation was not a confirmed threat until seven months after the actual march.

Equal Rights versus Special Rights

During the late 1980s and through the 1990s, the states became battlegrounds for gay rights, of which the most famous (in terms of affecting the 1993 march) were Measure 9 in Oregon and Amendment 2 in Colorado. Oregon's was the most restrictive. Measure 9 had the expected ingredients: the repealing of anti-discrimination ordinances and the barring of similar ordinances in the future. But it did not stop there. Measure 9 explicitly classified homosexuality as "abnormal, wrong, unnatural, and perverse." It mandated for this to be taught in all public schools and prevented government funds from being used for programs that depicted lesbians and gay male sexuality as a viable alternative to heterosexuality. Oregon's lavender scare failed in a close race: a 57 to 3 vote.[41]

The biggest success for opponents of gay rights came with Colorado's Amendment 2, a constitutional provision that nullified all existing protections and banned new anti-discrimination measures from ever being passed in the future. During the nine days of testimony, the presented evidence "attempted to sift through all that was known about gay people—from ancient history through the latest scientific research—to determine where and how gay people fit into the body politic." In addition to legal questions, Amendment 2 also sought "to answer another question: Who are gay people?" Redolent of *Bowers,* the very souls of gay people were again on trial. In a 53 to 47 vote, Coloradans approved Amendment 2. In response, lesbians and gay men organized a national boycott of the state of Colorado in an effort to use gay economic clout to dissuade other states from considering similar measures. Nineteen ninety-three marchers carried placards supporting this boycott. However devastating in the short-term, gay activists would challenge the case all the way to the Supreme Court. In the landmark 1996 case of *Romer v. Evans,* the Supreme Court struck down Amendment 2 for violating the Constitution's Equal Protection Clause.[42] These and other state-level cases that acquired national resonance—especially painful defeats, as in Colorado—ensured the fires of progressivism would continue burning bright amid steadfast strides into the mainstream.

The Religious Right was an influential player in this process. The Right has always blasphemed gay people. What was different in the early 1990s was the rhetoric they used to persuade the public to repeal and block pro-gay legislation. Demonization was no longer the key; the Right now warned against providing special rights to gay people. Discrimination against lesbians and gay men, the argument went, was not the same thing as that against other minorities, as activists had argued during the days of the second march.[43] Gay people sought preferential treatment for their (debased) lifestyle choice. Just as the Supreme Court did not confer a "fundamental right to sodomy" in its 1986 *Bowers v. Hardwick* decision, so too the government should not confer special rights to a lifestyle group that chose to be that way. Recall that during the organizing for the second march, activists worked tirelessly to link with other progressive causes to situate themselves as a social justice bloc. The Right's special-rights strategy endeavored to bulldoze this edifice. The distinctiveness of gay people, they responded, was not their similarity with other groups but rather their inherent depravity and thus unworthiness for legal protections.

Amendment 2 became an engine through which the special-rights debate was fought. The group, Colorado for Family Values, produced literature supporting the amendment that declared, "Stop special class status for homosexuality." The subtext read, "Special rights for homosexuals just isn't fair—especially to disadvantaged minorities in Colorado."[44] The Right's strategy unleashed raging debates. What are civil rights? Do gay people deserve them? Or are they asking for special rights? How do we distinguish the two? Claiming to represent the majority of Americans, the Right argued that homosexuality was morally wrong. Gay ac-

tivists responded by claiming to constitute a minority, that being gay
was no more or less moral than being straight, that those in the majority could not dictate private matters such as the right to love, nor deprive
any minority group of their civil rights, including those based on sexual
orientation.

Much was at stake in Amendment 2. Tracing the pathways of the debate is outside the scope of this narrative.[45] What is relevant is that lesbians and gay men were forced to defend claims to equal, not special
rights. This is nowhere more apparent than in the title of the march:
"The 1993 National March on Washington for Lesbian, Gay, and Bi
Equal Rights and Liberation." This was the only march that specifically used the phrase *equal rights* in its title. The debate can therefore
be seen as a pivotal moment in the life course of lesbian and gay politics that called into question the viability of an entirely progressive, social justice stance. The Right attacked activists' earlier strategy of lump-
ing gay rights with other civil rights, especially those of people of color
and women. It therefore no longer seemed effective for lesbian and gay
activists' to situate themselves as different from straight people. Thus, in
the uproar over special rights we see a more aggressive shift toward the
mainstream.

The language of *special rights* resonated with a societal dialogue on
the origins of sexuality. Four groundbreaking studies were published in
the early 1990s. The media took immediate interest when an NIH study
showed a possible genetic basis for sexual orientation. *Newsweek* ran a
front-page story depicting the face of an infant with the headline, "Is
This Child Gay? Born or Bred: The Origins of Homosexuality." The article cited the research of neuroscientist Simon LeVay, who found that a
tiny area in the brain (the hypothalamus) controlled sexuality. If this was
true, then "it could undercut the animosity that gays have had to con-
tend with for centuries." If gays were born that way, then they were entitled to legal protections based on an indisputable minority status and
claims to equal—not special—rights. According to coauthor Dr. Richard Pillard, "A genetic component in sexual orientation says, 'This is
not a fault, and it's not your fault.'" Instead of conciliating the debate,
however, the studies exacerbated it. Some scientists took issue with Le-
Vay's interpretations: "Of course it [sexual orientation] is in the brain,"
retorted Johns Hopkins University psychologist John Money in response
to LeVay's finding that gay men's hypothalamuses were similar in size to

straight females. "The real question is, when did it get there? Was it pre-
natal, neonatal, during childhood, puberty? That we do not know."[46]

The born-versus-bred debate (and thus the special-versus-equal-
rights wrangle, as well) fractured the "hardly monolithic" gay community. Many felt the search for a cause implied that homosexuality was a
defect and thus curable:

> In our rush to embrace biological explanations because of their political
> utility, let's not forget that an earlier generation of gay rights advocates, in
> Germany in the first part of the twentieth century, argued tirelessly for a con-
> genital explanation of homosexuality. They believed it would promote toler-
> ance. Their efforts came to naught after Hitler's rise to power when the Nazis
> decided that these congenital "defectives" ought to be eliminated for the sake
> of the master race.[47]

Why did it matter whether gay people were born or bred? The *Newsweek* article cited a 1989 study for answers. In that comparative research
of four countries, those who believed that gay people were born gay were
least homophobic. Especially given American's self-conception of fairness, the "born gay" basis for homosexuality would make it unfair to discriminate "for being true to nature's ways."[48] These debates were never
resolved—indeed, they persist to this day. The special rights dialogue,
along with conversations about the origins of sexual orientation, suggests America's lingering ambivalence with its new neighbors. As such,
it may be more appropriate to situate lesbians and gay men on what I call
the *mainstream margins,* suspended in a tension between two competing
impulses: conservative/centrist (we are just like you and only want equal
rights, as we declare in the title of our third march) and progressive/left-
ist (we are different from you and maybe instead what we want is liberation, as we also demand in the title of our third march).

Must Identity Movements Self-Destruct? A Queer Dilemma

The Challenge of Queer Politics

Sociologist Joshua Gamson provocatively asked, "Must identity movements self-destruct?" In articulating this "queer dilemma," Gamson
mused over the political utility of sexual identities. He drew inspiration

from the rise in the late 1980s and early 1990s of queer politics on the ground and queer theory in the academy. The major tenets of each suggest that sexual power relations are omnipresent and discursively organized through binary divides (e.g., man versus woman; gay versus straight); a skeptical and distrustful stance toward an essential logic of all identities (e.g., there is no such thing as man, woman, gay, or straight as a naturally existing entity; everything is socially and historically constructed); a rejection of mainline civil rights strategies in favor of a carnival-like politics of confrontational, transgressive, and parodic cultural display in the streets (e.g., do not lobby, take to the streets instead); and an infusing of sexuality into domains one would not traditionally consider it to affect or be affected by (e.g., sex is everywhere and in every interaction). Queers, or those who subscribe to queer politics, enacted what some call a "cultural politics" that was directed at "regulative norms," "disciplinary mechanisms of power," and other systems of meaning that organized how rights and responsibilities were distributed.[49]

In examining the 1993 San Francisco Gay Freedom Day Parade that had as its theme "The Year of the Queer," Gamson uncovered a paradox of identity-based organizing, namely, an identity's "made up yet necessary character" in which it is often "as liberating and sensible to demolish a collective identity as it is to establish one." There is a tension, in other words, between the politics of identity-blurring (fueled by a logic of deconstruction and the loosening of categories) and the politics of identity-building (fueled by claims of ethnic/essentialist group membership and the tightening of categories).[50]

As queer theory settled into the academy, some simplified it as an anti-identity politics:

> Under the undifferentiated sign of Queer are united all those heterogeneous desires and interests that are marginalized and excluded in the straight and gay mainstream. Queers are not united by any unitary identity but only by their opposition to disciplining, normalizing, social forces.[51]

Queer symbolized the unity of people around a shared rejection of identity categories. Queer was achingly paradoxical, leaving scholars puzzled with its theoretical purchase. This paradox is seen most forcefully in Queer Nation, a group founded in 1990 in New York. Queer Nation formed as a result of complaints from lesbians, gay people of color, leftists, radical AIDS activists, and non-gay sexual minorities who, at that historical moment, jelled into their own, self-named group. "The very name 'Queer Nation,'" notes sociologist Elizabeth Armstrong, "suggested a more straightforward endorsement of identity building." Other scholars concurred, arguing that "Queer Nationals are torn between affirming a new identity—'I am queer' and rejecting restrictive identities—'I reject your categories.'"[52]

The currents of queer theory today have all but dissipated, leaving the framework suspended in a tension between identity-building and -blurring. Armstrong has come closest in replying to Gamson's question of whether identity movements must self-destruct. She reconciles this tension by suggesting that the lesbian and gay movement defined diversity as its strength, thereby making space for all identity variants, no matter how challenging or anti-identity they may be. The annual Gay Freedom Day parade exemplifies this unification. The parade allows for the display of shared identity as gay and the secondary elaboration of those identities (e.g., gay women, queer nationals, bisexuals, transgenders, etc.). It brings together the colorful and collective diversity of the movement into a symbolic celebration of an all-embracing gay identity. Argues Armstrong, "By participating in the same parade, the contingents appeared unified. . . . *Everyone* brought one or more additional identities into the community with them. . . . The existence of many organizations was now seen as evidence of community richness and strength rather than as evidence of fragmentation and division."[53]

The parade provides a conceptual tool for considering how the movement responded to the challenge of queer politics—indeed, it provides a tool for considering how the movement responded to a host of internal dissents. The queer challenge, like others that came before it, did not reorganize the logic or workings of the movement. This is not to say that infighting had no impact. Subgroup challenges have always catalyzed border skirmishes over the meanings of group membership. The queer challenge, Armstrong asserts, was "domesticated. It was reduced to simply another of many ways to express gay identity." Queers penetrated movement boundaries that, plastic as they sometimes were, stretched to accommodate their challenge without crumbling. Evidence of queer politics' domestication is seen in how the word *queer* has become interchangeable with *lesbian and gay* by movement insiders and outsiders alike.[54]

The Communitarian Ruckus of Representation

Gamson and others who quested toward or questioned queer theory found motivation in the multiplication of identities. Identity specialization is one key difference between the second and third marches. Nineteen eighty-seven witnessed an increase in all types of gay organizations, especially those that served gay people of color. This growth continued unabated throughout the late 1980s and 1990s, especially for African Americans, Asian Americans, Native Americans, and Latinos. Similar to activists in the late 1970s but now backed by a more developed organizational base, activists of color challenged the mainstreaming of the movement, pushed leaders to think radically, and continued to emphasize the importance of coalition-building.[55] By 1993, in particular, we see the rise of bisexual and transgendered organizations, which represent increasingly specialized subtypes of gay identity.

Bisexual communities developed slowly through the 1980s, suppressed by societal debates on whether sexuality was determined by nature or nurture. As fundamentalists argued that the gay lifestyle was chosen and therefore morally reprehensible, gay leaders responded by asserting that they were born gay and could not change their sexuality even if they so desired. This generated a historical moment when it became popular and politically expedient to argue that people were either straight *or* gay, polarizing identity into a rigid dichotomy. Discourse was binary and oftentimes biphobic, with not a lot of flexibility. For bisexuals, this meant there was little to no space in which to be open. They were at once excluded from gay groups and reduced to gay from mainstream America. Both sides deemed them "confused."[56]

AIDS ironically helped consolidate bisexuals as a distinct group especially when, in the late 1980s, the Centers for Disease Control (CDC) identified them as a special risk group that could introduce HIV into the general population. In 1987, *Newsweek* ran a story that "branded bisexuals societal 'pariahs.'"[57] This finger-pointing increased bisexual militancy, generated bi pride, and further crystallized bisexuals as a distinct community. Bisexual politics imagined a world "free from constricting gender and sex classifications."[58] The *Chicago Tribune* interviewed bisexual activist Loraine Hutchins, a coordinator for BiNet USA, a national bisexual rights organization, for her thoughts on why lesbian and gay leaders were reluctant to embrace bisexual concerns. The undertones of queer theory are unmistakable: "The gay community has trouble accepting bisexuals for the same reason that straights do. Because if we admit it's not an either-or world, then we might have to deal with a little more complexity in our lives."[59] Hutchins's sentiment resonated with queer theory in their common quest to blur categories—especially either-or dichotomies (e.g., gay *or* straight). Bisexual activists envisioned a world characterized by what we might call a "both-and paradigm" that emphasized sexual diversity without forced choice.

The different role of bisexuals in the second and third marches also captures their emerging power. The 1987 march marked the first time that there was a national contingent of bisexuals present on the mall. By the 1993 march, however, bisexuals had successfully campaigned to have their name included in the march's title: the 1993 National March on Washington for Lesbian, Gay, *and Bi* Equal Rights and Liberation. Bisexual activists also successfully demanded a speaker during the post-march rally. They chose D.C.-based bisexual and AIDS activist Elias Farajaje-Jones to help carry the banner and Lani Ka'ahumanu, a bisexual organizer from San Francisco, to speak at the rally, where she proclaimed:

Bisexuals are here,
and we're queer.

Bisexual pride
speaks to the truth
of behavior and identity.

No simple either/or divisions,
fluid—ambiguous—subversive
bisexual pride challenges both
the heterosexual *and* the homosexual assumption.

Bisexual activists agree that Ka'ahumanu's speech at the 1993 national march marked a major turning point in bisexual political history.[60]

Transgender activists share a similar story as bisexuals, albeit comparatively less successful. Transgenders were included in all 1993 march literature and the demands, but did not find their way into the title. Some activists perceived a "'divide and conquer' politicking by transphobic gays and lesbians that pitted bisexuals against transgenders. They told the bisexual community members who were also working toward official inclusion that it was either transgender or bisexual, but not both."[61]

Transactivists have always been met with confusion and resistance by lesbians and gay men. During the organizing for the first march, trans-people were not included because many activists admitted to not under-standing the term. Confusion persisted fourteen years later. *Transgender* is used today as an umbrella term to include all individuals who experi-ence their gender as partially or fully reversed. Although the term is con-tested, the most accepted current definition includes "people who were assigned a gender, usually at birth and based on their genitals, but who feel that this is a false or incomplete description of themselves." Some activists use *transgender* to broadly refer to anyone who transgresses so-cietal norms of sex and gender.[62]

Transgender is distinct from *transsexual,* a term that characterizes people who desire to have, or have achieved, a different anatomical sex from that which they were assigned at birth. *Transsexual* was originally a medical term coined in the 1950s to describe the process of changing one's sex, which included hormone replacement therapy and sometimes genital reassignment. Once someone underwent sex reassignment, they might call themselves *MTF,* for "male to female" or *FTM,* for "female to male," to designate the direction of their transition. The former some-times refer to themselves as transwomen and the latter as transmen.

Transgender and *transsexual* are both distinct from *cross-dresser.* This term describes a person of any sexual orientation who wears cloth-ing generally worn by an individual of the opposite gender (i.e., men who dress like women and women who dress like men). Cross-dressers may or may not adopt the mannerisms of someone of the opposite sex, and generally do not desire sexual reassignment surgery. Cross-dressing is also distinct from drag. Cross-dressers are generally straight, whereas individuals who do drag are overwhelmingly gay. Drag is an exagger-ated (and sometimes political) form of cross-dressing.[63] A man who ex-aggerates the dress of a woman is called a *drag queen,* and a woman who exaggerates the dress of a man is called a *drag king. Cross-dresser* and *transvestite* are related terms, with the latter originating in the medical literature. Today, *transvestite* has been replaced almost entirely by *cross-dresser* in usage and meaning. Both are distinct from *hermaphrodite* and *intersex,* which refer to people born with genitals that are neither fully male nor female. Given the variety of terms, confusion seems inevitable, which prompts debate over representation and inclusion.

Virginia Prince first coined the term *transgender* in the United States during the 1970s. Prince sought a term to contrast with *transsexual,* which referred to someone who desired sexual reassignment surgery. *Transgender* was intended for those who did not desire surgical intervention—those who felt their gender identity fell somewhere in between genders, and so for those who did not identify as either a man or a woman. This last depiction of *transgender* as "in between" has stayed with the movement over the years. This may be due to its overlaps with queer theory, seen in the rise of a newer term in the 1990s: *gender queer,* which highlights the blending and blurring of traditionally male and female qualities.[64]

Homosexuality, bisexuality, transgenderism, and queer politics have each been met with confusion and resistance. If a bisexual man is dating a woman, is he no longer gay? What about a transwoman who is romantically involved with a man? Some activists believe that if a transgender person does not have a gay or lesbian orientation, he or she is not part of the movement. When a transgender person does not also have a gay sexual orientation, adding transgender concerns to gay concerns may mean inadvertently advocating for heterosexuals. Transgender activist Riki Wilchins, executive director of the gender education and advocacy group GenderPAC, responds by claiming that "gayness used to be about both orientation and gender." Phylis Frye, another prominent transactivist, went a step further by holding a workshop titled "Is Sexual Orientation a Subset of Gender Identity?" at the annual Creating Change workshops sponsored by the NGLTF. Such concerns still elicit more confusion than clarity, which breeds conflict. It reveals that lesbians and gay men can sometimes be just as biphobic and transphobic as straight America.[65]

Transactivists have had an especially difficult time finding representation in Washington marches. One cannot help but notice the irony here, given that transindividuals were integral in the Stonewall Riots that activists and scholars credit with the birth of the modern movement.[66] Some of the difficulty transactivists experience is due to the distinctions between gender identity and sexual orientation. In the early days of gay liberation, gay men were stereotyped as effeminate and lesbians as masculine, thereby conflating gender and sexual orientation. Today, transgenders are assumed to be gay, even though they may not self-identify as such. And so the conflating continues. Lesbians and gay men have worked hard to dispel stereotypes about their gender identity. According to Wilchins, gays launched what has proven to be a successful, even if internally divisive, public relations strategy in winning support from heterosexuals: "We look like you. We act like you. We're just like you. Give us our rights."[67] Transpolitics pose an assault on this assimilationist strategy while remaining dependent on lesbians and gay men, evidenced by a rainbow flag as part of the logo of the national transgender advocacy organization.

Leaders of the trans and lesbian/gay movements recognize their connections. Transactivists claim the lesbian and gay movement was hijacked and sacrificed for political expedience, with transactivists working toward reintegration. The two movements are also philosophically linked, argue transactivists, because leaders are fighting the same battles against sexual prejudice and discrimination. Activists further argue that lesbian/gay and trans identities can remain separate while recognizing a common bond. The larger political movement should be based on what is shared, rather than what divides. Kerry Lobel agrees: "NGLTF believes there is one movement, the GLBT [gay, lesbian, bisexual, and transgender] movement."[68]

So must identity movements self-destruct? They do seem to be programmed with self-erasing tendencies. Identities can exaggerate differences: lesbians are quick to point out how they are different from gay men, both of whom identify differences from bisexuals and transgenders. Transgender persons may not have been represented in the title of the 1993 march, but they were included in the demands. Lesbians, gay men, bisexuals, and transgenders are all fighting a cultural battle asphyxiating sexual diversity that is further manifest in a host of discriminatory legislation. The point may not be to compare how different groups structure their lives, but the common political *limits* imposed on them. Not who one is, but rather who one *cannot* be.

The People Next Door on the Steps of the Mainstream Margins

Gay people were everywhere in the early 1990s: film, television, magazine covers, ballot measures. Visibility, however, came with a price. Republicans launched cultural warfare on gays, and the Religious Right championed a vicious rhetorical backlash. By 1992, twenty-four states had active statutes outlawing sodomy. Of these, nine states prohibited only gay sodomy. Although there was more AIDS funding, people were still dying. Between 1990 and 1991, there was a 31 percent rise in anti-

gay hate crimes reported in New York, San Francisco, Boston, Minneapolis–St. Paul, and Chicago.[69] Although the people next door were moving in, they were still kept at bay, on the mainstream margins. Visibility
collided with the culture war. As a result, activists found themselves suspended in competing impulses: do we emphasize the many ways in which
we are distinct (we are different and want liberation) or blur our differences and assimilate (we are the same and want equality)?

The title of the 1993 national march—"For Equal Rights and
Liberation"—suggests the movement endeavored to walk the line between these polar positions despite pushes and pulls in both directions.
On the one hand, the dialogue between the Religious Right's accusations
of "special rights" and activists' replies of "equal rights" is evidence of
pressure to lean into the mainstream. We cannot simply conclude that
the Right *caused* this redirection from periphery and progressive (1979
and 1987) toward mainstream and moderate (1993). Using the national
marches as an interpretive lens, history suggests the Right's influence
more likely turned up the volume on tendencies that had been a long
time simmering. For instance, activists' response of equal rights paralleled in some ways 1970s activists' pleas for human rights. The Right,
however, clamored that gays were not like other minority groups—which
was the premise for the human rights argument—and so this comparison, while analytically useful, is still imperfect. Despite drawing similarities to straights, most gay people believed their sexual orientation was
genetic. This born-versus-bred conversation, along with persisting state-
level threats, on the other hand, sustained the notion of difference. Thus,
in this historical moment, mainstream and liberation impulses coexisted
in a productive, albeit tenuous, tension.

Gays also became more aware of their internal diversity during this
era, evidenced by the rise of queer theory and the demands of bisexuals and transgenders. Organizing among gays of color flourished, as well.
Throughout the 1990s, there was a rise of "ever-more specific identities,
while also trying to define a common ground agenda for a united gay
community." Although "diversity has been a source of strength," it has
"inevitably created tensions." The slow and steady march into the mainstream met with boisterous dissent. Were centrism and leftism compat-
ible? Would the mainstream flatten or flow with the movement's rich diversity? Could there even be such a thing as unity through diversity?
Fabricating unity through diversity and dissent has always been a challenge for gay activists, especially in organizing the national marches.

Veteran activist Urvashi Vaid summed it up best: "Trying to organize the lesbian and gay community is like trying to organize the Milky Way galaxy."[70] I turn next to the disputatious constellation of this galaxy, seen through the lens of the 1993 National March on Washington for Lesbian, Gay, and Bi Equal Rights and Liberation.

A Simple Matter of Justice: The 1993 National March on Washington for Lesbian, Gay, and Bi Equal Rights and Liberation

During San Francisco's 1992 Freedom Day Parade, activists Roger Doughty and Rebecca LePere were passing out neon orange stickers declaring, "I'll be there!" for the upcoming 1993 march. One man in the crowd hesitated, "Why go back?" he asked, to which a nearby woman shouted in reply, "Because rights don't show up all wrapped up in a bow! We'll keep going back until we get what's ours!" "That about summed it up," recounted Doughty and LePere. "We've come a long way since October 1987. . . . But we still live in a world . . . in which we are viewed with such hatred that our very existence has become the centerpiece of a presidential campaign," they noted, referencing the barrage of anti-gay epithets uttered at the 1992 Republican National Convention. "We need to march because . . . nothing else so loudly shouts to America . . . our absolute determination to accept nothing less than equal rights."[1] It was an idea whose time had come. Again. For the third time.

Organizers constructed what turned out to be a titanic third march along opposing tensions that had in some respects always been in place: Does this march reveal to the country that we are no different than anyone else—that we, like other minorities, deserve basic human rights and freedom from discrimination? Or does this march instead affirm that we are a progressive group of liberationists fighting to redress deeply situated inequalities, fighting for a fundamental transformation in how society is structured, and fighting to reconfigure how society distributes rights and responsibilities to its citizens? Activists' calculus swung like a pendulum from favoring the former in the first march to the latter in the second. The 1993 march, as an interpretive lens, shows how activists were able to finally strike an optimal balance between these two seemingly polar positions.

The Invitation[2]

This time, veteran activist and then executive director of the National Gay and Lesbian Task Force (NGLTF) Urvashi Vaid carried the torch. The idea for a third march was born of conversations she, Brian Coyle, an openly gay city councilmember from Minneapolis, and other activists had during NGLTF's annual Creating Change Conference in Minneapolis in November 1990.[3] In response, Vaid mailed an invitation dated January 24, 1991, to activists across the country to attend a one-day meeting to brainstorm possibilities. "Activists throughout the country have started discussing different proposals for the next March on Washington," Vaid said in her letter. "I have received a number of calls and am concerned that we must coordinate our concepts and ideas about the next march." Activists cited the success of the Great March as reason to go back. Organizers of the 1987 march claimed it drew more than a half-million people, making it the world's largest gay rights demonstration at the time.[4] Energy from that march continued to effervesce, evidenced in an organizing flier that declared, "For Love and For Life, Here We Come Again,"[5] alluding to the theme from the second march.

Vaid sent the invitation to national and grassroots, regional and state organizations, requesting each to send no more than two representatives to the meeting. To enhance a sense of ownership, she urged invitees to "feel free to share the fact that this meeting is happening with organizations in your communities. We hope to gather the broadest input possible. Organizations who cannot send representatives are encouraged to send a letter with your group's views to me, and I will take responsibility to share it with the attendees." This would be a community-wide affair.

The Initiating Meeting[6]

Seventy-eight activists from over thirteen cities attended an all-day meeting on March 9, 1991, in Washington, D.C. There was a five-part agenda:

1) How did we get here? 2) What major gay events are projected between March 1991 and July 1994? 3) What lessons did we learn from the 1987 March? 4) How do people feel about a march before June 1994? 5) Are there other possibilities instead of, or in addition to, Washington?[7] Vaid emphasized that the meeting was not intended to reach final decisions but to begin a conversation.

Being the third potential Washington march, questions related to the efficacy of the tactic were inevitable. To consider them, meeting facilitators requested 1987 organizers who were also present to report lessons learned. Steve Ault (who cochaired the 1979 and 1987 demonstrations), Lee Bush (the office manager from 1987), Michelle Crone (who helped with the CD action from 1987), Joyce Hunter (who cochaired the 1979 event), Morris Kight (longtime activist), and Kay Ostberg (cochair from 1987) shared their perspectives (see table 7.1).

Table 7.1 delineates portions of the cultural template activists constructed across their first two demonstrations and on which they were hoping to rely for the third. It classifies their lessons into four categories—organizing, finances, focus, and strategy/identity—and weaves political, cultural, and practical concerns to describe a fundamentally grassroots endeavor. Their blueprints specify a decentralized network of local organizing committees that experience collective ownership of the march.

After this discussion, delegates reconvened to hear proposals for other possible actions. Fourteen proposals were offered, including one from Howard Armistead of either a biennial or quadrennial march on Washington; proposals to march in spring 1992, fall 1992, or in 1993; a fifty-state march on every state capitol; a march in Houston at the Republican National Convention or New York for the Democratic National Convention; a 1997 march to commemorate the tenth anniversary of the second march, and a "Stonewall 25" march in New York City to celebrate its twenty-fifth anniversary. This list suggests that the 1993 Washington march was not inevitable and, instead, had to be justified amid a flurry of other compelling options.

After lunch, each participant summarized his or her reactions in two-and-a-half minutes or less, after which a two-hour collective discussion ensued. The views were all over the map, from complete opposition to those who wanted the march but were concerned it might distract from Stonewall 25. The idea of a fifty-state march was also popular since much activity was transpiring in the states. This elicited unanimous support, and delegates agreed to organize it either the year before or after a

TABLE 7.1. **Lessons Learned by Previous March Organizers**

Organizing

        Allow at least one year to plan. Two-year lead time is better.
        Work out structure and governance early.
        Regionality: decentralize as much as possible.
        Need over two hundred local organizing committees.
        Early participation from different regions and cities is helpful.
        Recognize and appreciate regional work and leadership.
        Accommodate quick decision-making and local autonomy.
        Use large national planning conferences.
        Obtain the support of the national organizations.
        Confer with experienced individuals and groups.
        Best if organized during a non–election year.
        Integrate all activities, e.g., civil disobedience, fund-raising, etc.
        Flexibility is a value.

Finances

        Need seed money early.
        Good financial planning and contributions to committees.

Focus

        The focus needs to be a compelling political purpose to march.
        Don't have *Hardwick* (1986) decision as impetus.
        View the march on Washington as an empowerment tool.
        View the march as generating, not depleting, resources.

Strategy and
Identity

        Diversity: include all communities.
        Ownership by all: the march should not be "owned" by national groups.
        Recognize differences five years later with AIDS and the movement.
        More and stronger gay/lesbian, AIDS organizations today.
        Gay/lesbian community is easier to reach today.
        Work on mainstream media's coverage of gay/lesbian issues.

Source: Report on March 9, 1991, Meeting Concerns: A March on Washington.

Washington march. Virtually all attendees expressed that going back to D.C. was wise.

The question of when to march was the greatest source of division at the initiating meeting, with attendees split between 1992 and 1993. Coyle advocated 1992, arguing it would put AIDS and gay rights on the election agenda. He suggested springtime (instead of fall, as were the first two marches) to ensure Congress would be in session, which would maximize impact in the November elections. Steve Ault and Joyce Hunter disagreed, arguing that a 1992 march would conflict with a national health-care march planned by a coalition of gays and non-gays. ACT UP and other HIV/AIDS groups supported the health-care march, further dissuading a 1992 date.[8] Here we see march organizing directly affected by a competition between centrist impulses (e.g., lobbying to effect gay-specific policy changes) and leftist impulses (respect for other coalition-based events such as the health-care march).

Those who favored a march in 1993 argued that it would take more than a year to organize. Given 1987's success, a third march would have to draw at least a half-million people to do the same. This turnout could not be achieved by 1992. Nineteen ninety-three advocates also argued that a 1992 march would complicate efforts to elect openly gay delegates to the Democratic and Republican conventions and, related to this, deflect energies needed for the election itself. Although the springtime comment was savvy (it seems like a good idea to hold a demonstration in D.C. when Congress is in session), the election was framed as at once advantageous and untimely. An election-year march would put gays on the agenda, yet deflect energies for election activities.

After an exhausting eight-hour day, attendees realized that they could not make a final decision. They decided by consensus that a wider outreach effort was required, that they were not representative enough, and that more diversity in decision-making was the order of the day. A planning committee formed for a follow-up grassroots conference in Washington, D.C., over the weekend of May 11–12, the purpose of which would be to address the two most formative organizing tasks of whether and when to march.[9]

The Grassroots Planning Meeting

A press release soon announced, "Planning Meeting Called for National March on Washington for Lesbian and Gay Rights."[10] Between 90 and 150 activists attended the May 11–12 grassroots planning meeting, representing more than twenty-two states from Florida to Alaska.[11] Enclosed in their registration packet was a flier that asked, "Why a national planning meeting?" A cover letter replied, "In March 1991, nearly one hundred lesbians and gay men responded to the call of the National Gay and Lesbian Task Force to discuss the possibility of a march on Washington for lesbian and gay rights. Those present decided to convene a national meeting of lesbians and gays where final decisions can be made as to where, when, and how millions of lesbian and gay voices will be heard."[12] The conference was a vehicle to vote on questions of whether and when to march.

Whether to March

Ongoing phone calls to Vaid, her January invitation, the initiating meeting in March, and now the grassroots meeting generated a sufficient buzz
to conciliate most disagreements on whether to march. Some still questioned the utility of a third march, couching their skepticism in the lack
of a mandate, as existed in 1979 with the assassination of Harvey Milk
and the Anita Bryant imbroglio, and in 1987 with AIDS and *Bowers*.
Why should we march again? Such objections were generally brushed
aside, with the majority "citing the continued existence of anti-gay violence and discrimination, state sodomy laws and the AIDS epidemic" as
compelling reasons to return.[13] Agreeing to march despite the presence
of discrete threats comparable to what activists experienced in 1979 and
1987 suggests that they may have perceived the event as a "habitual routine" to affirm their visions of strategy and identity.[14]

Those in favor of returning to D.C. argued that "activists outside
the country's major urban areas are crying for another march."[15] Activism is difficult to sustain. People burn out. As reported in the gay
press, "Nearly four years later [after the 1987 march], these same local
activists are still running their groups alone and are facing the possibility of burn-out unless they get another infusion of newly invigorated
activists."[16] The 1993 march, in other words, brought a different mandate. The first two marches were in response to discrete threats. No new
(similar) conflict surfaced in 1993. Rather, there was continued federal
inaction externally, and activist burnout internally. March proponents
reminded attendees that "the 1987 march [was] a major success and a
dramatic turning point in gay politics because it attracted large numbers
of new people into the gay movement." They further noted that "activists returned from the 1987 march to form an unprecedented number of
AIDS and gay rights groups."[17] The discussion of whether to march yet
again was anchored in the perceived success of the 1987 event. This is evident in an organizing flier later circulated throughout the country that
read, "For Love and For Life, Here We Come Again," which references
the 1987 theme. The flier continued, "Organizers around the country
have called for this [the 1987] march to be repeated in 1993."[18]

The 1993 march was therefore mandated by movement revival: to re-
build and embolden the rank and file. Those in attendance agreed that
the movement needed an internal jumpstart, an activist defibrillator. A
Washington march would deliver a high-energy organizational current

to resuscitate political organizing. This idea found its way into a press release announcing the first meeting of the national steering committee in Los Angeles in January 1992. The release quoted Robin Tyler, "Many who attended in '87 took the incredible energy of that March back to their communities and started the local organizations which have become the backbone of our movement. This will be the booster shot our movement needs."[19] This difference in mandate affected debates on whether to march. In 1979 and 1987, activists drew on discrete events to justify going to Washington. In their absence, they drew on the previous march as a reason to return. In considering whether to march, the debate did not wrestle with the severity of threat to which the movement was responding; rather, it addressed the strategic utility of the tactic itself.

When to March

Much of the grassroots meeting wrestled with the timing of the march. Should we march in 1992, prior to the election, in 1993 after the election, or sometime later, in light of other key events? Nineteen ninety-two advocates argued for the march's ability to influence presidential and senatorial elections. The elections, however, were used to support *and* refute 1992. Proponents of a 1993 march said many lesbians and gay men would be involved in campaign activities and thus be incapable of investing time. A 1992 march would compete with the election cycle, in terms of activist energy and news media coverage, more than be helped by it. Media attention was especially important, given frustrations with inadequate coverage of the first two marches.[20] Concerns of how long it would take to build the march also informed this cost-benefit analysis. A successful march, the argument went, would take more than just a quick year to organize. A 1993 march would enable more activists to get involved, would not compete with the election, and sidestep an "overcrowded agenda."[21]

A 1994 march was eliminated from consideration because New York City activists were organizing Stonewall 25, an international event for June 26, 1994, to commemorate the twenty-fifth anniversary of the famous riots. This coincided with two other international events: the Fourth Annual Gay Games, an international celebration of gay sporting events, and the Fifteenth World Conference of the International Lesbian and Gay Association. Delegates voted 72 to 7 (with 11 abstaining) for an April 1993 March on Washington. April was chosen so that the march would occur when Congress was in session (which it was not over Columbus Day weekend in October, when the prior two marches were organized).

By the end of the weekend, those who advocated march organizing around the election cycle abdicated on two grounds. First, Native Americans in coalition with other people-of-color constituencies were organizing a 1992 "March for the Survival of Indigenous Cultures" to protest the quincentennial (five hundredth) anniversary of the arrival of Christopher Columbus. The Indigenous Cultures March was to protest this "anniversary of colonialism and imperialism" and to counter the government-sponsored "celebration of Columbus's discovery of America." "Nineteen ninety-two is about oppression," said black lesbian delegate Sabrina Sojourner. "It's about five hundred years of imperialism. . . . The whole thing about Columbus 'discovering' America is the very root of oppression. Join us in our agenda. Do not force us to compromise our agenda for you."[22] The social justice self-definition affirmed by the 1987 march affected debates on when to march the third time around—and even trumped the value of an election cycle. Thus, the cultural template activists sketched from the prior marches (that valorized other progressive causes) did more than guide articulations of strategy and identity; it also influenced the nuts and bolts of organizing on the ground.

Once the media announced the date, reactionary letters flooded editors' offices. One Chicago letter expressed, "While I believe there are many issues justifying a national protest march, I am dismayed and find it unbelievable . . . to hold it in April 1993."[23] The writer aligned himself with Coyle, who asserted the value of an election year. In April 1993, the next president, members of the senate, and members of the House of Representatives would all have already been sworn in and seated for three months. "Even if one million protest marchers descend on Washington on April 25, 1993, how receptive will these newly entrenched incumbents be to hear/reply to whatever message the marchers may be trying to convey?" And then came the punch line: "A protest march before a major election . . . makes much more sense" since politicians would be more likely to listen in light of reelection pressures. The writer astutely questioned, "Will a march held at such an inopportune time be better than having no march at all?"

This concern was echoed in the surrounding public forum. In more than one hundred newspaper articles written about the march in Chica-

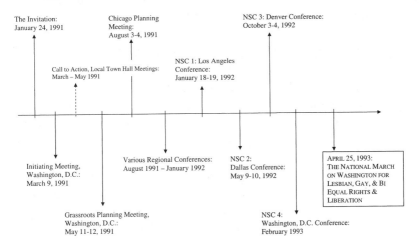

FIGURE 7.1. An Organizational Timeline of the 1993 March.

go's gay press and the *Advocate,* 62 percent articulated sore spots related to the date or title (an issue that would be addressed at the upcoming Los Angeles Conference). Neither the 1979 nor the 1987 march was organized during an election year, giving activists an opportunity to experiment. It is notable that none of the demands from the first two marches were met, calling into the question organizing during a non-election year. We again see evidence that activists' cultural template strongly influenced their actual decisions.

Thirteen hours of discussion over two days ended with a nearly unanimous decision to return to Washington. At Sunday's end, a loud cheer went up from the crowd, with people rising to their feet and a few attempting to start a group wave similar to what one might see at a sporting event. Meeting facilitator Michelle Crone exhaled, "There's just something about consensus. . . . When you wait for the end, you reach consensus by endurance." Consensus by endurance concluded with a collective sigh and was comically characterized as including "occasional outbursts, hours of debate, and at least one vaginal diagram."[24] Delegates concluded the two-day affair by calling a national planning meeting during the weekend of August 3–4 in Chicago. The Chicago Planning Meeting would decide an exact date and select a steering committee, once again signaling activists' allegiance with the structure they used in their first two marches. Figure 7.1 details an organizational timeline for the 1993 march.

The Cultural Template

Before chronicling each conference, as I have done for the first two marches, it is instructive to first reflect on emerging patterns, or what I call the *cultural template,* across the first three marches. This template prescribes guidelines for how gay people should enact their vision and values for social change in a way that can accomplish their strategic objectives (i.e., are our efforts viable?) while also remaining sensitive to identity concerns (i.e., are we being accountable to our internal diversity?). Activists drafted this template in the back and forth between dissent and decision-making that transpired at the national conferences they used to assemble their marches. The very idea of a cultural template provides for reflection on the relationship between theory and action. It suggests that, through infighting, activists converged on a cluster of assumptions, agreements, and meanings which (sometimes unconsciously) structured their future conventions of argumentation, disputation, and decision-making. The cultural template facilitates sensitivity to how emergent culture in one era structures configurations in subsequent time periods. By comparing Washington marches, we see clearly how cultural forms and conventions in earlier deliberations become constitutive templates (or at least ideas exceedingly difficult to ignore) in the next round.[25] Infighting, then, does more than just carry and make concrete cultural conceptions of strategy and identity; it also influences how on-the-ground organizing will proceed from one march to the next.

By 1993, the cultural template was firmly established. Even as activists continued to disagree over the six organizing tasks, they did *not* quarrel over the procedure itself. In many ways, the fourth march broke form from the prior three, as organizers did not receive either a mandate from local lesbian and gay communities to march in the first place nor did they manage to achieve consensus over what it means to be gay and what gay people want in the twenty-first century. It therefore speaks to consequences of *rupturing* or violating this template. Historical comparison across all four marches suggests that adherence to the cultural template increases the probability that dissent will yield its dividends. Let us now briefly pause to take a closer look at the lesbian and gay cultural template.

Across the first three events, a core group of activists, identifiable through leadership positions in local and national organizations, initiated a call to consider whether and when the movement ought to march.

These stalwarts organized early meetings of around one hundred organizational representatives to assess whether a collective wisdom confirmed or disputed the need to march. The first three marches were grassroots in part because of their adherence to this process of communitarian input. From this nucleus, each march flowed forward.

Each demonstration also adopted a participatory-democratic decision-making structure that activated leadership bonds once the sociopolitical climate was facilitative of mobilization.[26] This structure encouraged the expression of dissent, which helped facilitate the distillation of its dividends. Prior to agreeing on this structure and template, dissent proved less productive, evidenced in lack of organizational consolidation (Urbana Conference, 1973) and dissolution (Minneapolis Conference, 1978). A participatory-democratic decision-making structure, in other words, is a critical component to access the potential rewards that inhere in deliberative debate. Abruptly changing the structure without consensus from the community deflects the potential value of infighting.

In the late 1970s, the idea for a march was widely shared in the New Left repertoire of contention. Harvey Milk successfully harvested it for the gay community, after which activists assembled national meetings to assign organizing responsibilities. For the second march, Steve Ault and Joyce Hunter (who were co-coordinators of the first march) organized an initiating meeting. They circulated an invitation at a leadership conference and mailed it to leaders of gay organizations across the country. Ault and Hunter waited for endorsements, used that to assess the collective buzz, and only then organized a national planning conference. For the third march, veteran activist Urvashi Vaid combed initial interest. She tossed around the idea at Creating Change (as Ault and Hunter did at their leadership conference, as Milk did in his speech at the 1978 Gay Freedom Day Parade) and organized initiating and grassroots planning meetings to feel the pulse. Once a representative body of delegates voted, the process commenced.

Each march had its own call to action that reflected the sociopolitical context and developmental features within the movement. The call urged people to attend a large national planning conference where organizing officially launched. The call and the national planning conferences were instigated by an "originating spark," "triggering event," or "precipitating factor" that catalyzed collective behavior.[27] In 1979, Anita Bryant and Senator Briggs enraged local communities. With the level of assault rising, Harvey Milk's death sealed the deal.

In 1987 Ault and Hunter sounded a call in light of AIDS and *Bow-ers*. A national planning conference was soon organized where formal organizing began. In both cases, a call went out *after* an initiating meeting had already transpired and generated a buzz (the Minneapolis meeting in 1979, New York in 1986). Although there was no formal call in 1993, Vaid followed a similar procedure. Her invitation gathered people to an initiating meeting, where delegates assessed interest. Attendees organized town-hall meetings to galvanize people for a follow-up grassroots meeting. The call in 1993 was aired symbolically through a network of local meetings, where lesbians and gay men discussed why they should reconsider returning to Washington. If town-hall meetings can be collectively construed as an equivalent to the call, then they too were held after an initiating meeting. In all three cases, once the organizing began, delegates used the first national planning conference to establish an organizing structure. Each march incorporated decentralized, participatory-democratic national, regional, and local committees that required gender parity and racial representation (20, 25, and 50 percent, respectively).

The nature of the originating spark differed between the first two and the third marches. The first two responded to discrete threats. Although Bryant and Briggs were local culprits in 1979, Harvey Milk's death operated as a national trigger, throwing the movement over a threshold, as did AIDS and *Bowers* in 1987. In 1993, there was no new, tangible national threat. Instead, activists were responding to a culturally diffuse backlash generated by an increasingly influential Religious Right, continued federal stagnancy toward granting lesbians and gay men equality, and internal activist burnout. The core group of organizers—many of whom were involved across the first three marches—had learned what marches could accomplish, which also provides evidence for leadership continuity. Because movement architects were more or less the same for the first three demonstrations, each adopted a formulaic organizing process. By the early 1990s, the core group realized that, although marches were useful to respond to external threats, they could do more: they could defibrillate indigenous organizational activity and jump-start political sensibilities with renewed fervor. The fact that the AIDS crisis continued to worsen as anti-gay hate crimes rose were also convincing motivators, suggesting an internal-external balance in analysis.

There have also been important differences surrounding the political/cultural status of gay people, the nature of threat, consciousness, and organizational development across demonstrations. During the first two marches, lesbians and gay men were situated at the periphery of American life and had moved to the mainstream margins by the third march with the rise of gay visibility. During the first march, conflict was discrete and concentrated at the local level with the likes of Bryant and Briggs. In 1987, conflict was still discrete, but moved to a national level with AIDS and *Bowers*. In 1993, conflict was a diffuse backlash that defined gay rights as special rights or preferential treatment. Finally, there was no consciousness of a national movement during the first march, which corresponded to a weak organizational infrastructure. Between the first and the second marches, the movement became increasingly self-aware as it underwent organizational expansion. This development continued through the third march with the rise of bisexual and transgender groups. A new voice of identity-blurring also entered this period in the form of queer politics. These four dimensions influenced how activists constructed, modified, and enacted their cultural template over time. Having provided some texture to the generation and evolution of the cultural template, I now discuss each of the national conferences activists used to assemble the 1993 march (see fig. 7.1).

The Chicago Planning Meeting

During the weekend of August 3–4, 1991, activists flocked to Chicago to begin building their third march. Approximately 120 to 180 delegates met at the Allerton Hotel on Chicago's Magnificent Mile for a summer organizing meeting to vote on the date and structure for the march.[28] One of the most important outcomes of Chicago was agreeing on an organizing structure. Once this was in place, delegates elected an interim committee they charged with local outreach to ensure more activists would attend the first nationally representative organizing meeting in Los Angeles the next year.

The Date

The meeting opened amiably with a discussion on setting an exact date. Activists had decided at the grassroots planning conference, amid a flurry of debate, to hold the march in April of 1993. Those at Chicago finalized the date as Sunday, April 25, 1993.

The Organizing Structure

The most contentious issue in Chicago was the organizing structure. Delegates adopted a modified version of what they used in 1979 and 1987, favoring the preexisting blueprints for its built-in democratic principles. Activists agreed that however the structure was modified, it must prioritize diversity and empowerment over efficiency.[29] Without this, "marginalized people will be positioned once again to fight for their place at the table. The organizational structure cannot allow the final process to commence while anyone is still outside the table." Some asserted that "the success of the 1993 March—how many thousands show up in D.C. in April—hinges directly on our commitment to diversity and empowerment, as well as efficiency." The principle of empowerment-through-diversity set the terms of debate.

Activists agreed on a three-tiered national structure that would maintain a decentralized relationship with regional and local committees entrusted with outreach. At the base was a large, policy-setting national steering committee (NSC) composed of four representatives from each of the country's seventeen regions. This was an augmenting move, given the country was formerly divided into seven and eleven regions for the 1979 and 1987 marches, respectively. Above the NSC base was a twelve-member executive committee (EC) that monitored and implemented the decisions of the NSC. Finally, above the EC were the national cochairs whom the NSC formally elected. In addition and as a modification from 1987, delegates agreed on an advisory group comprised of members of the executive and steering committees from the second march. This group of march elders ensured the preservation of the cultural template.

Having agreed on a three-tiered structure (NSC, EC, cochairs), activists tackled the goals of representation required to seat a delegation at any given conference. In the second march, this was operationalized as gender parity and 25 percent representation for people of color (up from 1979's 20 percent) at all levels of organizing. This system upheld the spirit of inclusion, a cultural convention that "ensure[d] that all persons in our community have an opportunity to be represented."[30] Based on 1987 blueprints, activists Roger Doughty and Hilari Lipton proposed a 50 percent gender parity rule and 25 percent for people of color (POC). In what was the most important and incendiary discussion at Chicago, delegates modified the "Doughty-Lipton plan" to increase the POC requirement from 25 percent to 50 percent, making it on par with gender.[31]

Many felt that 25 percent was appropriate, a sentiment rooted in statistics produced by the U.S. Census. The POC caucus effectively argued that 25 percent representation extended minority status in decision-making. Whites would still have a majority representation (at 75 percent). Symbolically, 25 percent POC representation put primary ownership of the march in white hands. If the march drew ethnically diverse participants, then one could attribute it to successful organizing by whites. Chicago activist Daryll Gordon voiced this concern when he said, "Decisions made four years ago [for the last march on Washington] were made mostly by white gay men and there wasn't much input from people of color. . . . We will make sure that more people of color . . . will be part of the march."[32]

Those in favor of 50 percent used a *principle of parity* that emphasized equal power in decision-making. As one delegate explained, "I fear that without these requirements, it will end up being a bunch of white males. By mandating a certain amount, that will ensure representation from groups that are often unfairly overlooked."[33] Scout Weshchler, who would become one of the cochairs, agreed: "This is a formula for bringing a million lesbians and gays to Washington."[34] In reminiscing about the conference years later, cochair Billy Hileman mused, "Adoption of the modified . . . proposal (with the minimum 50 percent POC amendment) was [the] best thing that happened. . . . The fact that one of the nation's largest civil rights demonstrations was based on this structure, I believe, is not a coincidence. . . . The equality that was at the heart of our organization was an example of what we were asking of our government and should be working for in our community." Racial and gender parity, continued Hileman, "meant that women and men, people of color and white people jointly owned the process and *began* to organize together."[35] The rise of gay people of color organizing provided delegates the prerequisite empowerment to persuasively argue for parity in ways they may have felt unable to before.

Passed by consensus, the 50 percent rule was envisioned as a national model for affirmative action. Some delegates, however, disagreed, sometimes vehemently. Boston activist Alan Rueckgauer felt it was an "unnecessary quota system that could lead to paralysis in the organizing process."[36] Others expressed milder objections: "I voiced objection to raising the percentage from 25 to 50 percent for practical reasons," recalled Tim Drake, then director of the privacy and civil rights project at the NGLTF. "It did not represent the demographics of our community, and therefore I thought it would be difficult to implement, and it might cause some public relations problems."[37]

Similar debates erupted across the country. A *Windy City Times* letter to the editor from Jeff Richards, titled "National Lesbian and Gay March Structure Undemocratic," asked, "Is this fair?" According to his letter:

> Strict racial and gender quotas may be appropriate to remedy intentional discrimination; absent such past discrimination, the proposal discriminates against whites. . . . Is there some evidence that organizers of earlier marches . . . have engaged in intentional discriminatory behavior? . . . Isn't it hypocritical and embarrassing to organize a march that will address civil rights issues along strict racial . . . lines? It is precisely this kind of politically correct behavior which . . . causes so may of our leaders to "not see the forest for the trees": it is undemocratic . . . it is racist.[38]

Halfway across the country, Rick Rosendall submitted a similar op-ed piece to the *Washington Blade*: "A 50 percent goal for people of color is blatantly unrealistic, since the population figure for ethnic minorities is less than half that." Rosendall then identified its penalizing possibilities:

> The people-of-color rule . . . suggests, insultingly, that ethnic Gays cannot be expected to look after their own interests, but must be coddled with special advantage and more-correct-than-thou rhetoric. . . . A person's leadership ability should not be judged—either positively or negatively—on the basis of irrelevant criteria. . . . Those who seek an authentic national consensus should not attempt to impose a false one by means of restrictive quotas which . . . discriminate . . . in the name of fairness.[39]

These are familiar arguments against affirmative action.[40] Rosendall, however, connected this to gay identity and strategy:

> Only by meeting as equals can men and women of different backgrounds join in common cause. . . . This is impossible if one habitually cries "Racist!" whenever anyone strays from the One True Path of Political Correctitude. . . . Many white Gay men have been intimidated into silence or non-involvement because they are tired of being accused of racism, sexism, and classism before they can open their mouths. . . . The Gay rights movement's mainstream

workers . . . cannot be expected to keep bailing out the out-of-touch, socialist ideologues who are hell-bent on taking the Gay community in a direction the bulk of it doesn't want to go.

This dialogue conflated percentages with ownership and exhibited different operational assumptions that cultivated dissent. On the one hand were those proceeding with a definition of representation vis-à-vis the American population. This group used the Census to determine delegate composition. Twenty-five percent composition was allegiant to a *principle of proportions*. An inclusive delegation was one that reflected the demographics of American society. On the other hand, and as already mentioned, was a group that proceeded using a *principle of parity*. This group believed 50 percent composition ensured equality of ownership and equal power in decision-making. The two groups therefore differed on definitions of inclusion: did it mean parity or proportions?

This same debate had recurred over the last three marches. In 1979, the disputes were muted due to a lack of precedent. The pioneers defaulted to a principle of proportions. Organizers debated this during the second march and once again settled on proportions, although they increased the requirement from 20 percent to 25 percent to flag their commitment to social justice. In 1993 we see a leap to 50 percent defended by a principle of parity. We can better understand the move from proportions to parity by examining two factors: a 1987-induced mentality of belonging to a social justice movement and a 1993 response of equal rights to the Religious Right's crusade to frame gay rights as special rights. Empowered by their internal growth and enmeshed within these two currents, the POC caucus blended their own version of social justice and equal rights that white delegates were now positioned to hear. This dialogue reveals how activists once again used dissent over practical tasks (the organizing structure, in this case) to carry cultural concerns (interracial working relationships, in this case).

The Los Angeles Conference[41]

During Martin Luther King Jr.'s birthday weekend on January 18–19, 1992, the full NSC met for the first time to begin constructing the 1993 march.

The Title, Part One

Delegates went into the first afternoon brainstorming titles in what was "by far the most contentious issue"[42] in LA. Table 7.2 lists some suggested names.

A title expresses the purpose and constituency of an event (or organization). In this capacity, the twenty-one proposals in table 7.2 are instructive. The word *bisexual* occurs in six, or 29 percent, of proposals, followed closely by *queer,* which occurs in five, or 24 percent. *Transgender* (or its variant) surfaces in three titles (14 percent). Although transgroups were gaining voice, they had neither acquired equal prominence with bisexuals nor disabused confusion, reflected in inconsistent word choices—for example, *transgenderal, transsexual, transvestite, trans,* and *other gender persons.* The nondescript *sexual minority* occurred in two instances (10 percent) along with two faceless titles that did not make reference to any group (e.g., "The Love March" and "1993 March for Liberty and Justice for All"). Queer theory manifested in occurrences of *queer, sexual minority,* and titles without any reference, for a total of nine, topping the list at 43 percent of proposals. Queer-related titles embraced identity-building and -blurring. "Queer March" and "Colorful Queer March" muted internal differences, while "Queer Civil Rights," "Queer Liberation," and—most notably—"Family of Queers" implied a queer nationality, the paradoxical identity of an identity-less group. Compare this with titles that only used *lesbian and gay* (or vice versa), as did the first two marches. These occurred in three suggestions (14 percent), less than the 29 percent for *bisexual* and dwarfed by *queer*'s 43 percent. Even if one did not know the final decision, the numbers reveal that delegates drew upon shared cultural scripts, that is, the rise of bisexual groups, queer politics, and, to a lesser extent, transgender groups.[43]

These are not the only cultural scripts. The title "The 1993 MOW for Gay and Lesbian Rights" paid homage to the titles of the 1979 and 1987 marches which provided path-dependence, that is, organizational continuity.[44] "Lesbian, Gay, and Bisexual March for Human Rights" echoed a 1979 suggestion to define the march broadly for human rights. The title "1993 March for Liberty and Justice for All" emphasized a patriotic American identity for the people next door. "The 1993 MOW for Lesbian, Gay, and Bisexual Liberation," on the other hand, is considerably more progressive than the notion of rights or civil rights for gays or human beings in general. Thus, even the titles reflect the tenu-

TABLE 7.2. **Proposed Titles for the 1993 March**

The 1993 March on Washington for Lesbian, Gay, and Bisexual Rights
The Colorful Queer March for America 1993
March on Washington for Queer Civil Rights—1993
The 1993 March on Washington for Gay and Lesbian Rights
Queer March
March on Washington for Sexuality-Related Rights
The 1993 March on Washington for Lesbian, Gay, and Bisexual Liberation
Lesbian, Gay, and Bisexual March for Human Rights
Gay and Lesbian 1993 March on Washington for All Rights for All People
Gay, Lesbian, Bisexual, Transsexuals, Transvestites, and Other Gender Persons March on
Washington
March on Washington 1993 for Queer Liberation
March on Washington for Lesbian, Gay, Bisexual, Transgenderal Rights 1993
1993 March on Washington for the Civil Rights of Sexual Minorities
The Love March
The Translesbigay March on Washington 1993
Gays and Lesbians United for their Rights March on Washington 1993
Dyke Sluts from Hell Take Over D.C., Fags Can Come Too, Fuck Me Silly in the Nation's
Capital
Rivers of the Rainbow Queer March on Washington
1993 March for Liberty and Justice for All
The 1993 Family of Queers March on Washington
March on Washington to End Homophobia

Source: 1993 March on Washington National Steering Committee Meeting Summary

ous coexistence of centrist and leftist impulses and between deemphasis and difference. Finally, "Dyke Sluts from Hell Take Over DC, Fags Can Come Too, Fuck Me Silly in the Nation's Capital" was "the wildest suggestion," according to the gay press. It was "greeted with laughter and much applause" amid an otherwise divisive discussion. This title animates Bakhtin's "carnival spirit," in which the intention of dialogue is to include many voices while maintaining a playful and skeptical attitude through laughter. Diversity is the desired end, humor the facilitating lubricant.[45]

Delegates proceeded with a straw poll to see "what the group could live with." Fifty-five voted to only use *gay and lesbian* in the title; 68 for *gay, lesbian, and bisexual*; 45 for *gay, lesbian, bisexual, and transgenderal*; 17 for *gay, lesbian, bisexual, transgenderal, transsexual, transvestite*; 25 for using the word *queer*; and 41 for the title "March on Washington to End Homophobia." After this, came another vote to select among the top three—*gay, lesbian, and bisexual* (68); *gay and lesbian* (55); and *gay, lesbian, bisexual, and transgenderal* (45). To simplify the process, delegates moved from tallying more than one hundred individual votes to aggregating the seventeen regions and fourteen constituency groups present at the conference. The size of each group determined the relative weight of its title preference (one, two, three, or four votes). With three regions and three constituency groups abstaining, the final tally came to 32 votes for *gay and lesbian*; 17 for *gay, lesbian, bisexual, and transgenderal*; and 8 for *gay, lesbian, and bisexual*.

Because none received a two-thirds majority, delegates continued to vote, feverishly pitting titles against each other. Some wanted to keep the name short and sweet, as it had been for the first two marches, whereas others wanted to broaden it to represent the increasingly diverse movement. One delegate chided, "To exclude bisexuals and transsexuals from the title is to exclude them from the march, because the public is not being made aware that bisexuals and transsexuals are out there. In a sense, it's the same kind of exclusion that hets [heterosexuals] do to gays and lesbians." Another supporter of broadening the title drew connections to Stonewall, "The people who've always been beaten up first, the transsexuals and transgender people" should not be excluded.[46] Attendees were not able to establish a two-thirds majority that day and decided to schedule another vote for the next day to give time for informal lobbying.

Even before we consider how the chips fell, the debates themselves illustrate that activists used their dissent over the title to engage in a cultural conversation over the meaning of gay identity. Infighting over the title carried this identity work, as delegates vied to include bisexuals and transgendered people. Their reticence was also clear. The influence of bisexuals and to a lesser extent transgenders, however, was unmistakable. The scene was set for an explosive debate.

The Title, Part Two

The next day, delegates first focused on the presumably simpler question of purpose: was the march about the pursuit of "rights," "civil rights," "human rights," "equal rights," "liberation," "rights and liberation," or something else?[47] Delegates began with a vote to identify their top four choices. Another round of two-thirds majority voting ensued and failed as it did the day before. Delegates then changed the procedure to permit individuals to vote for a name on a "you can live with this" basis. After a couple of burdensome hours, "For equal rights and liberation" received more than a two-thirds majority. Similar to Saturday, the results from this debate also reflect activity in the sociopolitical context. The move from "rights" (used in the title of the first two marches) to "equal rights" makes sense in light of the Religious Right's special-rights crusade, activists' response of equal rights, and the born-versus-bred hysteria. It also reveals a delicate balance between mainstream ("equal rights") and leftist ("liberation") impulses within the movement that would burst from the seams during the fourth march.

Delegates resumed after lunch with another "you can live with this" vote to settle the front end of the march's title. *Lesbian, gay, and bi* received greater than two-thirds majority over both *lesbian and gay* and *lesbian, gay, bi, and transgender.* Delegates finally established the official title: "The 1993 March on Washington for Lesbian, Gay, and Bi Equal Rights and Liberation."

But why *bi* and not *bisexual?* According to lesbian activist Shirley Lesser, "The committee decided to use 'bi' instead of 'bisexual' . . . because a number of delegates felt 'bisexual' had a sexual connotation."[48] The word *bi,* in other words, deemphasized sex (the proverbial "ick factor"), a strategic move activists felt would bolster their efforts to be treated like everyone else—that is, to secure equal rights. What we see here is that every decision, down to the choice of each individual word, is deliberate. The end result suggests that activists augmented conceptions of both categorical commonality (or shared attributes) and relational connectedness (or shared networks), the two ways of thinking about identity, through their title debates. After years of struggle, bisexuals were now officially included as part of the national movement. Even if they were stripped of their sexuality.

Controversy lingered long after the Los Angeles conference. One letter to the editor in the *Washington Blade* titled "Major Mistake" opined, "The purpose of the 1993 March is to send a clear signal to straight America. Confusing the March title to make it an umbrella for every minority group is a major mistake."[49] Another writer was "really getting fed up with all the catering going on in the Gay community for bisexuals. . . . From the time of that fateful night in 1969 when the Gay Liberation Movement as we know it began, Gay men and Lesbians have fought long and hard to get where we are today. Now, the bisexuals are crawling out of the woodwork to reap the benefits."[50] These are expressions of cultural skepticism over the augmenting of gay identity.

To the gentleman who was fed up, another writer replied, "I too am 'fed up'. . . . What I'm fed up with is her/his attitude and misinformation!

Bisexuals were at Stonewall. Bisexuals helped build the Gay movement. The movement belongs to us as much as anyone. . . . Our Gay community needs to expand its definition and our goals if we are to succeed."[51] Yet another writer, titling her thoughts "Same Struggle," succinctly said, "Bi inclusion boils down to one basic premise: our struggle is exactly the same. . . . Bis are not the enemy. . . . We are on the same side of this struggle. . . . We are you."[52] Proponents used the title to carry identity work, that is, to expand the category *gay* by equating lesbians and gay men with bisexuals.[53]

The successful incorporation of bisexuality into the title was an artifact of the considerable growth of bisexual organizations between the second and third marches. One bisexual delegate argued that bisexuals became more organized and visible during the past six years. This made it difficult for lesbians and gay men to deny their existence: "We were getting fed up with being told by the lesbian and gay community and the straight community that we didn't exist. . . . We had no choice but to come out as bisexuals."[54]

Although bisexuals and transgenders were both heavily debated, it is notable that delegates only included the former. As suggested in a *Windy City Times* editorial, "Gay and lesbian organizations throughout the country long have been wrangling over whether to add 'bisexual' to their titles or to develop programs geared toward bisexuals. But, unlike transsexualism or transvestism, bisexuality, like homosexuality, is a sexual orientation."[55] Here we see the limits of identity expansion achieved by effectively drawing *differences* between sexual orientation and gender identity.

The Dallas, Denver, and D.C. Conferences

The NSC met for the second time during the weekend of May 9–10, 1992, in Dallas, Texas. Each conference for each march addressed one or more signature debates. The 1993 initiating meeting addressed the question: should we march? The grassroots planning meeting that followed picked up the next question: when should we march? In Chicago, the organizing structure was the focal point of friction, and for L.A. it was a teething of the title. Dallas had two objectives: to elect cochairs, which was fairly benign, and to draft the platform, which was far more bellicose.

Cochairs

Determining cochairs was decidedly the easier of Dallas's two tasks, although it was not devoid of dissent. The first march had two co-coordinators, whereas the second march had three cochairs. The question now arose of how to maintain gender and racial parity with three individuals (recall that Chicago delegates increased the people-of-color requirement from 25 percent, as it had been during the second march, to 50 percent for the third march). In response, some delegates proposed that the 1993 march should have four cochairs instead of three. Not everyone, however, was on board. Those who opposed four cochairs were in favor of "go[ing] with the original concept,"[56] that is, maintaining allegiance with the cultural template. After a short discussion, delegates decided by consensus to have four cochairs, as the number was a clean way to ensure racial and gender parity. The floor then opened for nominations, followed by one-minute nominee speeches. After some discussion, delegates elected Billy Hileman, Derek Livingston, Scout Weshchler, and Nadine Smith. A young, new guard, with the assistance of an advisory group of the old guard, was ready to take the helms to D.C.

Platform/Demands

Ten months before Dallas, Urvashi Vaid predicted the pains that would be associated with the platform. To simplify the process, she "urge[d] the body [of delegates] to not re-invent the wheel on demands. The seven demands of 1987 are all relevant today. None should be dropped. . . . If we drop those demands, we ignore not only the political realities of the day . . . but we will alienate a lot of people's support—including mine personally, and this organization's [NGLTF's] politically."[57] The platform committee heeded some of her advice, but veered away enough to generate an onslaught of criticism.

The committee solicited input from individuals, organizations, and regions across the country and presented a draft to the NSC at the Dallas conference. To do this, they mailed a form letter to organizations and asked them to return platform ideas under the header, "I believe that the following concerns must be incorporated into the platform [of] the 1993 March on Washington."[58] Here we see a move away from pursuing a lowest common denominator that could unite the community toward

expansion instead. In other words, instead of starting from a narrow base
with one or two broad issues of interest to a large constituency (e.g., the
Five Demands from 1979), the committee started from a broad base and
later struggled to narrow, in what turned out to be a very bitter process.

Similar to 1987, the 1993 platform committee proposed the demands
open with (instead of conclude with) an action statement, or philosophical preamble. This was followed by an astonishing fifty-five-item laundry
list of demands. For the next several hours, delegates debated wording.
For example, anywhere the phrase *sexual orientation* was mentioned,
some delegates successfully argued to modify it to *sexual orientation/
identification, identity, gender, and gender expression.*[59] At the close
of the fifty-fifth item, delegates had meditated on twenty-six gay rights
objectives (e.g., repeal of state sodomy laws) and twenty-nine coalition
items (e.g., affordable access to health care for all). Similar to 1987, demands were organized into seven topical planks that included civil rights
(seven items), people of color (eight items), education/students (four
items), universal health care (fourteen items), reproductive freedom (five
items), family (seven items), and discrimination (nine items). Single- and
multi-issue demands, corresponding to centrist and leftist impulses, remained in productive tension in the platform as mainstream and social
justice inclinations had in the title (e.g., "equal rights and liberation").

After a ninety-minute discussion, and through consensus, the delegates approved the list with little to no opposition.[60] Despite this ease
in production, platform reception by the rank and file was not calm and
cool. Although platform skepticism was familiar from previous marches,
in 1993 it picked up three new voices: the debate was inflected with a
mainstreaming rhetoric, it focused on the issue of transgender inclusion,
and it was recast in periphery-center terms after an unexpected endorsement from the National Association for the Advancement of Colored
People (NAACP). Activists used the platform and its associated dissent
to give voice to concerns of strategy: Are we a mainstream movement, in
which case we should assemble a single-issue platform? Or are we a social justice movement seeking coalitions with others?

The Platform: The "Looney Left" versus the Mainstream

After Dallas, some delegates criticized the platform for alienating mainstream gays, which would deter them from attending the march. The
draft was accused of being "a laundry list for the left" that "represents a

fringe group within a fringe group." Although activists once again used an organizing task to give voice to strategy, it sounded different this time. A structurally familiar debate about single- versus multi-issue politics became inflected with a culturally modern hue of the mainstream.

As the planks marinated, they absorbed more and more controversy. Within two weeks, D.C.'s local committee refused to endorse the draft, urged the EC to rescind the entire platform, and replace it with a single statement of purpose: "Because of the great diversity within our community . . . we recommend that the Executive Committee declare that the sole purpose of the 1993 March on Washington be for 'the equal rights and liberation of Lesbian, Gay, and Bisexual People.'"[61] Here we see activists using the platform to speak to strategic disagreements over diversity. The statement of purpose suggests a lowest-common-denominator logic, that is, "equal rights and liberation." Some activists argued that diversity management required unity around a single, all-encompassing demand. Longtime activist Frank Kameny captured this position best: "There is an old saying: 'Shoemaker, stick to your last.' Our 'last' is gay rights, and that alone. Let's stick to it in our platform."[62]

Ironically, activists intended the platform draft—adopted unexpectedly with few to no objections—to be inclusive: "The long list of demands represents the diversity of our community," expressed one letter to the editor.[63] This wide-net logic supported a far-reaching platform. A single-issue platform "would divide our community because it would ignore the needs of people of color, women, and those of limited economic means."[64] This side also mobilized the rhetoric of diversity, although in a very different way. Diversity was now justification for pursuing many demands.

The controversy snowballed into a national dialogue that asked, "What are we marching for?" Commentators recognized some demands as "the common currency of gay advocacy." Others were less clear and compelling. In attending the march, an individual was demanding the legalization of polygamy and polyandry, an end to economic injustice internationally, laws that recognize sexual relationships among youth, restoration and enforcement of bilingual education, an end to poverty, and an end to institutionalized racism. Some felt that the platform committee "just could not bring itself to care about enough of our issues because it had too many other agendas." Quickly, "the suspicion grows that members of the committee frankly did not know what 'our' issues are."[65] At one level, this conversation was about the logistics of organizing: what should we include in our platform? At another level, however, activists were engaged in culture work, that is, with meaning-making over questions such as: Who are we? And what do we want?

Within a month, the EC organized an emergency meeting to review, revise, and resubmit the demands. Platform committee cochair Chip Wells noted, "The task of producing a platform that is acceptable to everyone in a community as diverse as ours [is] almost impossible. . . . Growing and expanding our consciousness is not always an easy or painless process."[66] The EC tailored the platform in several ways. First, they deleted the most controversial (and notably most progressive) item that called for the "legalization of multiple partner unions." The EC also modified the wording of two supporting statements on age of consent and medical treatment for transgender persons. The more heated of these two originally read "implementation of laws that recognize sexual relationships among youth, between consenting peers." It was revised to "passage and implementation of graduated age of consent laws."[67] The preamble to the platform was maintained. In finalizing the document, cochair Nadine Smith asserted, "Our priority has from the beginning been one of inclusivity. The march platform is the result of our grassroots organization's commitment to diversity. No one is on the outside of this movement."[68]

These disputes speak to disagreements over strategy. According to one editorial, "Some people think the march should focus on the issues everybody agrees are common to lesbians and gay men. Others think it must raise other issues which only some of us think are intrinsic to lesbian and gay freedom. This question has been around a long time. The same question split the movement against the Vietnam War. I didn't know the answer in 1965 and I don't know it now. I *do* know the question won't be resolved before April."[69] For some, the platform was a "joke," while for others it was no quibbling matter. The Log Cabin Republicans, for example, withdrew their support from "any and all" march activities unless the platform was rescinded and revised.[70]

Those who favored a single-issue march accused multi-issue supporters of being out of step with a mainstreaming movement, with being "ideologically rigid march organizers."[71] Single-issue advocates believed the platform "does not reflect a march for gays and lesbians but one for the lost children of the '60s, with its call for a return to indigenous populations of their lands."[72] Others, such as Frank Kameny argued, "Our march has ceased to be a march of gay rights and has been successfully hi-jacked by the 'looney left'. . . . Our march has . . . become a march for a national utopia, or a march for a perfect society, or a march against all oppression—or a cure-everything march. It has ceased to be a gay-related march at all."[73] Kameny was furious:

> The platform and its introductory paragraph sound like something left over from the '60s. The '60s were a wonderful era which left us a priceless legacy, but they were also an era of unparalleled slovenly, sloppy thinking and impractical activism by well-meaning, idealistic people who had not the slightest idea of how to accomplish real gains in a real world. This platform is a perfect example of the latter. . . . I marched in the famous 1963 march on Washington for civil rights for blacks. I am sure that Martin Luther King was well aware of the veils of both anti-Semitism and sexism (to name but two) and disapproved of both. He did not mention them, nor should he have. He properly left anti-Semitism to the B'nai B'rith and others, and sexism to the then still-formative feminist movement. We should follow his lead.

Kameny had three concerns with the platform. The first was over breadth: "If you try to do everything, you end up doing nothing well." Kameny also accused the platform of "ideological orthodoxy, fascism, and enforced political correctness." He and Nadine Smith both identified a tension between grassroots commitment, pushed by the "looney left" and an evolution into the mainstream. Kameny's final point concerned reciprocity and currying favors: "If gays are going to be the saviours of all the world's oppressed, that those oppressed would reciprocate and try to be saviours of gays. They do not." Kameny's article made a splash in local gay newspapers across the country.

As the controversy bubbled, it spoke to the tenuous center-left tension. Some D.C. residents complained that the platform "provides ample ammunition and some justification for those who accuse us of seeking special privileges." A rank-and-file Chicago resident agreed: "If retained, the seven main demands and the fifty-five 'support items' of the march will provide unlimited anti-gay fodder for the right-wing and may reverse years of hard-fought political gains. . . . Jesse Helms, Patrick Buchanan, and other anti-gay leaders will use this platform against us for years to come."[74] Yet another writer expressed the same complaint: "We remain concerned that the right wing will use the platform to stymie gay and lesbian political gains" since certain demands will become "ammunition that the right can, and almost surely will, use against us."[75]

Not only did activists use platform debates as a culture carrier for a meta-conversation over strategy, they also used it to make sense of the sociopolitical context. Supporters used the language of *equal civil rights* in the planks. Those who opposed the platform drew on the same debate. The platform is dangerous, said opponents, because it would prove that gays were indeed pursuing special rights. Platform debates therefore corresponded to activity in the sociopolitical context where a mainstreaming movement was fighting to define its struggles as the pursuit of equal rights while not abandoning its rich, liberationist history.

The Platform: Transgender Inclusion

The platform controversy was central at the third and fourth NSC meetings in Denver and D.C. Recall that Dallas delegates did not include the word *transgender* in any of the planks. During a question-and-answer period at the third NSC meeting held October 3–4, 1992, in Denver, transactivists expressed feeling left out and demanded change.[76] Delegates were caught off guard and without reply. Transactivists persisted, voicing feelings of exclusion from the "headlines" (i.e., the planks). They threatened a boycott if their demands were not met.[77] In response and because there was so much controversy already, the EC met later that night to try and find a resolution.

The next day, the EC presented a statement on transinclusion to the NSC: "It is in the spirit of inclusivity, cooperation, and good faith expressed at the Los Angeles NSC meeting to include 'transgendered people' extensively in March on Washington literature, that we, the Executive Committee acknowledge our oversight in the platform document and correct this oversight." After apologizing, an EC member read the revised platform, in which trans concerns were explicitly incorporated into four of the seven planks and the supporting items (see table 7.3).

It is noteworthy that transgender concerns were included in the platform but not the title. During the fourth NSC meeting in Washington, D.C., over the weekend of February 6–7, 1993, transactivists tried to reopen a title discussion.[78] Princess, a self-identified transactivist, began by educating delegates on the similarities between trans and lesbigay concerns: "We've always been around this LGB movement." Trina, another transactivist, emoted that "this imbalance [of inclusion] is causing geno-

TABLE 7.3. **Demands, 1993 March**

ACTION STATEMENT PREAMBLE TO THE PLATFORM

The Lesbian, Gay, Bisexual, and Transgender movement recognizes that our quest for social justice fundamentally links us to the struggles against racism and sexism, class bias, economic injustice, and religious intolerance. We must realize if one of us is oppressed we are all oppressed. The diversity of our movement requires and compels us to stand in opposition to all forms of oppression that diminish the quality of life for all people. We will be vigilant in our determination to rid our movement and our society of all forms of oppression and exploitation, so that all of us can develop to our full human potential without regard to race, religion, sexual orientation/identification, identity, gender and gender expression, ability, age, or class.

1. WE DEMAND PASSAGE OF A LESBIAN, GAY, BISEXUAL, AND TRANSGENDER CIVIL RIGHTS BILL AND AN END TO DISCRIMINATION BY STATE AND FEDERAL GOVERNMENTS INCLUDING THE MILITARY; REPEAL OF ALL SODOMY LAWS AND OTHER LAWS THAT CRIMINALIZE PRIVATE SEXUAL EXPRESSION BETWEEN CONSENTING ADULTS.

Passage of the Civil Rights Amendment Act of 1991 (HR 1430 & S574).
Repeal of Department of Defense directive 1332.14.
Repeal of laws prohibiting sodomy, cross-gender expression (dress codes) or non-coercive sexual behavior between consenting adults.
Amendment of the Code of Federal Regulations to recognize same-sex relationships.
Passage of the Equal Rights Amendment.
Implementation of, funding for, and enforcement of the Americans with Disabilities Act of 1991.
Passage and implementation of graduated age-of-consent laws.

2. WE DEMAND A MASSIVE INCREASE IN FUNDING FOR AIDS EDUCATION, RESEARCH, AND PATIENT CARE; UNIVERSAL ACCESS TO HEALTH CARE INCLUDING ALTERNATIVE THERAPIES; AND AN END TO SEXISM IN MEDICAL RESEARCH AND HEALTH CARE.

The provision of responsive, appropriate health care for people with disabilities, deaf and hard of hearing people.
Revision of the Centers for Disease Control definition of AIDS to include infections particular to women.
Implementation of the recommendation of the National AIDS Commission immediately.
A massive increase in funding for AIDS education, research and care—money for AIDS, not for war. This money should come from the defense budget, not existing social services.
An increase in funding and research to provide an independent study of HIV infection in women, People of Color, Bisexuals, Heterosexuals, children, and women-to-women transmission.
Access to anonymous testing for HIV.
No mandatory HIV testing.
A cure for AIDS.
The development and legalization of a national needle exchange program.
Free substance abuse treatment on demand.
The re-definition of sexual re-assignment surgeries as medical, not cosmetic, treatment.
The provision of appropriate medical treatment for all transgendered people in prisons and hospitals.
An increase in funding and research for chronic illness, including breast, ovarian, and other cancers particular to women.

(continued)

TABLE 7.3. *(continued)*

The right of all people with chronic illness, including HIV/AIDS, to choices in medical treatment as well as the right to end such treatment.

3. WE DEMAND LEGISLATION TO PREVENT DISCRIMINATION AGAINST LESBIANS, GAYS, BISEXUALS, AND TRANSGENDERED PEOPLE IN THE AREAS OF FAMILY DIVERSITY, CUSTODY, ADOPTION, AND FOSTER CARE AND THAT THE DEFINITION OF FAMILY INCLUDES THE FULL DIVERSITY OF ALL FAMILY STRUCTURES.

The recognition and legal protection of the whole range of family structures.
An end to abuse and exploitation of and discrimination against youth.
An end to abuse and exploitation of and discrimination against older/old people.
Full implementation of the recommendations contained in the report of the Health and Human Services Task Force on Youth Suicide.
Recognition of domestic partnerships.
Legalization of same-sex marriages.

4. WE DEMAND FULL AND EQUAL INCLUSION OF LESBIANS, GAYS, BISEXUALS, AND TRANSGENDERED PEOPLE IN THE EDUCATIONAL SYSTEM, AND INCLUSION OF LESBIAN, GAY, BISEXUAL, AND TRANSGENDER STUDIES IN MULTICULTURAL CURRICULA.

Culturally inclusive Lesbian, Gay, Bisexual, and Transgender Studies program; and information on abortion, AIDS/HIV, childcare and sexuality at all levels of education.
Establishment of campus officers and programs to address Lesbian, Gay, Bisexual, and Transgender students' special needs.
The ban of all discriminatory ROTC programs and recruiters from learning institutions.
An end to discrimination at all levels of education.

5. WE DEMAND THE RIGHT TO REPRODUCTIVE FREEDOM AND CHOICE, TO CONTROL OUR OWN BODIES, AND AN END TO SEXIST DISCRIMINATION.

The right to control our bodies.
Unrestricted, safe, and affordable alternative insemination.
An end to sterilization abuse.
That access to safe and affordable abortion and contraception be available to all people on demand, without restriction and regardless of age.
That access to unbiased and complete information about the full range of reproductive options be available to all people, regardless of age.

6. WE DEMAND AN END TO RACIAL AND ETHNIC DISCRIMINATION IN ALL FORMS.

Support for non-racist policies and affirmative action.
An end to institutionalized racism.
Equal economic opportunity and an end to poverty.
Full reproductive rights, improvement of pre-natal services, availability of alternative insemination for Lesbians and Bisexual women of color.
Repeal of all "English Only" laws and restore and enforce bilingual education.
Repeal of all discriminatory immigration laws based on race and HIV status.
A commitment to ending racism, including internalized racism, sexism, and all forms of religious and ethnic oppression in our communities and in this country.
An end to the genocide of all the indigenous peoples and their cultures.
Restoration of the self-determination of all indigenous people of the world.

TABLE 7.3. *(continued)*

---

7. WE DEMAND AN END TO DISCRIMINATION AND VIOLENT OPPRESSION
BASED ON ACTUAL OR PERCEIVED SEXUAL ORIENTATION/IDENTIFICATION,
RACE, RELIGION, IDENTITY, SEX AND GENDER EXPRESSION, DISABILITY, AGE,
CLASS, AIDS/HIV INFECTION.

An end to anti-Semitism.
An end to sexist oppression.
An end to discrimination against people with disabilities, deaf and hard of hearing people.
An end to discrimination based on sexual orientation in all programs of the Boy Scouts of
America.
An end to economic injustice in this country and internationally.
An end to discrimination against prisoners with HIV/AIDS.
An end to discrimination against people living with HIV/AIDS, and those perceived as having
HIV/AIDS.
An end to consideration of gender dysphoria as a psychiatric disorder.
An end to hate crimes including police brutality, rape, and bashing.
An end to censorship.

Source: Official Program of the 1993 National March on Washington for Lesbian, Gay, and Bi
Equal Rights and Liberation. Primary source materials. GLBT Historical Society of Northern
California.

cide. We come from the same closet. I'm transgender and lesbian. We're
fighting for the same thing. . . . Look at Stonewall, that was transgender people." These relational debates sought to reconfigure how different types of gay people were connected to each other.

Trina picked up Princess's direction and took it one step further by
invoking the closet and Stonewall to draw links between transgender
and lesbian/gay political organizing. Marisa Cheryl Lynn, founder and
president of a national transgender magazine, agreed: "We want a better
relationship with the LGB and women's movements. Our issues are the
same: intolerance, hatred, etc. Be supportive of my people." Well-known
transgender rights activist Phyllis Randolph Frye agreed that anti-gay activity and anti-trans activity share homophobia in common: "The March
on Washington for Lesbian and Gay and Bisexual (and should also be
for Transgender) Rights is the place for any freedom-loving person to
be. . . . As most prejudice against transgendered persons is based on homophobia, any 'sexual orientation' gains made in laws by lesbians, gays,
and bisexuals may assist in attitude—but not necessary legal—changes
regarding transgenderals."[79]

Transactivists specified that their issues, while similar, were not identical to those of lesbians and gay men. This was all the more reason why
they demanded full inclusion, since their rights would not automatically
be achieved by going in the back door of lesbian and gay demands. Ac-

cording to Princess, "Sexual orientation doesn't cover transgender people. It's gender identity, not sexual identity."[80] Princess then called for a vote to "add our name, to be included on this march. We are this march! [But] we're not on the name." Cochair Billy Hileman expressed the delegates' appreciation for trans issues. He noted that four of the seven planks were modified to include transgender concerns. "What about the name of the march?" retorted Princess. "The name of the march is a separate issue. That's what transgenders want."

Not everyone was convinced. One delegate noted, "While this statement might not be popular, it needs to be made and listened to. . . . A vast majority don't know about the transgender label. That has been somewhat forced on all of us, and some don't want to be associated with this word. . . . We need more discussion among ourselves." Much of the rank and file agreed. Similar to 1979, hesitation around transgender issues was due to lack of information and multiple, inconsistent terminology. One letter to the editor of Chicago's local gay newspaper chided that "anyone marching in Washington on April 25 will be 'demanding' that straight men who wear pantyhose be added to the gay and lesbian civil rights bill. They will be demanding that schools adopt 'transgender studies' programs. They will be demanding that transgendered people be added to legislative proposals that would allow gay and lesbian people to adopt children. . . . We are certain that the vast majority of gay and lesbian people would strongly object to the inclusion of transgendered people in this platform."[81] For whom was this march? Were transpersons part of the movement? If lesbian/gay and trans concerns were indeed different, could they nonetheless coexist in the national march?

Definitional distinctions between straight transgender persons and the lesbian and gay movement became particularly pronounced, as captured in another Chicago editorial: "The issue here is not transgendered rights. The question is whether it is appropriate to make a straight transvestite's concerns a priority in the movement. (Studies have shown that most transvestites are straight.) Transvestism and transsexualism are not the same as sexual orientation, and transgendered concerns should not be part of a march for gay and lesbian rights."[82] An NGLTF spokesperson summarized the bottom line, "People are just becoming familiar with gays and lesbians. . . . That [transgender inclusion] would certainly require further education."[83] The inclusion of bisexuals but not transgenders in the title reveals limits to boundary elasticity. Although transgender visibility had increased over the course of the first three marches, they had not achieved the same presence as bisexuals. Continuing misinformation about transgender concerns also inhibited full inclusion, evidenced by persisting debates over whether transpersons were more similar to heterosexuals or lesbigay people.

But still, the three national marches reveal that the boundaries of erotic life are plastic enough and do stretch over time to include new groups. Trina articulated this process of boundary evolution at the NSC meeting in D.C.: "First it was gay and lesbian and then bisexual. We need to be included too." Phyllis Frye also tuned into this process of rhetorical expansion:

> At the planning meeting for the first March on Washington, I had to visibly boycott the meeting to get "transgender" recognized in the brochure. During the second march, I noticed that the transgender community was once again given a short shrift by those in charge. Now I note a third march: the transgender community was omitted one more time from the name. . . . Insist that the term "gender identification" is included. Insist that the term "transgender" is included. They used to say gay. Then they learned to say lesbian and gay. Now they are learning to say lesbian, gay, and bisexual. Insist that they learn to say lesbian, gay, bisexual, and transgender.[84]

Frye's comment underscores a process of boundary expansion that included some (bisexuals) but not others (transgenders). Although one step closer, transgendered persons were still several more steps behind.

Stretching takes time, evidenced in the response of D.C. delegates. Those who advocated including transgender in the title argued that they were part of the march. They had, after all, helped us establish our rights (via Stonewall). We have included them in the literature, so why not extend it to the title? Those who opposed inclusion argued that the issue was difficult for everyone and that delegates were going to pit themselves against each other. *Transgender* means different things to different people, leaving its ultimate meaning unclear. After this discussion of cultural politics and disputes over meanings, delegates voted on "whether or not to reopen the issue." This was not a vote on whether to include but instead to reengage the deliberative process. Fifty-two delegates voted no, thirty-one voted yes, and two abstained. Because a two-thirds vote was not achieved, the issue was silenced.

The various controversies associated with the platform garnered so much steam that some advocated ignoring the document altogether. The platform "was designed to please everyone, and it ended up not pleasing anyone," in the words of Victor Salvo, a key organizer of the second march. Continued Salvo, "We had a cockamamie platform in 1987, too, but people didn't pay attention to it. The platform is irrelevant, and no one will remember what it said. If you don't like the agenda, ignore it."[85] A call to ignore the politics of the event, extolled in the platform, defaults to the cultural dimensions of political organizing. Lori Cannon, who helped organize the 1987 march, attested that people "were transformed by it [the march]. If you go to this march, you will not come back the same person." Marches on Washington have a defibrillating, cultural effect that can serve as the primary incentive to march. Another writer captured this sentiment: "I was at the previous lesbian and gay march on Washington, and I was at the one before that. I don't remember the formal platform or demands from either march. Does anybody? . . . I *do* remember two . . . magnificent milestones in the growth of our . . . power."[86] It seems that politics and culture collide in Washington marches.

The Platform: The NAACP Endorsement

One month prior to the demonstration, organizers received an unexpected and unprecedented endorsement of the march from the NAACP, the country's largest and oldest civil rights advocacy group. The forging of this "historic coalition," in the words of cochair Nadine Smith, marked a major moment in the movement's history. This was the first time that the NAACP officially supported—and unanimously, at that—the repeal of anti-gay laws. Dr. William Gibson of the NAACP remarked that the endorsement "marks the beginning of a new and very important coalition. The NAACP supports efforts to end discrimination against gay men and lesbians in areas of American life where all citizens deserve equal protection and equal opportunity under the law." The NAACP also agreed to speak at the march as a testament to their commitment.

Responses to the endorsement are noteworthy. Although Gibson used the word *coalition,* gay rights activists reframed the endorsement as confirming their *mainstream* status. According to Nadine Smith, "The lesbian and gay movement has moved from being viewed as a special interest fringe group to being in the mainstream of America. . . . We're now seen as part of the broader civil rights movement."[87] This idea was echoed two weeks later in a Chicago editorial, "The March on Washington could illustrate our resolve to achieve basic civil rights. . . . With the participation of the NAACP . . . the message that gays and lesbians are only asking for the same rights that others have—and not special rights—will be loud and clear."[88] Whereas activists used similar debates in the second march to self-define as a social justice movement, organizers of the third march used them to reframe their strategy away from seeking social justice toward the pursuit of equal rights in the mainstream.

Even when 1993 organizers used the word *coalition,* they did so differently than their predecessors. The third march did not identify the need to build coalitions in the face of a hostile, unresponsive domestic and international political climate. Instead, coalitions were framed as evidence of the movement's maturity, that it had moved from the periphery to the center of American consciousness, and that it had become a mainstream civil rights entity. The title of a post-march article in the gay press succinctly confirmed: "The March's Legacy: Mainstreaming the Movement."[89] Changes in the sociopolitical context account for this difference. The roaring special rights–equal rights debate exerted assimilationist pressures that compelled the movement to blur its differences from straight America—that is, to self-define as the people next door who were fighting for equal rights. The NAACP's endorsement solidified the veracity of this struggle and self-definition.

Conservative currents charged that it was an insult to compare gays and blacks. Jesse Jackson and Dr. Gibson of the NAACP disabused such notions in their rally address. Gibson quoted from Martin Luther King's "I Have a Dream" speech. The poignant symbolism of this address—delivered by Dr. King thirty years earlier from the steps of the Lincoln Memorial—was unmistakable. Said Gibson, "As Martin Luther King said, 'Justice denied anywhere diminishes justice everywhere'. . . . The NAACP will not sit in silence while our fellow Americans are denied full civil rights because of their sexual orientation."[90] Jackson and Gibson called for black and gay groups to work together. According to Torie Osborn, "That really launched us into the more broad-based civil rights movement."[91] The dawn of the mainstream had arrived.

The 1993 March on Washington for Lesbian, Gay, and Bi Equal Rights and Liberation

On April 25, 1993, nearly one million lesbians, gay men, bisexuals, and transgender persons descended on the nation's capital to declare,

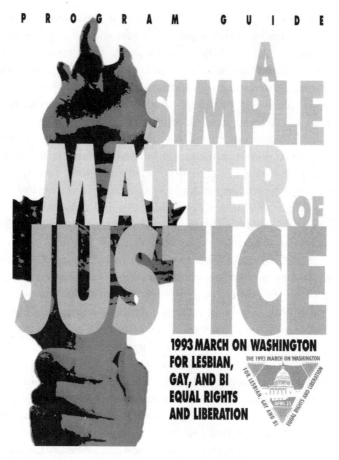

FIGURE 7.2. A Simple Matter of Justice. Source: GLBT Historical Society of Northern California.

"Our Time Has Come," as headlined in Chicago's local gay press.[92] The movement was assembled in full force, surrounded by C-SPAN cameras (who, for the first time, were providing a live broadcast), gay and straight presses from across the country, and, of course, rainbow flags. This was the largest gathering of LGBT persons in the history of the movement—and one of the largest gatherings of its kind in D.C.'s history, surpassed only by two anti–Vietnam War marches and a 1992 abortion rights march.

Participants were overwhelmed by the titanic turnout, with contingents from states where few even imagined gays to live. "Tell your ma, tell your pa, you saw queers from Arkansas," chanted hundreds behind their state's banner. The people next door had arrived, declared the *New York Times,* in an era of "unprecedented national debate on whether gays and lesbians deserve equal rights under the law."[93] LGBT folks testified that this was not a matter of special rights; it was "a simple matter of justice," heralded as the theme of the march, uttered by cochair Derek Livingston during Dallas, widely circulated as the march poster, and also powerfully displayed on the cover of the official program (see fig. 7.2; an image of the march banner follows in fig. 7.3).[94]

Getting to D.C. was fraught with infighting. Months after the march, some wondered whether the movement was successful in its "attempts to satisfy all factions." Titling their thoughts, "Destruction from Within," one group of writers felt that "the energy activists spend on destroying each other is mind-boggling" as leaders "call each other 'enemy' or 'traitor' because of minor differences that are magnified into battles of monumental proportions."[95] Although infighting was often painful, activists still generally perceived it as beneficial. As Derek Livingston argued, "For a year, we have debated the racial and gender composition of regional representatives; we have debated the platform; we have debated the March's name. These debates we have among ourselves are healthy and welcome; they are a testament to what a diverse, vibrant community we are."[96] The rank and file agreed, especially in the gay press's willingness to air the debates: "I have been glad to see the continuing debates in *Windy City Times* about . . . the March on Washington. *WCT* is filling

FIGURE 7.3. 1993 March Banner. Photo © 2004 Patsy Lynch.

one of the most important roles of the community newspaper by carrying this kind of discussion."[97]

Similar to the 1979 and 1987 marches, infighting in 1993 was connected to the same six organizing tasks: whether and when to march,
how to organize it, what to title it, what to include in its platform, and
who to invite to speak. Dissent over these tasks concretized cultural concerns of strategy and identity. By the third march, however, the conversation sounded different. This is exemplified, for instance, in how 1987 and
1993 organizers used the word *coalition*. In 1987, activists used it to self-
define as a social justice movement committed to eradicating interconnected oppressions, whereas in 1993, activists redefined themselves as a
mainstream movement in pursuit of equal rights.

Infighting revealed the gradual augmentation of identity. In the 1970s,
gay was the lowest common denominator and was assumed to reflect everyone's experiences. Feminists stretched the nomenclature to gay *and
lesbian,* which stayed in place through the second march. Activists once
again expanded the phrase during the third march to include bisexuals:
lesbian, gay, *and bi.* Although the bisexual challenge was successful, the
one posed by transgender activists was less so. That is, although transgender individuals were included in the platform, they were excluded
from the title, evincing limits to the plasticity of identity. Transactivists
would continue this identity work throughout the 1990s and, as I will
show in the next chapter, were finally successful (after failed attempts in
1979, 1987, and 1993) in the Millennium March.

Infighting also captured a movement strategically marching into the
mainstream, educating society that gays were like straights, and demanding equal rights. Invoking the spirit of Harvey Milk, one activist
expressed that Milk "would probably remind us of the incredible opportunity we have to show the whole world 'the truth about homosexuals,'
that we are basically like everyone else."[98] Chicago's gay press agreed:
"Straight America saw that most of their gay neighbors looked just like
themselves." An Alabama lesbian also said, "We must be visible. . . .
People don't want to be full of hatred. . . . They're just scared of what
they don't know. Once people realize that we're their neighbors, their
sisters, their brothers, their children, that will get rid of their fears and
things will be all right."[99] One week later, another news article reported
the same theme: "Straight America saw that most gay and lesbian people
look a lot like themselves, not the monsters that the right paints gays as."
The message filtered into the mainstream media as well. Noted Chicago's

Rick Garcia, "The media stories talked about the mainstreaming of the community and how the 'fringe elements' seemed out of place."[100] Several weeks later, the theme persisted, attesting to its tenacity: "One vision for the March is to put a face on gay America . . . a face that may be your brother, sister, friend, uncle, clergyman, doctor, soldier, co-worker, carpenter, senator, or teacher."[101]

This mainstream strategy clashed with persisting liberationist impulses. The early question of when to march, for example, was hotly debated as activists juggled competing progressive causes such as the March for the Survival of Indigenous Cultures to protest what some activists revealingly described as the "anniversary of colonialism and imperialism." The decision to work out the timing of one march around this other exemplifies sensitivity to a social justice self-definition established by 1987 organizers, an impulse that weighed in as more important than the potential (heretofore untested) value of organizing during an election cycle. Recall also how a left orientation explicitly wrestled its way into the title. This march was not just about equal rights but also about liberation, a sensibility activists additionally codified in the action preamble in their platform, along with the various supporting items that, despite fantastic resistance, were inescapably progressive amid an increasingly firm, mainstream grip.

Debates over the representation of people of color provide a vivid example of just how rarified was the space in between these two positions. Recall that activists fought to expand POC representation from 25 percent (used in 1987) to 50 percent (in 1993). Was this evidence of a social justice (left) or equality (center) orientation? Activists embraced a principle of parity that reflected both. It at once resonated with the special- versus equal-rights debate, externally in the sociopolitical context (thereby capturing inclinations toward the center), and the rise of POC organizations within the movement (which more readily expressed social justice overtones). As these and other examples chronicled in this chapter suggest, activists organized the 1993 march in a special historical moment when the "looney left" danced side by side with "the people next door." The expression of dissent, the media's willingness to provide a public forum, and openness norms in a participatory-democratic decision-making structure sustained, in a productive tension, these two impulses for a brief period of time.

CHAPTER EIGHT

Vertigo: Lesbian and Gay Life at the Dawn of the Millennium

"It has been said that the past, the present, and the future are all happening at the same time," reflected the editor of the *Advocate*. "It
isn't too difficult to understand that something we did yesterday is shaping our lives today—and therefore still going on today. . . . Clearly it's all
connected."[1] Although the Clinton years ushered in unprecedented feelings of hope, gay life during the time of the fourth march oddly resembled the late 1970s: the landscape was replete with anti-lesbian/gay laws;
Congress had not passed a comprehensive lesbian and gay civil rights
bill, nor was there a federal anti-discrimination statute in place; sodomy
remained a felony in many states; and societal attitudes were fraught
with stereotypes and moral judgments.

Veteran activist Robin Tyler recognized the past in the present, the
seeming illusion of movement, of vertigo: "We've got visibility. We've
developed a GLBT industry. But we don't have one basic thing that we
asked for in 1979. . . . We've got to go back to Washington."[2] The ambi-
tions of the cultural refrain, "We Are Everywhere," had been achieved.
Yet none of the Big Five—the demands from 1979—had been procured,
forcing lesbians and gay men to battle many of the same issues that gave
birth to their national movement, albeit with a contemporary twist. This
is the story of the Clinton years, when promise marched side-by-side
with pain in a present that reflected images from the past.

The lesbian and gay movement organized its fourth march—the Millennium March—on Sunday, April 30, 2000, immersed in an era distinct from, yet eerily redolent of, the past. Culturally, gay visibility developed along the trajectory established in the early 1990s. According to *US* magazine in 1995, there were fifteen recurring lesbian and gay characters on prime-time shows.[3] In 1997, there were reportedly twenty-two lesbian or gay characters on television, marking an almost 50 percent increase in a short two-year time span.[4] The 1990s were an explosive era for gay visibility. Lesbians and gay men—especially new gay celebrities—frequently appeared on the covers of prominent magazines such as *Time* and *Newsweek* and were regularly reported in the *New York Times,* the *Washington Post,* and other mainstream media outlets. As a point of departure, the late 1990s witnessed the emergence of a distinct gay marketing niche, consolidating gays as an economically distinct and potent subgroup. This otherwise positive development was met with an opposite: the rise of a new ex-gay movement characterized by the belief that lesbians and gay men could be "cured."

Politically, the late 1990s continued to be a battleground on local, state, and federal levels. Prominent issues included gays in the military, gay marriage, adoption, employment non-discrimination, and the fight to extend hate crimes legislation to cover sexual orientation. Apart from a handful of national measures, much of this confrontation was waged on the state level. This obsession with sexuality propelled internal development, with a notable rise of professional, bureaucratic organizations that claimed to represent the movement at a national level. Although this afforded some mobilization potential, it also created complications for activists who struggled to incorporate bisexual, transgender, gay youth, queer, and ally identities into an ever-expanding umbrella of sexuality.

Visibility prompted backlash, with the Religious Right continuing its special rights crusade and launching an outright holy war against gays. This fueled more attacks on gay people, with an increase in hate crimes and exponential military discharges. Fortunately, advances in medical technology alleviated some of the impact of AIDS, allowing activists to turn their attention to these matters. These four factors—movement consciousness (emergence of a marketing niche and celebrities); organizational development (rise of transgender organizing and the development of national, bureaucratic organizations); threat (discrete and diffuse, local and national); and political/cultural status (now mainstream center)—affected the organizing and infighting of the Millennium March.

Besides establishing the context within which the fourth march was organized, in this chapter I also seek to understand the positioning of the movement as firmly within the mainstream, despite continued legislative obstacles and setbacks. By the turn of the century, activists had shifted the calculus of their prior program of simultaneity (deemphasis *and* distinctiveness) from the third march decidedly in the direction of the mainstream. The long-standing quest to assimilate had oscillated over the years between distinction and difference. On the one hand, lesbians and gay men had sought to be treated like everyone else, to secure basic human or equal rights that all people deserved, to be the people next door, and to be considered a mainstream civil rights movement. This conservative/centrist impulse, on the other hand, regularly collided with a progressive/leftist one: We are *not* just like you. We are a distinct and organizable minority. We are furious with systematic federal neglect. And we want liberation for *our* people. Between the third and fourth marches, however, the mainstream impulse had acquired a centrifugal force that seemed unstoppable.

A Burst of Lavender-Green: Gay Culture and Consciousness

USA Today observed that in 1990, "ABC lost half its advertisers and $1,000,000 for an episode of *Thirtysomething* showing two men in bed. Just a few years ago, *Roseanne* was slammed for an on-screen lesbian kiss with Mariel Hemingway, and the Fox network got cold feet and cut a gay kiss from its *Melrose Place*. That was then. This is now."[5] *Entertainment Weekly*'s "Gay '90s" feature story proclaimed, "In 1995, the gay stream flows freely into the mainstream,"[6] while *USA Today* declared, "Gays and lesbians are moving from the media margins to the media mainstream at a fast and furious pace."[7]

Trends toward heightened visibility that defined the early 1990s continued unabated through the decade. For example, the hit television series *Friends* proudly displayed a loving lesbian wedding in which Candace Gingrich, the openly lesbian half-sister of then Speaker of the House Newt Gingrich, officiated as minister. Transvestite RuPaul found her way on *The Crew* as a guest flight attendant. On Father's Day in 1995, *CBS Evening News* covered a story about two gay men who were raising their two sons together. The sounds of gay artists k. d. lang, Boy George, Janis Ian, Melissa Etheridge, Indigo Girls, and George Michael flowed freely over the airways. The list was lengthy, prompting *Entertainment Weekly* to ask, "Is your TV set gay?"[8]

The mid- to late 1990s witnessed two developments that distinguished it from the earlier part of the decade: the public coming out of celebrities and exclusively gay television sitcoms and movies. The trend of straight actors playing gay parts continued as well, for example, with Tom Hanks and Antonio Banderas portraying a gay couple, with one partner infected with HIV, in the award-winning *Philadelphia* (1993). A less-mainstream, though still-widely-circulated, film starred Steven Weber and Michael T. Weiss as an amorous, serodiscordant couple in *Jeffrey* (1995). AIDS helped open America's squeaky closet doors. Jess Cagle of *Entertainment Weekly* commented, "It is, in fact, the AIDS epidemic that has exponentially increased the visibility of gays in the mass media." Cagle quoted playwright/screenwriter Paul Rudnick (*Addams Family Values, Jeffrey*) saying, "AIDS has given gay life a very serious subtext. . . . It makes it impossible to use gay characters as only comic relief."[9]

Some began to wonder whether "straight actors in drag" were "the gay equivalent of minstrel shows," an allusion to blackface minstrelsy that personified and blurred racial tendencies by transgressing the color line.[10] As if a corrective response, the mid- to late-1990s marked the rise of gay celebrities—those whose fame derived specifically from being openly gay. In wondering, "Can gay stars shine?" Dana Kennedy of *Entertainment Weekly* observed, "America's living rooms have begun to see a growing populace of TV actors who are gay or bisexual on screen and off—from *Roseanne*'s Sandra Bernhard to *My So-Called Life*'s Wilson Cruz and *Kids in the Hall* cast member–turned–*Larry Sanders Show* regular Scott Thompson."

Other standouts included: Amanda Bearse from *Married with Children* who made headlines in 1993 when she became the first primetime actress to publicly come out of the closet as a lesbian; singer and songwriter Melissa Etheridge, who came out to hundreds of guests at a January 1993 Triangle Ball in Washington, D.C., the first inaugural ball ever to be held in honor of gays and lesbians; singer and songwriter Elton John who made public his long-term relationship with David Furnish and revealing himself as strictly gay (and not bisexual, as he initially declared in an interview with *Rolling Stone* in 1976); singer and songwriter George Michael, who inadvertently came out as gay on April 7, 1998, after being arrested for having sex with another man in a public restroom in Beverly Hills; gay comedian Lea DeLaria, who generated quite a buzz

in 1993 when she became the first openly gay comedian to appear on national television; and last but not least, the rise to stardom of RuPaul (full
name RuPaul Andre Charles), a six-foot-five-inch tall African American
drag queen and singer who popularized drag with movie appearances
(e.g., Spike Lee's *Crooklyn* in 1993 and Beeban Kidron's *To Wong Foo,
Thanks for Everything, Julie Newmar* in 1996), music albums (e.g., *Su-
permodel of the World* in 1993 and *Foxy Lady* in 1996), and, from 1996
to 1998, a talk show called *The RuPaul Show* that aired six days a week
on VH1 and featured gay-celebrity and gay-friendly guests such as k. d.
lang, Eartha Kitt, and Dennis Rodman.[11] These developments pushed
gays deeper into the mainstream. For a group that had long struggled
with invisibility, there was enormous appeal to all this publicity, even if it
was of a particular kind.

Although other minority groups had been "deemed worthy to headline their own show," by the mid- to late 1990s, no gay character occupied
a similar position. That is, until Ellen DeGeneres's public coming out on
an episode of her own show, landing her as the first openly gay lead character on television. The Friday, April 30, 1997, fourth-season episode of
Ellen had then thirty-nine-year-old actress and comedian announce to
her friends, family, and therapist that she was a lesbian. Rumors of just
this possibility circulated for over half a year. One commentary noted,
"Though it seems strange in hindsight, the possible coming out of one
fictional TV character on a series with middling ratings was front-page
news intermittently from September 1996 to April 1997, bumping more
urgent stories to the insides of respected periodicals." DeGeneres's coming out gripped the national imagination because she was the first openly
gay star of a television series *and* because she herself was a lesbian. As
Alan Klein, communications director for the Gay and Lesbian Alliance
Against Defamation (GLAAD), observed, "If the character Ellen does
come out, it would be a milestone for network television because never
before has a lead character been out of the closet."[12] This was no straight
actor *playing* gay. This was a *real* gay person.

"The *Ellen* phenomenon," as it was notably dubbed, "was groundbreaking" and as an "event," "stands out, surely, as a defining moment in
the history of gay and lesbian cultural visibility." With its expansive news
coverage, DeGeneres's coming out on national television "rocked American culture, setting off pervasive public debates over homosexuality and
gay visibility. . . . The *Ellen* controversy became the news story that no
one could escape. It was everywhere." San Francisco–based freelance

writer Malindo Lo observed, "There are a few television events that will go down in history as watershed moments marking significant changes in American culture. In 1968, *Star Trek* aired television's first interracial kiss . . . one year after the Supreme Court ruled that barring interracial marriage was unconstitutional. . . . And in 1997, Ellen DeGeneres came out on her sitcom *Ellen* and in real life."[13]

Ellen paved the way for gay characters to inhabit lead roles, and since her, several other shows have featured coming-out storylines, including *All My Children, Buffy the Vampire Slayer, ER,* and *The O.C.* Then, in 1998, along came a new show that radically featured an always-out gay character. The 1998 NBC sitcom *Will & Grace* became a representation of a particular type of gay visibility. *Will & Grace* chronicled the lives of Will Truman, a gay lawyer (Eric McCormack, who is straight off screen), and his best straight friend Grace Adler (Debra Messing, also straight off screen). According to communication scholar Larry Gross, *Will & Grace* "combines familiar elements from TV's armory of sure-fire devices with a new twist. An 'odd couple' for the 1990s, Will and Grace are best friends who share an apartment, end each other's sentences, commiserate over their recently ended relationships with other people, and generally center their lives around each other. But they're not romantically involved."[14] What separates them is their sexual orientation. Will is gay. And Grace is straight.

Although *Will & Grace* was path-breaking, it remained stereotypical. Besides Grace, Will's other best mate is flamboyant and campy Jack McFarland, unabashedly effeminate and obsessed with money and consumption. Sociologist Suzanna Danuta Walters describes him as "the narcissistic, shallow, Cher-loving, boy-chasing, fashion-obsessed, showtune-singing Jack of *Will & Grace*—a sturdy stereotype if ever there was one." Neither Will nor Jack is connected to any gay community, however defined, nor do they ever have sex, despite Grace's regularly occurring sexual forays and eventual marriage. Will's asexual character, Walters asserts, functioned to make "gays safe for middle America through his resolute sameness and blandness, his asexuality, his ordinariness," while Jack's character serves the same purpose, though he is palatable "for middle America through his outrageousness, his snappy repartee."[15] Stereotypes aside, *Will & Grace* won twelve Emmys over its first seven seasons, testifying to the status gay people could occupy in American culture, contingent on their mainstream (and thus selective) appearances.

Gay visibility was not accompanied by proportional tolerance. A nationwide Gallup poll showed that "a significant minority still finds the prospect of gay stars distasteful," with attitudes varying according to age demographics. On average, 60 percent of young viewers (eighteen to twenty-nine-year-olds) expressed that they would not be offended by seeing a gay kiss on television, whereas 80 percent of those fifty and over said they would be "disgruntled" with such an image. Furthermore, one-third of everyone surveyed felt that there were "too many" homosexual characters and situations in today's movies. *Entertainment Weekly* concluded, "One thing is clear: The majority of Americans are *not* condemning this revolution. . . . The voices opposing this cultural shift are being drowned out."[16] Public opinion affected the viability of real-life gay people playing the gay parts depicted on the silver or television screen. Although Will and Jack of *Will & Grace* were gay on television, neither was gay in real life, perpetuating the overwhelming trend whereby "of all social groups, we [lesbians and gay men] are among the least permitted to speak for ourselves in public life, including the mass media."[17]

Gay cultural visibility also found its way onto the covers of prominent newsmagazines that featured stories such as: the battle for acceptance in schools, churches, marriage, and the workplace (*Newsweek,* March 20, 2000, headline: "Gay Today"); the rise of gay parenting (*Newsweek,* November 4, 1996, headline: "We're Having a Baby: Can Gay Families Gain Acceptance?"); and the public observation of the mainstreaming of gay people (*New York* magazine, September 30, 1996, headline: "When Did Gays Get So Straight? How Queer Culture Lost Its Edge"). Visibility prompted an expected anti-gay backlash, which also found its way onto magazine covers, including hate crimes (*Time,* October 26, 1998, headline: "The War Over Gays") and the mobilization of an ex-gay movement (*Newsweek,* August 17, 1998, headline: "Gay for Life? Going Straight: The Uproar Over Sexual 'Conversion'").

What prompted this cultural "revolution," in the words of *Entertainment Weekly* reporter Jess Cagle? Was it "a mission by Hollywood to (a) eradicate all forms of bigotry and homophobia, or (b) to destroy the values upon which society rests?" she asked. "Quite simply, gay sells. . . . It's no accident that advertising was at the vanguard of the gaying of America as the first business to realize that homosexuals comprised a very desirable demographic. Not the largest demographic, but one with powerful hands of disposable income."[18] Some have argued that "of all the representations circulating in the 1990s, perhaps none was more striking than the image of gay men and lesbians as the latest, the ultimate, the yet-untapped niche market." By 1993, *American Demographics, Wall Street Journal,* the *New York Times, Advertising Age,* and other mainstream publications featured news stories of a gay niche market.[19]

Going from movement to market is not unique to gays. As individuals coalesce around a shared stigma, they jell into an identity movement that seeks expansion of political rights. Increased visibility is a common method to seek legitimacy, which establishes these movements as "worthy of acceptance into mainstream U.S. culture," according to Alexandra Chasin. It is at these moments of enfranchisement that movement members are identified as potential market niches. Throughout the twentieth century, "political rights have been increasingly recast as economic liberties,"[20] says Chasin, as market forces facilitate assimilation into a seemingly desirable, homogenous national culture. It is here that we ironically see the operations of an identity-erasing impulse (in efforts to become mainstream, i.e., like everyone else).

Landmines: Lesbians and Gay Men in Politics

Gay visibility developed alongside almost daily political fights at the local, state, and national levels. By the end of the decade, this "battle for acceptance," noted *Newsweek* on its "Gay Today" cover story, had "moved to schools, churches, marriage, and the workforce."[21] Despite nationally prominent political events—such as attempts to pass an employment non-discrimination measure, the military issue, a Supreme Court case that put to rest the Religious Right's special rights crusade, and a national anti–gay marriage measure—the "center of gravity on gay issues," according to the NGLTF, "has shifted to state capitals across the country."[22]

Historian John D'Emilio agreed: "By the mid-1990s, state capitols had become the site of ongoing legislative debate on gay issues, but the measures that were introduced and passed were equally likely to be gay-friendly or gay-hostile."[23] In the last five years of the decade, there was an escalation in the number of pro- and anti-gay bills introduced in state legislatures. Pro-gay bills increased over 350 percent from 1996 to 2000, while anti-gay bills increased 110 percent, although not all passed into law. Pro-gay bills that passed into law increased by more than 450 percent, while anti-gay bills that passed increased by a smaller 8 percent. Figure 8.1 details legislative trends at the state level from 1995 to 2000.

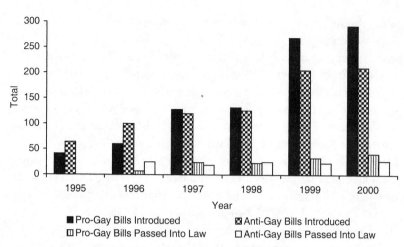

FIGURE 8.1. Pro- and Anti-Gay Bills Introduced and Passed across Fifty States, 1995–2000. Source: "Capital Gains and Losses: A State by State Review of Gay, Lesbian, Bisexual, Transgender, and HIV/AIDS-Related Legislation." National Gay and Lesbian Task Force. Information compiled from separate 1995–2000 reports. Data on bills passed into law not available for 1995. No information available for years preceding 1995.

The Employment Non-Discrimination Act (ENDA)

A handful of national measures seized Americans' attention and found their way onto the rally stage of the Millennium March. The first was the Employment Non-Discrimination Act, or ENDA, a bill that, if passed, would prohibit employment discrimination based on sexual orientation, making it a legally protected category. According to the *Advocate,* "Among the rights lesbians and gay men are fighting for—same-sex marriage, the ability to be out in the military, domestic partner benefits, and the outlawing of job discrimination—the last is clearly the most critical. Regardless of relationship status or level of patriotism, all gays need a livelihood."[24] Although a sweeping gay civil rights bill had been introduced in Congress every year since 1974, ENDA's scope was more modest.[25] It isolated the workplace as its battleground, whereas prior legislation attempted to encompass issues of housing, public accommodation, and others, as well.

Modeled after the Civil Rights Act of 1964, the bipartisan ENDA was first introduced on June 23, 1994, by Representative Chris Shays (R-Conn.) in the House (H.R. 3285) and Senator Edward M. Kennedy

(D-Mass.) in the Senate (S. 1705). While the 1964 Civil Rights Act protected against discrimination based on race, religion, color, national origin, and gender, it remained silent on sexual orientation.[26] President Clinton endorsed ENDA in October 1995, stating that if passed, the bill would ensure that "all Americans, regardless of their sexual orientation, can find and keep their jobs based on their ability to work and the quality of their work."[27] Other prominent figures also went on record in support of ENDA. Coretta Scott King declared, "I support the Employment Non-Discrimination Act because I believe that freedom and justice cannot be parceled out in pieces to suit political convenience. As my husband, Martin Luther King Jr., said, 'Injustice anywhere is a threat to justice everywhere.' Like Martin, I don't believe you can stand for freedom for one group of people and deny it to others."[28]

Several major opinion polls also revealed support for ENDA. A 1995 and 1996 *Newsweek* poll showed that 84 percent of respondents supported equal rights for lesbians and gay men in the workplace. A June 1996 ICR Survey Research Group (whose results are accurate within 3 percentage points, 19 out of 20 times) found an 85 percent support rate for employment non-discrimination. A separate June 1996 poll by the Associated Press found the exact same approval rating. Finally, an election time (November 5–8, 1996) survey conducted by Greenberg Research Inc. of 1,007 American Christians found that 70 percent believed lesbians and gay men were entitled to equal protection in the workplace.[29]

Despite its popular support, when ENDA first came to vote in 1996, the Senate fell short by one from passing it. Every year since then, ENDA has resurfaced in revised form, only to be defeated time after time, even with enduring popular support. A 1997 public opinion poll that asked whether an individual supported a federal law to "prevent job discrimination against gays and lesbians" showed that ENDA had 68 percent support nationally. A 1998 Princeton Survey Research Associates poll (with a 4 percent margin of error) found that 83 percent of Americans believed that lesbians and gay men deserved equal rights in their pursuit of employment. Winnie Stachelberg, then legislative director of the Human Rights Campaign (HRC), one of the largest national lesbian and gay civil rights groups in the U.S., argued, "Employment protections have really emerged as a mainstream, bipartisan issue." In September 1996, Matt Coles, then director of the Lesbian and Gay Rights Project of the American Civil Liberties Union, said, "We are on the verge of passing legislation that will finally ensure fairness for all American workers, regardless of sexual orientation."[30] Although its support continues to increase year after year, at the time of this writing, it has not yet passed. Currently, there is no federal law that protects against employment discrimination based on actual or perceived sexual orientation.

Similar measures have received more success in the states. By 2000, eleven states plus D.C. had enacted statutes prohibiting workplace discrimination based on sexual orientation: California (1992), Connecticut (1991), the District of Columbia (1977), Hawaii (1991), Massachusetts (1989), Minnesota (1993), Nevada (1999), New Hampshire (1997), New Jersey (1992), Rhode Island (1995), Vermont (1992), and Wisconsin (1982).[31] Because such discrimination had not been outlawed by the time of the Millennium March, the demonstration was flooded with HRC-sponsored signs that demanded: "End Workplace Discrimination."

Don't Ask, Don't Tell

The issue of gays in the military continued to make newspaper headlines through the decade, although with comparatively divided support. A Gallup poll showed that in 1992, 57 percent of Americans supported gays serving in the military.[32] Democratic candidate William Jefferson Clinton favored lifting entirely the ban against gay service members. Recall, however, that Clinton broke his promise to American gays by implementing instead the infamous compromise, "Don't Ask, Don't Tell" (DA, DT), a policy codified into law on November 30, 1993. Accordingly, the Pentagon would not ask soldiers and recruits whether they were gay, and those who self-identified would have to remain in the closet. If anyone dared to disclose, he or she risked almost certain discharge.

DA, DT passed despite numerous independent reports that found little to no evidence for its claims: four reports commissioned in 1957 by the Department of Defense found no evidence to support a gay ban; the Navy's 1957 Crittenden Report challenged claims that gays were a security risk; a 1988 and 1989 report by Personnel Security and Education Research Center found that gay and straight people performed equally well in the military and concluded that there was no empirical evidence to support a gay ban; and finally a 1994 Rand Corporation report commissioned by the Department of Defense found that gays in the military posed no threat to military readiness and concluded that there was no

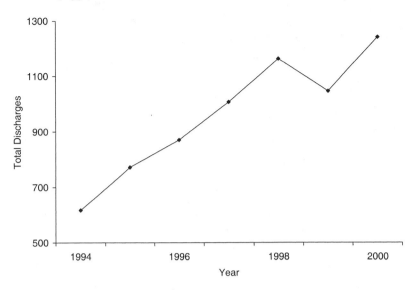

FIGURE 8.2. "Don't Ask, Don't Tell" Military Discharges, 1994–2000. Source: Department of Defense, United States Army, United States Air Force, United States Navy, United States Marine Corps, United States Coast Guard, Unofficial Congressional Sources, and the Servicemembers Legal Defense Network.

reasonable justification for continuing the ban on gay military service.[33] The military disregarded these reports, Congress shrugged them aside, and thus they played an inconsequential role during the hearings.[34] Because Clinton felt he was going to lose on lifting the ban, he deemed the DA, DT option a lesser of two evils.[35] Clinton intended the compromise to better serve gays than the previous blanket ban. This intention, however, was at odds with the subsequent realities of discharges (fig. 8.2).

Figure 8.2 reveals that in the years following codification of the policy (1993), the annual number of gay people discharged *rose* from 617 in 1994 to 1,241 in 2000, representing a 101 percent increase in policy-related discharges. Based on such figures, the Servicemembers Legal Defense Network, a national, nonprofit legal service, watchdog, and policy organization working to repeal DA, DT, released a study in February 1995 that framed DA, DT and its effects as amounting to "Ask, Pursue, and Harass."[36]

DA, DT was met with lawsuits. In 1989, Colonel Margarethe Cammermeyer from the Army National Guard came out as lesbian during a security-clearance interview. Three years later, she was discharged, despite a highly acclaimed military career. Her lesbian identity trumped her Bronze Star accolade for service in Vietnam. Cammermeyer became the highest-ranking officer to challenge the military's anti-gay policy.[37] She ultimately won a nationally scrutinized civil lawsuit, which allowed her to be reinstated to the Washington State National Guard as an openly lesbian officer. Cammermeyer's story—documented in a 1995 award-winning book, *Serving in Silence,* and in a similarly titled television movie in 2000—highlights another disturbing trend of the policy: its disproportionate impact on women.

Tori Osborn, then executive director of NGLTF, objected that the policy was "simply a repackaging of discrimination," while Tim McFeeley, then executive director of the Human Rights Campaign Fund (HRCF), dubbed it a "shattering disappointment." Even conservative writers felt wronged. Author and columnist Bruce Bawer lambasted the policy: "This compromise . . . would essentially write into law the institutions of the closet: while heterosexuals would continue to enjoy their right to lead private lives and to discuss those lives freely, gays would be allowed to remain in the armed forces only so long as they didn't mention their homosexuality to anyone or have relationships on or off base." Even President Clinton declared the policy a failure in his second term.[38]

The policy has also cost the very lives of military personnel in one hate crime after another. Twenty-two-year-old Allen Schindler was one such victim. Schindler was brutally beaten to death in a public restroom on October 27, 1992, by two of his navy shipmates (Apprentice Terry M. Helvey and Airman Apprentice Charles E. Vins) in Sasebo, Japan. Schindler became "a cause celebre and a symbol of hostility to gays and lesbians in the military."[39] Schindler's mother, Dorothy Hajdys-Holman, was able to identify her son only by the remains of the tattoos on his arms. The medical examiner likened Schindler's injuries "to those sustained by victims of a fatal airplane crash or a high-speed automobile accident—all but two of Schindler's ribs had been broken, his penis bore cut marks and his liver contained holes that allowed the pathologist to see straight through it."[40] Although the military tried to cover up the murder by attributing it to a "difference of opinion," horrid details leaked, and Helvy was sentenced to life in a military prison in Fort Leavenworth, Kansas. Vins was released after three months in confinement in exchange for his testimony describing the lurid details of the gay-bashing. Allen's mother Dorothy has since become a spokesperson against the DA, DT policy and was featured at both the 1993 and 2000 marches.

A *New Republic* editorial artfully captured the dizzying sense of vertigo animated within the pages of the DA, DT: "And the most demeaning assumption about the new provisions is that they single out the deepest moment of emotional intimacy—the private sexual act—as that which is most repugnant. Its assumption about the dignity and humanity of gay people, in and out of the military, in public and in private, is sickening."[41] The *New Republic* editorial is redolent of an image from the 1979 march that equated gay rights with the right to love (see fig. 3.2).

Romer v. Evans *(1996)*

The year 1996 began an epochal moment in gay politics, with two major events marking it as such. First, on May 20, 1996, the Supreme Court handed down *Romer v. Evans,* a 6–3 decision that overturned Colorado's Amendment 2, a statute that prohibited municipalities in the state from banning discrimination against gay people. *Romer* struck down Amendment 2 for violating the Constitution's Equal Protection Clause of the Fourteenth Amendment. In effect, *Romer* asserted that civil protections for gay people were not special rights, as the Religious Right had decreed. Instead, gay people were entitled to the same, equal protections enjoyed by every other American. In a scathing denunciation of Amendment 2, Justice Anthony M. Kennedy declared in the majority opinion, "Amendment 2 classifies homosexuals not to further a proper legislative end but to make them unequal to everyone else. This Colorado cannot do. A state cannot so deem a class of persons a stranger to its laws." An academic book, titled *Strangers to the Law,* that paid homage to Kennedy's words, remembered *Romer* for bringing a "cultural war to court" as it "attempt[ed] to sift through all that was known about gay people—from ancient history through the latest scientific research—to determine where and how gay people fit into the body politic."[42] The breakthrough case hit the front page of the *New York Times,* the *Washington Post,* and other national and local newspapers.

Amendment 2 was a vehicle for debating whether gays were asking for equal or special rights. Literature produced by Colorado for Family Values supporting the amendment declared, "Stop special class status for homosexuality." The text beneath read, "Special rights for homosexuals just isn't fair—especially to disadvantaged minorities in Colorado."

Romer "effectively halted the use of this strategy by the Religious Right."
As Justice Kennedy argued:

> We cannot accept the view that Amendment 2's prohibition on specific le-
> gal protections does no more than deprive homosexuals of special rights. To
> the contrary, the amendment imposes a special disability upon those persons
> alone. . . . We must conclude that Amendment 2 classifies homosexuals . . . to
> make them unequal to everyone else.[43]

The 1996 *Romer v. Evans* case settled once and for all the special
rights–equal rights debate. It reverberated across the country, impact-
ing a number of pending anti-gay cases in several states. *Romer* gave gay
people a glimmer of hope in their struggles for equality.[44]

Gay Marriage

The Defense of Marriage Act (5/96 H.R. 3396), or DOMA, was the second major legal event responsible for marking 1996 as a momentous
year in gay politics. On September 21, 1996, four months after *Romer,*
President Clinton signed into federal law (with overwhelming support)
the Republican-sponsored Defense of Marriage Act. DOMA, itself defensive, sought to define and protect the institution of marriage by en-
abling states to *not* honor a same-sex marriage legally performed in any
other state. The law circumvented Section One, Article Four of the U.S.
Constitution—the Full Faith and Credit Clause—which provides for continuity and enforcement across states. DOMA, in other words, allowed
states to disregard a same-sex marriage performed in another state. Although objections are accumulating of DOMA's potential incompatibil-
ity with the Constitution, at the time of this writing, the Supreme Court
has refused to hear any case challenging it.

DOMA defined *marriage* as "a legal union of one man and one
woman as husband and wife" and specified that *spouse* "refers only to a
person of the opposite sex who is a husband or a wife." Like the military,
DOMA was another instance in which Clinton let down the American
gays who helped to elect him. Clinton developed a reputation as a liar,
and so it was not uncommon to see Millennium marchers holding up parodic placards of a Pinocchio-esque president with a protracted nose.
This use of protest art to indicate disdain for a president has a marked
resemblance to 1987 marchers holding up signs of Reagan and "AIDS-

GATE." Again the lesbian and gay movement faced a sense of vertigo, wondering what progress it had made.

Same-sex marriage debates did not begin in the 1990s; some have traced their deliberations back to Plato's *Symposium*. In musing on the enigma of love and in particular the mysteries of his same-sex desires toward Aristophanes, Plato recites a parable on the origins of human beings. According to the myth, there were once three sexes: those with two male halves, those with two female halves, and those with one of each. The God Zeus punished humans for their misbehavior by cutting them in two. Since then, humans have been cast across the globe with the curse of wandering in search of their lost other half. This search manifests just as naturally in heterosexual pairs as it does in homosexual male and female pairs. Plato poeticizes, "And so, when a person meets the half that is his very own, whatever his orientation, whether it's to young men or not, then something wonderful happens: the two are struck from their senses by love, by a sense of belonging to one another, and by desire, and they don't want to be separated from one another, not even for a moment."[45] In Plato we hear early articulations for the right to love.

The American marriage battles erupted circa 1990 in Hawaii, before which, even if the idea was entertained, it was generally perceived as implausible. At that time, two lesbian couples and one gay male couple applied for a state marriage license. Like others, they were denied. Unlike others, however, they filed suit against the state for denying their civil rights. The three couples pursued the suit on their own, against the discouragement of the established lesbian and gay political organizations, who felt they were engaging in a losing battle that would hurt rather than help the movement. Three years later in May 1993, the supreme court of Hawaii decided *Baehr v. Lewin,* declaring that the denial of marriage licenses on the grounds of same-sex application violated the equal protection clause of the state's constitution that outlawed sex-based discrimination. In "the ruling that roiled America," Hawaii's supreme court established a legal precedent for the issue. The court decreed:

We hold that sex is a "suspect category" for purposes of equal protection. . . . It therefore follows, and we so hold, that (1) HRS § 572–1 is presumed to be unconstitutional . . . unless Lewin, as an agent of the State of Hawaii, can show that . . . the statute's sex-based classification is justified by compelling state interests. . . . Whether the legislation under review is wise or unwise is a matter with which we have nothing to do. . . . The only legitimate inquiry we can make is whether it is constitutional. . . . If the provisions of the Constitution be not upheld when they pinch as well as when they comfort, they may as well be abandoned.[46]

Baehr dictated that the State must show a compelling interest in prohibiting same-sex marriage. The case concluded that if the plaintiffs were opposite-sex couples, they would be allowed to marry. Sex, therefore, was "a suspect category." The Hawaii Supreme Court remanded the case back down to the trial court for the state to articulate its compelling interest. Although the decision was not definitive, it was the first time in American history that a court placed same- and opposite-sex couples on a potentially even legislative playing field.

Three years later in the fall of 1996, the remanded trial court heard *Baehr*. In constructing its compelling interest for limiting marriage to a union between one man and one woman, the state argued that gay marriage would facilitate greater instances of gay parenting and, given this, it had a viable interest in ensuring that children were raised in families that had one male and one female parent. Trial Judge Chang ruled that such arguments were unsatisfactory due to the fact that lesbians and gay men were fit as parents and that their children were developmentally on par with those reared in heterosexual families: "Children of gay and lesbian parents and same-sex couples tend to adjust and develop in a normal fashion. . . . In Hawaii, and elsewhere, same sex couples can, and do, have successful, loving, and committed relationships." Between 1993 and 1997, every session of the state legislature entertained new perspectives and potential responses to gay marriage, while local newspapers ran articles every week, cumulating in the hundreds over a short four years.[47]

Opponents increased organizing efforts in response to the remand. In 1997, the legislature introduced a constitutional amendment that defined marriage as the union of one man and one woman, which voters approved in the November 1998 elections. To overcome gender as a suspect category, the legislature enacted the Reciprocal Beneficiaries Act, a law that provided to same-sex couples many of the benefits conferred by marriage. Although full legal marriage in name for same-sex couples ultimately failed, the Reciprocal Beneficiaries Act was the first state law that allowed same-sex couples to legally register their relationships and obtain benefits. By 1993, gay marriage had replaced the military's DA, DT policy as the center of the gay political agenda and became the most visible gay issue in the national news media.[48]

The Hawaii case generated a political ripple effect: it formed the backbone of DOMA's support along with a flurry of similar state constitutional amendments. Speaking on behalf of the American Center for Law and Justice, Jay Alan Sekulow, the chief lawyer for the Religious Right, defended DOMA in a written testimony to the House Judiciary Committee on May 15, 1996: "A decision for the same-sex couples who are plaintiffs in *Baehr* will, very likely, have nationwide ramifications. . . . The threat that same-sex couples married in Hawaii will seek to have their marriages recognized in other states is real. . . . Some have predicted not a trickle of such Hawaii same-sex marriage junkets, but a flood. . . . The strategy to recognize same-sex marriage is nothing less than a strategy to discard the traditional idea of 'family' that has served to hold this society together."[49]

Sekulow hit the bull's-eye in predicting that *Baehr* would have national ramifications. Over the years, and in an attempt to deflect the case's imminent impact, over half the state legislatures enacted laws to prohibit same-sex marriage. In 1996, same-sex marriage cases "overshadowed all other gay-related legislative issues." Of the 32 measures that were ultimately signed into law, 18 (in 15 states)—or 56 percent—concerned marriage. A total of 25 anti-gay measures were signed into law, of which only 7 did not relate to the issue of same-sex marriage.[50] In 1997, state capitals witnessed 50 marriage bills that represented nearly a fifth of the 248 total bills tracked. The 46 unfavorable marriage bills represented a third of the 120 total unfavorable bills introduced and more than half of the bills that were actually signed into law (10 out of 19).[51] Given this quick trend, the NGLTF concluded, "Without question, same gender marriage occupied the center stage in the 1996 state legislative sessions. Last year, anti-gay forces chose one central issue to rally their troops around the country. That issue was marriage. . . . This campaign was organized in response to a Hawaii court decision."[52]

Inspired by *Baehr* and DOMA, another state battle began in Vermont on July 22, 1997, when two lesbian couples and one gay male couple brought a lawsuit to procure denied marriage licenses. On December 22, 1999—a fortuitous (for organizers) four months before the Millennium March—the Vermont Supreme Court released a unanimous decision on *Baker v. Vermont,* a landmark case that declared the state's marriage laws unconstitutional due to its violation of a two-hundred-year-old Common Benefits Clause of the Vermont Constitution that read, "Government is, or ought to be, instituted for the common benefit, protection and security of the people, nation, or community, and not for the particular emolument of any single man, family, or set of persons who are a part only of the community."[53] Like *Baehr,* Vermont also argued that the existing marriage statutes served the public interest by promoting "the link between procreation and child rearing." Gay families were again under fire.

At the hearings, the plaintiffs drew an analogy between gay marriage and antiquated miscegenation laws. Beth Robinson, who argued the case, noted a 1950s California Supreme Court ruling that struck down a ban on interracial marriages due to its unfounded claims of harm to children and parenting aptitude. After hearing arguments on both sides and in December 1999, the Vermont Supreme Court issued a unanimous decision that found the state's marriage statute unconstitutional. Writing for the majority, Chief Justice Jeffrey Amestoy uniformly rejected all arguments presented by the state, "May the State of Vermont exclude same-sex couples from the benefits and protections that its laws provide to opposite-sex married couples? . . . We hold that the State is constitutionally required to extend to same-sex couples the common benefits and protections that flow from marriage under Vermont law. Whether this ultimately takes the form of inclusion within the marriage laws themselves or a parallel 'domestic partnership' system or some equivalent statutory alternative, rests with the Legislature."[54]

In considering the link between marriage and child-rearing, the court observed that Vermont allowed same-sex couples the right to adopt children while denying them (and their children) the benefits of marriage. The court additionally recognized that not all opposite-sex couples desired children or were biologically able to procreate. "Therefore," observed Amestoy, "if the purpose of the statutory exclusion of same-sex couples is to 'further the link between procreation and child rearing,' it is significantly under-inclusive. The law extends the benefits and protections of marriage to many persons with no logical connection to the stated governmental goal." Amestoy concluded that arguments concerning the "stability" of same-sex relationships were too nebulous and speculative to merit serious consideration. And even if they were entertained, they could just as easily be applied to opposite-sex couples. In a rousing conclusion, the Vermont Supreme Court decreed, "The past provides many instances where the law refused to see a human being when it should have. . . . The extension of the Common Benefits Clause to acknowledge plaintiffs as Vermonters who seek nothing more, nothing less, than legal protection and security for their avowed commitment to an intimate and lasting human relationship is simply, when all is said and done, a recognition of our common humanity."

Despite this stirring conclusion, the court did not require the state to issue marriage licenses. Instead, it required the state to issue equivalent benefits to same-sex couples that marriage confers to male-female marital relationships. This, the court ruled, could be done by extending marriage to same-sex couples or by creating a "parallel domestic partnership system or some equivalent statutory alternative," to be done within "a reasonable period of time." The legislature reconvened immediately in January 2000 to consider a response. After a series of public meetings held by the House and Senate Judiciary Committees and attended by hundreds of state residents, the committee enacted "civil unions" that would be available exclusively to same-sex couples and that would confer every benefit and responsibility that came with a marriage contract. The bill passed by a narrow margin; Governor Howard Dean signed it into law on Thursday, April 27, 2000. It went into effect on July 1, 2000.[55]

Some scholars argue that the Vermont case "is about the power of the word." Governor Howard Dean has delivered many addresses in which he publicly stated that, "like anyone else," he was uncomfortable with the idea of gay marriage. He would, however, support domestic partnerships for gay couples. "What counts most," argues law professor David L. Chambers, "is the name." Evan Wolfson, a Lambda attorney, agreed, "One of the main protections that comes with marriage . . . is the word marriage, which brings clarity and security that is simply not replaceable by any other word or by a sheaf of documents." The reasons for the decoupling of the name from legal benefits remain unclear. What *is* clear is that *marriage* is a keyword that delineates cultural fault lines. Different groups (e.g., lawmakers, gay rights activists, the Religious Right, etc.) use it in tailored ways to promote or prohibit social change. It was not uncommon in the late 1990s to see activists frame civil unions as the gay equivalent of Jim Crow's separate but equal provisions. A Toronto equal marriage battle capitalized on this similarity in a print campaign that captivatingly asked, "Let two gay men marry? Next thing you know blacks will be drinking from the same fountains as whites."[56]

The marriage battles underscored that "families matter a great deal to LGBT people, as they do to society at large."[57] As the NGLTF noted, "While marriage took center stage in the 1996 state legislative battles, there were related family measures being considered as well: the right of gay people to parent; [and] regulations concerning adoption and foster care." The mainstream media also ran cover stories on gay relationships and families. *Newsweek,* for example, ran a feature in November 1996 depicting Grammy Award–winning singer Melissa Etheridge with her pregnant partner Julie Cypher that declared, "We're Having a Baby." The byline wondered, "Can Gay Families Gain Acceptance?" and "What's It Like for the Kids?" The Etheridge-Cypher story was part of a late-1990s national obsession with gay families.[58] As such, it was not surprising that Millennium March organizers mused over the possibility of "Faith and Family" as the march's theme. It was equally unsurprising to see marchers holding up grateful placards at the demonstration that read, "Thanks Vermont."

The fervor over same-sex marriage continued unabated through the decade. Gay political commentators and academics remain divided on its effect: as an issue, have same-sex marriage debates helped or hurt the movement? In a commentary revealingly titled, "The Marriage Fight Is Setting Us Back," historian John D'Emilio provides an unexpected yet observant response, "The battle to win marriage equality through the courts has done something that no other campaign or issue in our movement has done: it has created a vast body of *new* anti-gay law." Despite seeming progressive on the surface, D'Emilio concludes that "the campaign for same-sex marriage has been an unmitigated disaster. Never in the history of queerdom have we seen defeats of this magnitude."[59] The marriage debates, in other words, converge on a sensation of several dizzying steps forward and back.

Threat: The Holy War on Gays

The growth of gay visibility spawned an incensed backlash, the intensity of which compelled some to describe it as "the holy war on gays" that germinated "inside the war rooms of evangelical intolerance." The Religious Right conceded to launching the war. Focus on Family's *Citizen* magazine featured a cover that tagged 1990s as "the Civil War Decade." Writing for *Citizen,* Dr. James Dobson argued that, with the fall of the Soviet Empire, America's cold war was replaced by a culture war staged on three fronts: abortion, public education, and homosexuality. In a 1992 fund-raiser for Concerned Women for America, then president Beverly LaHaye agreed: "We are at war in America today. . . . We don't want our children taught that the sin of homosexuality is an acceptable life-style 'choice.' "[60] Thus, although *Romer* may have put to rest the cacoph-onous special-rights conversation, it did not prevent the Religious Right from continuing on with its unholy crusade. The battle redirected along three major fault lines: the Right proliferated anti-gay hate speech, aired a slanderous radio talk show that denounced homosexuality, and mobi-lized an ex-gay movement of people who claimed to have somehow been cured of their homosexuality.

Dr. Laura and the Ex-Gays

Lesbians and gay men encountered a new form of antipathy in the 1990s—hate speech—delivered en masse to American living rooms with the release of the syndicated *Dr. Laura Show*. Laura Schlessinger (Dr. Laura) considered her call-in show as radio therapy, characteriz-ing it as a "moral health program." She became a popular, conservative critic of practices she deemed over-prevalent in American culture: sex outside marriage, living together before marriage, single parenthood, women working outside the home, and same-sex marriage. In 1997, Dr. Laura began condemning lesbians and gay men, characterizing them as "abnormal," "aberrant," "deviant," "disordered," and "dysfunctional." On December 8, 1998, in one of her most inflammatory comments, she defined homosexuality as a "biological error": "I'm sorry—hear it one more time, perfectly clearly: if you're gay or a lesbian, it's a biological er-ror that inhibits you from relating normally to the opposite sex." To cor-rect this "error," Dr. Laura teamed up with the ultraconservative Family Research Council and advocated "reparative" or "conversion" therapy to help resume a "normal" life.[61]

Lesbians and gay men organized to get Dr. Laura off the air. They noted that she did not have a medical degree, that instead she had a Ph.D. in physiology (not psychology), thereby calling her credentials into question. A Stop Dr. Laura campaign assembled almost-daily demon-strations in major cities across the country and constructed a Web site (stopdrlaura.com) that claimed to receive more than 1.4 million hits. The *Advocate* noted, "StopDrLaura.com has become one of the most im-pressive weapons in the American lesbian and gay activism arsenal. Like a cyber machine gun, it has hit its targets with precision: the people and institutions involved in the creation and distribution of homophobic ra-dio talk-show host Laura Schlessinger's planned syndicated talk show for Paramount Television."[62] Gay activists generated a fulminating national dialogue that found its way onto nightly television news, major papers such as the *New York Times,* and critical commentaries in *The Nation,* which featured a story a couple of days before the Millennium March titled "Dr. Laura, Be Quiet!"[63] Dr. Laura issued a public apology, stating that she did not mean to "contribute . . . to an atmosphere of hate or intolerance," as reported by *Newsweek.*[64]

Dr. Laura contributed to a noxious national trend that pushed gay people to "convert" to a "normal" heterosexual lifestyle. This dialogue spawned the ex-gay movement, an international network that believed lesbians and gay men could convert to heterosexuality either through religion or what was known as reparative, or conversion, therapy.[65] The conversation gathered sufficient momentum for *Newsweek* to put it on its cover and ask: "Gay for Life? Going Straight: The Uproar Over Sexual 'Conversion.'" Reparative therapy included a combination of drugs, electroshock, and even testicular transplants to help (re)configure a heterosexual orientation. Social interventions included sexual abstinence (which consisted of refraining from fantasizing and masturbation), reforming one's gender disposition through activities such as participation in sports (for gay men), and heterosexual marriage. Although discussions of reparative therapy can be traced to the early 1980s, the dialogue gained momentum when the ex-gay movement consolidated into an institutional voice in 1992 with the founding of the National Association for Research and Therapy of Homosexuality (NARTH), an organization whose "primary goal is to make effective psychological therapy available to all homosexual men and women who seek change." NARTH's Web site further states, "We want to clarify that homosexuality is not 'inborn,' and that gays are not 'a people,' in the same sense that an ethnic group is 'a people.' . . . Most NARTH members consider homosexuality to represent a developmental disorder."[66]

Another influential ex-gay organization formed in 1998. The Parents and Friends of Ex-Gays and Gays (PFOX) provided services to the "ex-gay community and families touched by homosexuality."[67] PFOX's name deliberately alluded to a much earlier-formed (in 1972) pro-gay organization: the Parents, Families, and Friends of Lesbians and Gays, or PFLAG, a national, nonprofit, grassroots organization dedicated to promoting the health and well-being of LGBT individuals, their families, and their friends. In contrast to PFLAG, whose mission was to celebrate sexual and gender diversity, PFOX's objective was to suppress and condemn it.

The theocratic ex-gay movement germinated in a context in which both straights and gays were questioning the origins of sexuality. The familiar born-versus-bred debates had emerged in the late 1980s and become popularized by the early 1990s. In this manner, PFOX's Web site asserts that "no one is born gay." After *Romer* defused the special rights conversation, the Right successfully repackaged it to the viability of reparative therapy to cure homosexuality.[68] A 1998 Princeton Survey Research Associates poll found that 33 percent of the American population felt homosexuality was a genetic trait present at birth, not the result of environmental or social factors. In contrast, 75 percent of gay respondents felt their sexuality was genetically predetermined. The poll also found that an astonishing 56 percent of the overall population felt that gay men and lesbians were able to change their sexual orientation through therapy, will power, or religious intervention, whereas 11 percent of gay respondents felt similarly.

Newsweek cover story writers John LeLand and Mark Miller note that the ex-gay movement, along with the airing of anti-gay epithets on a nationally syndicated radio talk show, constituted a backlash whereby "straight America has reached some kind of tipping point, a limit to its tolerance for gays." Evidence for this included the rise in anti-gay hate crimes, the successful implementation of Don't Ask, Don't Tell, and preemptive outlawing of gay marriage via constitutional amendments. It therefore remained unclear the extent to which the lesbian and gay movement had disabused misconceptions about what it meant to be gay—especially given ex-gay voices that refuted the premise that lesbians and gay men even comprised "a people," in their words. In many respects, the ex-gay movement's labeling of homosexuality as a "biological error" and "developmental disorder" paralleled the pre-1973 American Psychiatric Association's stance on homosexuality as a mental illness. Kevin Jennings, then executive director of the Gay, Lesbian, Straight Education Network, mused on this overwhelming sense of vertigo that characterized gay life in the late 1990s: "This is the best of times and the worst of times for the gay community."

Hate Crimes

The national obsession over understanding who gay people were and what they wanted generated an anti-gay backlash that took a variety of forms. One particularly disturbing trend that characterized the late 1990s

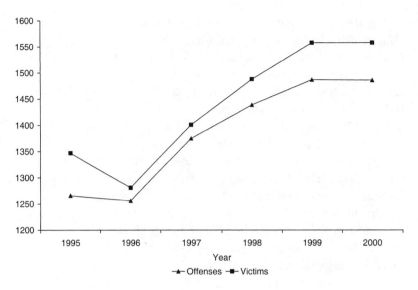

FIGURE 8.3. Anti-Gay Hate Crime Trends, 1995–2000. Source: Federal Bureau of Investigation (FBI).

entailed a spiking of anti-gay hate crimes, including murders. Throughout the 1990s, lesbians and gay men on the ground lived with the threat and realities that being perceived as gay or expressing any same-sex affection might put them at risk for being attacked. Figure 8.3 depicts anti-gay hate crime trends from 1995 to 2000.

The dramatic increase in anti-gay hate crimes, along with the development of a distinct anti-violence movement, inspired Representative John Conyers (D-Mich.) in 1988 to introduce the Hate Crimes Statistics Act, legislation that would require the Department of Justice to collect and publish annual statistics on crimes motivated by social bias. An impressive number of organizations showed support for the inclusion of sexual orientation, including the American Baptist Church, the NAACP, the AFL-CIO, the ACLU, and others. The bill passed both houses in the 101st Congress, when President George Bush signed it on April 23, 1990, as Public Law 101–275. The Hate Crimes Statistics Act of 1990 (later amended in 1994 and 1996) defined a hate-motivated attack as "a crime that manifests evidence of prejudice based on race, religion, sexual orientation, or ethnicity, including murder, non-negligent manslaughter, rape, assault, arson, and vandalism."[69] It was the first national law in the country that identified the needs and rights of lesbians and gay men in a favorable light.

The Hate Crimes Statistics Act compelled the federal government to track hate-related criminal activity. Similar statutes were non-uniformly in place at the state level, which the NGLTF described as the center of gravity for gay issues at the turn of the century. By April 2000, the month and year of the Millennium March, ten states did not have any hate crime laws, two states had laws that did not specify any target groups, and seventeen states had hate crime laws that did not include sexual orientation. Only eighteen states had laws that tracked crimes against lesbians and gay men.

The Millennium March galvanized support for hate crimes legislation by drawing attention to one particular murder. At around midnight on October 6, 1998, a frail, then twenty-one-year old University of Wyoming student, Matthew Shepard, left Fireside Lounge, a gay bar, with two other young men—twenty-two-year-old Aaron McKinney and twenty-one-year-old Russell Henderson—to a place a mile outside Laramie, Wyoming. Four months after that night, Americans watched in disbelief as the mainstream media uncovered what happened. The Albany County Court filing of first-degree murder, kidnapping, and aggravated robbery charges described what transpired after Matthew confessed to Aaron and Russell that he was gay: "After Mr. Shepard confided he was gay, the subjects deceived Mr. Shepard into leaving with them in their vehicle." According to a CNN report, during the drive, McKinney pulled out a revolver and told Shepard to hand over his wallet. When he refused, McKinney hit him with the gun. McKinney then instructed Henderson to drive to a remote area. Henderson pulled over in a secluded area just east of Laramie, at which point McKinney pulled Shepard out of the truck and brutally beat him with the .357 Magnum pistol butt. McKinney then pulled out a rope from the back of the truck and tied a bleeding Shepard to a nearby wooden fence post, after which he resumed pistol-whipping him. A tied-up Matthew was left to die in the near-freezing night temperatures.[70]

A cyclist, who nearly rode past Matthew, mistaking him for a scarecrow, found him the next morning at 6:22, eighteen hours after the initial attack. After taking him to the hospital and six days later at 12:53 AM on Monday, October 12, 1998, Matthew Shepard died, never having regained consciousness from the initial beatings. According to a CNN report, "Doctors said Shepard's skull was so badly fractured they couldn't operate; an autopsy showed he received eighteen severe blows to the head and bruises to his groin and inner thighs."[71] Russell Henderson pleaded guilty to the murder and was sentenced to two consecutive life terms without parole. Aaron McKinney was also found guilty and sentenced to two consecutive life terms without parole.[72]

Sheppard's murder was labeled a lynching to drive home the fact that "when push comes to shove . . . this is what we have in mind for gays."[73] *Vanity Fair* memorialized the gruesome incident as "The Crucifixion of Mathew Shepard."[74] Matthew's murder left activists disillusioned. The NGLTF commented on it impact: "Ironically, 1998's vicious and highly publicized murder of Wyoming college student Matthew Shepard did little to change the hearts and minds of Rocky Mountain lawmakers about the need for hate crime laws. Efforts to pass penalty enhancement laws [in 1999] in Idaho, New Mexico, and Wyoming all failed." The report noted that Wyoming actually introduced an *unfavorable* hate crimes legislation that *excluded* lesbians and gay men in their list of covered groups.[75] In an interview with *Time* magazine, then House minority leader Dick Gephardt agreed, "Matthew's death shows how much further we have to go."[76] Vertigo was exacerbated when, at Matthew's funeral, anti-gay zealot Fred Phelps and his supporters picketed with placards that read, "Matt in Hell," as reported by CNN.[77]

Matthew Shepard is one among thousands of similar such stories that narrate the torture and murder of men and women for being perceived as or actually being gay. The mainstream media featured these occurrences on covers that characterized the hysteria as the "War Over Gays" (*Time* magazine). Another prominently publicized horror story included the December 31, 1993, murder of twenty-one-year-old Brandon Teena (born Teena Brandon), a cross-dressing young woman who was raped, stabbed, and eventually shot to death by two men (John Lotter and Marvin Thomas Nissen) who discovered her discordant anatomical sex in Falls City, Nebraska. At the time of this writing, Lotter is on death row and Nissen is serving a life sentence without parole. Brandon's death was historically preserved in an award-winning independent film, *The Brandon Teena Story* (1998), which later inspired the critically acclaimed, Oscar-winning *Boys Don't Cry* (1999). Brandon's death also galvanized transactivism. These and other gruesome acts were featured at the Millennium March, as well, with demonstrators displaying signs that declared, "STOP HATE CRIMES."

AIDS, 1993–2000

Lesbians and gay men had to confront this backlash while continuing to manage HIV/AIDS. Much had changed between the third and fourth marches. For the first time diagnosis rates and new AIDS-related deaths decreased (see fig. 8.4). Despite the decline in deaths, the CDC announced in 1994 that AIDS was the leading killer of all Americans aged twenty-five to forty-four. AIDS remained the leading cause of death until 1996, at which point it became the leading cause of death specifically for African Americans within the same age group. In 1995, Olympic gold-medal diver Greg Louganis disclosed he was HIV-positive, prompting a public debate on the disclosure of HIV status.[78] In the same year, the media reported on the deaths of prominent figures such as Randy Shilts, author of *And the Band Played On* and *Conduct Unbecoming*, who died at the age of forty-two. Americans became more knowledgeable about HIV as a disease due to the advent of new medical technologies, public health campaigns, and cultural productions such as Tony Kushner's Tony Award– and Pulitzer Prize–winning play *Angels in America* (1993).

On December 6, 1995, the FDA approved saquinavir (Invirase), the first protease inhibitor (PI), a new, magic-bullet class of medications to treat HIV. This ushered in the era of highly active antiretroviral therapy (HAART), a treatment regimen that combined three or more drugs. HAART slowed the rate at which HIV multiplied, contributing to the decrease in deaths in the latter portion of the decade. The unprecedented success of PIs prompted *Newsweek* to run a feature story that asked the unthinkable: "The End of AIDS?"[79]

Prior to the first PI, treatment options were limited to a class of medications known as nucleoside reverse transcriptase inhibitors (NRTIs), including drugs such as AZT (released March 19, 1987), ddl (released October 9, 1991), ddc (released June 19, 1992), and d4t (released June 24, 1998). After saquinavir, other protease inhibitors were also released, including ritonavir (Norvir) (March 1, 1996); indinavir (Crixivan) (March 13, 1996); and nelfinavir (Viracept) (March 14, 1997). The medical breakthroughs continued through the late 1990s, with the discovery of a third class of medications, nonnucleoside reverse transcriptase inhibitors (NNRTIs). Within each class, the FDA approved new drugs every year, providing HIV-infected individuals unprecedented treatment options. Although newfound opportunities for health generated additional

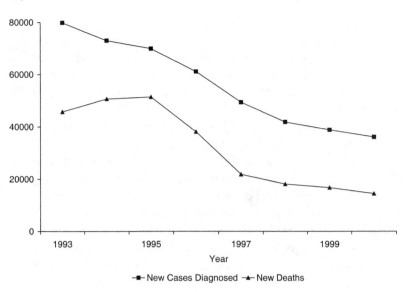

FIGURE 8.4. New AIDS Cases Diagnosed and New AIDS-Related Deaths, 1993–2000. Source: Centers for Disease Control and Prevention. *HIV/AIDS Surveillance Report,* 2001; 13(2):30.

challenges, they nonetheless allowed activists to augment their attention to other concerns.[80]

Of Rainbows and Bureaucracies: Internal Organizational Development

Heightened political and cultural visibility, along with the backlash it spawned, facilitated internal organizational development and advocacy. In this regard, the late 1990s witnessed contradictory currents. One the one hand, the diversification trends witnessed during the third march continued into the fourth. New constituencies (such as gay youth, same-sex parents, and straight allies) demanded and procured a place at the table. Self-identified queer, bisexual, and transgender individuals, in particular, gained considerable representational momentum. This diversification, however, developed alongside the bureaucratization of national organizations that exerted a homogenizing influence over the movement.

The Many Colors of the Rainbow

The late 1980s and early 1990s witnessed a multiplication of gay identities. Individuals that self-defined as queer, bisexual, and transgender experienced sizable organizational growth that continued throughout the 1990s, illuminating the many colors of the sexuality rainbow. Queer politics, in particular, "neutralized" as it became evident that it "offer[ed] a thin politics as it problematiz[ed] the very notion of a collective in whose name a movement act[ed]." Although *queer* provided a boisterous critique of identity politics, it did not offer an alternative that could be organizationally sustained. The effect, argues Elizabeth Armstrong, was "the domestication of queer politics," that is, the interchangeable use of *queer* to signify *lesbian* and/or *gay*. Not all identity movements, it seems, were destined to self-destruct; only those who, in their quest to blur identity, failed to provide an institutionally viable alternative.[81]

Similar to queers, "the challenge posed by bisexuality" was also "neutralized." Bisexuals achieved prominence within the movement, evidenced by their contingent in the second march and their representation in the title of the third. Bi activists successfully lobbied to have a speaker during the post-march rally, as well. This differing involvement across marches provides evidence of their gaining visibility and voice. Bisexual influence grew dramatically in the 1990s, with the consolidation of a distinct, international movement. By 2001, just one short year after the Millennium March, the *Bisexual Resource Guide* listed 352 bisexual and 2,134 bi-inclusive organizations in sixty-eight countries. This movement succeeded in pressuring many previously lesbian and gay organizations to change their names and mission statements to include the term *bisexual*.[82]

The transgender movement developed at a comparatively slower pace. As shown throughout this book, transactivists have always been met with confusion and resistance by lesbians and gay men, giving rise to an internal "politics of social erasure," in the words of transactivist Viviane Namaste. Like bisexuals, transgender influence was also neutralized, evidenced by the fact that, similar to the word *bisexual,* formerly lesbian and gay–titled organizations steadily made space for *transgender* in their names and mission statements. In 1997, the NGLTF became the first national lesbian and gay organization to amend its mission statement to include bisexual and transgendered people. Over the years, activists realized that "people who hate . . . do not distinguish among the categories of queers. . . . All transgenders, lesbians, gay men, and bisexuals are labeled *queer.*"[83] The monikers *LGB* and *LGBT* were increasingly standardized in organizational names and colloquial speech patterns, as well. This recognition helped usher full bisexual and transgender inclusion in the fourth march.

The transgender movement achieved significant attention in the late 1990s. New books provided a conceptual framework that was absent before (e.g., Leslie Feinberg's *Transgender Warriors: Making History from Joan of Arc to Dennis Rodman* [1996]; Ricki Anne Wilchins's *Read My Lips: Sexual Subversion and the End of Gender* [1997]; Pat Califia's *Sex Changes: The Politics of Transgenderism* [1997]; Vivane K. Namaste's *Invisible Lives: The Erasure of Transsexual and Transgender People* [2000]; Kate Bornstein's *Gender Outlaw: On Men, Women, and the Rest of Us* [1994] and also her popular *My Gender Workbook: How to Become a Real Man, a Real Woman, the Real You, Or Something Else Entirely* [2000]). Independent films (e.g., *Different For Girls* [1996]; *Ma Vie En Rose* [1997]; *The Brandon Teena Story* [1998]) and Hollywood films (e.g., *Boys Don't Cry* [1999]) appeared that sensitized mainstream, American audiences to transgender issues. Many cities and states incorporated anti-transgender bias in their local hate crime and anti-discrimination statutes. By February 2000, twenty-six localities had enacted a trans-protective law.[84] Powerful new organizations formed, such as GenderPAC, The Intersex Society of North America, and Transsexual Menace. Challenging courses appeared in American universities. The transgender movement, therefore, advanced by leaps and bounds in the seven years between the third and fourth marches. This may account for there being virtually no debate in including *transgenders* in the title of the fourth march. Indeed, near the banner that commenced the march, one could see a splattering of GenderPAC-sponsored signs that declared: "Gender Rights are Human Rights." Although there was still work to be done, transactivists finally secured their long-fought-for representation.

An Organizational Movement

Constituency diversification was met with an opposite force: the bureaucratizing and strengthening of national organizations, most of which exerted mainstreaming (read: homogenizing) pressures. Three organizations—which might be called the Big Three in lesbian and gay political

organizing—wielded the most influence: the United Fellowship of Metropolitan Community Churches (MCC), the National Gay and Lesbian
Task Force (NGLTF), and the Human Rights Campaign (HRC). According to historian John D'Emilio, "The fundamental way in which the
movement has changed over a long decade . . . is that it is so institutionalized now. . . . It's a different world. . . . Unaffiliated people—who are the
people that organized the other marches, and many of the people opposing this [the Millennium] march—find themselves out in the cold." Sociologist Joshua Gamson concurs, "The LGBT movement has shifted from
one of loosely affiliated activists to one of organizations." Organizations
are of course key to the survival of any political organizing, as they me-
diate between the rank and file and demands for change while providing
human, economic, and communication resources—"mobilizing structures," in other words.[85] Therefore, one way to assess changes in political
organizing is to assess changes in organizational composition.

The late 1990s witnessed a transition from "the role played by organizations" (in the first three marches) to "an organizational movement" (in
the fourth). This exacerbated internal dissent, especially a long-standing
divide between assimilationists fighting for insider political access and
liberationists fighting for cultural change and solidarity across movements. These and other debates centered on the role of national organizations and provided a vehicle for activists to wonder, "Who is even positioned to ask and answer questions about vision and strategy?"[86]

THE METROPOLITAN COMMUNITY CHURCHES   On Sunday, October 6,
1968—nine months before Stonewall, when homosexuality was still considered a mental illness—twelve people gathered in then twenty-seven-
year-old Reverend Troy Perry's living room in a small pink house in Hun-
tington Park, California, for the first worship service of what launched
an international religious movement of the Universal Fellowship of Metropolitan Community Churches (UFMCC, or just MCC). Perry titled
his first sermon, "Be True to You." Inspired by Polonius's advice to his
son Laertes from Shakespeare's *Hamlet,* Perry opened, "This above all:
To thine own self be true, And it must follow, as the night the day, Thou
canst not be false to any man." Perry moved to the Book of Job, followed
by the story of David and Goliath. The message was the same: "Be true
to you. . . . You have to believe in yourself as a human being first, and
then God is able to help you." Perry closed with the Epistle of St. Paul:
"I can do all things through Christ, which strengtheneth me!" In recall-

ing his first sermon years later, he fondly mused, "There wasn't a dry eye in the place. . . . After I finished preaching . . . one young man came up to me and said, 'Oh Troy, God was here this morning!' "[87] Realizing most people consider homosexuality and religion impossible bedfellows, the MCC sought a spiritually blessed marriage of the two. Perry's objective was to "ensure that religion will continue to play a significant role in the determination of LBGT identities in the future."[88]

The MCC played a major role in calling for and organizing the Millennium March. Indeed, the march was called in a top-down fashion over a lunch between Troy Perry of the MCC and Elizabeth Birch of the HRC (and unaffiliated Robin Tyler). This departure from prior marches confirms the influence exerted by national organizations to shape gay identity and strategy. The heavy hand played by a religious organization, in particular, testifies to the strength of mainstream sensibilities within the movement, codified in an early (and highly disputed) theme of "Faith and Family."[89]

THE NATIONAL GAY AND LESBIAN TASK FORCE   Each of the Big Three fulfilled a unique role in the movement. The MCC was the voice of religion. The second organization, the National Gay and Lesbian Task Force (NGLTF), filled a different niche: it was the oldest and most prominent national *grassroots* organization self-consciously dedicated to the movement's diversity—especially at the local levels. NGLTF was founded in October of 1973 (as the National Gay Task Force, or NGTF) as a joint effort of seven individuals from the Gay Activists Alliance in New York (Dr. Howard Brown, Martin Duberman, Barbara Gittings, Ron Gold, Frank Kameny, Nathalie Rockhill, and Bruce Voeller). In 1985, it renamed to the National Gay *and Lesbian* Task Force (the Task Force, for short) to signal commitment to gender parity and lesbian issues. D'Emilio suggests that "no account of the changes in the laws and public policies that shape gay and lesbian life in the United States would be complete without attention to the Task Force."[90]

NGLTF's competitive advantage was its focus on developing grassroots political strength through its annual Creating Change Conference, "the premier national organizing and skills building LGBT conference," in its own words.[91] NGLTF also established a policy institute in 1995— "the community's premier think tank"—which provided social science research, policy analysis, strategy development, and public education on LGBT issues. NGLTF's mission statement embraces the movement's di-

versity: "As part of a broader social justice movement, we work to create
a world that respects and makes visible the diversity of human expression and identity where all people may fully participate in society."[92] In
1997, the NGLTF amended its mission to include bisexual and transgender people, marking it as the only organization of the Big Three that included transgendered people in its mission statement.

Despite progressive overtones, the NGLTF did not recraft its name.
Organizational renaming would provide the symbolic architecture to assert that 1) bisexual and transgender experiences were distinct; 2) their
experiences were as universal and specific as those of lesbians and gay
men; 3) bisexual and transgender issues were of equal importance for
movement politics; 4) an organization could not claim to represent bisexuals and transgenders without including them in its name; and 5) organizations that claimed to represent bisexuals and transgenders had to have
them as members and leaders.[93] Because the late 1990s saw the growth of
an organizational movement with resource-rich centers in D.C., and because the NGLTF was committed to the local grassroots, it strongly resisted the fourth march.

THE HUMAN RIGHTS CAMPAIGN (FUND)   NGLTF's organizational niche
was fertilizing the grassroots rather than lobbying Congress. Another
organization of the Big Three, the Human Rights Campaign Fund
(HRCF), filled this void. The NGLTF and HRCF developed in opposition, with the culture and identity of one serving as a foil for the
other. As D'Emilio observed, "In the effort not to become, as the Human Rights Campaign appeared to be, a tool of an unreliable Democratic Party, NGLTF moved far in the other direction. It saw itself only
as oppositional, and it seemed to regard marginality and outsider status
as valuable."[94]

Founded seven years after the NGLTF on April 22, 1980, by Steve
Endean, the Human Rights Campaign Fund raised money for gay-
supportive congressional candidates. Over the years, it became the largest national gay advocacy organization that provided financial support
for pro-gay candidates. This mission soon expanded to lobbying congressional representatives and disseminating educational materials to
sway public opinion. The organization symbolically marked the expansion of its mission statement on August 7, 1995, by dropping the word
Fund from its name, making them the Human Rights Campaign (HRC).
HRC launched a new Web site, a flashy magazine, and engineered a slick

logo consisting of a block yellow equal sign against a dramatic, navy blue background. The symbol of the equal sign was simple and bold—prerequisites for any memorable logo—and littered the Millennium March. On April 30, 2000, the lambent logo was everywhere on the most political patch of grass in the country.

The HRC has had a conflicted relationship with the movement for a long time. Through the late 1990s, transgender activists criticized them for refusing to support trans inclusion in ENDA. This critique was symbolic of a larger image the rank and file had developed of the organization: to many, it seemed to exclusively represent the interests of middle- to upper-middle-class, white gay Americans, motivating some to resignify the organization's acronym of "HRC" to "Headed by Rich Caucasians," or, in the earlier days when it was "HRCF," to "Human Rights Champagne Fund."[95] The HRC recognized these complaints and posted on its Web site, less than a year *after* the Millennium March, a document titled "Focus on Diversity: The Human Rights Campaign's Work with Communities of Color." Underneath its name, the organization states, "Working for lesbian, gay, bisexual, and transgender equal rights."

Grassroots activists also criticized the HRC for its national structure, especially in light of the local- and state-saturated political center of gravity in the 1990s. This critique increased in volume on October 20, 1998, when the HRC endorsed and donated $5,000 to New York Republican Senator Al D'Amato, the incumbent, over Chuck Schumer, a Brooklyn-based congressman with a progressive record who had supported gay rights for years prior to D'Amato. According to then executive director Elizabeth Birch, "These are troubled times and our community has endured unprecedented attacks from both religious political groups and the Republican leadership. Senator Alfonse D'Amato has stood up to and challenged this ignorance and prejudice, and championed many of our issues. We hope this endorsement tells Republican candidates that if they oppose the bigotry of extremism and the ignorance of their leadership, they can look to us for support. We will not turn from them on partisan grounds."[96]

HRC's decision caused a "firestorm"[97] from which the organization arguably never recovered, including one board member who resigned and hundreds of former members who cancelled their memberships. Within minutes of the endorsement, "gay New York began buzzing with a fury."[98] A *Nation* article titled "Rebuilding the Gay Movement" suggested that this "appalling decision" to endorse D'Amato "crystallized for many gay activists around the country the disconnect they feel with national, Washington-based organizations operating on a top-down and elitist corporate model. . . . Those close-to-the-ground organizers rightly argue that the lion's share of gay resources should go into creating political and electoral power at the state and local level."[99]

Local activists agreed. HRC was repeatedly lambasted at NGLTF's November 1998 Creating Change Conference in Pittsburgh. In one plenary panel titled, "What Is This Movement Doing to My Politics?" activists used "the D'Amato Factor" to vent frustrations of participating in progressive politics in a movement that was becoming "mainstream," "corporatized," and "marketed."[100] New York activists were particularly incensed. "This is an awful decision that destroys all of HRC's credibility," noted Stephen Gendin, a longtime local AIDS activist. Bill Dobbs, who would go on to lead resistance efforts against the Millennium March, concurred: "At some point . . . people will throw their hands up and take these organizations back. I'm elated there's a big backlash."[101] In the end, the powerful gay voting bloc spoke at the polls: on election day, Schumer defeated Republican incumbent D'Amato 55 percent to 45 percent. Activists argued that this reversal was due to a "boomerang effect," in which lesbians and gay men mobilized to vote *against* HRC's endorsement. The voter turnout was a result of people feeling "intense anger generated by the D'Amato endorsement," in the words of Matthew Foreman, then executive director of Empire State Pride Agenda in New York.[102]

Vertigo: The Metamorphosis of the "Gay Moment"

The Gay '90s were the best of times and the worst of times. Although the "gay moment" had arrived for the people next door, the vagaries of gay life evolved firmly toward a mainstream project in the seven years between the third and fourth marches. The delicate balance between assimilation and liberation established during the 1993 march proved unsustainable. This was evidenced by the strengthening of normative media trends from the earlier part of the decade, by the rise of gay celebrities, and by the development of a gay market niche. Political developments in the mid- to late 1990s emphasized a conservative and nationally debated agenda over gay marriage, gay families (and adoption), gay spirituality, employment non-discrimination, and military service (at the expense of pressing for sexual freedom, universal health care, or the abolition of racism and sexism, for instance). The mainstreaming project manifested internally, as well, with the rise of professional and powerful social movement organizations such as the Big Three, which, as we will see in the next chapter, played a heavy hand in the Millennium March.

In September 1996, *New York* magazine ran a cover story revealingly titled, "When Did Gays Get So Straight? How Queer Culture Lost Its Edge."[103] Writer Daniel Mendelsohn observed that as the movement had "matured" over the past twenty-five years since Stonewall, its substance and style "are increasingly hard to differentiate from those of the straight mainstream." Once upon a time, gay politics had an edge and radically enforced the right to have sex in public places, bath houses, and sex clubs, and the morality of outing as a strategy. ACT UP made use of dramatic, theater-as-protest tactics such as disrupting Easter service at St. Patrick's cathedral. At the dawn of the new millennium, gay politics focused on family issues such as marriage and adoption, inclusion in the armed forces, and employment non-discrimination. This calculus favored a strategy of "treat us like everybody else." Mendelsohn, like many other commentators, activists, and everyday people, could not help but experience a dizzying sensation: how did all this visibility happen, what does it mean, and for whom?

Mendelsohn defined this "dramatic cultural assimilation" as the "heterosexualization of gay culture," a phenomenon that implicates trends in gay strategy (our values and visions for social change) and identity (who we think we are). Some have called this mainstreaming millennial movement *embourgeoisement,* or the acceptance over time of mainstream, cultural norms by those who were once revolutionaries. Embourgeoisement is no fiction; it is a nomenclature that, for example, captures the emergence of a gay market niche in the late 1990s. Hence book titles such Alexandra Chasin's *Selling Out: The Gay and Lesbian Movement Goes to Market.*

Mendelsohn is not at a loss for synonyms for the heterosexualization of gay culture. It is an artifact of the historical shift from the "gay outside" to the "institutional inside," or the transition from the periphery (1979 and 1987 marches), to the mainstream margins (1993 march), and now to the mainstream center (2000 march). Gay politics lost its edge and became "indistinguishable from the mainstream" as it was "pasteurized into total consumer-culture irrelevance." One cannot help but wonder, "Is gay identity . . . much more than a set of product choices?" Mendelsohn may not reply, but he does make a counterintuitive observation: having moved from the "exoticized gay margin to the normalized straight center" is an artifact of acceptance (read: assimilation). In the late 1990s, gay culture suffered "a classic assimilationist ailment (c.f., Jews): You can't take away what was most difficult about being gay without losing what made gay culture interesting in the first place. . . . You realize that, at least culturally speaking, oppression may have been the best thing that could have happened to gay culture. Without it, we're nothing." In Mendelsohn's analysis, "a gay cultural ethos made sense only when gays were 'chained to the gates.'" Conflict can certainly be generative. Here we see what happens in its absence: oppression's unexpected twist.

Pundits asked similar questions: Where should the movement go? What do we want? Who are we? And who have we become over the years? These questions of strategy and identity implicate a long-standing struggle to achieve what Urvashi Vaid describes as the "dream of a common movement," a struggle replete with infighting. In her provocatively titled book *Virtual Equality: The Mainstreaming of Gay and Lesbian Liberation,* Vaid suggests that despite, or perhaps because of, the impressive gains made by the movement, gay people find themselves at a Dickensian juncture, that is, the best and worst of times. Gays remain second-class citizens who have achieved little more than what she calls "virtual equality," that is, a state of conditional and simulated equality based more on the appearance of acceptance by straight America than actual civil equality. While there has been progress "over the profound denial and silence that surrounded gay and lesbian existence before the modern gay rights movement evolved," questions beg to be answered about whether the ultimate goal for the movement is some illusory mainstream status or whether this represents a marker to be passed along "a longer road to fuller human dignity and freedom."[104] Is the mainstream a road stop or final destination?

The pursuit of equality, like the proverbial dangling carrot, is virtual for Vaid, an apparition of equality that pushes the movement down the mainstream. This can throw the movement off balance and propagate a sense of vertigo since gays are still "at once marginal and mainstream, at once assimilated and irreconcilably queer."[105] Although Vaid's assertions "ring with conscience and common sense," in the words of Armistead Maupin, she may mistakenly suggest that activists need to transcend internal divisions altogether. "In order to move beyond the current stalemate," Says Vaid, the movement needs "to wake up and face the forces that divide it and to consider what gays and lesbians stand for, as individuals and as a people."[106] But infighting does not always present a divisive impasse. Activists can capitalize on it to carry and concretize their self-conceptions of what they stand for and who they think they are. They can paradoxically, though powerfully, actually make use of infighting to bring into focus the "dream of a common movement."

"The Event in 2000": The Millennium March on Washington for (Lesbian, Gay, Bisexual, and Transgender) Equality

Staged on April 30, 2000, the Millennium March on Washington for Equality (MMOW) was the fourth national event that "addressed the unfinished agenda of the gay rights movement," noted the *New York Times*.[1] Although in some ways it was "your standard, good old-fashioned mass march on Washington," in the words of sociologist Joshua Gamson, in many respects, it was the first of its kind: "It's the first gay and lesbian march dot-com, organized more through Web sites and advertising than grassroots mobilization. It's the first called by a handful of people from two national organizations, who then invited everyone else to come along. It's also the first in which bisexual and transgender people have been included as a matter of course, the first in which around half of those running things are people of color and also the first that many people-of-color, bisexual, and transgender groups have consistently and angrily refused to endorse."[2] The most revealing first was the high level of opposition it spawned. This was not championed by anti-gay forces, as one might expect, but from within gay activist ranks themselves. Political cartoons flourished that depicted the fourth march as fraught with infighting (see fig. 9.1).

The mainstream press also noticed. The *Washington Post* published "March Shows Gays Taking Different Roads" in which it observed, "When hundreds of thousands of gay men and lesbians marched on

FIGURE 9.1. The Centrality of Infighting in the Millennium March. Cartoon by Ron Williams, © Rich Williams.

Washington seven years ago, they worried that conservative, anti-gay groups would disrupt the gathering. This time around, the bitterest fighting is among gay rights leaders [themselves]."[3] In "Millennium March: Gay Rally Bares Deep Divisions," the *San Francisco Chronicle* noted, "It is hardly surprising that there is opposition to tomorrow's rally by gays and lesbians. . . . What is astonishing is that the most vocal critics of 'The Millennium March' come from within the gay community itself."[4] The *New York Times* chimed in: "Rather than unite and galvanize the gay, lesbian, bisexual, and transgender community, the march's organizers . . . have created divisions."[5]

Infighting has been part and parcel of every Washington march the movement organized. It seemed inevitable as activists hashed out what they wanted, how to best secure that which they wanted, who they thought they were, and how different contenders were connected as part of the same movement. But there was something different about this fourth event. Of all the marches, this last one (and, to a lesser but notable extent, the first one, as well) provides caution for not overstating the dividends of dissent. Like the prior three, Millennium March debates gave voice to competing meanings of gay strategy and identity. Unlike the others, however, we now see more clearly the circumstances under which infighting, despite this positive rhetorical outcome, may still lead to a defection of sorts. I say "of sorts" because what was new, as Gamson alluded to earlier, was the development of an organized boycott—by gay people—of a national protest event that purported to be in the name of those very same people. This allows us to expand our question from the earlier "what role does infighting play in political organizing?" to now also consider, "under what conditions might dissent escalate into an organizational splinter?" Sometimes infighting can indeed snowball to less-than-desirable outcomes. Infighting was responsible for dissolving the earliest organizing committees from the 1979 march as much as it contributed to the formation of a factional boycott against the event in 2000. We can now more carefully consider the conditions under which different outcomes result.

The MMOW was embroiled in controversy since its inception in 1998 when the Human Rights Campaign (HRC), a political lobbying organization, and the Universal Fellowship of Metropolitan Community Churches (MCC), a gay and lesbian–focused group of churches, announced top-down plans to hold the march without input from state organizations—a departure from how the prior marches were organized and at odds with the political center of gravity at the time. Organizers Elizabeth Birch, then–executive director of HRC and Troy Perry of the MCC boldly asserted, "The priorities of our community have changed dramatically [toward the pursuit of] stability in our relationships . . . the desire to legally marry, [and the return to] the churches of our youth."[6] This position had *mainstream* written all over it.

The announcement "set off a controversy of biblical proportions."[7] Immediately after Birch and Perry put out the call, a flurry of vituperative e-mails, letters to the editor, op-ed pieces, and public statements screamed in the gay and mainstream presses. Within a few short months, an official opposition group formed, the Ad Hoc Committee for an Open Process (AHC), that charged Millennium organizers of being anti-democratic, elitist, financially unaccountable, racist, sectarian, conservative, and hypernormative.[8] In several press releases issued one month before the march, the AHC urged that fellow gays and lesbians "should sit this one out," rhetorically asking, "Who shall speak for us?"[9] AHC member Bill Dobbs, in an interview with the *New York Times,* confirmed that the rift was about "who speaks for the movement and how decisions are made."[10] Dobbs flagged attention to critical questions of identity and strategy.

An unprecedented volume of state press releases—from San Francisco to D.C.—attacked the march and urged gays at the local level to "put the march on hold,"[11] if not flatly "boycott the Millennium March."[12] Editorials imploring "don't go to the march"[13] and invidious remarks proclaiming that the movement was "marching to nowhere"[14] were commonplace. Mocking titles such as "Millennium March Madness,"[15] "What march?"[16] and "Millennium What?"[17] took position along the indigenous battle lines. Even organizers of past marches joined the boycott to ask in the *Washington Post,* "Why are we marching?"[18] Commentators rightfully observed that "the march has sharply divided the U.S. gay movement."[19]

The National Association of Black and White Men Together (NABWMT) voted unanimously to *not* endorse the march when it became apparent that people of color had not been part of the planning leading up to the march, even though they were eventually represented on the "board of directors," the march's self-named organizing committee. A Chicago letter signed by several prominent local organizations argued that "participation in this march uncritically replicates and propagates the racism, elitism, and consumerism that need to be confronted if we are to achieve the justice our movement seeks. We urge our fellow LGBT brothers and sisters to sit this march out."[20] "The main story the march opposition wants to tell," observes Gamson, is "of a movement dominated by arrogant, corporate style, money-driven organizations geared toward assimilation through the marketing of acceptable gayness," that is, "the . . . marketing of a particular kind of gayness."[21]

Infighters focused on the elitist decision to hold a march without community input. Birch said in hindsight that issuing the call was "a colossal error in judgment"—an error, that is, to articulate on behalf of "the community" of "what it means to be gay in this nation at the turn of the century."[22] Birch's comment highlights the consequences of ignoring the cultural template established by the prior marches. Each was grassroots in nature and assembled using a participatory-democratic decision-making structure executed at large national conferences open to the public and press. The fourth event, in contrast, was top-down and was inspired by a corporate model with a board of directors as its primary decision-making body. The board often met behind closed doors that were not open to the public or press.

The self-named "Boycott the MMOW Coalition" echoed implications of this organizing process: "The MMOW erases most of us. It erases us in its political foundation. It erases us in its practice. It erases us in its weak rhetoric about 'equality.'"[23] In an *Advocate* commentary titled "Cease Fire!" Richard Goldstein defined this moment as gay people's own culture war:

> We are gay in many different ways, but we are all subject to homophobia, and we have always depended on the hatred of strangers to keep us together. So it's no surprise that our battles with each other reflect the structure of our oppression.
>
> But this latest ruckus [surrounding the MMOW] is part of a larger culture war raging in our community. Like the culture war in American society, this conflict is ultimately about control. Behind the sound and fury lies a perennial question: Who owns gay liberation?[24]

Through their Washington marches, gay people had established a tradition of using dissent to help them understand who they thought they were and what they thought they wanted, and so infighting in the MMOW was neither new nor surprising. There was, nonetheless, something different this fourth time. The MMOW broke stride from the beginning when Robin Tyler, Elizabeth Birch, and Troy Perry arranged a private meeting in a hotel room where they decided a fourth march was a good idea. From there, the MMOW morphed into something that hardly resembled its predecessors. Three days before the event, the *Windy City Times* ran an opinion piece written by Billy Hileman, one of the national cochairs from 1993. Titled "Top 5 Reasons to Skip MMOW," Hileman boldly declared, "The Millennium March on Washington is not the fourth national mobilization for the rights of lesbian, gay, bisexual, and transgender people. It was not called by our community. It is not accountable to our community. It is obligated to corporations, not to individuals. It does not represent our community. . . . History should not record the MMOW in the same vein as the 1979, 1987, and 1993 MOWs."[25]

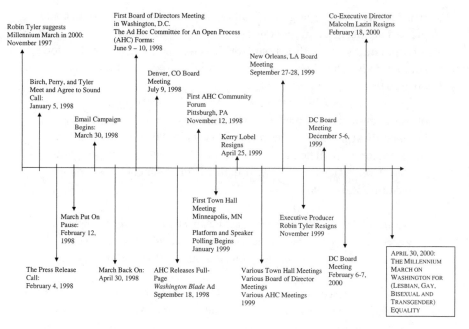

FIGURE 9.2. An Organizational Timeline of the Millennium March.

Years later, Hileman dubbed the MMOW the "event in 2000," an "imitation" that was distinct from the first three "real" marches:

> The first three were the real deal. This last one was an imitation. . . . There are only three marches. . . . That executive committee of that event in 2000 . . . did not know how the marches were organized. . . . [The MMOW] was a way to put on a show and call it a march. . . . You're not going to quote me calling it a march. . . . Nobody will ever quote me saying the 2000 event was a march. It wasn't. . . . It was a party by HRC which made them a lot of money. . . . It's not the same event; it's not the same thing.[26]

Hileman's insistence on not calling it a march is due to the many ways it abandoned the cultural template sketched by prior activists in consultation with their community (see fig. 9.2).

Absent in figure 9.2 are the national conferences that were the staple of prior marches, replaced instead by board of directors meetings that were generally closed to the press, asphyxiating the sharing of information that was customary in the past. The timeline is littered with other anomalies, such as putting the march on hold and then turning it back on, several resignations, and the "Ad Hoc Committee for an Open Process," a formal organization of past march leaders who boycotted the Millennium March, exposing an intensity of infighting never before seen.

Whether and When to March

The most explosive debates during the MMOW concerned the formative questions of whether and when to march. In dissenting over whether to march, activists aired concerns about the direction in which LGBT political organizing was and should be headed. Millennium March organizers, however, deliberately departed from the cultural template to pacify the infighting they perceived as problematic in the past. The case of the MMOW reveals that either circumventing or, worse, muting dissent only inflames it by eliminating the forum in which activists converged around shared ideologies of political organizing.

The family feud began in November 1997 at NGLTF's Creating Change Conference in San Diego. The Millennium March was the brainchild of Robin Tyler, who had also been involved with organizing the past three marches—but who wanted to do it differently this time:

> I'm sitting there thinking, "You know what? We don't have one civil right. It's the year 2000. It's gonna be twenty-five years or twenty-two years since the first march on Washington. . . . What the hell are we doing? We've gotta go back. What are we waiting for?" . . . But I didn't want to do it the same way. I didn't want the same fifty people meeting in every city . . . and voting on four people that had not had any experience whatsoever [in the 1993 march]. So I said, "No. This time, I'm going to go to [the Creating Change conference]."[27]

At six o'clock one morning of the conference, Tyler called her friend Nicole Ramirez-Murray, another veteran activist, and asked him to come to her room. Tyler recalled, "I said 'Nicole, we have to go back to Washington. We have to march on Washington again. We have to go back to Washington.' He said, 'You're right.' I said, 'Okay, I'm gonna try to organize it here.'" Throughout the weekend, Tyler approached other activists to test the waters. Informal conversations suggested that some loved the idea, while others were reticent. Urvashi Vaid (who initiated conversation around the 1993 march) and Kerry Lobel (then executive director

of the NGLTF), in particular, resisted, noting that the NGLTF was organizing fifty state marches in 1999 in an event called Equality Begins at
Home. Ramirez-Murray encouraged Tyler to proceed, anyway, recom-
mending the year 2000 to prevent conflict with NGLTF's event in 1999.
By the end of the month, Tyler had officially registered the name "Millennium March on Washington" to prevent the Religious Right from securing it, given its inescapably theist connections.[28] Tyler was motivated
by an impression that the word *millennium* was sexy and competitive
and that gay people ought to be the first to stage a Washington march in
the new century.

On December 7, 1997, Tyler called her old friend Reverend Troy
Perry and Elizabeth Birch, whom she had not met prior, to talk over the
idea. Both loved it: "I called up Elizabeth Birch. I said, 'It's Robin Tyler; we don't know each other.' She said, 'Hi, Robin, I've heard of you.'
I said, 'Elizabeth, how many rights do we have?' And she said, 'None.'
I said, 'Well, then we need a march on Washington.' She said, 'You're
right; we need to march on Washington.' I was so thrilled. I said, 'Okay,
let's meet.' So I said, 'I wanna do this with Troy Perry and HRC. And
we'll use those two organizations as the hub.'"[29] After hanging up, Tyler organized a meeting for January 5, 1998, in Washington, D.C., with
Perry and Birch.

On January 5, 1998, Robin Tyler, a longtime lesbian comic and events
producer, Troy Perry of the MCC, the largest gay religious organization,
and Elizabeth Birch of HRC, the largest Washington-based gay political
lobbying organization, met for lunch. They decided among themselves
that a fourth march was a good idea, and that the MCC and HRC would
officially sponsor it. They agreed at their lunch to call the event the Millennium March and stage it sometime in the spring, and discussed plans
for forming a corporation and assembling a board of directors to over-
see the event.

Tyler was not interested in a grassroots event that she felt (and history confirmed) would be fraught with bickering. Frustrated with the
election of new-guard cochairs in 1993 whom she felt had little prior experience, Tyler also did not want neophytes at the helm. She modeled
her vision after the National Organization for Women (NOW), which,
as a centrist organization, elected members to a board: "NOW usually
put on the marches in Washington by themselves, alone, as an organization. . . . So I looked at this feminist prototype of how the marches had
been put on, and I thought, 'What we should do is go through an orga-

nization because it seems to be less conflicting, and we could have more accountability.'" Tyler circumvented the cultural template used by previous marches: "They [the leadership and board of directors of the Millennium March] weren't voted on. . . . I was looking for more . . . being professional, so we didn't have the fight. Then you bring people on board to decide the stage, the issues, whatever."[30] Ironically, Tyler had hoped to *reduce* infighting.

For the final touches, Tyler asked Birch on February 2 to call seven organizations for endorsements to legitimate the call. Birch returned with eight: the Gay and Lesbian Victory Fund; the National Black Lesbian and Gay Leadership Forum; the National Latino/a Lesbian and Gay Organization; the National Gay and Lesbian Task Force; the National Gay and Lesbian Alliance Against Defamation; the National Center for Lesbian Rights; the National Youth Advocacy Coalition; and Parents, Families, and Friends of Lesbians and Gays. The pace was frenetic, as the *Gay Community News* also observed, "According to a number of organizations listed as endorsers, the sponsors of this event contacted them less than twenty-four hours before press time to sign on to this proposal." One day later (February 3), they drafted a press release. And one breathless day after that, on February 4, 1998, the HRC and MCC issued the fated press release that unveiled the Millennium March on Washington, with Robin Tyler as executive producer:

> WASHINGTON—The nation's largest gay and lesbian political organization and the nation's largest gay faith-based movement announced plans today to sponsor a march on Washington in the spring of the year 2000. The event will be produced by veteran march organizer Robin Tyler who brought the organizations together to formulate planning . . . for the "Millennium March on Washington for Equal Rights."

The press release also quoted Birch, "This march will set a new tone for a new century," and Perry, "This march will set the pace for social justice and human rights."[31]

And so went flying the sparks of controversy around a situation that activist Mandy Carter called "a defining moment for our movement."[32] A Chicago letter signed by several progressive activists noted the original sin: "Despite sentiments against a national march at a 1997 Creating Change Conference . . . top leaders of the Human Rights Campaign (HRC) and the Universal Fellowship of Metropolitan Community

FIGURE 9.3. The "Meaninglessium March." Cartoon by Ben Carlson. Courtesy of the *Bay Area Reporter*.

Churches (MCC) unilaterally decided to hold and name the march without consulting other national, state, or local LGBT organizations."[33] The democratic process previously in place had been abandoned. Political commentators criticized the "Meaninglessium March" as frivolous, elitist, top-down, and removed from the realities of gay life at the time (see fig. 9.3).

Tyler dismissed the early rumblings of dissent: "There's never been an entire rising up of a group of people to call for a march. . . . It begins with a few people with a good idea."[34] Her observation has merit, which journalist Lisa Neff conceded: "March organizers emphasize that controversy often surrounds national marches, including the landmark 1963 civil rights march on Washington, and has been a factor in each of the national gay civil rights marches. In 1993 activists questioned the logic of holding a march a year before the celebration commemorating the twenty-fifth anniversary of Stonewall Inn riots. In 1987 activists argued whether a march would pull money away from the fledgling battle against HIV/AIDS. In 1979 activists debated whether to march at all."[35] Neff and Tyler's observations overlook the same question: what channels and norms have leaders created for airing dissent? Before, leaders implemented a participatory-democratic process that embraced public debate. The MMOW hijacked this process and dissolved the cultural template that productively linked infighting with clarifying the contours of what it means to be gay.

The aftershocks continued: "No sooner had the February 4 press release gone out than the nation's largest gay political group [the HRC] was deluged by criticism—much from local gay groups who would be conduits to any march on Washington,"[36] noted the *Advocate*. Within a week, on February 12, 1998, the quickness and intensity of resistance forced Birch to place the Millennium March on hold. One *Washington Blade* article was revealing in its title: "March Is Put on 'Pause': HRC Agrees to Open Up a Discussion with Other Groups."[37] The HRC and MCC paused the march so activists could discuss "its timing, its purpose, and its message." Writers Lisa Keen and Lou Chibbaro Jr. quoted Birch, "It's very obvious to me that the time for the next march is at the dawn of the new Millennium." But there was still a problem: "People just want more dialogue. . . . We agreed to just pause and have more people at the table." Birch's commentary is problematic. What is "obvious" to her is distinct from a grassroots consensus and thus what appears to be an empty table. It is notable that Birch and Perry *later* agreed to invite people to the table, when this was the way grassroots activists had always *begun* discussing the possibility. There were different mobilization mechanics at work that put into the hands of a few the power to mold the entire movement.

The *Washington Blade* noticed early departures from the cultural template, that is, "the prevailing sentiment" that HRC and MCC had "jumped the gun" since they "had not given other organizations enough information about the proposed Millennium March nor enough opportunity to explore the feasibility, timing, and goals for the march." Chicago's *Windy City Times* observed that "the directors at many of the nation's gay and lesbian organizations were publicly complaining that they hadn't had enough time to weigh the merits of a national march before committing to the concept."[38] The *Blade* confirmed: "Many of the representatives were angry that HRC had called their organizations to sign on as supporters of the march less than twenty-four hours before a press release went out announcing that the march would take place."

Some organizations, like the Federation of Statewide Gay, Lesbian, Bisexual, Transgendered Organizations (the Federation, for short) and the NGLTF, reversed and placed their endorsements on hold. According to Kerry Lobel, "To date, the process has been hasty and lacked accountability. . . . We continue to advocate that the center of gravity for our movement is in the states, not Washington, D.C."[39] Five other organizations drafted a letter that, on March 4, 1998, was printed in gay presses across the country. Signed by the Gay and Lesbian Alliance Against Defamation, the Gay and Lesbian Victory Fund, the Los Angeles Gay and Lesbian Center, the Lambda Legal Defense and Education Fund, and the National Black Lesbian and Gay Leadership Forum, the letter conceded that "the symbol of a new century can be a powerful one for all of us to bring the civil rights struggle for the lesbian and gay community front and center." Having made this gesture, the leaders asked about strategy, "How do we best utilize the valuable resources of our community to maximize the opportunity presented by the millennium?" Such questions, and the resulting deliberative process, had been suppressed, which was a matter of grave concern. "We believe strongly that decisions are richer for the debate. Further, we ask community leaders to recognize our responsibility to engage our constituents in a public conversation on issues such as these, and we commit to developing both formal and informal mechanisms for that conversation. . . . We must all be careful to avoid setting our tactics before we have agreed on our goals."[40]

Birch, Perry, and Tyler worked to garner public support between February 12, when the march was put on pause and April 30, when they once again pushed play. To do this, they responded in one day to the March 4 letter described earlier: "In the year 2000, the entire nation will be looking for new trends and fresh messages. We have an opportunity, if not an obligation, to use this wave to effectively shift the paradigm of perceptions about gay people." They had a dream of a new movement: "We believe that in the early 1990s, gay America entered an entirely new period that has gone largely unlabeled and unanalyzed. . . . The priorities of our community have changed dramatically. We are looking for ways to find stability in our relationships, health, homes, and communities. . . . The desire to legally marry has emerged as an extremely important goal for many gay Americans. Many of us are returning to the churches of our youth or finding new ways to express our spirituality."[41]

Birch and Perry then took steps that had lasting repercussions. They asserted themselves the architects of the "largely unlabeled and unanalyzed" new movement: "The shift we have described has NEVER been effectively communicated on a mass scale to the American people. A Millennium March provides a remarkable opportunity to dramatically demonstrate what it means to be gay in this nation at the turn of the century. This march is an unprecedented opportunity to celebrate our diversity as a community of family, spirituality, and equality." The contradictions are unmistakable. They acknowledged the importance of "celebrat[ing] our diversity" yet narrowly (and without input) defined it as "a community of family, spirituality, and equality." A *Gay Community News* editorial chided this as the "Birch of a Nation."[42]

Birch and Perry flatly dismissed dissent: "Rather than become mired in the mud fight that has emerged among those who would criticize this idea, we would like to invite them—and you—to participate in what we believe will be the most exciting demonstration of our unity and power at a seminal moment in time."[43] The duo was once again burdened by contradictions. How could the MMOW be "the most exciting demonstration of our unity" when dissent was glibly reduced to a "mud fight"? Dissent carries and concretizes, rather than undermines and muddies, visions of unity. Political scientist Cathy Cohen articulated a similar insight about the dividends of dissent, namely the ability "to define who we are and where we struggle":

> Refining our political analysis forces us to reexamine the basis of our unity and explore just how far we can proceed with our current political configurations. . . . We're confronted with difficult choices but also wonderful opportunities to rebuild our organizations, reevaluate our politics, and, most importantly, recommit ourselves to the communities that help to define who we are and where we struggle.[44]

If "dissent is the highest form of patriotism," in the words of historian Howard Zinn, then Birch and Perry's efforts to denigrate infighting as a "mud fight" is evidence of their efforts to hijack a formerly democratic movement.[45]

The "high-stakes mud fight"[46] did not subside. One notable event occurred on March 30, 1998, when Perry initiated an "e-mail action alert" in which he urged individuals to contact national organizations that were withholding endorsements: "Perhaps the most important thing you can do to help move this forward is to send an e-mail message to the National Gay and Lesbian Task Force and the National Black Lesbian and

Gay Leadership Forum. . . . Tell them you are the grassroots and that you support the march. If you are a contributor, member, or supporter of these organizations, be sure to mention that too. . . . Ask them to come on board and to endorse the march. . . . Let them know how much we want and need—and expect—their support."[47] Perry's e-mail action alert paralleled in audacity the call to action and the "mud fight" comment when he singled out the need to convince lesbian and gay organizations of color to support the march. It was equally audacious in its vision for building grassroots support by commanding the rank and file to tell national organizations that their support was "expected." This is a confused conception of the grassroots. In the past, it grew organically, without command, as gays arose in critical numbers to assess the collective wisdom of marching. The grassroots was not instructed to grow from the top, as Billy Hileman noted: "Right now, Perry, Birch, and Tyler are . . . trying to prop up grassroots support for an event only they had input on. . . . And now that people are voicing their concern about the process, Birch, Tyler, and Perry are putting a call out to the grassroots groups instead of the other way around."[48]

Birch cornered herself, as well. On April 4, 1998, D.C.'s local community organized a gospel concert that six hundred black lesbians and gay men attended. Birch was there and at the closing conveyed to the audience, "We have not always done our best. We have not always been a good neighbor. But this year, you will see us at the Black Lesbian and Gay Pride weekend and at other major events."[49] Black lesbian activist Barbara Smith took umbrage: "Being 'a good neighbor' and showing up at black events is besides the point. The point is the articulation of a serious anti-racist activist platform that would lay out specific strategic actions for challenging racism both in society as a whole and within the white lgbt movement. . . . Institutionalized white supremacy is hardly a problem of good and bad 'neighbors.'" Smith concluded, "The fact that the forum and other people of color were not communicated with from the very beginning when the Millennium March was being conceived, but are now expected to sign on after the fact is the epitome of undemocratic tactics as well as of racism."[50]

A month after the march was put on hold and after all but one organization withdrew support, the *Washington Blade* reported, "Birch said plans for the event would move forward and that the National Latina/o Lesbian, Gay, Bisexual, and Transgender Organization (LLEGO) would become a . . . sponsor."[51] The choice to spotlight LLEGO—the only organization that did not withdraw support—was sly. LLEGO's founder, Nicole Ramirez-Murray, attributed its genesis to the 1987 march. He used this to defend the MMOW: "It is hoped that the march will spawn other gay and lesbian groups, in the same way as the 1987 march inspired the creation of LLEGO."[52] Ramirez-Murray also happened to be close friends with Robin Tyler, who, as discussed, marinated the idea in a private conversation with him at 1997's Creating Change Conference. These events—the way the call was sounded; Perry's e-mail action alert; Birch's "mud fight" and "good neighbor" comments, and her indication that the march was back on, given LLEGO's (insider) support—suggest the trio had not learned from their mistakes nor internalized the cultural template past organizers toiled to craft. They also incorrectly assumed that departures as dramatic as the ones they had initiated would be without consequence.

"After two months of debate," noted Chicago's *Windy City Times* on May 7, 1998, "the Millennium March on Washington for Equal Rights . . . [was] placed on the calendar last week."[53] The April 30, 1998, press release declared that the fourth national march would take place on April 30, 2000, exactly two years later. The HRC-MCC-Tyler trio pressed forward, having decided the march would in fact occur, when it would be held, and what it would be called. They also established "a nonprofit organization to handle planning, production, and finances." Such decisions—deliberated in the past by elected members of a national steering committee—were made unilaterally this time. Nadine Smith, 1993 cochair, voiced in the *Washington Blade* that MMOW disputes were over the state of the movement. In "March Moves Forward on Misguided Course," she asserted, "There is much more at stake here than hammering out the logistics of a march. In fact, what is at stake is the very heart of our movement." Questions such as "how we decide when and if the time is right for a march" (along with the date and title) mattered and, if mismanaged, could mistake "style for real substance," where "true activism" was traded "for occasional access at the national level."[54]

To Smith, the discrepant way the fourth march was being organized suggested troubling trends. "Our biggest problem," she provocatively noted, was that "too many people are wondering how they can become the Martin Luther King Jr. for our movement when we are in desperate need of a million Rosa Parks." Smith criticized the call and leadership for compromising effectiveness for who would be "the great man" of the movement. She then connected this to the values of dissent: "Those of us

who believe that our movement should not be strong-armed have a responsibility to speak up instead of accepting this as a 'done deal.'" Smith
expressed concern that "the movement is being hijacked" and implored,
"For our community's benefit, we need to make clear that this march
will not go on as it is now conceived. . . . This is not the way for us to
greet the next millennium."

Other activists also took issue with Birch, Perry, and Tyler's silenc-
ing of debate. Billy Hileman observed, "The current debate of an LGBT
civil rights event in Washington, D.C., in 2000 may look like 'political infighting' if one only takes a quick glance. But just below the surface is
one of the most important community discussions to occur in decades."
In dissenting, lesbians and gay men were "redefining the movement."[55]
"The tragedy of this situation" was their being "the willing architects of
this attack on queer democracy." This was beyond arrogant. "Arrogant
is not the word," noted Hileman. "Only sheer contempt for democracy
can describe their organizing style." Hileman concluded by identifying
more contradictions: "Organizing a national civil rights event without a
grassroots 'call' is exclusive no matter how much multicultural rhetoric
they try to pour over it."

Some of the whether-to-march debate was redolent of past discussions on whether to endorse other events (e.g., Stonewall 25). In light of
the sociopolitical context, this structurally familiar debate was culturally
recast to question where to invest resources. A Chicago editorial wondered, "A question of great importance faces this community: Do we
march on Washington in 2000 or on our state capitals in 1999?"[56] U.S.
Representative Barney Frank (D-Mass.) argued that a $2 million march
would be a diversion of resources better used on grassroots politicking.[57]
Others, such as Brian Bond, then executive director of the Gay and Lesbian Victory Fund, agreed. He circulated a memo to local leaders across
the country blasting the MMOW: "The key to success of the gay rights
movement is now local." Kerry Lobel concurred: "The center of gravity
is in the states."[58] The collective wisdom to march was in question.

Recall that a fifty-state march was also proposed during the third
march. The idea was voted down when leaders decided by consensus to
go to Washington instead. In 1997, the Federation formed to respond to
the shift of political power from the federal government to state legislatures. Leaders of state organizations, along with the grassroots NGLTF,
embraced Equality Begins at Home—it was not tabled as before. Activists planned the event for 1999. That the fifty-state march made the

FIGURE 9.4. National versus Local Organizing. Cartoon © 1999 David Brady.

calendar this time but not before speaks counterfactually to the current lack of consensus to defer to Washington. A fourth march was not mandated by the grassroots. One political cartoon portrayed the debate as a tyrannical MMOW commanding the locally overwhelmed rank and file to obey (see fig. 9.4).

Birch dubbed the local-versus-national tension a "false dichotomy." "The problem," according to her, "is that we have all failed to build a meaningful relationship between state and national organizers."[59] Tyler agreed: "This should not be a battle over state marches vs. a national march."[60] But when considering limited resources, was this dichotomy really false? In an op-ed piece titled, "March to Nowhere," Chicago writer Paul Varnell answered: "Plans for the national march will inescapably draw some time, energy, and money away from the marches planned for each state capital. All talk of coordination, synergy, and so forth between the plans makes no sense. There is only so much time and money around, and states are where most important gay issues are decided. . . . Forget the national march. Do something useful instead."[61]

In the article "A March Divided?" Diane Hardy-Garcia, cochair of the Federation and director of the Lesbian and Gay Rights Lobby of

Texas, agreed with Varnell: "We just can't afford not to include state movements anymore. . . . I don't want another project where there's millions and millions spent on a big party."[62] Kerry Lobel pointedly asked, "We've marched on Washington three times. What's different now?"[63] Drawing on the wealth of experiences as a U.S. Congressman, Barney Frank answered, "Frankly, I think the march is a mistake. . . . The National Rifle Association is the most successful militant organization in the country. They don't put their rifles on their shoulders and go marching around the Mall. . . . There was a period in our movement when we needed to get out there and say, 'Here we are!' But visibility is not enough anymore. Too much of what we do now helps us feel better but doesn't help politically."[64] Conservative critic Andrew Sullivan dismissed the march as a waste of time, succinctly claiming that at the turn of the century the movement was "post-march."[65]

Others were skeptical of organizing during an election year, a debate which had also surfaced in the past, but which always concluded with a vote to stage the demonstration in an off-year. This time there was no vote, as the trio decided an election year would be best (even if untested). With previously implemented channels (of open national conferences) for debating eliminated, journalists turned to academic insights. In an article titled "March Madness: Political Infighting Raises Questions about the Worthiness of a Millennium March on Washington," the *Advocate* quoted sociologist Todd Gitlin: "National marches may not serve the crucial role of advancing gay causes the way they once did" since the "political currency of marches has diminished since the heyday of antiwar and civil rights marches of the 1960s and '70s." The article concluded with considerations of timing: "Staging a march in the middle of an election year is especially risky business. . . . If Americans don't like what they see on CNN or if political candidates feel forced to take a side, it could result in backlash."[66]

These beginnings at once resemble and depart from how the other marches were organized. In each case, one or more person was responsible for articulating the possibility of marching. For the first march, Harvey Milk harvested an idea already prominent in the New Left repertoire. In 1987, former co-coordinators Steve Ault and Joyce Hunter brought the conversation to the table at an initiating meeting. And in the third march, Urvashi Vaid assessed similar sentiments. In this capacity, Tyler's actions were consistent with how things had been done before. The idea had to come from somewhere, after all.

In the past, however, activists organized national meetings where leaders brainstormed and voted on the wisdom of marching. Once this participatory process yielded a favorable response, leaders were elected onto a national steering committee that decided major issues such as when to march, what to title it, how to organize it, how to assemble the platform, and who to invite as speakers. None of this happened the fourth time. From day one, Tyler knew there was resistance. This did not stop her from proceeding. Although she did consult a handful of close friends and activists, Tyler did not organize an initiating meeting. She, Perry, and Birch unilaterally decided whether to march (yes), when to march (April 30, 2000), and what it would be called (the Millennium March on Washington for Equal Rights). "The event in 2000" ruptured the cultural template of past marches and unleashed a movement civil war.

The Title and Theme

Title critiques focused on its religious overtones (i.e., the 2,000th *anno Domini*) and the lack of an identifiable constituency. A *New Republic* article captured the sense of bewilderment in its headline: "Backward March: Why Are Gays Protesting a Gay Rights March?" The article quoted leaders of past marches lambasting use of the word *millennium*. It was denounced as "a specifically Christian marker of history [that] leaves many feeling uneasy and many non-Christians feeling they don't belong."[67] A *Bay Area Reporter* article also supported this argument in its coverage of the Gay and Lesbian Atheists and Humanists (GALAH). Titled "Queer Atheists Raise Objections to Millennium March," the article quoted representatives as saying: "The very conception of the rally is discriminatory to non-believers. The millennium has Christian context based on the supposed date of Christ's birth. . . . The emphasis on faith and spirituality rather than diversity is a major problem. . . . The word 'millennium' would be better replaced with words such as 'lesbian, gay, bisexual, transgender' which would have the added benefit of bringing this march out of the closet."[68] Thus, the first part of the title debates took issue with the relationship between sexuality and religion.

The second aspect of the debate focused on the lack of identity in the title: "It has not been lost on many gay civil rights advocates that the 'Millennium March' does not even contain the words gay or lesbian in its title, much less bisexual, transgendered, or intersexual,"[69] noted *The*

Data Lounge. Some accused the march of being "closeted."[70] Identity-less titles were also proposed for the 1979 march, where an activist suggested "Human Rights March," and the 1993 march (see proposals in table 7.2). The debate was more thunderous this time perhaps because the title was announced without community input, a process that created feelings of ownership.

HRC spokesperson David Smith revealed to the *Washington Blade* that "HRC and MCC decided on the name 'Millennium March on Washington for Equal Rights' because keeping it simple adds to its strength."[71] Smith's defense of the title on the grounds of simplicity-as-strength is redolent of HRC's choice of its logo. Both suggest the subordination of politics to marketing. Alexandra Chasin asserts that these were "economic maneuvers cloaked in the guise of politics" driven by "the manipulation of money in the name of identity."[72]

Title debates were aggravated when a New York journalist followed up with Smith about the march's theme. Published two days after the February 4 call, the article was subtitled, "Organizers say 'Millennium March' will bring themes of 'families' and 'faith' to the forefront."[73] Another New York gay newspaper suggested that Troy Perry defended the uniqueness of the MMOW by showcasing gay expressions of "faith and family." "The organizers," noted the journalist, "justify the march's theme by explaining that 'many of us are returning to the churches of our youth.'" Writer Alisa Solomon made clear the growing public restlessness in her article title: "Whose Faith? The Next Gay March on Washington Could Be a Boon to the Christian Right."[74] Once again we see activists questioning the title to grapple with complex questions of what it means to be gay at the turn of the century.

Perry replied in September 1998 by refuting that "faith and family" was ever the theme, despite Smith's assertion above that it was: "This is false. This has never been the theme, the proposed theme, or the goal of the Millennium March. . . . It is not true."[75] As Chasin explains, the veracity of "faith and family" was never settled:

> By some accounts, the theme for the march was "Faith and Family"; by other accounts, no theme . . . had been announced. . . . Even if faith and family had never been the intended themes, the very name of the march caused some to look deeper into the MCC's leadership in the event: "Millennium," wrote Stephanie Poggi [in her notably titled article, "Onward Christian Soldiers?"], referred to "a thousand years of 'Christ's' reign on earth in which holiness

is to prevail. HRC and UFMCC are clearly not adverse to conjuring up this particular sense." MCC's own literature did not reassure on this score . . . MCC's explicit statement that people of all religions were welcome had an unwelcoming effect, of course, as it suggested that they saw themselves as gatekeepers.[76]

As these debates reveal, activists used the title to make tangible otherwise abstract concerns of gay identity (for whom is this march?) and strategy (does "faith and family" adequately represent what gay people across the country want?).

Organizing Structure

After the April 30 press release that finalized the march, organizing proceeded fast and furiously—and in ways that hardly resembled prior marches. The MMOW also spawned an organizational entity whose sole purpose was to challenge the march. The intense opposition was a consequence of millennial leaders shattering the cultural template. In responding to "Why has the planned Millennium March on Washington . . . caused so much controversy?" Michelangelo Signorile argued:

> March organizers consciously abandoned our movement's democratic traditions, and chose to employ a corporate-style, top-down leadership structure which excluded democratic input from the lgbt community at large. Cut off from us and making closed-door decisions, there was simply no way MMOW could unite a community as diverse as ours behind a truly inclusive and representative national political agenda. Without a grassroots organizing strategy and a democratic structure in place for people to air their aspirations and concerns, MMOW was destined for failure from the very beginning."[77]

It started at an invitation-only (i.e., closed to the public and press) meeting.[78] The march's planning committee invited thirty-five to forty local and national representatives of major gay organizations to attend a Washington, D.C., meeting the weekend of June 9–10, 1998. This self-defined "broad and diverse" coalition convened to "collectively design" an inclusive and diverse organizing structure.[79] The meeting was the first in a series of closed-door board of directors meetings. Activists did not fail to notice the secrecy. "If it was hard to get much information about the millennium march in the past two months, and it was," noted one Chicago writer, "it was now even harder."[80]

Those gathered sought to draft an organizing structure and to respond to mounting criticisms. The facilitators embraced their first objective by posing a series of rhetorical questions followed by a brainstorming session: How do we establish a working model for operating the march? How do we become inclusive? How do we resolve our conflicts in a healthy way? How do we take into account the history of our marches? Posing the questions confirmed widespread disaffections with the Millennium March. One might expect this to prompt reparative gestures in light of the cultural template. This, however, did not happen. Those in attendance proposed a corporation-like board of directors (BOD) to replace past steering committees. Unlike those large, 164-person decision-making bodies, the BOD would be comprised of ten to fifteen people. This significantly smaller governing body would assume fiduciary and legal responsibility, facilitate conversation around the platform, lead fund-raising efforts, and arrange committee work. Birch noted that in the past large steering committee meetings were overcrowded, and there were many who could not afford the travel costs to attend. This created the dual problems of unmanageability (due to large numbers) and inadequate representation. The BOD was designed to rectify both these shortcomings.

The delegates approved the structure along with a later motion to incorporate an explicit diversity requirement: "The BOD is mandated to place people in decision-making positions who represent diversity in geography, race, culture, class, sexual orientation, age, gender and gender identity, disability and spirituality." An ancillary "friendly amendment" also passed in which the BOD "will strive for 50 percent gender parity and will strive for inclusion of youth, bi, elder, trans, heterosexual, immigrant and 50 percent POC [people of color]." Attendees also agreed on a leadership council (LC) that would be "communicating the March to the country," with secondary responsibilities for local and regional organizing, supporting the mission, goals, and platform of the march, engaging in fund-raising efforts and determining profits post-march (should there be any). The LC would be comprised of representatives of all major regions in the country and was required to "represent diverse constituencies." *Diversity* and *inclusion* became buzzwords organizers used to defend the march's legitimacy and accountability. Delegates agreed to hold elections that same day to fill the ten slots and "hold five places open."

This style of organizing departed from the cultural template in two ways. First, a board of directors symbolized a different framework compared to the grassroots steering committees from prior marches. It is also telling that the current structure became legally registered as the "Millennium March on Washington for Equality, Inc.," or just "the Corporation" for short. What we see here is the borrowing of a private-sector approach to assemble a mass protest event. Second, and of more consequence, was the issue of appointment. In the past, activists staged open meetings where representatives from across the country attended and lobbied to get *elected* onto the steering committee. This time, however, the board was populated from a *self-selected* list of invited activists. These differences suggest a shift in strategy away from grassroots toward corporation-inspired politics. It also suggests closure on a social-justice identity and an embracing of one that was professional and market-driven instead.

Figure 9.5 illustrates the never-before-used structure, replete with paid positions. The board adopted an open-door policy in which all meetings were ostensibly open to the public.[81] The gay press, however, reported that they were in fact "closed-door meetings."[82] The leadership council was structured "to encourage as many community activists as possible to work directly with members of the MMOW Board of Directors to develop the MMOW platform and plan official MMOW events; organize local, state, and national activities in support of the Millennium March on Washington; update the GLBT community and allied individuals and organizations on all Millennium March on Washington activities." The LC included representatives from "every local, state, and national organization that officially endorses the March in writing." Council members were responsible for publicizing the march, soliciting endorsements, promoting attendance, sharing information, and fund-raising.[83]

The executive and associate producers were on the next level down. In concert with the stage production staff, they were responsible for the "organization, planning, promotion, execution, and completion of the event."[84] The director of field organizing and the communications director were responsible for mobilizing the rank and file to bolster attendance, with the former working on the ground and the latter devising a motivational media strategy. Underneath the former was the campus organizer, who would "coordinate youth participation . . . by contacting and or visiting GLBT campus organizations." The volunteer coordinator recruited and managed volunteer efforts, assuring that "volunteers

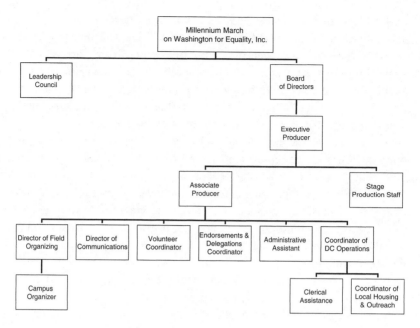

FIGURE 9.5. Millennium March Organizing Structure. Source: author's adaptation from "MMOW Organization Chart," personal papers of Ann DeGroot.

are reflective of GLBT community and communities of color." The endorsement and delegations coordinator was "responsible for monitoring, tracking, and soliciting endorsements from GLBT, progressive, feminist, union, and people of color organizations." Finally, the administrative assistant, coordinator of D.C. operations, clerical assistant, and the coordinator of local housing and outreach were responsible for general administrative functions.[85]

Attendees next turned to community input where the "facilitator invited uninvited guests to comment." Enter the Ad Hoc Committee for an Open Process. These "uninvited guests"—ten seasoned activists and architects of the prior three marches—had been in touch for some time prior to this June meeting. The group coalesced into what they called the Ad Hoc Committee for an Open Process (AHC). The AHC "came together to challenge the Millennium March organizers on their refusal to integrate a nationwide, community-based discussion about whether we want to march on Washington, and if so, when, why, around what demands, etc. . . . The time has come to build a movement that is truly inclusive, committed to democracy, and politically progressive."[86] In an interview with the *Windy City Times,* group member Leslie Cagan explained their name: "That's why we call ourselves an Ad Hoc group. . . . We did not start as a new civil rights organization. Rather, we want to spark discussion . . . about the state of [the] gay movement."[87] Even in its many ruptures—most notably in efforts to stifle the expression of debate (recall the "mud fight" comment), activists and rank and file alike once again turned to infighting as a culture carrier to articulate and reflect on their movement.

The conversation—perhaps better called a confrontation—began immediately. The AHC presented a proposal with more than sixty-five supporting signatures.[88] Titled "The Call for an Open Process," this document urged organizers to "initiate a movement-wide process to discuss the pros and cons of another march on Washington."[89] The AHC began with a history lesson:

Each march was very different as were the times in which they were organized. However, each one was run democratically with mass, grassroots involvement, and each followed a similar organizing scenario. A committee . . . organized a national meeting to which representatives of all lesbian and gay . . . organizations—local, state, and regional as well as national—were welcomed. . . . Here, the primary decision whether to have the event was made first, followed by deliberations on the name of the event, the politics, structure, leadership, and the organizing strategy. Then, throughout the country, open, democratically run meetings selected delegates, with mandates to include women and people of color, to a national steering committee, the highest decision-making body. Many of these meetings were at times contentious and chaotic. But in the end the decisions were accepted because the process was fair and inclusive.[90]

The cultural template was inviolable: "Now, as a fourth march on Washington is being proposed, we must summon the legacy of the previous three for the process by which this discussion proceeds will define not only the nature of any event that may follow, but more importantly, that of the lesbian/gay/bisexual/transgender movement itself." The AHC concluded with their own call to action: "We, the Ad Hoc Committee for an Open Process . . . are calling for an open process to engage our movement in a serious, national discussion on whether or not we want to go to Washington, what's the purpose, when do we want to go, what would we be calling for, and how do we insure the maximum, most diverse participation in any planning process." In bold-type, the call asserted, "Let the Community Decide!" Do not jettison the cultural template, warned the AHC.

The AHC's primary objection was how the MMOW had been called— that is, the formative question of whether to march. Process mattered because it was "a reflection of our politics," in the words of AHC member Leslie Cagan.[91] The AHC wanted millennial organizers "to start over from square one, to consider whether there was a sound political purpose for the march in the first place."[92] The way organizers had circumvented the cultural template undermined the democratic basis for the march and dissolved "ownership of decisions" and the "sense of solidarity and commitment" that accompanied it.[93] The tried and true procedure ensured that "people from all over the country were motivated to commit their time, energy, and resources to build the marches because they realized that they were both heard and represented."[94]

The meeting minutes reveal an intense struggle over process. AHC spokesperson Barbara Smith noted that "Ad Hoc does not want to throw out [the] model used in previous marches." Cagan agreed: "We need to discuss when we go . . . how we go . . . why we go. . . . The march as proposed is top down." Barbara Smith clarified that these debates over organizing tasks spoke to cultural concerns over how to define the state of the movement: the "process will not only define the event, but also the future of the movement." Although "chaos is part of the democratic process," the current "model is too corporate" and "chaos is preferable to the process outlined today."

After a fifteen-minute break, the planning committee responded. They stubbornly maintained that the year 2000 "offered a key opportunity for the community." They advocated for process evolution and asked the AHC to "not . . . underestimate them." The AHC should "honor [the] validity of different models of organizing." Lobel described various "ways our community is changing" and that "inclusiveness by itself does not translate to social change." The board, in other words, asked for flexibility and change, although they had yet to establish that there was any kind of national consensus on modifying how it had been done in the past.

Robin Tyler interjected, trying to move the conversation away from individual impressions. She cleverly observed that the *Advocate* and *Data Lounge* conducted an online poll in March 1998 to assess march support.[95] The *Advocate* poll found 84 percent in favor while *Data Lounge*

found 73 percent "strongly supported" the march and another 22 percent
"supported" it. The polls also attested to changes in the state of the movement. Over 65 percent of respondents indicated that they would support
a Washington march behind the themes of "gay families" and "faith," (as
the scaffolding of the new gay identity) and 58 percent agreed that "presenting a conservative or 'safe' image of the gay and lesbian community
is politically desirable" (as the strategic framework). From this statistical
vantage point, the planning committee felt it was marching side-by-side
with the rank and file. Indeed, Birch, Perry, and Tyler often used these
poll results "to show the grassroots support for the march."[96]

Numbers are a tricky business. Tyler failed to mention two mislead-
ing statistical trends. First, the demographics of those who visit the *Data
Lounge* Web site (where they cast their votes) were 75 percent men, more
than half of whom had managerial, professional, or computer tech jobs,
and the majority of whom made an annual income of at least $30,000.
The results, therefore, were biased against racial, gender, and class diversity and thus not representative. Especially around the millennium, online access and use was not normally distributed in the American population or the gay community. This "digital divide" further biased the
results.[97]

In addition to *Data Lounge,* the *Advocate* poll may have also been biased. The national newsmagazine was an official sponsor of the MMOW
and had donated $425,000 of in-kind services, including printing full-
page color ads in twenty issues. According to AHC activist Bill Dobbs,
this "corporate mindset" had "compromised its editorial integrity." *Advocate* editor in chief Judy Wieder, however, dismissed this as "'growing
pains' for the movement. . . . It's difficult for certain people in our read-
ership to see the magazine rise up into the mainstream." Wieder also denied that sponsorship had "affected its editorial coverage." According to
her, "If I compromise as the editor in chief . . . if I sell out, then I've lost
the product that everyone wants. I hope that we hold on to our integrity,
and I will die doing that."[98]

The total number of articles the *Advocate* published pertaining to
the marches increased over the course of the four events, with a notable
jump for the MMOW (N = 21, 25, 24, and 56 articles for 1979, 1987, 1993,
and 2000, respectively). The percent that addressed infighting, however,
increased across the first three yet *declined* for the fourth (38 percent,
44 percent, 50 percent, and 41 percent for 1979, 1987, 1993, and 2000,
respectively). This proportional decrease in articles pertaining to inter-

nally conflicting matters is not attributable to less overall discord. This possible description bias in reporting questions the relationship between corporate sponsorship and editorial integrity.

The *Advocate*'s sponsorship may also have introduced selection bias into the poll results. As noted by *Gay Community News,* "The favorable vote of the *Advocate* poll was in part the result of a campaign by HRC to get their members to vote, including sending them the Web site address." Analytically, these biases all work in the same direction and thus diminish validity.[99] The disagreement over numbers and whether they accurately represented the rank and file illustrate a cultural contest over defining "the grassroots" in the first place.

Back to the AHC-BOD confrontation. The dialogue continued for another half-hour, at which point the attendees broke for lunch. After lunch, the planning committee offered the AHC to "designate one person to sit at the table with [one] vote." Mandy Carter replied that the AHC did not desire a vote (a co-opting maneuver) but rather sought the opportunity to address the issues they raised in the early afternoon. The PC rejected this suggestion, at which point the AHC left.

AHC members did not hesitate to speak with the gay press about the closed-door meeting. "Three organizations have said that the march is going to take place—no matter what—and this is a very bad dynamic," expressed Steve Ault.[100] Nadine Smith addressed concerns over movement ownership: "This is about whether our movement is up for grabs to whomever has the most cash or whether it's a real movement that incorporates diverse points of view." John O'Brien, then executive director of the ONE Institute in Los Angeles, agreed. He suggested that the event's original three sponsors (Birch, Perry, Tyler) controlled decisions about who participated in the process and under what circumstances. "It's a group of people who know each other and want to work together . . . but don't want to work with other people."

PC member Lori Jean offered the most revealing insider interview: "We had pretty much agreed that [the march] was going to happen. . . . We can't go back and revisit that." Jean's comment erased the AHC and the once-revered cultural template. It made valid Cagan's fear that the MMOW was "eclipsing a grassroots movement."[101] It also contradicted the BOD's claim to be representative of and accountable to the national community. MMOW executive director Malcolm Lazin inadvertently confirmed this fear when he provided a curt response to AHC charges about the grassroots commitment of prior marches: "What past marches did is not relevant."[102]

Between the June and September board meetings, the AHC agreed to do something about the PC's dismissive stance. The AHC "decided to make our concerns even more public" by running a two-page centerfold ad in the September 18, 1998, issue of the *Washington Blade*. This ad, later reproduced in gay presses across the country, bellowed their concerns alongside three hundred supporting signatures. The September 18 ad was "the largest public outcry to date and represents an unprecedented critique of some of our national organizations."[103] It was caustically titled, "They Say It's a March on Washington, We Say It's Trampling on Our Movement." The text lambasted the Millennium March's definition of the movement:

> Since February, when the Human Rights Campaign and the Metropolitan Community Church initiated their call for an event in the year 2000, there has been a disregard for our movement's history of grassroots empowerment. . . . Yes, we want the process opened—but much more is at stake. This is about re-claiming the heart and soul of our fight for equality, justice, freedom. This is about power and how it is wielded, manipulated, and abused. Who sits at the table and who decides how the table is set. This is about the direction of our grassroots movement and what we are fighting for.[104]

Even with three hundred signatures, the BOD still did not listen, somehow convinced that they knew best the sensibility of the grassroots (even if their actions flew in its face). The AHC began organizing community forums to mimic the old cultural template whereby the rank-and-file could contribute their voice.

Internally, the BOD agreed that "this is not the time to become mired in a defensive response to the ad hoc committee." They tried instead to extend a proactive message about their work, realizing that "we haven't done this yet in any real form." In a personal e-mail to the HRC, MCC, and others, Kerry Lobel agreed with the AHC: "We also haven't scheduled community meetings, put into place a mechanism for input, etc." In another e-mail, Rea Carey of the National Youth Advocacy Coalition added that the board needed to move forward "and regain the trust of many in our communities (not just Ad Hoc members)."[105] Finally, some within the board were beginning to take notice.

The HRC and MCC responded with a press release that again casti-
gated dissent in the public forum: "Sadly, the so-called *Ad Hoc Committee* chose to invest resources in a media campaign at a time when our
community can least afford such internal attacks. . . . The resources ex-
pended by the Committee would have been better directed toward the
true opposition, the extreme right. The broadside served no purpose but
to perpetuate misinformation and divide our community." Organizers
(yet again) contradicted themselves by observing, "We realize that at the
core of the sentiments expressed by the *Ad Hoc Committee,* there are
some legitimate concerns. On these matters, reasonable people can disagree."[106] These statements prevented readers from assessing whether
the AHC's concerns were valid ("misinformation" versus "there are
some legitimate concerns") and whether dissent had any value ("internal
attacks . . . divide our community" and waste resources versus "reasonable people can disagree").

The jousting continued through community forums and town-hall
meetings. The AHC organized the former to educate the public about
the MMOW's unforgivable ruptures to the movement's cultural template. The BOD countered with town-hall meetings to respond to AHC's
concerns and symbolize their commitment to the grassroots. As with the
board's other efforts, this one too was riddled with contradictions. In
"An Open Letter to the Lesbian, Gay, Bisexual, and Transgender Community," eleven progressive Chicago organizations commented on the
BOD's town-hall meetings: "These meetings were not publicized and
few were actually held. Only twenty-five people showed up at the first
meeting in Minneapolis, home to one of the march's cochairs. The second meeting was scheduled for Chicago. There were no announcements
in the local LGBT press about the event, but approximately seventy-five
people showed up (most learning about the event through E-mail posts),
almost all voicing opposition to holding a march."[107] Was this how the
board demonstrated its commitment to the grassroots? It unfortunately
sounded like another substitution of "style for real substance," to allude
to Nadine Smith's earlier remarks. Some of these town-hall meetings
erupted with fury. March cochair Donna Redwing recalls:

> In my community, the only time I have ever been afraid was once when a
> group of neo-Nazis came to my house and threatened the life of my child.
> The only other time was when I was in Chicago, and these people were shout-
> ing us down and hurling, I think, the most amazing epithets, and we actu-

ally had to have someone walk us to our car. So, what I saw was this division in our community that I don't think I've ever quite understood. I understand why people didn't want the march. I don't understand why they would find the resources to literally track us, shout us down.[108]

In response to the AHC, march organizers announced efforts to create a "diverse" and "inclusive" board of directors. The board drafted "MMOW Board Resolutions" that outlined these commitments.[109] Their first resolution was racial justice: "*Acknowledging* the expressed concerns of our community regarding the perpetuation of racial justice, and *Realizing* the need for and the obligation of the Millennium March to identify and embrace the struggle for racial justice as an integral part of achieving equality for all people, *Be it hereby resolved that the Millennium March on Washington formally incorporates racial justice into the Millennium March Platform as follows:* The theme of striving for racial justice will be integrated into every aspect of organizing and staging the Millennium March on Washington for Equality" (emphases in original). To achieve this goal, the board restructured to include 50 percent people of color. And to strengthen people-of-color communities, it decided to donate 30 percent of the profits from the march (assuming this would happen) to POC organizations.

The board also incorporated an additional resolution concerning gender equality that used the same language, but substituted the phrase *gender equality* in place of *racial justice*. To achieve this goal and similar to its POC resolution, the board decided to be 50 percent women. Finally, the document outlined a concern for "visible gender variance" in their very next resolution that acknowledged transgender discrimination. These resolutions collectively helped organizers assemble "a fourteen-member board of directors which includes representatives of many of the nation's largest gay organizations and which represents a broad cross-section of the gay, bisexual, and transgender communities."[110] At a press conference in April 1999, and as if displaying a prized trophy, organizers announced that their BOD consisted of 60 percent women, 60 percent people of color, and only one white gay man, Reverend Troy Perry. They hoped this "would pacify loud and persistent critics who question[ed] the timing and need for the march as well as its self-appointed leadership."[111]

These events provide evidence for the Millennium March being "the first in which bisexual and transgender people have been included as a matter of course, [and] the first in which around half of those running things are people of color."[112] Hardy-Garcia noted, "I will admit that in the beginning the organization of the march was problematic. . . . But we should also get credit for some of the positive changes we have made, like our inclusion of racial issues."[113] The critics, however, were not mollified. The problem stemmed from the realization that minority groups did not decide for themselves, on behalf of their respective communities, what *inclusion* meant. The AHC explained:

> People of color and other constituencies must be selected by and from their communities. . . . The MMOW board asserts the MMOW has been made inclusive by expanding the board of directors to include over 50 percent people of color. . . . The people of color—and everyone else—serving on the board are being selected by a body that is itself self-selected. One can only guess at the criteria for selection. In contrast, in our three marches on Washington people of color—and everyone else—were selected by and from their own communities.[114]

According to this perspective, accountability and representation must rise up from within the ranks of the respective communities. In past marches, people of color willingly attended meetings where they were *elected* to leadership positions. They then went back to mobilize the communities they now felt compelled to represent. This fourth time around, the BOD *self-selected* (in an unknown process) its POC delegates. As black lesbian activist Mandy Carter summarized, "If I continue to hear about the 50 percent people of color on the MMOW board, I'm going to scream. With all due respect, there is a qualitative difference between being a person of color and representing a people-of-color constituency."[115] Thus, dissent over the organizing structure captured tensions over representation. This bespoke concerns of how different types of people (whites versus nonwhites) shared a common identity as lesbian or gay, and how they then came together to set the strategic direction of their movement.

There is additional evidence that diverse board composition was not perceived as equivalent to being representative or accountable. The majority of lesbian and gay organizations of color did *not* endorse the march. The National Association of Black and White Men Together, for example, slammed the march by moving its national spring meeting in D.C., initially scheduled to overlap with the march to enhance POC visibility, to two weeks earlier.[116] Activists and the rank and file also dissented with their feet. "While the march saw diversity in terms of interests, areas, and agendas," noted the *Windy City Times* about the actual demonstration, "there was not much racial diversity, and the crowd was a strikingly white one, with only a smattering of people of color. Some activists have even speculated that the march and rally drew only 1 percent people of color."[117] One letter to the editor noted, "LGBT persons of color were obvious by their absence" and that this "omission is a form of racism."[118] Chicago's *Free Press* agreed, "The march was overwhelmingly white in color."[119] The idea is the same: through dissent, gay people participated in the construction of the state of their movement.

The Platform and Speakers

The BOD's most pronounced efforts to appease critics involved the platform. In January 1999, they decided to fertilize the grassroots with technology by polling thousands in what they anticipated to be "the largest gay community survey ever conducted." The BOD distributed the survey through mailing lists supplied by national groups (mostly HRC), through inserts in gay publications (mostly the *Advocate*), and through gay community centers and other foci of gay congregation such as bars, bookstores, and coffee shops. As explained by Hardy-Garcia, "We'll be asking people for their input on where the movement should go and what they think are the most important issues for this march."[120]

The AHC retorted that the survey would be an inadequate substitute for an open meeting at which delegates could determine whether to have the march in the first place: "It appears that almost all attempts at organizing the Millennium March have taken place over the Internet. While the Internet is a powerful tool, a Web site is no substitute for a national, grassroots organizing campaign. In addition, there are many in our community who cannot afford a computer and are left out of the process entirely."[121] Bill Dobbs likened the survey to a "business reply card" the BOD would ignore.[122]

The strategy winnowed to Internet ballots posted on the Web sites of the *Advocate* and PlanetOut.com, both of which were financial sponsors of the march.[123] This caused a resurgence of validity criticisms given biases that inhered in the method of data collection. Less than two months before the march, the platform and political agenda were still not final-

ized, leading some to question the premise of the march: "Why even begin planning a march before having an agenda?" asked a progressive coalition of Chicagoans. "Why expect folks to make plans to attend the
march now when they don't even know what they are to be marching
for?"[124] As Steve Ault sarcastically put it, "Let's have a march on Washington and figure out why—later why. . . . That was a joke."[125] This became a fatal flaw in the eyes of the AHC:

> Marches on Washington are generally called by constituencies or coalitions
> of constituencies to address a critical political situation of a national charac-
> ter. . . . In the three marches organized by the LGBT community, the specific
> language articulating these issues (why we are marching) was decided early
> on. It seems obvious that calling a march and having some idea why should go
> hand in hand. With the MMOW, twenty-three months have passed and still
> there are no demands. . . . It becomes obvious that a march was called and
> then a process initiated in an attempt to find a political rationale for doing so.
> Great idea—call a march and then conjure up the reason why twenty-three
> months later. . . . The entire concept of initiating a march without a clear po-
> litical context is fatally flawed.[126]

Inserts and Internet polling sites followed the same procedure. At the
top, in bold letters, was the assertion, "Let Your Voice Set the Agenda
of the Millennium March." The survey overview stated, "We are asking
you to make your voice heard by identifying the issues that are most important to you when you dream of ending discrimination that is based
on sexual orientation." Then followed, "When I dream of ending discrimination that is based on sexual orientation, these issues are most
important to me: (Please pick your top three.)"[127] After this came nine
pre-selected categories with check boxes: hate crimes, equal marriage
rights, non-discrimination in education, health-care funding, AIDS/
HIV issues, family protections (child-custody rights and ability to
adopt), non-discrimination in employment, economic equity, and domestic partnership benefits. "Other" was not an option. With more than five
hundred responses, the board completed balloting by December 1999
(see table 9.1).

The board's approach was again riddled with contradiction. Although
they used the survey to symbolize a grassroots commitment, it isolated "discrimination that is based on sexual orientation," and therefore
muted the possibility of a multi-issue, coalition platform. Response cat-

TABLE 9.1. **Final Tally of Millennium March Platform Balloting (%)**

Hate Crimes Legislation	73
Non-Discrimination in Employment	72
Right to Marry	64
Overturning Anti-LGBT Laws	62
Child Custody and Adoption Rights	56
AIDS Issues	34
Youth Issues	33
Right to Serve Our Country	24
Privacy/Choice Issues	22
Lesbian Health Issues	13
LGBT Aging Issues	12
Immigration Rights	10
LGBT Global Issues	4

Source: Personal Papers of Robin Tyler and Ann DeGroot.

egories were also close-ended and *pre-selected*. This, as the AHC noted, was inadequate: "Clicking on a few pre-selected items cannot replace the community-wide discussion, the give-and-take required to determine what issues are considered important."[128] Three months later, the AHC reiterated, "A handful of people have set the agenda, highlighting topics important to some while excluding issues important to others. Demands pertaining to the issue of racism were included in the platforms of both the '87 and '93 marches. . . . Now, with the MMOW, it's entirely off the radar screen."[129]

Despite the forced choice, table 9.1 includes items not part of the original nine categories. This is because 3.2 percent of the respondents hand wrote additional issues, even though they were not given that option. Items ranged from additional gay rights issues (e.g., transgender issues, right to public sex) to coalition issues (e.g., classism, racism, networking with other social justice organizations). Concerns that likened the survey to a "business reply card"[130] the board would ignore proved false. The board finalized the platform and speakers at their D.C. meeting in December 1999 where they incorporated all but two of the items from the tally (see table 9.2). Departing from the prior two marches, the millennial platform was overwhelmingly single-issue.

The board used a similar procedure to determine speakers. More than 2,300 individuals responded online to the open-ended question, "Who would you like to see perform or speak at the rally?" and identified more than one hundred different prospects. Many were gay celebrities such as Melissa Etheridge (who received more votes than anyone else, at

TABLE 9.2. **Demands, Millennium March**

Though our community is comprised of people of incredible diversity, we are united by our struggle against the oppression of GLBT people and in our dream for a future of equality. Through community polls, surveys, and ballots, the following eight topics were identified among a host of concerns as the paramount issues facing our community today. On April 30th, we will march on Washington to demand resolution to these issues. On November 7th, we will go to the polls to do the same.

HATE CRIMES
Hate crimes are crimes which are motivated by animus toward a person based on his or her actual or perceived race, color, religion, natural origin, sexual orientation, gender, or disability. Sadly, GLBT people, like members of other minority groups, have historically been targeted for violence because of who we are. In our case, we are subject to attacks based upon our sexual orientation or visible gender variance. According to FBI statistics, hate crimes based on sexual orientation are the third highest category of reported hate crimes, following those based on race and religion, respectively.

Hate crimes against GLBT people result in both physical and psychological damage to the individuals who experience the crimes; in worst cases, such as those of Billy Jack Gaither, Brandon Teena, and Matthew Shepard, hate crimes result in death. Hate crimes destroy our community by taking from us people that we love and making us feel unsafe. Knowing that we can be targeted for injury or death simply because of who we are and who we love makes us feel vulnerable and insecure, even within our own communities.

At the national level, U.S. law permits federal prosecution of hate crimes only if the crime was motivated by bias based on race, religion, national origin, color, and if the attacker intended to prevent the victim from exercising a federally protected right, such as the right to vote. Hate crimes based on animus towards the victim's perceived sexual orientation or gender identification cannot currently be prosecuted at the federal level. The Hate Crimes Prevention Act of 1999 sought to change this; however, Congress rejected this legislation.

At the state level, protection for victims of hate crimes based on sexual orientation varies greatly. Twenty-two states and the District of Columbia have hate crime laws which include sexual orientation. Twenty states have hate crime laws which exclude victims of hate crimes based on sexual orientation. Eight states have no hate crime laws whatsoever.

We must lobby Congress to pass the Federal Hate Crimes Prevention Act and lobby our state legislatures to ensure that every state has a comprehensive hate crime law which includes sexual orientation and gender variance. Additionally, if you, or someone you know, is a victim of a hate crime, it is vital that you report it. Hate crimes against GLBT people are historically underreported, often because victims reasonably fear the reaction of the police and/or of their family, friends, and coworkers, if they are outed. Hate crimes can also be reported to specific agencies which advocate for GLBT rights, such as your local anti-violence project or community center. Gathering the statistics on these hate crimes increases our power to lobby for appropriate legislation to combat them.

EMPLOYMENT DISCRIMINATION
A workplace environment free of discrimination is something that most people take for granted. Unfortunately, GLBT people too often face harassment and discrimination in the workplace. In addition, many GLBT people live in fear of losing their jobs if their employer discovers they are gay, lesbian, bisexual, or transgendered, continuing to confine too many of us to the closet.

Only 11 states and 118 cities and counties have comprehensive protections against employment discrimination on the basis of sexual orientation. Protections on the basis of gender identity are

TABLE 9.2. (*continued*)

even more scarce, with citizens of Minnesota enjoying the only statewide protection, joined by only three counties and 20 cities.

Employment protection is on the agenda of most state, local, and national organizations working for GLBT rights. At the federal level, the Employment Non-Discrimination Act (ENDA), if enacted, would provide protection on the basis of sexual orientation. Though gender identity/variance is not covered by ENDA, a coalition of groups is working to rectify this. Most statewide organizations in states not already covered are pushing a bill in their state legislatures.

To advocate for ENDA, contact the Human Rights Campaign, the National Gay and Lesbian Task Force, or GenderPAC. To work for state or local protections, contact your statewide political organization for information on lobbying the state legislature. If you experience workplace discrimination based on your sexual orientation or gender variance, contact your local legal services organization, the ACLU, or Lambda Legal Defense and Education Fund.

GLBT FAMILIES
Family issues have moved to the forefront of the battle for GLBT civil rights. As more GLBT people come out and courageously fight for the equal treatment of our families, we continue to face challenges at the national, state, and local levels. We are fighting for equal marriage rights, domestic partnership protections, and the right to obtain or maintain custody of our children.

Although we've had successes, we've also seen setbacks. In a recent historic ruling, the Vermont State Supreme Court ruled that gay and lesbian couples should not be denied the same rights and responsibilities granted to legally married heterosexual couples. At the same time, GLBT Californians faced the virulently anti-gay Knight Initiative that sought to limit marriage rights to unions between one man and one woman. Twenty-nine states have enacted anti-marriage laws targeting gay and lesbian couples, and the federal Defense of Marriage Act (DOMA) allows all 50 states to deny recognition of gay marriages performed in other states. Additionally, DOMA enables the federal government to deny legal rights to same-sex couples which are given to their heterosexual counterparts.

As psychological research negates the myths of the dangers of GLBT parenting, more GLBT-parented families are coming forward to demonstrate the happiness, health, and love that they have experienced together. Nevertheless, a backlash against gay and lesbian families—led by religious and political extremists—has manifested in recent years. Landmark court cases across the country have shown that GLBT families are not assured the same legal protections as straight families. In the wake of such attacks, many family-focused organizations have mobilized to become more politically active.

The Human Rights Campaign notifies members of updates, information, and specific actions that unfold regarding marriage and family rights. In addition, the National Gay and Lesbian Task Force; Parents, Families, and Friends of Lesbians and Gays (PFLAG); the Family Pride Coalition; and Children of Lesbians and Gays Everywhere (COLAGE) provide resources for individuals who wish to become involved in national, statewide, and local movements for civil rights or need information about parenting and adoption. The Freedom to Marry Coalition and the Partners Task Force for Gay and Lesbian Couples provide outreach, education, and advocacy for same-sex couples and those who serve them.

RACIAL JUSTICE
The fight for racial justice is a central focus of the Millennium March on Washington. The pervasive existence of racial oppression has run a close parallel to oppression based on sexual orientation in the United States. In two highly publicized cases in 1998, two men in this country

(*continued*)

TABLE 9.2. *(continued)*

were tortured and murdered—one because he was gay and the other because he was black. And unfortunately, there have been too many others. The passage of strong hate crime legislation and the desire to live our lives free from violence are just two of the many concerns that these two communities share.

Respected civil rights leaders such as Coretta Scott King and Cesar Chavez have recognized the intrinsic link between discrimination based on race and discrimination based on sexual orientation, and have therefore stood in solidarity with the GLBT community. The struggle for racial justice and the struggle for justice based on sexual orientation are integral parts of a broader struggle for social justice for all people.

There are many ways for people to get involved with this struggle. The National Gay and Lesbian Task Force runs the Racial and Economic Justice Initiative, and national people of color organizations such as LLEGO, the National Latina/o Lesbian, Gay, Bisexual, and Transgender Organization and the Black Lesbian and Gay Leadership Forum do critical work for racial justice. Many statewide organizations and people of color organizations have built strong coalitions and work closely together on legislation critical to both communities. Statewide organizations are also a good source of information for local organizing.

HEALTH
The health-related issues of the GLBT community have emerged as one of the areas most in need of community action. Even as we make strides in the political arena, a range of health concerns from anti-gay violence to substance abuse, from AIDS to breast cancer, from mental health to STDs continue to negatively impact the well-being of GLBT people.

AIDS and breast cancer are among the most devastating illnesses to affect our community. According to the World Health Organization, it is now estimated that 40 million people worldwide are living with HIV/AIDS. In a disturbing trend, HIV infections worldwide rose 10 percent between 1997 and 1998, indicating a failure of effectiveness in prevention; an estimated 16,000 people become infected every day. Finally, according to the U.S. Centers for Disease Control, more than 110,000 young people between the ages of 13 and 29 had been diagnosed with AIDS as of December, 1998.

Breast cancer is a serious issue confronting all women, particularly lesbians. According to the National Cancer Institute, one in every three women will get cancer in her lifetime; one in every nine women will get breast cancer (1990). According to the Mautner Project for Lesbians with Cancer, lesbians are at greater risk for breast, cervical, and ovarian cancers. Furthermore, lesbians are less likely to seek health care due to discomfort with coming out to health care providers, and they are less likely to visit a doctor for routine gynecological services, and therefore less likely to have cancer detected at earlier, more treatable stages.

Growing awareness and pressure from GLBT health activists is challenging agencies to begin to fund research into GLBT-specific health issues. Funding is also needed for prevention programs that target the GLBT community. While a few larger cities such as New York, Los Angeles, San Francisco, Chicago, and Boston have lesbian- and gay-specific health clinics, most cities do not. In most cases, if GLBT health is dealt with at all, it is through HIV/AIDS organizations.

Both the National Gay and Lesbian Task Force and the Human Rights Campaign address health policy. The Gay and Lesbian Medical Association focuses specifically on our health concerns. Statewide organizations may be willing to take on other GLBT health issues. Local, state, and federal representatives must also be made aware of the need for funding for specific GLBT health research and services.

TABLE 9.2. *(continued)*

YOUTH AND AGING

A new generation of GLBT activists are joining those who have been a part of this movement since the fires of the Stonewall Riots, at the Millennium March on Washington. Those who, in 1979, were a part of the first march on Washington will be standing side-by-side with those who had not yet been born.

GLBT youth continue to come out younger and have won more victories than most people would have imagined possible just a few years ago. They are the future activists and organizers of this movement and must play an integral role in creating its future. At the same time, they represent a segment of our community that is in crisis. A 1997 survey conducted by the Massachusetts Department of Education found that 46 percent of gay, lesbian, and bisexual youth had attempted suicide in the past year, while 22.2 percent had skipped school in the past month because they felt it was unsafe. Lack of education on, or support of, GLBT issues in our nation's school systems is one of the most pressing concerns facing queer youth today. GLBT youth must also deal with harassment and violence, unsupportive families (and the homelessness that sometimes results), as well as HIV/AIDS.

At the same time, many of the activists who began this era of the movement are aging and find themselves facing the same problems as other seniors, with some unique differences. There is a void in retirement-related information and services that are sensitive to the needs of the GLBT community. The need for adult living communities that support a positive GLBT environment is in high demand, yet very few facilities exist. Health concerns become more pronounced in the GLBT aging community. In addition, the importance of visitation rights for partners grows in significance as one ages.

The National Youth Advocacy Coalition (NYAC) serves as a national clearinghouse for information about local youth service providers. The Gay, Lesbian, Straight Education Network (GLSEN) advocates on GLBT issues in our nation's K–12 schools and coordinates a network of Gay/Straight Alliances in high schools across the country. Parents, Family, and Friends of Lesbians and Gays (PFLAG) has been working, through its local affiliates, for safe schools for almost a decade. Any of these organizations, or your local community center, could tell you how to support GLBT youth in your area. To get involved with issues around GLBT people and aging, contact the Gay and Lesbian Association of Retired Persons or Golden Threads.

RIGHT TO PRIVACY

The Right to Privacy is one of the most fundamental rights guaranteed by the Constitution and impacts all aspects of American life. The protections of life, liberty, and property enshrined in the 5th and 14th Amendments have been interpreted to create a sphere of privacy protecting a diverse range of activities, from access to contraception to a parent's right to control the education of his or her child.

Central to the struggle for GLBT rights is the issue of privacy. In 18 states and the Uniform Code of Military Justice (UCMJ), sodomy is criminalized. The Supreme Court's decision to uphold the criminalization of sexual acts between consenting adults in its 1986 *Bowers v. Hardwick* decision is the foundation for much of the legalized discrimination directed at the GLBT community. From denial of the right to serve in the military to bans on adoption to the boy scouts, opponents of equality cite the "tendency" of GLBT people to engage in "criminal acts" in their arguments against equal treatment.

Over the last several years, the momentum to secure privacy rights has shifted from the federal arena to the states. Court challenges to sodomy laws and other invasive statutes using state (instead of federal) constitutional protections continue to proliferate and recent successes in

(continued)

TABLE 9.2. (*continued*)

Georgia and Montana bode well for eventual victory. In addition, in many states with sodomy laws, legislative challenges are underway.

Lambda Legal Defense and Education Fund, the National Center for Lesbian Rights and the ACLU's Lesbian and Gay Rights Project coordinate the national strategy of court challenges to sodomy and other invasive laws. In states with sodomy laws, the statewide political organization can tell you how to get involved in your area. Servicemembers Legal Defense Network is the principle organization working on amending the UCMJ.

THE RIGHT TO SERVE
GLBT Americans have served this country with honor and courage throughout the history of the United States military. They have done so under the threat of abuse and/or discharge should their sexual orientation become known to, or suspected by, their colleagues, officers, or commanders.

The military's first formal ban on GLBT service members began in 1943, when revised Army regulations documented the procedure for rejecting gay draftees based on their status as homosexual. Legislation to overturn the ban was introduced in 1992, and President Clinton asked the Secretary of Defense to draft a new, anti-discriminatory policy. Unfortunately, this initiative was met with extreme opposition. A resulting policy, labeled "Don't Ask, Don't Tell, Don't Pursue," was developed as a compromise. It is this policy that remains in effect to this day.

Under the "Don't Ask, Don't Tell" policy, service members may not be discharged for being gay, but may be discharged for engaging in sexual conduct with a member of the same sex. Despite the fact that the "Don't Ask, Don't Tell" policy was intended to reduce discrimination and discharge based on sexual orientation by prohibiting only homosexual conduct, as opposed to status, the policy has resulted in nearly double the amount of discharges than the previous policy and has been widely criticized due to inconsistent enforcement. Nonetheless, the policy has been upheld in several court cases.

In addition to the threat of discharge, GLBT service members suffer harassment and physical abuse for being gay. In a tragic recent example, Pfc. Barry Winchell was beaten to death in 1997, because he was suspected to be gay. Although some branches of the military, such as the Air Force, have since adopted strengthened anti-discrimination policies that include prohibitions on discrimination based on sexual orientation, anti-gay harassment persists in all branches of the military.

Despite the continuance of the "Don't Ask" policy here in the United States, there is cause for optimism: increasing numbers of our international allies have recently eliminated similar bans on gays in the military. For example, in September 1999, the European Court of Human Rights ruled in favor of four British enlistees discharged for being gay, thereby effectively ending Britain's ban on gays in the military. All of our NATO allies, with the exception of Turkey, allow GLBT people to serve in their armed forces.

You can fight the ban by contacting your Congressmember and urging them to remove the ban. You can also donate your time and/or resources to organizations fighting the ban. If you are a member of the armed forces and fear or are facing investigation, contact the Servicemembers Legal Defense Fund or Lambda Legal Defense and Education Fund, both of which have provided legal services to gay and lesbian military personnel.

Source: Official Program of the Millennium March on Washington for Equality. *Advocate,* April 30, 2000.

16.1 percent), Ellen DeGeneres (4.3 percent), Elton John (3.2 percent), and George Michael (1.0 percent). Other nominees included Bill and Hillary Clinton (2.2 percent and 2.9 percent, respectively), Whoopi Goldberg (1.2 percent), Madonna (.9 percent), and Coretta Scott King (.7 percent). The board created some speaker segments that paralleled the platform (e.g., hate-crime speakers, health-issue speakers, etc.) and others that did not (e.g., faith, art, international, etc.).[131] It is notable that speaker selection remained open-ended, whereas the platform was forced choice. This may be because the latter was perceived as having higher stakes (and thus generated tighter control) in its ability to communicate the state of the movement both to the rank and file and straight America.

Despite claims of being "the most democratic" march, the board never disclosed the process by which the final seven platform planks and 120 speakers were selected. Such decisions, along with others that pertained to electing the cochairs[132] (from within the board), securing a permit, finalizing the route, and stage arrangements, among others, were made at four board meetings in Denver (July 9, 1998), New Orleans (September 27–28, 1999), and D.C. (December 5–6, 1999, and February 6–7, 2000). The board said meetings were open, whereas the gay press disputed them as "closed-door meetings."[133]

The marginal media trail focused on board restructurings and personnel issues. On April 25, 1999—one year before the march—Kerry Lobel resigned from the board. Lobel's was the second resignation, which followed the February 1999 resignation of Rea Carey. Lobel's resignation letter was "sharply critical of the very idea of the Millennium March as well as its controversial planning process." A front-page *Washington Blade* article described her letter, in which she blasted the board for having "largely ignored the fundamental issues that led me into becoming involved: why we should march, the agenda, and the involvement of the entire GLBT community." Lobel continued, "I cannot serve on a board that will not open itself to greater input and scrutiny from the communities we claim to represent."[134] AHC members interpreted this as insider confirmation that "a handful of people—not a broad cross-section of the LGBT community—decided it was time to march on Washington."[135]

Lobel and Carey's resignations began a dizzying series of leadership restructurings and secretive BOD meetings. Given mounting criticisms and negative publicity, the BOD communicated through unadvertised conference calls and e-mails that totaled more than 1,100 in number. Critics recognized this: "The Millennium March still lacks community support and has been hobbled by a small self-selected board making decisions in secret."[136] The board was criticized for this mode of communication since e-mail "cannot replace a democratic, inclusive process."[137] After Lobel, and just five months before the event, Robin Tyler also resigned. During their closed-to-the-press New Orleans meeting, the board hired Philadelphia activist Malcom Lazin as co–executive director, a position that absorbed some of Tyler's responsibilities. The board felt that planning and organizing was "too much for one person" (Tyler). They wanted Tyler to focus on stage production and Lazin to concentrate on fund-raising, media, and speakers.

The board also expressed frustration with Tyler's decision-making. Speaking "only on condition of anonymity," one member explained that the board was "stunned" when Tyler unilaterally decided several of the march's speakers, as well as six comedians who would emcee the event. "We were in a state of shock," the board member explained. "I do not want to see six comedians emceeing this march. . . . The entire board should make these decisions." The board's anger prompted them to restrict Tyler's power and their eight-to-four decision to hire Lazin.[138]

Tyler expressed displeasure with the board's action, reporting to the gay press that Lazin's appointment was "unethical and illegal" given contractual obligations between her and the board.[139] She was "not willing to work under an executive director."[140] Citing "conceptual and creative differences,"[141] Tyler's departure from the board in November "reflect[ed] internal discord in an organization that has faced severe external criticism since march plans were first announced."[142] Unbeknownst to the board at the time of hire, Lazin would also abruptly resign—eight weeks before the event—over disagreements as to which company should produce the event. The board silenced his resignation as "a personnel matter that I would rather not talk about in detail," said Ann DeGroot, one of the national cochairs, to the *Washington Blade*. The *Blade* reported that "neither Millennium March officials nor Malcolm Lazin . . . would confirm whether he voluntarily quit or was asked to resign, or what prompted the departure."[143] The secrecy continued.

The board's limited reliance on community input fed the fires of controversy. At the New Orleans meeting, they decided to completely do away with a physical march and instead hold a massive rally on the Mall. According to Lazin, "We feel that a demonstration will be more effective than a parade or march."[144] This odd decision took the march out of the Millennium March. Letters to the editor wondered, "What is the

Millennium March on Washington really? Is it a Gay civil rights rally? Is it a gathering on the mall? Is this for everyone, processed by consensus? Or is it proclaimed from on high with the Human Rights Campaign and the Universal Fellowship of Metropolitan Community Churches pulling the strings?"[145]

With criticism mounting, and similar to the call itself, the board reversed its position. A November 23, 1999, press release declared the event "would include a procession through the streets of Washington."[146] To ensure that people were made aware, MMOW board chair Ann De-Groot circulated a letter to the editor in gay papers across the country: "March or rally? That's been a key question about the Millennium March. . . . Now it's official. Like past marches, the Millennium March will feature both a civil rights march through the streets of Washington, D.C., and a massive rally on the National Mall."[147] It is striking that the decision to make the Millennium March a march was not officially announced until December 1999, four months before the event—or that it could even be described as a "key question."

The Millennium March on Washington for (Lesbian, Gay, Bisexual, and Transgender) Equality

On April 30, 2000, in a journey that revealed "the internal strife of the Gay civil rights movement [had] spiked to a new high,"[148] anywhere from 125,000 to 800,000 lesbian, gay, bisexual, and transgender individuals returned to Washington in a revealing sea where HRC's block-yellow equal sign was just as visible, if not more prominent, than the rainbow flag. HRC's symbol was so ubiquitous that some described the Mall as "verg[ing] on becoming a live commercial for the Human Rights Campaign."[149] Compared to prior marches, the MMOW felt less political. "The march itself," noted the gay press, "was relatively quiet, with minimal chanting." Many saw it as just a party. Equality Illinois executive director Rick Garcia bluntly asked, "Why are we here? It's more like a fund-raiser for the Human Rights Campaign. . . . This is not a political event."[150]

The MMOW was the first to be staged during an election year and the first at which the president of the United States delivered an address, albeit via videotape. Attendance figures varied more than for any of its predecessors, capturing competing claims of power and effectiveness. Mem-

bers of the AHC issued a detailed explanation that put the crowd size
at 125,000, whereas march cochair Donna Redwing estimated 800,000.
Law enforcement officials, the Associated Press, and most media estimates fell nearer to AHC's at 200,000. There was no official count since
the U.S. Park Police stopped releasing such estimates in 1995 after pro-
moters of the Million Man March filed suit over attendance figures.

Title debates surfaced in day-of media coverage. The *San Francisco
Chronicle* observed, "Even the Millennium March title—which has no
mention of gays, lesbians, bisexuals, or transgenders—is an affront to
some activists." The article proceeded to quote AHC member Bill Dobbs
for an explanation: " 'It's a way to hide the identities,' Dobbs said. 'They
are trying to water it down.' "[151] Unlike prior marches, the title kept mor-
phing. It began as just the "Millennium March on Washington," without specifying the marchers' identities or the movement's strategy. For
whom was this march? Was it for equal rights? Equality? Liberation?
Then, at some later, undisclosed point, it evolved to "Millennium March
on Washington for Equality." Now there was strategy, but still no identity. The final metamorphosis gave birth to an identity by tagging on "for
Lesbian, Gay, Bisexual, and Transgender Equality," as seen in the banner carried notably by gay celebrities and board members (see fig. 9.6).
Hoisting the banner was a group that looked very different from 1979's
Salsa Soul Sisters (see fig. 3.4).

Similar to the title, the board also never effectively communicated the
new theme (or the process by which it was chosen): "Equality: Nothing
More, Nothing Less." Many infighters were not able to move beyond the
controversial "Faith and Family," which might explain why so few people were aware of the new theme. Unlike prior marches, it was hardly
even visible at the demonstration.

The MMOW was an excruciating experience for many. Elizabeth
Birch reflected that "the March on Washington of 2000 was the single
most painful experience . . . of my whole professional life."[152] Six months
after the march, one board member wrote a handwritten letter to a cochair that declared, "Having gained your friendship will be one of the
few 'benefits' from MMOW."[153] Some, like 1993 march cochair Billy
Hileman, were so inflamed that they did not want history to even record it as a march. What was it? In Hileman's words, it was "the event
in 2000."[154] He circulated this view three weeks prior to the march in
gay newspapers across the country. Boldly titled, "MMOW Is Not the
4th Gay-Rights March," Hileman asserted, "The Millennium March

FIGURE 9.6. Millennium March Banner. Photo by Richard Renaldi for the Human Rights Campaign.

on Washington is not the fourth national mobilization for the rights of lesbian, gay, bisexual, and transgender people. It was not called by our community. It is not accountable to our community. . . . It does not represent our community. It demands nothing from our government. History should not record the MMOW in the same vein as the 1979, 1987, and 1993 marches on Washington."[155] Nothing like this had ever happened before.

Even some post-march rally speakers commented on the cacophonous infighting. Keith Boykin delivered perhaps the most controversial speech. In "Poem for the Millennium March," Boykin first addressed the striking absence of people of color: "I speak so that the presence of people of color will not be tokenized and the absence of people of color will not be trivialized." He then moved to strategy: "I speak because two people sitting in a hotel room should not be able to dictate the entire lesbigaytrans agenda . . . [and] because our community has a right to know how decisions are made, and a responsibility to hold our leaders accountable."[156] Boykin concluded with a commentary on identity: "I speak as a member of the family because there are problems in the family that cannot be healed by sweeping them under the sterilized, sanitized rug of homogenized homosexuality."[157] At times, the speeches felt like a battle, for example, when Birch appeared to respond to Boykin and others, "Some people, even in our community, didn't want you to be here today. . . . But you voted with your hearts . . . and you voted with your feet."[158] This was a very public fight.

In an unprecedented state of affairs, infighting congealed into a formal march boycott, consolidated in the "Boycott MMOW Coalition." One month before the march, the group disseminated a press release that pointedly declared, "Boycott the MMOW." According to the release, the movement must not become a stranger to itself:

> There are times when a unified "movement" is a façade for a void of critical, principled, and justice-seeking leadership. . . . These are such times. . . . The MMOW constricts justice. The MMOW erases most of us. It erases us in its political foundation. It erases us in its practice. It erases us in its weak rhetoric about "equality". . . . We cannot, in the name of our own liberation, perpetuate those things which . . . make us strangers to ourselves. . . . We cannot submit to erasure and constriction.
> The MMOW lurches forward and will . . . happen. This . . . does not mean that any of us must or even should attend. We can all refuse to be pimped by this big-dollar hustle cloaked as a movement for equality. . . . We are being encouraged to assimilate. . . . The true leaders are eclipsed by celebrities.
> We the people of the community have not made the decision to march, have had no true voice in choosing this direction. . . . The means by which the MMOW robs us, each of us, of our rightful voice in our own lives demands a response. It mandates our resistance. . . . Each of us can take back our voice. . . . Each of us can reclaim the movement and set it on the path that we choose as a people. The Boycott MMOW Coalition calls upon all members of the lesbian, gay, bisexual, transgender, two-spirit community and our allies to stay away from the activities of the MMOW. The failure of the MMOW will be a victory for the cause of liberation. . . . A failed MMOW will make it possible for us to reclaim our movement.[159]

The AHC, although part of the Boycott Coalition, distributed its own press releases as well. One, titled "Why We Aren't Marching," outlined the MMOW's "Four Fundamental Flaws."[160] Topping the list was "No Democracy": "How can we have a 'Millennium March on Washington for Equality' without a democratic decision-making process open to all?" Second was "No LGBT Community Mandate." Here, the AHC emoted that the "MMOW had the arrogance to expect that the entire LGBT community would obediently follow its lead and shift local priorities and resources—without consultation, without discussion, and without a democratic process for making decisions." Next came "Racial and Community Tokenism," elaborated as follows: "MMOW asserts their Board was made more inclusive by expanding it to include over 50 percent people of color. . . . The Board itself is a body which is self-selected. In '79, '87, and '93, people of color—and everyone else—were selected by and from their own communities." The fourth and final fundamental flaw was "Marketing $$$ Rule," which took issue with the corporate sponsorship of the march.

This last item ("Marketing $$$ Rule") requires comment. The Millennium March debates focused overwhelmingly on process. But this was not the only sore spot. Another prominent area of dissent concerned movement marketing. Unlike prior marches, the MMOW was financed by corporate sponsors, some from within the community (e.g., the *Advocate*), and others that were external (e.g., United Airlines, the "official airline" of the march). This compelled some to ask, "MMOW: Is This a Gay March? Or a Gay Market?"[161] In another article, "Movement or Market?" writer Bob Roehr provocatively pondered, "[Corporate sponsorship] blurs the line between movement and market. It leaves one wondering what gays are fighting for, equal rights or the equal right to shop? When Martin Luther King Jr. said, 'I have a dream . . .' was he talking about the Abercrombie & Fitch catalog?"[162] Keith Boykin also addressed this issue in his rally speech: "I speak to resist the commercialization and commodification of the mainstream Gay lifestyle that enriches the privileged few and impoverishes the masses with a bankrupt culture of uniformity."[163]

The mainstream media facetiously renamed the event the "Militant Marketing March." The journalist asked, "Corporate America is herding thousands of gays, lesbians, and other gender outlaws into D.C. on April 30 for the latest March on Washington. Is the event really about social change, or mass-marketing?"[164] The article quoted Steve Ault's reaction: "This is what we've turned into thirty years after Stonewall? We're described as this commodity? We're being sold?" Nadine Smith concurred: "Does it all come down to dollars?"

Unlike past marches, the millennial BOD refused to release its financial records. The AHC urged the board to open their books to respond to concerns of financial accountability. Board cochair Donna Redwing sharply replied, "We are not going to release our financial statements to the Ad Hoc Committee. . . . Our contractual arrangements are none of their business." The AHC was shocked. Michael Castellano observed, "When MMOW says it's 'none of their business,' the 'their' refers to the entire LGBT community, the same community they purport to represent."[165] This trend continued up to one month before the march, at which time a Chicago letter noted, "There has also been no financial accountability. . . . [Th]e MMOW board refuses to release financial information."[166] Three days before the march and in an article titled "Top 5 Reasons to Skip MMOW," Billy Hileman declared, "The MMOW has refused to open its financial records to the community—MMOW leaders are annoyed by requests for financial disclosure."[167]

The BOD were jolted out of secrecy when, two weeks after the march, the gay press revealed that an astonishing $750,000 was missing from the "Millennium Festival," a two-day event produced by Jose Ucles, who stepped down from the board to assume responsibility for the for-profit venture.[168] The Festival was organized in conjunction with, though vividly fenced off from, the MMOW and asked a $5 donation to enter. To some, the dramatic chain-link fence signaled that the festival "seems profit motivated." Others remarked, "I think the fence . . . is very, very negative to the movement" since it felt like segregation rather than "a blending."[169]

The FBI became involved in what some described as "the largest financial wrongdoing ever in the gay community,"[170] a sentiment that found its way in a political cartoon that depicted a rainbow flag with the green stripe missing (see fig. 9.7).

No charges were filed on the "grand larceny."[171] Commentators threw up their hands in disbelief. Michelangelo Signorile sighed, "So much for the thought that our movement had created a well-oiled, well-financed machine that avoided these kinds of amateurish blunders or that we could afford to stop listening to the grassroots now that we have slick and more corporate Washington groups doing our bidding."[172] Bill Dobbs added, "It's hard to be shocked by this, especially after two years of march organizers refusing to divulge financial records to the public. You can't have a multi-million dollar event behind closed doors."[173] Some reduced "the march's legacy" to "a flood of red ink."[174]

The Millennium March lived and breathed despite the possible death of the grassroots. John D'Emilio refers to this tendency as "grassrootsism," a "kind of rigid, ideological allegiance to or claim to have allegiance to the grassroots."[175] The MMOW captures the rise of powerful and professional national movement organizations that are unafraid to utilize corporate sponsorship and corporate organizing structures. It also highlights the difficulties of believing that a self-selected board of directors can set the agenda from the top-down yet also claim to speak for everyone in what was touted as "the most democratic" march in the movement's history. These concerns aside, the MMOW signals a shift in strategy away from participatory and grassroots toward a bureaucratized

FIGURE 9.7. Who Took the Green? Cartoon by Ron Williams, © Rich Williams.

and corporate style that has "proved that the old way of doing things is not the only way to do things."[176] The historical record, however, does not shine favorably upon this alternate model.

The MMOW also exhibits changes in gay identity. The BOD minimized differences between gays and straights. This was evidenced in numerous ways, from early themes of faith and family that suggested gay people wanted to return to the churches of their youth and celebrate their families, just like everyone else. It was also evident in the *Advocate* poll in which 58 percent of respondents agreed that "presenting a conservative or 'safe' image of the gay and lesbian community is politically desirable." This minimizing is strikingly similar to the human-rights approach from 1979 and the queer challenge from 1993 that advocated identity-blurring. The case of the Millennium March challenges the idea of "unity through diversity,"[177] as board members struggled with the former, while the demonstration minimally exhibited the latter. Despite genuinely desiring unification, the board flattened (and dictated) diversity down to a homogenized image of conservative, hyper-normative, mostly white, middle-class gay people. It seems, at the dawn of the new millennium and as seen through the lens of the Millennium March, that gays had indeed gotten rather straight and that gay culture had become "heterosexualized," to allude to Daniel Mendelsohn's *New York* magazine cover story discussed in the previous chapter. History has yet to determine whether this transition from the "exoticized gay margin to the normalized straight center"[178] is sustainable, whether the grassroots has definitely been usurped by powerful corporate-styled social movement organizations, whether the grassroots will again rise up to reclaim what was hijacked from them, or whether the two can each contribute their respective strengths to what Urvashi Vaid described as "the dream of a common movement."[179]

Conclusion:
How Conflict and Culture Work
in Political Organizing

In this book, I have inquired into the prevalence, role, and pattern of internal conflicts, or infighting, across four lesbian and gay marches on Washington that span thirty years of political organizing. My story challenges infighting's "sorry reputation." As one listens to activist voices in these pages, it is not convincing that we hear "internecine dog fighting" that "hastens movement collapse" by rendering insurgent groups "impotent." Infighting in these particular Washington marches cannot be etched as the "cause of death upon [their] tombstones." There must be another explanation.

Infighting as a Culture Carrier

Dissent captures "the heart of the struggle to define what sort of politics gay people should promote" and "who is the 'we' on behalf of whom activists speak,"[1] to borrow from sociologist Steve Epstein. This *state of the movement,*[2] as I have called it, includes competing cultural or meaning-rich conceptions of strategy and identity, both of which activists carry to the table by fighting over logistical tasks. Through the voices of infighting, one can discern questions of strategy that include: Where are we headed? How do we get there? How are decisions made? Who controls the movement? Infighting also enables identity work, as activists seek answers to questions such as: What does it mean to be gay in America? And what subgroups are part of our movement?

As activists air and alleviate dissent at one moment in time, they consolidate their lessons learned into what I have called a cultural template that influences how future organizing will proceed (or how it ought to proceed). This template prescribes guidelines for how gay people should enact their vision and values for social change. Activists drafted this template in the back-and-forth between dissent and decision-making that transpired at national conferences. The very idea of a cultural template suggests that, through infighting, activists converged on a cluster of assumptions, agreements, and meanings that (sometimes unconsciously) structured their future conventions of disputation and deliberation. By comparing four Washington marches, we see how emergent cultural conventions in earlier periods become constitutive templates (or at least ideas exceedingly difficult to ignore) that structure the next round. Infighting therefore does more than just carry conversations of strategy and identity to the table; it also influences and monitors how organizing will proceed from one march to the next.

Infighting and Strategy

During the first march, activists argued that passage of local gay rights ordinances was no longer viable as a primary strategy, anchoring their rationale in the observation that no minority group had ever gained rights in this fashion. Infighting symbolized difficulties of moving from a local perspective, inspired by the Stonewall spark and which was firmly in place, to a national vision, which had no precedent. Stubborn debates over whether to march carried cultural anxieties about whether enough gays would show up, an indicator of deep skepticism in a national movement. If there was a poor turnout, the event would mark a black-eye on the movement. Questions of who controlled the movement materialized in regional critiques (for example, concerns that gays from urban areas exerted too much influence, leaving those in the Hinterlands without voice).

Debates over movement goals evolved over the course of organizing the first march. During the earlier days, activists proceeded with a logic of boundary-blurring that deemphasized the uniqueness of gay sexuality to external audiences. They drew on President Carter's foreign policy agenda to argue that gay rights were a part of human rights that all

people deserved and that, according to Carter, were absolute (read: universal and general). As organizing progressed, activists began to imagine themselves as an autonomous, national movement. This inspired a
single-issue march framed by the Five Demands and unified by a singu-
lar purpose: to "end all social, economic, judicial, and legislative oppression of lesbian and gay people." The aphorism "we are everywhere" was
part of the shared lexicon; the 1979 march gave it material credence and
proved that lesbians and gay men were indeed a force with which to be
reckoned. Activists staged the event on October 14, 1979, to commemorate the ten-year anniversary of Stonewall. By linking a local event to
a national demonstration, the decision of when to march was part of an
omnibus strategy to redirect away from a localities approach onto a national platform.

Activists assembled the second march using the nascent cultural template established by the first and staged it over Columbus Day weekend
(October 11, 1987) to provide continuity. With a national consciousness
in place, the movement was now able to augment its strategy. It departed
from the single-issue precedent of the first march and embraced instead
a coalition platform that was then considered the most progressive statement ever drafted. Infighting revealed a complex analysis that advocated
for the intersection of oppressions. The genius of this strategy was its
linking of homophobia with racism and sexism as a way to encompass a
broad spectrum of humanity—gay and otherwise—into the movement.
The transition from a single- to multi-issue platform was viable due to
the establishment of a national consciousness, the acuteness of external
threat, international political activity, and its resonance with gay people
of color. It signaled a transition away from national autonomy toward an
interconnected social justice stance. This was not inevitable, as infighting revealed.[3]

In contrast to 1979, second march activists found their sexual orientation to be a distinct source of oppression. The decision to link with other
movements and to draft a multi-issue platform did not imply boundary
permeability as did the decision to subsume gay rights under the rhetoric of human rights in 1979. The diminishment strategy of the first march
made sense in light of an underdeveloped national consciousness. This
time, activists were keenly self-aware, sought strength through an additive constellation of groups, and hardened boundaries vis-à-vis external
agents, thereby reversing what they did before. A recalibration was necessary given the shifting sociopolitical context. Government neglect of

gay people as they became infected with HIV and died of AIDS, along with a trial over the very souls of gay people in the halls of the Supreme Court, made the second march fundamentally and irreducibly *about gay people*. An era of war and protest inspired gay distinction.

The titanic 1993 march captured activists fighting once again over strategy. Activists stitched deeper into their cultural template by agreeing on a coalition platform, something they affirmed by changing the date to not conflict with an Indigenous Cultures March protesting the arrival of Christopher Columbus. The idea of social justice, however, had morphed. Organizers reframed the same decision (i.e., we should link up with other movements) away from a self-definition as a social justice movement and instead toward a mainstream civil rights project. This reframing made sense in light of developments in the sociopolitical context. The threat of AIDS and *Bowers* in the 1980s made social justice more viable, so the movement could present a formidable front, whereas the culturally diffuse nature of external threat in the 1990s (recall the special rights fiasco) along with visibility trends (the "Gay '90s") allowed the movement to opt for the mainstream. Activists underscored their new centrist strategy in press releases that defined the NAACP endorsement, in particular, as evidence that the movement was no longer on the fringe. Seeds for this strategy were also visible in the second march's official endorsement of the Wedding, one of many weekend events, but one that was resoundingly normative. The people next door had arrived. Being new to the neighborhood, they were still situated on the mainstream margins and rigorously promoted the rise of respectability.

During the third march, centrist and leftist impulses were suspended in a productive (though tenuous) strategy of simultaneity that at once emphasized distinction and deemphasis. Activists argued that "we are just like you" and only want equal rights, as they declared in their title (and in contrast to the Religious Right's accusations that they sought special rights). The lavender left, however, was restless. And so we additionally hear activists declaring, "We are different from you and maybe what we want instead is liberation," as they also demanded in their title. The late 1980s and early 1990s were thus a special time in history when the progressive "looney left" and the conservative "people next door" organized in equal partnership.

Although the "event in 2000" also had a coalition platform (similar to the 1987 and 1993 marches), its construction was against the initial in-clination of organizers, evidenced by the survey instrument they used to solicit input that included only forced-choice, pre-selected, single-issue items. The change from single-issue to coalition did not occur until late in the organizing process and without widespread awareness. The Mil-lennium March mostly paralleled the first march in 1979 when the move-ment was breaking free from a localities strategy. Nearly twenty years later, the movement returned to this approach, revealed in the strong support for Equality Begins at Home, in which protests were organized in the capitals of every state. Although the full circle compounded a sense of vertigo, something was different. The program of simultaneity activists so carefully balanced in 1993 had decidedly shifted in the direc-tion of the mainstream by the millennium. This, in conjunction with the rise of powerful, bureaucratic, national, D.C.-based organizations, a gay marketing niche, and gay celebrities, put in place the conditions needed to organize a march that departed from its predecessors for a movement that now stood in the mainstream center.

The Millennium March reveals the consequences of rupturing the cultural template. The most forceful debates concerned the basic ques-tion of whether to march (i.e., a community mandate), an area of contro-versy that never resolved, and which affected the event's comparatively lower turnout. Unlike the prior three marches, the fourth was called and organized by a self-selected group that represented a handful of prom-inent national organizations. In the process, "presumptuousness mor-phed into power" and "began to look a bit monstrous, like it was sucking up the movement and spitting it out in its own image," in the words of so-ciologist Joshua Gamson.[4]

The eclipsing of grassroots politics and the dawn of organizational control suggested by the Millennium March unleashed a fury never be-fore seen. Some of it may have been tempered if organizers were trans-parent about what many saw the event plainly to be—a fund-raiser and party for the HRC. They chose instead to speak "on behalf of the com-munity" of "what it means to be gay in this nation at the turn of the century," in the words of then executive director Elizabeth Birch. The Millennium March suggests that activists cannot disregard a cultural template that embodies their own history. Doing so exacerbates infight-ing and shrinks its generative possibilities. Figure 10.1 summarizes the evolution of strategy across the four marches.

Single-Issue and Grassroots; From Localities to National Autonomy	Multi-Issue and Grassroots; From National Autonomy to Social Justice Coalitions	Multi-Issue and Grassroots; Equal Rights and Liberation on the Mainstream Margins	Mostly Single-Issue and Top-Down; From Mainstream Margins to the Mainstream Center
1979	1987	1993	2000

FIGURE 10.1. Strategy across Four Washington Marches.

Infighting and Identity

Activists also used infighting to define their identity by elaborating what attributes and relationships they shared (i.e., categorical commonality and relational connectedness, respectively). Organizers of the 1979 march equated sexual identity with family. A familial model for categorical commonality was evidenced in the slogan "We Are Family" and the pronounced language of *lesbian sisters* and *gay brothers*. This facilitated unification efforts by deemphasizing any single or distinctive characteristic gay people were presumed to share. Instead, activists emphasized their "family resemblance," to allude to philosopher Ludwig Wittgenstein.[5]

Siblings in a family are related as brothers or sisters; this then set the terms for debate on relational connectedness. Dissent in the 1970s encompassed fights to include lesbians underneath the otherwise unqualified gay umbrella. Hence debates to rename all organizations from gay to gay *and lesbian,* including the march title. This inclusion augmented identity boundaries. Early differences also pertained to people of color, although these debates were comparatively amiable, perhaps due to lesbians' and gay men's joint involvement in civil rights organizing, in contrast to lesbian separatism that wedged gender more widely apart. All delegations had to ensure 20 percent representation for people of color and gender parity to vote. Activists also demonstrated their commitment to racial inclusion by staging the march the same weekend as the first Third World Conference, a series of workshops and plenary sessions designed to address the special needs and experiences of gay people of color.

Debates during the first march suggest that boundary expansion was not without limits. Redolent of pressures for ideological purity in the women's movement, transgender people (*transpeople,* in the argot of the times) were excluded in the title and platform despite desiring recognition. This boundary-hardening vis-à-vis certain contending insiders was due to a lack of understanding about who transpeople were, what they wanted, and how they fit into the movement. Such uncertainties persisted for decades. Dissent during 1979 suggests that broad similarity, rather than specificity, facilitates unity in the earlier phases of mobilization.

Infighting over race and gender continued into the second march. Lesbians' demand for inclusion was initially met with increased sexism within the movement, and inclusion for people of color was initially met with heightened racism. That delegates voted to include the statement on racism and sexism in the 1987 platform suggests the salience of these issues. It also suggests the instability over time of a family-resemblance identity model. Although the language of *lesbian sisters* and *gay brothers* lingered, it did so with much less frequency than in the first march. Dissent in 1987 therefore reveals pressures away from generality and toward specificity instead. Mere resemblance is unsustainable. Who exactly are we? The decision to move away from a single-issue platform toward coalitions suggests social justice as a new basis for categorical commonality. Gay people were not just family members; they were family members who were sensitive to racism and sexism within and beyond the movement. Gay identity stretched beyond the narrower confines of sexuality, something activists additionally signaled by increasing the people-of-color representation requirement from 20 percent to 25 percent.

The redefinition of categorical commonality resonated with changes in relational connectedness. That is, a quest toward a social justice agenda (what the category *gay* meant) resonated with the notable growth of lesbian and gay organizations of color (how different gays were connected to each other). Although this suggests a degree of identity plasticity, 1987 march debates also reveal certain limits. The most vivid was around bisexual inclusion, a series of debates that paralleled those between lesbians and gay men during the first march. The 1970s witnessed the expansion of the moniker gay to gay *and lesbian*. In 1993, this expanded further to gay, lesbian, *and bi*. The requisite identity work began in the (transitional for bisexuals) second march.

The late 1980s and 1990s witnessed the blossoming of a bisexual culture and politics. Along with debates initiated in the second march, this gave them bargaining power in ways they did not have before, evidenced by their inclusion in the title of the 1993 march. Dissent and organizational development consolidated bisexuals as a distinct subgroup within what had previously been just the lesbian and gay movement; it was now a lesbian, gay, and bi march. The Religious Right's special-rights epithet propelled the movement down a mainstream path. As they attempted to blur differences between themselves and straights, activists at times deemphasized their sexuality. The decoupling of sex from gay identity explains why bisexuals were included in the title of the march, though reduced to asexual *bis*.

The struggle for equal rights also compelled the movement to consider what equality itself meant. This generated debates on the appropriate representation of people of color. Should they comprise 25 percent of delegates, as they did in 1987, or 50 percent? This question manifested as a tension between a principle of parity versus proportions. That organizers decided to increase the requirement to 50 percent reveals their commitment to equal rights, in terms of how they wanted to be perceived by Americans *and* how they wanted gay people to understand each other. For the first time, women and men and whites and people of color jointly owned the organizing process. Equality of internal diversity was born.

Boundary expansion in the early 1990s stopped again at transgender inclusion. Although this debate had lingered since 1979, there were notable differences by 1993. Fourteen years of organizing still had not disabused confusion. This is one reason why transgenders were not represented in the march's title. The movement's steady march into the mainstream along with their desire to blur differences vis-à-vis straight people provides additional explanations for boundary reticence. But rejecting transgender people was at odds with the movement's new principle of parity used to reconfigure people-of-color representation to 50 percent. This dissonance explains why transgender people were included in the platform and had a seat on the steering committee yet were not included in the title. Transgenders were at once a part of, and excluded from, the 1993 march.

Departing from its predecessors, the Millennium March in 2000 finally included transgenders in its title. Bisexuals were now granted their sexuality in the title as well, which listed them fully instead of reducing them to just *bi*. In terms of relational connectedness, the Millennium March evinces the most inclusive stance, "in which bisexual and transgender people [were] included as a matter of course." This matter of course came late and was accompanied by deafening debates. The event was originally titled "Millennium March on Washington for Equality." Early debates revealed activists affronted by this seemingly closeted title. Without debate, the Millennium March may have exhibited a symbolically backward, if not erasing, stance in its elimination of all identities in its title. It remains unclear whether this was what the organizers thought of as "acceptable gayness."[6]

The Millennium March was the first in which "half of those running things are people of color and also the first that many people-of-color groups have consistently and angrily refused to endorse."[7] The trouble lay in confusion between selection and representation. In the past three marches, people of color willingly chose to attend national meetings where they were elected to a steering committee and, as such, became accountable to the communities they represented. The fourth march jettisoned this cultural template in place of a corporate model that used a board of directors. The self-selected board comprised over 60 percent people of color. However, and as Mandy Carter summarized, "There is a qualitative difference between being a person of color and representing a people-of-color constituency." The Millennium March had incorporation without representation, evidenced by the lack of endorsements from most people of color organizations. Some, such as the influential National Association of Black and White Men Together, protested by moving its national spring meeting in D.C., originally scheduled to overlap with the march to enhance POC visibility, to a different date. This was in stark contrast to 1979 when the march deliberately coincided with the Third World Conference.

Title and theme debates illuminated categorical commonality as well. The word *millennium* in the title along with an early theme of Faith and Family ignited dissension. Some objected to the emphasis on faith and spirituality rather than diversity, advising organizers to replace the word *millennium* with others that could specify ownership, for example, *lesbian, gay, bisexual, transgender.* Again we see an impulse of identity erasure that corresponds with entrance into the mainstream. In this process, the Millennium March reconfigured the 1990s queer challenge. Whereas queer theory pushed for identity-blurring in the name of uncontainable diversity, the event in 2000 pushed for identity erasure in the name of being like everyone else. The new queer challenge manifested in the march's trying to clone its own image, which was less diverse than the reality of LGBT communities across the country.

Infighting in the 2000 march reveals three characteristics of the millennial movement. First, it is increasingly an organizational one, where enough power is concentrated in the hands of few that can run a national show—whether one calls it a march or an event or a party—without necessarily being accountable to those they claim to represent. Second, infighting reveals an increasingly diverse community, a dynamic that is sometimes at odds with an impulse to be just like straights, that is, less

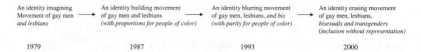

An identity imagining Movement of gay men and lesbians	→	An identity building movement of gay men and lesbians (with proportions for people of color)	→	An identity blurring movement of gay men, lesbians, and bis (with parity for people of color)	→	An identity erasing movement of gay men, lesbians, bisexuals and transgenders (inclusion without representation)
1979		1987		1993		2000

FIGURE 10.2. Identity across Four Washington Marches.

diverse. This tension fuels culture wars to define what it means to be gay and politically polarizes the grassroots from the organizational professionals. As Richard Goldstein observed, "As the community expands far beyond its original homosexual base to include transsexuals and even questioning straights, it's become impossible to control the meaning of queer."[8] Finally, infighting suggests that although power may be concentrated in the hands of a few, the hands of the many cannot be smothered. Organizational power cannot accumulate unabated and will not go unchecked. Kevin Danaher, cofounder of Global Exchange, once remarked, "In Ethiopia they have a saying, 'When spiders unite, they can tie down a lion.' . . . If all of us small citizen forces come together, we can force these guys to change."[9] The story of the Ad Hoc Committee for an Open Process reveals that although the grassroots may be circumvented, they cannot—indeed will not—be eradicated. Figure 10.2 depicts the evolution of gay identity across the four marches (with italicized items emphasizing historically specific developments). Together, figures 10.1 and 10.2 illustrate infighting's capacity to operate as a culture carrier for meaningful conversations of strategy and identity that together comprise the state of the movement.

The preceding discussion points to the possibility that, over time, dissent itself becomes the means through which activists understand what it means to be gay, that is, gay people are those who always fight with each other. Judy Wieder, former editor in chief of the *Advocate,* provocatively linked infighting to genetics: "It doesn't matter if you disagree. That's just your gay genes talking. Gays and lesbians will fuss with each other over anything." Turning to the Millennium March, she continued, "Yes, the march is controversial . . . (that ol' gay infighting gene again). But so what? We've always marched to different drummers."[10] Other commentators agreed: "Perhaps the impulse to divide and demonize is in the nature of being a minority," mused Richard Goldstein. Former U.S. Congressman Steve Gunderson (R-Wisc.) chimed in: "We in the gay community often want to be critical."[11] Are the dividends of dissent somehow connected to the genetics of sexual orientation?

Nineteen ninety-three march cochair Billy Hileman responded to Wieder's gay-genes comment:

> Why is there so much bickering in the LGBT community? Well, according to *The Advocate*'s editor in chief, Judy Wieder, the source of our unsettled community is that we carry in our DNA that "gay infighting gene". . . . Debate in our community is not controlled by a common heredity, and it isn't necessarily a destructive thing. . . . What is really going on here? Well, it's not bitchy DNA. The controversy surrounding the MMOW is a direct financial threat to *The Advocate*. *The Advocate* is committed to a 300,000 print run of the official MMOW program. No doubt they are busy selling ads. . . . To help protect their investment, any complaint about the MMOW is automatically characterized as "infighting" and is dismissed.[12]

Dissent is embedded into the pages of gay history. And the movement has benefited from this. As one activist remembered during the Millennium March, "Controversy and debate have surrounded every previous march on Washington. And that's not bad for our community—it's good. And healthy. All voices must be heard and all views must find expression."[13] Equating infighting with genetics, bitchiness, prickliness, or reducing it to mere personal attacks is a mistake. Airing dissent enables activists to carry on a more complex conversation for which there may not otherwise be space.

Culturally Varying Scripts for Structurally Similar Tasks

When activists look back on their four marches, they speak to what they and movements in general mean, that is, to their cultural template. According to activist Scott Tucker, "Every march had immediate existential worth: 'Here I stand, I can do no other'—to borrow Luther's words. But every march also existed, of course, on a historical and social timeline. The earlier national marches—in 1979 and 1987—left an imprint upon the later ones in 1993 and 2000."[14] The gay press contributed with stories titled, "Different Times, Different Marches" and "Four Decades, Four Marches."[15] These demonstrations are an important and heretofore neglected part of gay history.

Infighting in the organizing process erupted over the same six tasks across each of the four demonstrations: whether to march, when to

TABLE 10.1. **Dimensions of Difference across Four Washington Marches**

	1979	1987	1993	2000
Internal Dimensions				
Community Consciousness	Deemphasis (human rights)*	Distinction	Distinction and deemphasis	Deemphasis (heterosexualization)
Organizational Development	Lesbians and gay men	People of color*	Queers and bisexuals	Transgenders and national organizations
	Grassroots	Grassroots	Grassroots	Top-Down*
External Dimensions				
Threat	Discrete, Local	Discrete, National*	Diffuse, National*	Discrete and diffuse, Local and national
Political / Cultural Status	Periphery	Periphery	Mainstream margins*	Mainstream center*

Note₁: Developments within a particular category and march persist over time. Subsequent marches are characterized by additional trends, as opposed to replacement trends.
Note₂: * Denotes the variable(s) that exerted the most influence during the respective march.

march, the title and theme, speakers, platform/demands, and the organizing structure. To what extent were activists aware of this pattern? And if they were aware, why were they not able to preempt future fights? The story told in these pages reveals that structurally similar debates became inflected with culturally varying scripts based on the sociopolitical context and developments within the movement (see table 10.1). Four factors account for this, including the organizing group's consciousness or subjective state, their internal development, the nature of threat confronting the group, and their political/cultural status in society. These factors inflected different meanings (culturally varying scripts) to debates that otherwise looked the same (were structurally similar).[16] In this section, I report quantitative data to illustrate how this process unfolded across more than 1,100 newspaper articles that reported on all four marches.[17]

In 1979, the lack of a national consciousness exerted the most influence over whether-to-march debates. Activists marched to "build a national movement." Articulations of this goal were unevenly distributed in the public forum across the four marches. Activists mentioned it most in the first demonstration, when disbelief ran highest; did not over- or under-emphasize it in the second or third marches, when their attention had shifted to AIDS and *Bowers* and the special-rights crusade, respectively; and talked about it less than expected by the fourth march, when the veracity of a national movement was self-evident. This goal set the terms of debate. The most vociferous dissent in 1979 revolved around the question of whether to march. Would enough gays risk visibility? Could they successfully transition from a local to a national strategy? Because of the salience of lesbian separatism and charges of gay male sexism in the late 1970s, infighting was colored with charges of "gender inequality." The question of whether to march was not similarly gendered for the other three demonstrations.

Debates on whether to march were comparatively muted in 1987, as the first march consolidated a national consciousness and conflict became discrete and concentrated at the national level. The first mass protest event demonstrated gay autonomy. Eight years later as the movement continued building, activists had to decide whether to link with other causes or situate themselves as politically sui generis. They concluded that autonomy did not translate to power, evidenced by the one-two punch of federal inaction around AIDS and the *Bowers* ruling. "To fight AIDS," therefore, was a prominent reason to march in 1987. Activists did not mention it the first march, since HIV had not yet been discovered. It remained a prominent blip on activists' radar in 1993, suggesting its continued prominence, and was not particularly pronounced in the public forum during the Millennium March, suggesting a strategic shift. Besides AIDS and in response to *Bowers,* activists decided they needed to return to Washington "to celebrate and recognize gay relationships." This reasoning was over-prevalent during the second march, muted in 1979 (when concerns were primarily about imagining a national movement), and not particularly over- or under-pronounced in the third and fourth marches.

Besides activity in the domestic and international sociopolitical context, activists were also motivated to march and express dissent in 1987 based on internal developments. Here, it is instructive to recall U.S. intervention efforts in Central American countries and the dramatic growth of people-of-color organizations. These factors allowed new meanings to develop around platform and speaker debates. Activists dissented over these tasks to assert themselves as a social justice movement. Hence, "building solidarity with other groups" was disproportionately concentrated in 1987 as a reason for marching and dissenting. Although the idea also surfaced in other marches, its distribution was neither over- nor under-pronounced vis-à-vis other ideas. Because of the importance of coalitions, activists used platform and speaker debates in 1987 to emphasize the importance of remedying racism and sexism (i.e., "intra-community-isms"). In addition, debates over whether Jesse Jackson, Eleanor Smeal, and Cesar Chavez should speak at the rally resulted in their favor because they symbolized a progressive coalition between gay, black, women's, and farm workers' movements. Activists further signaled their progressive intentions by increasing the people-of-color requirement for delegate composition from 20 percent in the first march to 25 percent in the second (and maintaining the requirement for gender parity). While racism and sexism have always been prominent concerns, activists neither over- nor under-emphasized them in the other marches.

Platform debates erupted again in 1993 when activists deliberated whether or not to proceed autonomously or in collaboration with others. Similar to 1987, activists decided to connect with other groups. The special rights–equal rights debate, the rise of ex-gays, and the movement's own steady stride into the mainstream reconfigured the terms of debate. Fighting AIDS, celebrating lesbian and gay relationships, and building solidarity were no longer the primary reasons to march. To assert that gays wanted the same treatment as everyone else, activists focused on educating Americans about who gay people were and what they wanted. This gave rise to two rhetorical arguments. First, activists used the language of "educating society" more prominently in the third march than in any of the others. It was nearly absent in the first (when gays' concerns were linked more to each other), not particularly over- or under-pronounced in 1987, and far less than expected by the millennium, when the Supreme Court had put to rest the special-rights debate. Activists also demanded "social and cultural acceptance," an idea they articulated less in 1979 and in no patterned way during the second and fourth marches.

Because of the particular confluence of external and internal factors, activists redefined themselves from being a social justice movement that was building solidarity and coalitions with others to now being a mainstream movement in pursuit of equal rights. Thus, the language of "equal rights," despite being linguistically unremarkable, was over-concentrated in the third march and neither more nor less than expected for the others. Activists also reframed platform debates by deliberating whether to embrace a "single- or multi-issue focus." This language was almost entirely absent in 1979, when the movement was imagining its own autonomy, not over- or under-prevalent in 1987, when their concerns were framed instead as pertaining to coalitions, and silent in 2000, when top-down activists from national organizations set the agenda as single-issue. The debate in 2000 overwhelming concerned the question of whether to march, which further accounts for why the language of single- or multi-issue focus was under-articulated in its public forum.

In 1993 external and internal factors generated lively dissent over the title and organizing structure. Stepping into the mainstream ignited debates over "bisexual inclusion" and "transgender inclusion," both of which complicated a narrative of equal rights. Bisexuals sometimes suggested that sexuality was a choice, not a genetic orientation, which may have favored arguments for special rights and therefore inadvertently supported the ex-gay movement. Thus, bisexual debates were aggravated in 1993 in ways they were not for any of the other marches. Although they had made significant strides since the first march, transgenders were still burdened by confusion over who they were and their relationship to lesbian and gay politics. They were therefore included in the platform but excluded in the title. This, along with the fact that the title was augmented to include bisexuals for the first time, fueled additional debates over trans inclusion in the third march, whereas it was no more or less than expected in 1979, under-emphasized in 1987 (perhaps due the unifying properties of AIDS and *Bowers*) and also under-emphasized in 2000 since they were seamlessly incorporated in all aspects of organizing.

Dissent in 2000 was shaped by the movement's mainstream status and especially by the rise of powerful national organizations. Many struggles from the prior marches were settled. Although *equality* was part of the march's title, "equal rights" was hardly whispered in the public forum, and its corollary, "educate society," was dramatically under-articulated. Advances in AIDS medical technologies muted that issue, as well. The movement had succeeded in traveling from the periphery, where it was in 1979 and 1987, through the mainstream margins in 1993, and finally into the mainstream center by 2000. It had resolved many of its prior struggles with relational connectedness (i.e., activists had resolved how lesbians, gay men, bisexuals, and transgenders were related to each other as part of the same movement).

Given such resolutions and an established history of organizing, one might expect an uncontroversial Millennium March. If many prior issues were now successfully negotiated, what dissent, if any, persisted and why? In a strange resemblance with the first march, the main area of debate concerned the formative question of whether to march in the first place. This time, however, there was no concern about whether enough gays would risk visibility (gay visibility was at an unprecedented high during the millennium), whether a low turnout would give the movement a black eye (now unthinkable after successful 1979 and 1987 marches and a titanic 1993 march), or whether there existed something that could plausibly be called a national movement (now axiomatic). This structurally similar debate over whether to march was now culturally resignified to contest questions of ownership. Who will set the agenda and by what means? To grapple with such questions, activists dissented over the "organizing, planning, and leadership" of the march, an issue that burst at the seams of the public forum in 2000, whereas it surfaced less than one might expect in the first march, noticeably less than expected in the second march, and remained stable in the third. Until the day of the demonstration itself, there was never a community mandate, no collectively agreed-upon wisdom to return to Washington. That the march was organized nonetheless suggested to some that the movement had been hijacked by national organizations that exerted unilateral control. The Ad Hoc Committee, in particular, accused the march of being elitist and undemocratic. They felt organizers were erasing the movement's diversity by marketing an acceptable form of gayness. This is evident by the lack of certain motivations to march. For the 1993 march, the largest and arguably most internally diverse, activists were motivated to "build support for miscellaneous groups." This concern was neither prominent nor absent in the first march, when activists were concerned about the relationship between lesbians and gay men and whites and people of color instead. Its distribution in the public forum during the second march was the same, when activists were burdened by AIDS and *Bowers*. In 2000, however, this discussion was notably under-articulated. This march did not seem to be about lesbian and gay diversity. For that matter, it was never settled why the movement was returning to Washington.

The lack of community mandate reconfigured the same debate—whether or not to march—to now address resource allocation. Thus, sound bytes of "local versus national" and "resource allocation" buzzed through the public forum. This idea was not pronounced in the first march, given other sources of dissent. More striking is its significant under-representation in the second and third marches. That activists and the rank and file did not question directing their resources to D.C. for these two marches suggests greater consensus and unity. This never happened in 2000. Additional evidence stems from alternatives to a march on

TABLE 10.2. **Culturally Varying Scripts for Structurally Similar Debates**

	1979	1987	1993	2000	χ^2
Why March					
To build a national movement	6.2	−0.9	−0.8	−4.5	43.97***
To fight AIDS	−5.5	5.6	2.5	−1.9	54.04***
To celebrate and recognize gay relationships	−5.0	4.3	0.3	0.8	33.33***
To build solidarity with other groups	−0.7	4.2	−1.3	−1.9	18.29***
To educate American society	−2.9	0.5	6.7	−4.0	52.57***
To obtain social and cultural acceptance	−2.5	−0.2	4.1	−1.2	18.54***
To pursue equal rights	−1.7	−0.6	2.3	0.0	6.66*
To build support for miscellaneous groups	0.8	0.6	2.3	−3.5	13.38**
State-level activity	−3.6	−3.0	0.8	5.5	39.03***
Infighting					
Gender inequality	2.9	−0.6	−0.5	−1.9	9.119**
To build solidarity with other groups	−0.7	4.2	−1.3	−1.9	18.29***
Intra-community-isms	0.4	2.8	−1.8	−1.2	10.07**
Single- versus multi-issue	−3.5	1.7	4.1	−2.0	26.69***
Bisexual inclusion	−1.5	0.8	2.4	1.5	8.28**
Transgender inclusion	0.0	−2.0	4.5	−2.5	22.66***
March organizing, planning, and leadership	−1.9	−3.5	−0.5	5.4	33.07***
Local versus national, resource allocation	1.3	−2.9	−3.2	4.4	29.61***

Note: Except for the last column, numbers report adjusted standardized residual values.

* = $p < .08$, ** = $p < .05$, *** = $p < .001$

Washington. The public forum in 2000 was saturated with "state-level activity" as a counter-objective to a national political demonstration. This was nonexistent in 1979, given activists' desire to imagine and build a national movement. It was never articulated in 1987 when activists continued the project of movement-building and when conflict situations demanded a national response. The idea did surface in 1993, although not prominently. This may be because threat was less discrete and also because the third march marked the beginning of a shift in the center of gravity toward the states, a phenomenon that was in full force by the end of the decade.

In summary, four factors account for the pattern of infighting across the marches—that is, how and why new meanings (or culturally varying scripts) became associated with the same six organizing tasks (or structurally similar debates). These factors include consciousness, organizational development, external threat, and political/cultural status of the group. Certain factors exerted more or less influence at different moments in time. Community consciousness exerted the heaviest hand during the first march, organizational development and threat in the second, threat and political/cultural status in the third, and political/cultural status and organizational development in the fourth. It is no wonder activists struggled with the same debates: although they appeared similar in form, they meant very different things during the different marches. Table 10.2 consolidates statistical evidence for the claims made in this section.

Democracy and the Dividends of Dissent: Implications across Contexts

The United States was "founded by dissenters" when Protestants (meaning "protesters") settled in New England "as an act of intellectual opposition" given their "quarrel with Providence."[18] These beginnings have stayed with us. The First Amendment, for example, prohibits government from making laws that would "abridge the freedom of speech" or prevent its citizens from "petitioning the government for a redress of grievances." Freedom of speech and dissent go hand-in-hand, facilitating self-governance, accountability, the recognition of and tolerance for diversity, and the "discovery of truth," in the words of John Stuart Mill.[19]

American history is punctuated by the stories of "rebels and renegades" envisioning and enacting the best of all possible worlds.[20] The dividends of dissent are most lucid in a democracy in which civic debate is valued. Democracy withers in the absence of debate; people cannot rule unless they have access to a public forum in which information is readily exchanged. Pressing the mute button on the marketplace of ideas unleashes a "gag rule" of "audible silence" that signals tyranny rather than democracy: "The survival of American democracy depends less on the size of its armies than on the capacity of its individual citizens to rely . . . on the strength of their own thought. We can't know what we're about . . . unless we can see or hear one another think out loud."[21] Without dissent, we are in the dark about who we are and what we want.

The lesbian and gay movement, like others inspired by the New Left, prefigures democracy. Prefigurative politics, which activists implemented at their national conferences, "create and sustain within the live practice of the movement" a vision of the "desired society."[22] To borrow from Mahatma Gandhi, activists embody the change they wish to see in the world. In an opinion piece titled, "A Transformational Movement," Kerry Lobel, former executive director of the National Gay and Lesbian Task Force expressed this very same idea: "If we want to build a movement that is transformational, we will . . . take the risks that challenge conventional thinking. . . . We will seek out and lift up every voice, chal-

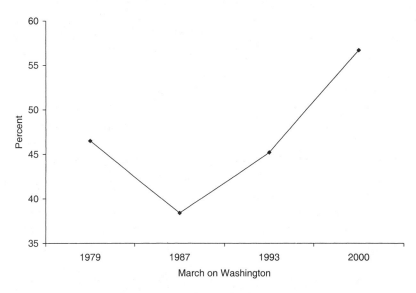

FIGURE 10.3. Infighting across Four Washington Marches.

lenged by what we hear but not afraid. . . . The true test of democracy is how it embraces those who look, act, and think differently, not just those who are the same. This is the world we dream of."[23]

That lesbians and gay men fight with each other does not mark them as different from anyone else. According to Sabrina Sojourner, former legislative aide to Representative Maxine Waters (D-Calif.), "I haven't found a movement yet that doesn't eat its leadership alive."[24] However, the American LGBT movement's "rampant diversity"[25] fuels rancorous infighting over what it means to be gay in America and where the movement is headed. It is therefore a typical case to empirically isolate and illuminate under-theorized meaning-making processes. During each march, activists devoted considerable resources to the problem of infighting (see fig. 10.3).

Figure 10.3 depicts the percentage of media reports that addressed infighting in each march. The numbers range from 38 percent in the second march to 57 percent in the fourth, averaging 47 percent across demonstrations. Infighting was least pronounced during the second march, possibly as a result of the unifying properties AIDS and the Supreme Court's *Bowers* decision. This would be consistent with conflict theorists' predictions. The numbers peaked during the fourth march, which never obtained a community mandate, that is, the formative task of whether to march. On average, the movement divested nearly half its communication resources to cover infighting.

Journalists marshaled a wealth of provocative and pithy catchphrases to muse on the problem of infighting: "that ol' gay infighting gene," "eating our own," "lavender fascists," "cannibalistic frenzy," "trashing and cannibalizing," "internalized homophobia," "oppression sickness," "horizontal hostility," "righteous skepticism," "internal lesbian and gay bashing," "culture war raging in our community," "cultural caste system," "pride and prejudice," "QUASH: Queers United Against Straight-Acting Homosexuals," "a formula for being gay," "queers are attacking other queers for being gay in an incorrect way," "the battle for the right way to be queer," "queer peer bashers," "the politics of divide and dis," "gay is dead," "the slash and burn approach to gay politics," "the impulse to divide and demonize," "a sadomasochistic style of politics," and "shredding the rainbow."[26]

In telling a story about this rampant infighting, I have suggested that dissent operates as a vehicle, or culture carrier, activists use to transport meta-meanings fashioned from the assemblages of practical organizing tasks. Figure 10.3, along with the above list of colorful descriptors, begs the question of whether and when infighting will hurt rather than help organizing efforts. There are two ways to approach this puzzle: by turning to empirically-observed outcome variation or extrapolating beyond to outline scope conditions under which one might hypothesize the findings to hold across contexts and cases.

My emphasis has been on situations in which infighting is generative by allowing activists to creatively express strategy and identity. To look for outcome variability, we need to shift levels of analysis away from the marches and toward the national conferences—the smaller, organizational units—responsible for march assembly (see fig. 10.4).

Figure 10.4 outlines a contingency theory of infighting that blends cultural, political, and organizational approaches to the study of social movements. It is premised on four observed outcomes (from left to right): 1) organizational nonconsolidation (i.e., activists failed to form an entity they could use to assemble the march—see 1973 Urbana Conference); 2) organizational dissolution (i.e., activists congealed but failed to sustain—see 1978 Minneapolis Conference); 3) the dividends of dissent (i.e., activists used practical tasks as a culture carrier to engage in conversations of strategy and identity—see 1979 Philadelphia and Houston Conferences, all 1987 national conferences, and all 1993

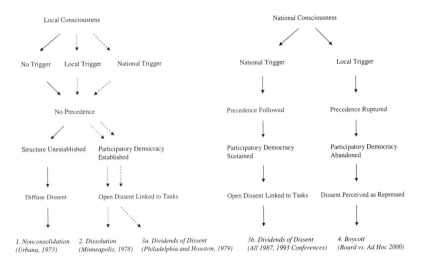

FIGURE 10.4. A Contingency Theory of Infighting.

national conferences); and 4) organizational boycott (i.e., activists boy-cotted the march—this is a version of, but not equivalent to, defection, seen in 2000). These varying outcomes suggest that infighting lies on a continuum of contention that includes these and perhaps other out-comes, such as organizational splits (plausible in unobserved regional and local conferences).

Under what conditions will infighting help rather than hurt organiz-ing efforts (paths 3a and 3b)? This outcome is determined by the config-uration of five factors along which there was variation across marches: movement consciousness (local versus national); triggering event (no trigger, local trigger, national trigger); whether there was a precedent and, if so, if it was followed; the type of decision-making structure; and whether there were openness norms for expressing dissent. Infighting will yield its dividends under one of two conditions. In the first instance, consciousness is still local, that is, the movement has not yet emerged as a national player. In this situation, local activists must confront a trigger-ing event that has national resonance, in response to which they decide, for the first time, to march on Washington. These early efforts must be guided by a commitment to participatory democracy, under which dis-sent becomes linked to logistical decisions and is perceived as a neces-sary component of decision-making (i.e., there are openness norms for its expression).

In the second condition, the movement is nationally situated (recall that the 1979 march consolidated a sense that lesbians and gay men comprised a national movement, where such a belief was lacking prior). In this situation, a trigger with national resonance is still required, to which activists respond by doing what is tried and true (i.e., they stick with their cultural template). It is especially useful for activists to continue embracing participatory democracy, though there is flexibility for tweaking it by making it more accountable as new constituencies become organized (e.g., augmenting the people-of-color requirement from 20 percent in the first march to 25 percent in the second and 50 percent in the third). Dissent should again be linked with practical tasks and, despite being at times uncomfortable, nonetheless still be perceived as welcome. Figure 10.4 suggests that other configurations will result in one or more of the three non-productive outcomes.

Both productive conditions share a participatory-democratic decision-making structure that incorporates openness norms for dissent. This implies that infighting does not result in defection or dissolution in those cases where it comfortably facilitates a higher order consensus about "who we are" and "what we want." Infighting in organizing lesbian and gay marches on Washington is highly predictable, even ritualized in some senses—it has pertained to the same general issues since at least the 1950s. Infighting establishes what we fight about (diversity in our visions of identity and strategy) and how we fight (the rules of engagement and styles of deliberation). This also suggests that infighting might generate defection or dissolution when people get tired of the same fight, do not find it meaningful, find it too painful, or no longer derive a sense of solidarity from it.

We can also extrapolate beyond empirical outcomes. Recall Sabrina Sojourner's comment: "I haven't found a movement yet that doesn't eat its leadership alive." The dividends of dissent are not restricted to the lesbian and gay movement nor to Washington march contexts. I hinted at the broader reach of infighting's culture-carrying capacity in the introduction, which provided vignettes across movements, time periods, and organizing contexts. Design limitations (the present study's narrower scope) restrict the extent to which findings can be definitively generalized. To speculate, however, I draw on a proximal similarity model of generalization that builds on a principle of surface, or proximal, similarity.[27] The analytic task is to extract similarities between the present research and the prototypical characteristics of the target of generalization. Four dimensions provide reliable (though still cautious) parameters: 1) conflict type; 2) movement type; 3) task type; and 4) decision-making type. I expect findings to generalize to expressions of dissent that either do not produce, or occur prior to, an organizational splinter (conflict type) within identity-based social movements (movement type) organizing non-institutionalized protest events (task type) using participatory-democratic means (decision-making type).

Secondary sources provide support for the robustness of this hypothesis. In *Freedom Is an Endless Meeting,* Francesca Polletta chronicles participatory democracy as a form across movement types, including labor, Southern civil rights, the New Left, women's liberation, and contemporary direct action and community organizing. Each movement organized non-institutionalized protest events and, along the way, experienced intense moments of disagreement that were central to articulating members' strategic and identity visions. For example, should labor organize around industrial or craft lines? is a question that "centered on just how inclusive unions should be." As another example: how were blacks and whites connected to each other as a "band of brothers" in the same civil rights struggle, especially when organizations such as SNCC used a deliberative style that came to be seen as white? The New Left struggled with the politics of launching an interracial movement as well, although they also had to manage social class, given so many members were students, lived at Berkeley's campus, and were trying to mobilize poor, neighboring residents. The women's liberation movement of the 1960s was often burdened by ideological disputes between "politicos," who connected sexism with capitalism and attempted to maintain ties with the Left, and "feminists" who wanted to sever all ties with men involved with the Left. Should the movement proceed autonomously or in coalitions with others? Conflicts within contemporary community organizing, often faith-based and premised on the principle of single-issue, direct action, were rooted in contentious conceptions of self-identify.[28] Infighting in lesbian and gay political organizing, it seems, has an affinity with many other movements.

In *Marching on Washington,* Lucy Barber moves us closer to the heart of this book by examining six Washington marches (other than the four chronicled in this book) over seventy-seven years. In each case, Barber identifies the centrality and symbolism that inheres in the six tasks isolated in the present study (what she calls "practical politics"). For example, in 1894 and before any precedent had been established linking

Washington with politics, Jacob Coxey and his "petition in boots" still recognized the importance of the title. Coxey termed his band of protesters the "Commonweal of Christ" to signal to lawmakers their "peaceful and godly" intentions. To indicate the gravity of his grievances, "Coxey's Army" decided to walk seven hundred miles on foot and horseback to the nation's capital. They commenced the march on Easter Sunday, connecting the two key tasks of the title and date (when to march).

As another example, the 1913 women's suffrage procession was burdened by representational politics that, similar to the lesbian and gay activists chronicled in this study, toiled over the inclusion of people of color. Organizers worried that their demands for suffrage would be diluted or misinterpreted by the presence of black women. In the end, "some black women did march," and organizers scattered them throughout the procession in an effort to subordinate "an identity based on race" to their master, gender identity. Here, too, infighting linked with practical politics to speak to identity.

Recall that activists dialogued organizing with the domestic and international political context (e.g., Carter's insistence on human rights, U.S. intervention in Central America, etc.). In a similar vein, A. Philip Randolph, in his proposed (though never actualized) 1941 Negro March on Washington manipulated his strategy to resonate with American political culture. Randolph emphasized economic rights (as part of his demands) to gain leverage from popular New Deal rhetoric and increasingly common hunger and labor marches. Similar to infighting over single versus coalition politics elaborated in this book, Randolph encountered internal resistance over his proposal to exclude whites from the march. Some attacked him for trying to fight "segregation . . . with a segregated march," to which Randolph responded by emphasizing "the importance of [African Americans] working for their own interests." Here infighting culturally enabled conversations of strategy.

Twenty-two years later, African American civil rights activists staged the 1963 March on Washington for Jobs and Freedom. Its modern-day renown obscures organizers' little-known struggle with the most formative organizing task of whether to march in the first place. The demonstration was the brainchild of "the Big Six": A. Philip Randolph, Martin Luther King Jr., Roy Wilkins, Whitney Young, John Lewis, and James Farmer. Bayard Rustin was involved as the deputy director.[29] Infighting found its way into this circle. Wilkins was perceived as the most cautious leader, perhaps as a result of being the executive secretary of the mainline NAACP. Wilkins (like Barney Frank in the present study) expressed "doubts about the practical outcome of protest," including Washington marches, which he did not believe were capable of securing real change. Wilkins preferred abandoning the idea altogether, urging others to channel their energies toward "analysis, understanding, and counter-maneuvers." Many "African American journalists blamed Wilkins and the NAACP for the lower-than-expected turnout" at past events. Early resistance to the question of whether to march affected organizational endorsements. Similar to the stumbling blocks of 1979 organizers (from the NGTF), Randolph also received a lukewarm initial response to the idea of the 1963 march. Few organizations sent representatives to planning meetings and withheld their endorsements.

Barber narrates these and other insightful histories, including the Veterans' Bonus March of 1932 and the Spring Offensive (i.e., the anti–Vietnam War march) of 1971. She tells a story about the history of the tactic itself, especially how it has come to symbolize American citizenship. Along the way, the reader encounters the problem of infighting coupled with the same six organizing tasks—her "practical politics"—outlined in the present study. And in each case, the dialogues speak to strategy and identity.[30]

But what about taking yet another leap and moving outside the scope of social movements and Washington marches?[31] Contemporary examples are illustrative. President George W. Bush has occupied a controversial administration and has spearheaded noxious battles across Democrats and Republicans over core issues of national security. In 2006, the terrain on Capitol Hill shifted unexpectedly when the president called for establishing military tribunals to try terror detainees. "The issue," MSNBC observed, "is the president's approach to fighting terrorism." Bush sought to reinterpret, if not sidestep, the sixty-year-old Geneva Conventions—a series of treaties that set international standards for humane conduct—to instead use "harsh techniques on terror suspects." Suddenly, "Republican Infighting" and "GOP Infighting" were making notable headlines in presses across the country.[32] In an odd turn of events, a Republican Bush had to negotiate with a Republican-controlled Congress on issues of human rights and civil liberties—what he called "alternative interrogation practices" for terrorism suspects. Former Secretary of State Colin Powell worried that Bush's redefinition efforts would compel the global community to "doubt the moral basis of our fight against terrorism" and "put our own troops at risk" for mistreatment abroad.[33]

Republican infighting also captured competing cultural visions of what could be called the "state of the party" or "character of the country" (to parallel what I have called "the state of the movement"). News analyst Carl Hulse of the *New York Times* observed, "At issue are definitions of what is permissible in trials and interrogations [read: strategy] that both sides view as central to the character of the nation [read: state of the movement]." The Geneva Conventions, which encapsulate a variety of smaller treaties [read: organizing tasks], became a lightning rod for "core principles" that would "send a signal about who America is [read: identity] in 2006," in the words of South Carolina Senator Lindsey Graham.[34] The example of Republican infighting over reinterpreting the Geneva Conventions illustrates a compelling, even if tentative, case for the robustness of my argument. Under certain conditions, infighting may operate as a culture carrier for involved actors to concretely discuss otherwise abstract concerns. It may also deliver for receptive audiences updates that, without dissent, remain inaccessible. Dissent demands a reconsideration of its unduly slanderous reputation.

Theoretical Implications: A Resinous Culture Framework

Scholars across disciplines often study social cohesion and solidarity at the expense of diversity and dissent.[35] Pierre Bourdieu, in his film *Sociology Is a Martial Art,* terms this a "principle of coherence" that exerts "a form of symbolic violence" due to the narrow questions and knowledge claims that may result.[36] This book offers an opportunity for theoretical redirection.

The four previously unstudied cases of mass protest I examine challenge that infighting is symptomatic of the death and decline of political organizing. Activists fight over recurring organizing tasks to carry on a cultural conversation that specifies what they want, how to procure it, who decides the terms, who speaks on their behalf, what it means to be part of their group, and how people who claim membership are connected (see fig. 10.5).

Rethinking infighting in this way affords an opportunity to reconceptualize how culture works in political organizing. *How culture works.*

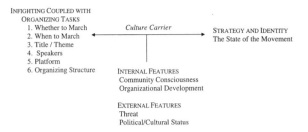

FIGURE 10.5. How Culture Works in Political Organizing.

These are three deceivingly simple words. What I mean by this is how systems of meanings influence what people think (empirically expressed in the articulation of their dissent) and how they act (empirically expressed in their actual organizational decisions). As figure 10.5 reveals, activists use infighting as a culture carrier to engage in a conversation about the meaningfulness of their identities and strategies. The mechanism by which this occurs is the coupling of infighting with a series of recurring organizing tasks. The bidirectional arrow suggests the viability of the reverse: instead of using the tasks to begin grappling with competing meanings of strategy and identity, some activists enter the dialogue with such notions pre-established, although they use the same logistical decisions to voice their opinions to the delegates present at respective national conferences.

Decisions made at each national conference for each march were deposited into a cultural template that informed future organizing. Infighting, in other words, does more than just give form to abstract concerns; it also affects how activists will organize in the future. Dissent in 1979 influenced how 1987 was organized, which affected conversations in 1993. The event in 2000 provides vivid evidence for the consequences of ignoring, rupturing, or rejecting the template. The imagery of infighting as a culture carrier incorporates the operation of ideas (in dissent itself) and action (in voted-on decisions and the template) and shows how culture is a type of learned behavior devoted at once to meaning-making and practice—that is, "willful action, power relations, struggle, contradiction, and change," in the words of William Sewell Jr.[37]

Despite or perhaps because of culture's being "one of the two or three most complicated words in the English language," the question of how it works has a long history in sociology.[38] In *The German Ideology,* Karl Marx asserted that the "ideas of the ruling class are in every epoch the ruling ideas," a culture-as-material-interests perspective that attempts to explain the historical prominence of certain ideas.[39] In *The Protestant Ethic and the Spirit of Capitalism,* Max Weber suggested that Protestantism provided its followers with an "ethos of the rational organization of capital and labor." Weber agreed with Marx that material interests mattered, but he went a familiar step further: "Very frequently the world images that have been created by ideas have, like switchmen, determined the tracks along which action has been pushed by the dynamic of interest."[40] This culture-as-ideas framework materializes world images through internalized individual ideas. In *The Elementary Forms of Religious Life,* Emile Durkheim observed that culture is constituted by "collective representations" through which groups ritualistically view and celebrate themselves. This culture-as-symbols perspective measured the "conscience collective" through totems.[41]

Many scholars have used these frameworks, including Parsons and his theory of values, Geertz, who redirected the study of culture to questions of meaning (rather than its effects on action) that inhered in public symbols, and Bourdieu's performative perspective in which culture is embodied in the habitus.[42] In common, classical studies investigate how culture (interests, ideas, symbols, values, meanings, habitus) affects action (what people do, their behavior). Gary Alan Fine, Robert Wuthnow, Ann Swidler, and Michael Schudson, among others, have paved the way for contemporary scholars interested in similar questions. Fine (1979) first articulated the problem I engage in this book: scholars must not treat culture as if it were "an amorphous, indescribable mist which swirls around society members." His solution was to study "idioculture," or small group culture. Fine emphasizes ethnographically studied, face-to-face interactions that transpire in local contexts.[43] Much of his work takes issue with culture creation, or why some objects become meaningfully incorporated into small groups whereas others do not. It provides a useful transition into my concern with how members of a larger imagined community imbue known but previously abstract ideas with materiality.[44] Scholars can therefore measure culture either through specifying a local, interacting small group as their unit of analysis, per Fine, or through operation mechanisms, as I have in this book.

Wuthnow examines the institutionalization of cultural forms, or why certain cultural objects (from bundles of discourse to religious ideologies) are produced and survive whereas others wither and die. His social ecology model emphasizes how ideologies (defined as "sets of statements" from pro-choice to Pentecostalism and Reformation) operate in "fields." This culture-as-language approach moves to a field-level of analysis to resolve measurement concerns. Wuthnow is not interested in why things mean what they do at the small group level, as is Fine, but rather the macro relationships between changing cultural forms and social contexts.[45] Bringing the level of analysis back down to the individual (but not in small groups), Swidler argues for the strategic use of cultural resources. Following Weber, she focuses on culture's ability to influence action over variable contexts of settled and unsettled times.[46] During settled, or stable, times, people choose among different ideologies to orient their actions. This is why when they are happily married, for example, people talk about love in contradictory ways, at times viewing it as prosaic (a lot of work) and at other times as mythic (it was meant to be). This variation decreases in unsettled times of separation or divorce when people gravitate toward fewer and explicit ideologies. Swidler's culture-as-toolkit perspective views individuals as instrumental actors who select from their repertoire that which will suit their needs. She moves the dialogue closer to concretization by emphasizing strategic malleability: how people actually use culture, although measurement directives for abstractions such as "society's core symbols" remain underspecified.

Students of social movements have taken a particular liking to Swidler. Given their emphasis on deliberative action, such as organizing a march on Washington, scholars have applied the culture-as-toolkit tradition to wide-ranging concerns. Some suggest that actors (pastors, for example) manipulate cultural elements such as institutional bundles of identities from their toolkit to solve organizational problems (in congregations, for example).[47] Others assert that successful campaigns for social change depend on the correspondence between activists' cultural understandings of the problems they seek to resolve and the organizational forms they build.[48] The wisdom here is to investigate the fit between culture and organizations.[49]

Assessing this fit implies the effectiveness with which culture works is itself an empirical question. In response, Michael Schudson offers five conditions that variably enable culture to influence attitudes and behavior. It must be "retrievable" (available), have "rhetorical force" (be memorable), "resonate" with the audience (be relevant to them), achieve "institutional retention" (become institutionalized), and have "resolution" (tell you what to do).[50] Schudson's framework comes closest in specifying how to precisely measure culture. A conceptual space nonetheless persists between his efficacy dimensions and what we might think of as the tactility of culture.

This book's comparative-historical analysis makes use of four previously unstudied protest cases to better understand questions of conflict and culture. At one level, the deliberations we have heard throughout these pages were ostensibly about fights over discrete tasks. At another level, however, activists were engaged in a process of meaning-making or culture work, wrestling for answers to competing claims of strategy and identity. The mechanism that enables infighting to operate as a culture carrier is its coupling with key, recurring decisions. This coupling of infighting with organizing tasks reconfigures the latter into symbols that enable cultural concretization. Activists therefore made cultural ideas concrete—that is, provided identity and strategy with a thingness—in the crucible of conflict. Said differently, fights over mundane tasks were proxies for deeper divisions about the role and meaning of sexuality in American life. This outcome transpired in debates activists had during their national conferences and was disseminated to the rank and file and in the public forum via media reports. For sociologists, this finding remedies a long-standing divide to attribute materiality to the social while leaving cultural matters comparatively misty.[51] It allows culture to be empirically observable with renewed operational rigor—that is, we can measure culture more effectively—by focusing on how it informs concrete conflicts tied to organizational tasks.

The idea of infighting as a culture carrier synthesizes the above reviewed classical and contemporary views. Activists use practical tasks to contest and clarify meanings (Geertz and Sewell) of strategy and identity at national conferences broken down into small, interacting groups (Fine). In this way, they construct strategies of action (Swidler), codifying, repeating, and institutionalizing those that are successful (Wuthnow). Retained ideas (e.g., the title reflects representation) are imprinted in a cultural template (Bourdieu) that, like a switchman, directs the tracks along which future organizing and infighting unfolds (e.g., title augmentation in 1993 was based on 1987 infighting) (Weber). Assembling the marches along six tasks at national conferences was ritualistically reenacted, which enabled activists to affirm and celebrate themselves (Durkheim). Infighting was omnipresent and captured a struggle to determine which are the ruling ideas and values and therefore which are the ruling, valued groups (e.g., grassroots versus national organizations) (Marx and Parsons).

In this book, I have shown that culture—defined as the symbolic expressions of a group of people—can acquire a materiality that generally evades it. In this manner, my culture carrier framework builds primarily off Schudson. For culture to be effective, that is, for it to influence what people think and how they act, it must meet six conditions: It must be retrievable, which activists ensured by organizing a handful of national conferences on which the media reported. It must also have rhetorical force, which activists ensured by arranging their dissent along symbolically charged tasks. Third, it must resonate, which activists ensured by aligning the march with activity in the sociopolitical context (recall the special-rights debate, for example). It must be institutionally retained, which activists ensured by codifying their lessons learned (for example, see fig. 7.1), referencing their cultural template, and making use of lesbian and gay archives as depositories. And fifth, culture must provide resolution, which was vividly ensured in the demand items that provided directives for legislative action.

In addition to Schudson's five Rs, my cases show that culture works better when it or its elements (e.g., ideologies, values, symbols, or other packages of meaning) can attach to organizing tasks. These provide a metaphorical resin that can concretize culture. Culture works better, therefore, when it is *resinous,* a sixth dimension to Schudson that is allegiant to his alliteration. Culture does not have to be "an amorphous, indescribable mist which swirls around society members." Its effective workings are enhanced when people find ways to make it tactile or sticky. Across the four Washington marches, activists ensured this by linking infighting with logistical decisions in a process that enabled major identities and strategies to emerge.

A resinous culture framework emphasizes that culture is clarified when abstract dialogues are tied to fairly mundane logistical decisions, such as titling a march and deciding its platform. Major cultural identities and strategic visions emerge from disputing a series of tasks that simply must get done. Organizing, in effect, does more than just get people from one point to the next: it also gives them a clearer understanding of who they are and what they want.

Of Schudson's five Rs, resinous most resembles institutional retention, in which culture works effectively when it is incorporated in the practices of social institutions such as the national steering committees (a type of social movement organization or SMO) that deliberated over the specifics of march organizing. This book suggests that cultural effectiveness requires more than mere presence within such institutions. Following Marx, who viewed proletariat organizing as disrupted by worker infighting, movement scholars have generally given internal conflicts a "sorry reputation" since they are presumed to "hasten movement collapse," in the words of William Gamson. Lessons learned from the decline of the American New Left, for example, point to activists' inability to placate conflict—despite various SMOs' willingness to make space for the fights. Why was infighting more destructive in the later years of the New Left than it was in the lesbian and gay Washington marches chronicled in these pages? Sociologist Todd Gitlin attributes the New Left's vulnerability in later years to a turn of events in which airing dissent became decoupled from specific organizing tasks. Absent this resinous condition (which provides a focus to the fights and thus enables cultural concretization), activists may become power-hungry and, according to Gamson, use "ideological postures as a means of gaining support."[52] It is here—even in the presence of institutions—that infighting may become destructive and culturally ineffective. Thus, resinous and institutional retention exhibit discriminant validity in terms of understanding how culture works.

In summary, a resinous culture framework speaks to measurement concerns by allowing the culture concept to be empirically observable with operational rigor. It can help sociologists distinguish culture from that which is not and to see from a fresh perspective how it might matter in social life.

Appendix A: Comparative Cultural Analysis

Overview

This is a comparative cultural analysis of four lesbian and gay marches on Washington staged in 1979, 1987, 1993, and 2000. I investigate the prevalence of internal conflicts or infighting and, having done so, move to identify its sources (why does it happen?), operations (what role does it play?), and patterns (does it take regular form?). This case-controlled, longitudinal design facilitates the identification and explanation of commonalities and differences across thirty years of one movement (1970–2000). Methodologically, I illustrate two ways of studying historical cases. Scholars can compare them analytically as semi-distinct, stand-alone episodes and can also (simultaneously, as I do in this book) tell a story that locates individual cases in relation to one another.

Cultural analysis examines meaning-making and the symbolic-expressive dimensions of social life. There are as many analytic techniques as methods, although some lack rigor in specifying steps for robust analysis.[1] The problem stems from conceptual confusion over the word *culture,* since how one defines it has consequences for studying it. Analysis may isolate cultural dimensions of movements and/or movement cultures themselves. I use infighting to assess how participants create and negotiate meanings of political organizing.

Research in the sociology of culture often describes specific cultural forms and practices. Scholars now emphasize uncovering generalizable and empirically verifiable mechanisms that specify the internal organization of culture. Such "endogenous explanation" proceeds by identifying "recurring features, distinctions, and underlying patterns which give form and substance to culture," in the words of sociologist Jason Kaufman. Following this advice, I uncover patterns in how activists organize (or produce) each Washington march and how people respond to (or receive) these efforts. I do this using a "tripartite model of cultural study" that investigates the production ("the activities through which it is created"), content ("what is being said in and through it"), and reception ("how those encountering it use and interpret it") of infighting.[2]

Data and Analytic Strategy

The present study is based on six types of data: 1) newspaper accounts from local and national, mainstream, and gay presses (N = 1,191); 2) interviews with every cochair from each demonstration, along with key local and national activists (N = 44); 3) archival documents from seven institutional archives and the personal papers of fourteen activists; 4) audio speeches from each march; 5) video documentaries of each march; and 6) photographs.

Newspaper Data

I collected 1,191 newspaper accounts from eight gay presses: the *Advocate* (national monthly); *Bay Area Reporter, Bay Windows,* and the *Sentinel*[3] (San Francisco weekly); *Gay Community News*[4] (Boston weekly); *Washington Blade*[5] (D.C. weekly); and *GayLife* and *Windy City Times*[6] (Chicago weekly). I also collected articles from mainstream sources, including the *Chicago Tribune, Chicago Sun-Times, Los Angeles Times, New York Times, San Francisco Chronicle,* and *Washington Post.* I used maximum variation (non-probability) sampling to diversify geographic representation. Random sampling was not feasible since population information was not available (i.e., information did not exist about every locale that printed a gay press in the 1970s).

Maximum variation was also desirable due to its theoretically focused nature. I sought to obtain "information-rich cases . . . from which one can learn a great deal about issues of central importance [in this case, infighting]," instead of "gathering little information from a large, statistically significant sample." This strategy approximates probability sampling by extending the statistical principle of regression to the mean. Sampling on diverse regions includes attitudes that are extreme while incorporating common practices. Maximum variation enhanced the geographic diversity of the sample while encompassing mean and modal attitudes and expressions.[7]

I conducted newspaper searches at Gerber/Hart Library (GH) in Chicago. Founded in 1981, GH is the Midwest's largest lesbian and gay library and archives. Their collection is not electronic. For each march, I fingered through every newspaper from each of the gay presses I used for this study. I began my search one full calendar year prior to each march (e.g., January 1978 for the October 1979 march) and ended at the end of the calendar year for a given march (e.g., December 1979 for the October 1979 march). For weekly presses, this meant that I individually searched 104 editions per march per press (52 editions per 12 months, 24 months total search, 4 marches, for a total of 416 total newspapers of each weekly publication used across all the marches). I modified this timeframe when I knew that organizing began over one year prior. For example, organizing for the Millennium March commenced in February 1998. I therefore began my search in January 1998. I photocopied all articles that had any connection to the respective march. Some articles were missing from GH's collection. I filled these in with electronic searchers at the Gay, Lesbian, Bisexual and Transgender (GLBT) Historical Society of Northern California. Many archives also housed mainstream clippings. I copied those where available.[8]

I sampled and content-analyzed 424 of the 1,191 articles (36 percent) I collected for the study. I first selected a computer-generated random sample to assess the extent to which they covered similar stories. This robustness test validated that factual news was stable across sources. Papers varied slightly in letters to the editor and opinion-editorial pieces. With these, the areas of debate were consistent (e.g., people across the country all debated the march's platform at one time, the speakers at another time, etc.). The final sample consisted of articles from the *Advocate* for all four marches. For 1979 and 1987, I included *Gay Community News*. For 1993 and 2000, I substituted *Windy City Times* for *Gay Community News* since the latter went out of print and the former resembled it most closely in content and structure (see table A.1). In line with a tripartite approach,

TABLE A.I. **Newspaper Data**

	1979	1987	1993	2000	Totals
Advocate	21*	25*	24*	56*	
Sentinel/Bay Windows/Bay Area					
Reporter	10	91	58	38	
Gay Community News	93*	61*	—	—	
Washington Blade	—	99	163	163	
GayLife/Windy City Times	72	73	80*	64*	
Totals:	196	349	325	321	1191
Sample Total:	114	86	104	120	424
	(58%)	(25%)	(32%)	(37%)	(36%)

*Newspapers used for quantitative content analysis.

news articles (and interviews) supplied a production-side perspective, while letters to the editor and opinion-editorial pieces filled in for reception. All data provided information on thematic and narrative content.

QUANTITATIVE ANALYSIS OF NEWSPAPER DATA   I coded articles for demographics (e.g., article type, length, location) and for two major themes: mobilization (why the movement should march) and infighting (the major sources of debate). *Mobilization* contained twelve sub-themes: AIDS, solidarity-building with other groups, community building, displaying unity, displaying diversity, displaying movement size/strength, educating society, equal rights/equality, federal activity, social/cultural acceptance, state activity, and other. The sub-theme *community-building* contained nine additional themes: bolstering local organizing, building miscellaneous constituencies, building a national movement, celebrating/recognizing gay relationships, creating new leaders, media representation, coming out, establishing a voting bloc, and other.

The category *infighting* contained ten sub-themes: organizing tasks; march effectiveness; finances; intra-community-isms (e.g., racism, sexism); local versus national allocation of resources; organizing, planning, and leadership structure; political logic (or march purpose); single- versus multi-issue concerns; subgroup representation; and other. *Subgroup representation* contained eleven additional themes: bisexuals, economic class, gender, lifestyle, political factions, AIDS, race, region, transgender, youth, and other.

I used quantitative content analysis to test a focused theoretical argument about culturally varying scripts for structurally similar debates. Such tests require statistically reliable coding: "Given that a goal of content analysis is to identify and record relatively objective (or at least inter-subjective) characteristics of messages, reliability is paramount. Without the establishment of reliability, content analysis measures are useless." I ensured this by computing Cohen's Kappa for each theme. This statistic assesses inter-rater reliability between two raters in the content analysis of categorical (often dichotomous) variables and is a more robust measure than the calculation of percent agreement since Kappa incorporates chance.[9] Kappa ranges from 0 to 1.00. An independent rater coded a 10 percent random sample across all four marches. Cohen's Kappa is considered the "standard measure of research quality" for content analysis. High Kappa values redress the common criticism of subjectivity and suggest strong, objective coding categories and definitions.[10] Appendix B details the coding manual and Kappas for each theme.

I tested whether certain themes were statistically over- or under-prevalent. To do this, I first report chi-square statistics to assert aggregate distribution of themes in the public forum. I then report adjusted standardized residual values (ASRs) for each march. These are similar to normally distributed z-scores and, when greater than the absolute value of 1.96, are significant at $p < .05$. A positive value suggests a statistically over-prevalent deviation from an assumption of independence (i.e., what we would expect if the talk was distributed by chance), whereas a negative value does the reverse. The advantage of this statistic over standardized residual values is that they allow for cross-category comparisons.

NEWSPAPER ACCOUNTS AS A PUBLIC FORUM   Journalism scholar Rodger Streitmatter argues that a rapidly growing gay press "created an arena in which lesbian and gay leaders waged their battles over what their social movement would be and where it was headed. . . . Writers stood at the front lines of the ideological warfare, defining the themes debated . . . across the country."[11] After the Stonewall Riots in 1969, through the 1970s and AIDS in the 1980s, the gay press "reflected its own political movement and community." Early editors embraced a responsibility for "building the movement" at a time when it was still "incipient."[12] The newspaper articles, in other words, represent a public forum.[13]

Movements and the media are longtime bedfellows. Scholars regularly turn to newspapers "to find protest events, to identify what occurred during the event, and to determine what the event was about."[14] The use of such data, however, has not been without concern. Early criticisms discouraged use to assess social psychological processes, especially in light of reporter distortion.[15] The present study's pursuit of the cultural level of analysis exempts it from these particular concerns. Prominent scholars such as Doug McAdam "highly recommend the methodological technique of content coding for the historical analysis of insurgency" for four reasons: 1) it facilitates replication; 2) it allows for formal hypothesis testing; 3) it can tap into macro currents operative in the sociopolitical context; and 4) it is practical, given the "extraordinary paucity of alternative data sources." McAdam concludes that "to exclude from use all newspaper data would thus seriously impair research into these important topics."[16]

Debate over the use of newspaper data persists.[17] A recent review argues that "newspaper content is not created for the purpose of conducting social scientific research." The main concern is about selection bias in reporting—that is, "how events are either selected into the media record or left unreported." A secondary concern is with description bias, or "how events are represented in the media record, given that they are reported." In response, researchers advise acknowledging limitations that inhere in such data, triangulating with other sources, using the data "to qualitatively examine understandings and definitions of events" and foregrounding concerns of sampling and sampling bias.[18]

The present study's use of newspaper data is justified for three reasons. First, scholars discourage using indices such as the *New York Times* to create a list of time-varying protest events. The most troubling studies are those that use newspaper data "to construct protest event counts as outcome variables."[19] I do not use newspaper data in this way. Second, it is virtually impossible to reconstruct LGBT history without consulting the gay news media. The mainstream media has a long history of neglecting to cover, or distorting in its coverage, gay issues. For years, gays have received "the cold shoulder from the media."[20] As late as 1993 the editor of the *Chicago Sun-Times* observed, "We're still self-conscious, still trying to decide how to cover gay and lesbian issues." A representative from the *Chicago Tribune* concurred, "There is probably no mainstream media outlet that does a good job of covering gay news on a regular basis."[21] Such sentiments account for the dearth of historical records on LGBT issues. Criticisms of newspaper data do not transfer neatly onto the gay press, for which similar methodological studies have not yet been conducted.

Finally, I use newspaper data as a Geertzian public forum. Activists have often turned to the gay media for such purposes, as indicated by a letter to the editor in the *Gay Community News*: "The service that's being provided by your organization to us in the gay community is one sorely needed: . . . the much needed information and something as fundamental as an open forum for us all across the country, to articulate our thoughts, feelings, and goals. . . . The gay media is practically fundamental to the realization of our needs and goals." The editor responded by acknowledging the paper's role as "a forum through which [activists] could communicate their concerns to other activists across the country."[22] This is a cultural use of newspaper data in line with a tripartite approach.

Archival Data

I conducted searches at seven institutional archives and using the personal papers of fourteen activists as follows:

1. Michael Armentrout, Personal Papers (Washington, D.C.)
2. Steve Ault, Personal Papers (Brooklyn, N.Y.)
3. David Aiken, Personal Papers (Washington, D.C.)
4. Paul Boneberg, Personal Papers (San Francisco, Calif.)
5. Ann DeGroot, Personal Papers (Minneapolis, Minn.)
6. Bill Dobbs, Personal Papers (New York, N.Y.)
7. Jeff Graubart, Personal Papers (Chicago, Ill.)
8. Billy Hileman, Personal Papers (Pittsburgh, Penn.)
9. Joyce Hunter, Personal Papers (Queens, N.Y.)
10. David Lamble, Personal Papers (San Francisco, Calif.)
11. Lesbian, Gay, Bisexual, and Transgender Community Center (New York, N.Y.)
12. Eric Rofes, Personal Papers (San Francisco, Calif.)
13. Gerber/Hart Library (Chicago, Ill.)
14. GLBT Historical Society of Northern California (San Francisco, Calif.)
15. National Lesbian and Gay Journalists Association (NLGJA) Collections (Washington, D.C.)
16. Nicole Murray-Ramirez, Personal Papers (San Diego, Calif.)
17. The ONE Institute and Archives (Los Angeles, Calif.)
18. Pacifica Radio Archives (North Hollywood, Calif.)
19. Rainbow History Project (Washington, D.C.)
20. Reverend Troy Perry, Personal Papers (West Hollywood, Calif.)
21. Robin Tyler Productions Inc., Personal Papers (North Hills, Calif.)

Interviews

I interviewed forty-four activists: all national cochairs from each march and a purposive sample of national and local leaders. Interviews lasted two to three hours and included the following individuals:[23]

1. Michael Armentrout (Washington, D.C.; 2000 treasurer/finance)
2. Steve Ault (Brooklyn, N.Y.; 1979 cochair, 1987 cochair; 2000 Ad Hoc)
3. Elizabeth Birch (Washington, D.C.; 2000 cochair)
4. Joan E. Biren (JEB) (Washington, D.C.)
5. Paul Boneberg (San Francisco, Calif.; 1979 lobby days)
6. Harry Britt (San Francisco, Calif.)
7. Lee Bush (postmortem, courtesy of the ONE Institute and ONE Archives; 1987 coordinator of national office)
8. Leslie Cagan (Queens, N.Y.; 1987; 2000 Ad Hoc)
9. Mandy Carter (Durham, N.C.; 1987; 2000 Ad Hoc)
10. Duane Cramer (San Francisco, Calif.; 2000 cochair)
11. Michelle Crone (San Diego, Calif.; 1987 civil disobedience; 1993, stage)
12. John D'Emilio (Chicago, Ill.)
13. Ann DeGroot (Minneapolis, Minn.; 2000 president of the board)
14. Juanita Diaz-Cotto (New York, N.Y.; 1979)
15. Bill Dobbs (New York, N.Y.; 2000 Ad Hoc)
16. Rick Garcia (Chicago, Ill.)
17. Gil Gerald (San Francisco, Calif.; 1979 Third World Conference; 1987)
18. Leticia Gomez (Washington, D.C.)
19. Jeff Graubart (Chicago, Ill.; 1973 NGMC meeting)
20. Eileen Hansen (San Francisco, Calif.; 1987 civil disobedience)
21. Diane Hardy-Garcia (Los Angeles, Calif.; 2000 co–executive director)
22. Billy Hileman (Pittsburgh, Penn.; 1993 cochair; 2000 Ad Hoc)
23. Ray Hill (Houston, Tex.; 1979)
24. Joyce Hunter (Queens, N.Y.; 1979 cochair; 1987; 2000Ad Hoc)
25. Billy S. Jones (Washington, D.C.; 1979; NCBLG)
26. Frank Kameny (Washington, D.C.)
27. Paul Kuntzler (Washington, D.C.)
28. David Lamble (San Francisco, Calif.)
29. Derek Livingston (Los Angeles, Calif.; 1993 cochair)
30. Deacon Maccubin (Washington, D.C.)
31. Mark Meinke (Washington, D.C.)
32. Pat Norman (San Francisco, Calif.; 1987 cochair)

COMPARATIVE CULTURAL ANALYSIS

33. Kay Ostberg (Santa Monica, Calif.; 1987 cochair)
34. Stuart Timmons (Los Angeles, Calif.)
35. Reverend Troy Perry (West Hollywood, Calif.; 1979; 1987; 1993; 2000 cochair)
36. Nicole Ramirez-Murray (San Diego, Calif.; 1979; 1987; 1993; 2000 cochair; LLEGO)
37. Donna Redwing (Evergreen, Colo.; 2000 cochair)
38. Eric Rofes (San Francisco, Calif.; 1979)
39. Scout (Boston, Mass.; 1993 cochair)
40. Nadine Smith (Tampa, Fla.; 1993 cochair)
41. Thomas Scott Tucker (Los Angeles, Calif.)
42. Robin Tyler (North Hills, Calif.; 1979; 1987; 1993; 2000)
43. Urvashi Vaid (New York, N.Y.)
44. Howard Wallace (San Francisco, Calif.)

Interview data, especially with multiple similar events that span many years, may contain the threat of recall bias. Reliance on memory, recollection, or retrospective self-report may pose a validity threat. Memories of one march may blur into another. But there are ways around this. Retrospective bias is reduced when interviews are anchored in discrete events, such as Washington marches and national conferences, identified by interviewees as important. It is also deflected by interviewing multiple individuals about the same event in the same way, a version of triangulation. And finally, I minimize recall bias by relying on interview data for the fourth march more than the prior three. This strategy shrinks the time interval between the event and the interview, thereby reducing the validity threat. Many quotes included in the analysis are taken from the newspaper data, when they were contemporaneous and therefore free from this particular bias.[24]

Other Data

I also consulted audio speeches from each march, video documentaries, and photographs. Audio speeches included the following: speeches from the National March on Washington for Lesbian and Gay Rights (1979, Pacifica National Archives, Los Angeles), *Harvey Milk Documentary* (David Lamble personal papers, San Francisco), *Harvey Milk Speech* (David Lamble personal papers, dated June 10, 1978, San Francisco), *Harvey Milk Interview with Howard Wallace and Ray Hill* (David

Lamble personal papers, dated June 10, 1978, San Francisco), *Fruit Punch: March on Washington* (David Lamble personal papers, dated October 21, 1987, San Francisco), the National March on Washington for Lesbian and Gay Rights (1979, Magnus Records, Gerber/Hart Library, Chicago), and speech recordings from the Third World Conference (Rainbow History Project, Washington, D.C.).

Video documentaries included: *Gay USA* (David Lamble personal papers, San Francisco), *Greetings from Washington, D.C.* (1979 march, Women Make Movies, New York), *1979 March on Washington for Lesbian and Gay Rights* (Eric Rofes personal papers, San Francisco), *Part of the USA! National March on Washington for Lesbian and Gay Rights* (1987 march, Eric Rofes personal papers, San Francisco), *March On!* (1993 march, Eric Rofes personal papers, San Francisco), *A Simple Matter of Justice* (1993 march, Billy Hileman personal papers, Pittsburgh), C-SPAN tapes from 1993 march, *C-SPAN 1993 Retrospective* (produced in 2003, National Lesbian and Gay Journalists Association, Washington, D.C.), and C-SPAN tapes from the 2000 march.

Appendix B: Coding Manual

Overview

The purpose of this analysis is to content code different types of newspaper articles (news, letters to the editor, op-ed pieces) relevant to the topic of a lesbian and gay march on Washington. News articles will address one or more of four possible Washington marches that occurred in 1979, 1987, 1993, and 2000, respectively.

News articles are coded for two main themes: 1) mobilization: why should lesbians and gay men organize a march on Washington? and 2) infighting: what internal disputes arose en route to staging the demonstration? News articles may contain other themes besides these two primary categories. Additional themes are considered extraneous for this analysis. We will use "presence-absence dichotomies." This coding scheme assigns the number 1 when an idea is present and the number 0 if it is absent.

How Newspaper Articles Are to Be Coded

Each article will be assessed along five broad, color-coded topical areas, within which there are more specific content themes. These areas include 1) article background/demographics (lavender), 2) mobilization overview (light green), 3) substance of mobilization (dark green), 4) infighting overview (light blue), and 5) substance of infighting (dark blue).

Codes are derived in one of two ways: keywords and/or inferential extraction. When inference is required, ask the article: what core concepts unify the central ideas in the paragraph? If doubt still persists, there are two options for proceeding: 1) See if the next paragraph builds on the first. Not every paragraph has to receive a code, and so reading the next paragraph may help extract a code shared by both paragraphs. 2) If the next paragraph is on a different theme, and you are sure that the prior paragraph under question contains a relevant theme, default to using the lead sentence or first two sentences for the code. More detailed information on how to code is outlined later in this codebook.

General Coding Guidelines for News Articles:
The Paragraph as the Unit of Analysis

Paragraphs are the textual unit of analysis for news articles. Although every paragraph has the potential to receive a code, not every paragraph will receive one. This analysis is only concerned with: 1) why the movement should organize a march on Washington (mobilization), and 2) the internal disputes associated with this organizing (infighting). And even within each of these, only certain themes will be coded, as specified below.

General Coding Guidelines for Letter to the Editor (LTE) and Opinion-
Editorial (OE) Articles: The Sentence as the Unit of Analysis

For LTE and OE sources, the sentence is the textual unit of analysis.

Specific Coding Guidelines for All Articles

The following are guidelines that may be helpful in identifying the presence of a code. These guidelines have been formulated in light of the structural features of American journalism.

1. Pay special attention to the lead and concluding paragraphs.
2. Pay special attention to *bold face sub-heads.*
3. Pay special attention to *bullet points and lists.*
4. Pay special attention to sentences prefaced with *first, second, third, next, finally,* etc.

5.   Pay special attention to sentences containing *superlative language.*
6.   Pay special attention to sentences containing the words *on the one hand* and *on the other hand.*
7.   Pay special attention to any sentence that contains a direct or paraphrased *quote.*

Section 1: Article Background

Codes

1.   Record number: a consecutive listing of all articles entered for analysis
2.   Which march? The respective march on Washington the story addresses
3.   Paper: the newspaper itself from which the story has been copied
4.   City: the city where the newspaper is published
5.   Date: the date of the story
6.   Story location: where in the newspaper is the story located? (front versus anywhere else)
7.   Author name: who wrote the story?
8.   Author affiliation: is the author representing any particular organization?
9.   Article type: what type of article is it? (news, OE, LTE)
10. Story title: what is the title of the story?
11. Number of codable units: how long is the story?
     ·   Count the number of paragraphs for news, sentences for LTE/OE
12. Does the story support or oppose the march? (OE and LTE articles only)
13. Does the story mention other marches on Washington?
14. If yes, which other marches are mentioned?
15. What is the writer's purpose in mentioning these other marches?

Section 2: Mobilization Overview

Every article must receive a code for EACH of the five categories in this section (present = 1; absent = 0).

Codes

16. Why march? Does the article talk about why the movement needs to march on Washington?
17. If not, purpose of story? What is the story's primary purpose?

18.   Explicit mention of identity or community?
       · Keywords: *identity, community, brothers, sisters, who we are*
19.   Does the article address external conflict confronting the movement?
20.   External conflict (elaborate): elaborate on the external conflict

Section 3: Infighting Overview

Every article must receive a code for EACH of the ten categories in this section (present = 1; absent = 0).

Codes

21.   Does the story mention unity/consensus in any capacity?
       · Keywords: *come/work together, solidarity, everyone support/get behind*
22.   Is the idea of unity/consensus central to the story?
23.   Does the story mention infighting in the current march?
24.   Does the story mention infighting in any prior marches?
25.   What sources of infighting from prior marches are mentioned?
26.   Is the discussion of infighting central to the story?
27.   What language is used to describe/discuss infighting?
28.   Is infighting described as good, bad, or neutral for the movement?
29.   Is there a suggestion made for how to resolve the infighting?
30.   If yes, what is proposed to help resolve the infighting?

Section 4: Substance of Mobilization

If the article did not address the question of "Why march?" (code No. 16 above), skip this section. If the article did address this question, assess the themes that were discussed. Note: there may be additional themes discussed than those listed here. Code those as "other" and make a note of what the theme is in the far right column titled "notes." Present = 1; absent = 0.

Codes

31.   AIDS (memorializing, education, research): we should march for reasons that have anything to do with HIV/AIDS (K = .737, p < .001)

32. Build solidarity with other groups: we should to march to build solidarity/
coalitions with other groups. (K = .712, p < .001)

33. Community-building: we should march to create, build, and celebrate our
own community (K = .738, p < .001). Specific codes are as follows:
- Bolster local organizing/organizational development (K = .429, p < .01):
  - includes discussions about the need to organize in non-urban
    places
  - includes discussions about the need to organize "back at home"
  - includes post-march discussions about wanting to keep up the politi-
    cal momentum
- Build support for miscellaneous constituencies (K = .737, p < .001):
  - includes discussions that we should march to advocate for various
    constituencies, such as gay youth, gay immigrants, gays of faith, third
    world, etc.
- Build a national movement (K = .651, p < .001):
  - includes discussions about "determining the direction of the
    movement"
- Celebrating/recognizing gay relationships (K = .760, p < .001):
  - includes general discussions that we are marching for "love"
  - this will often be associated with the "Wedding" as a weekend event
- Create new leaders (K = 1.0, p < .001):
  - includes discussions that marching helps build new leaders and
    leadership
- Media (K = 1.0, p < .001):
  - includes any discussion of the march's media coverage (whether or
    not it was done; how it was done; how to get it done; whether it will
    be done)
- Self-recognition/visibility, coming out (K = .659, p < .001):
  - includes discussions about the need to come out
  - includes discussions about the need "to learn more about ourselves"
  - includes discussions about the need to feel empowered
  - includes discussions about "celebrating our queerness" or "celebrat-
    ing sexuality"
  - includes discussions that "we are everywhere"
  - includes discussions about "what gay people look like"
  - includes discussions about building, solidifying, or affirming one's
    identity
- Voting bloc (K = 1.0, p < .001):
  - includes discussions about the need to establish a gay voting bloc

· Other (community building): other reasons why we should march
($K = 1.0, p < .001$)

34. Display or build our unity/solidarity/pride: we should march to build or
display our unity/solidarity/pride and/or work through our differences
($K = .815, p < .001$):
    · Keywords: *pride, proud, unity, solidarity* (with other gay people only)
    · Includes discussions about "joining in together" or "working together"
    · Includes discussions that we need to "end infighting" or to put an "end
to all factions"

35. Display our diversity: we should march to display our diversity ($K = .667$,
$p < .001$)

36. Display our strength/force/size: we should march to display our strength,
size, and/or force ($K = .870, p < .001$):
    · Includes discussions about attendance figures
    · Includes discussions about what it was like to be "among so many
queers" or "so many of us" or "so many lesbians and gay men"

37. Educate society: we should march to educate mainstream society
($K = .793, p < .001$):
    · Educating society by dispelling stereotypes about gays
    · Americans suffer from "misconceptions about us"
    · Includes discussions of putting a face on gay America
    · Includes discussion about bringing gay issues to "national attention"

38. Equal rights/equality: we should march for equal (legal, political) rights:
($K = .700, p < .001$)
    · Keywords: *rights, human dignity*
    · Includes general references to politics or political issues
    · Includes general references to "our cause" and position
    · Includes general references to ensuring or quickening progress
    · Includes general references to demanding freedom

39. Federal activity/oppression/ban discrimination: we should march to oppose federal oppression and/or federal discrimination ($K = .615, p < .001$):
    · Includes a variety of perceived problems at the federal level, including
AIDS, employment, housing, public accommodations, federal employment, etc.

40. Social/cultural acceptance/visibility: we should march to become more
socially/culturally accepted or to become visible to America ($K = .302$,
$p < .061$):
    · This code is about cultural visibility and acceptance (whereas equal rights
and federal discrimination are about political visibility and acceptance)

- Keywords: *acceptance, tolerance, attitudes, understanding*
- Includes discussions about how "normal" we are—or how gays are like straights
- *Educate society* is about providing information and dispelling false beliefs, whereas *acceptance* is about rectifying discriminatory tendencies/homophobia
- Includes discussions that we need to march because "people still hate us"

41. State-level activity: we should march to oppose activity in individual states (K = .783, p < .001):
    - We need to march because of activity in individual states
42. Other: we should march for other reasons (K = 1.0, p < .001)

Section 5: Substance of Infighting

If the article did not address the question of infighting (code No. 23 above), skip this section. If the article did address this question, assess the themes that were discussed. Note: There may be additional themes discussed than those listed here. Code those as "other" and make a note of what the theme is in the far right column titled "notes." Present = 1; absent = 0.

Codes

43. Organizing tasks: is the conflict a result of specific organizing tasks? (K = .942, p < .001)
    - Includes a discussion of any of the following: whether to march; when to march; title of the march; theme of the march; speakers; demands/platforms; general organizing structure
44. Effectiveness: is the conflict a result of concerns over whether the march will be successful or effective? I.e., what will be its *effects*? (K = .936, p < .001)
    - Concerns related to the tactical effectiveness and effects of the march: Is this going to work? What it will accomplish? Are those viable objectives? And is it is it worth the effort?
    - Concerns that not enough people will attend the march
    - Includes discussions about whether a march on Washington is an effective strategy/tactic for us to be using or whether we should try other tactics (like the fifty-state march)

· Includes discussions about disagreements over particular march events (e.g., a gay wedding)

45. Finances: is the conflict a result of concerns over financial accountability? ($K = 1.00$, $p < .001$)

· Includes discussions about the disclosure of money/finances/profits

46. Intra-community-isms: is the conflict a result of intra-community-isms? ($K = .918$, $p < .001$)

· Racism, sexism, classism, ageism within the gay movement

47. Local versus national (resource allocation): is the conflict a result of disagreements over whether resources are better spent at the local or national level? ($K = .773$, $p < .001$)

· Includes all general discussion about where to invest resources (e.g., money, time, energy)

48. Organizing, planning, and leadership: is the conflict about the organizing, planning, or leadership structure of the march? ($K = .828$, $p < .001$)

· Includes discussions about decision-making, the organizing body, and leadership

· Includes discussions about "credentials" (e.g., racial and/or gender composition)

· Includes discussions about who ought to be the "spokespersons" for our movement

· Includes discussions about "the process," in the 2000 march

49. Political logic: is the conflict about the *purpose* of the march? ($K = 1.00$, $p < .001$)

· Entails the point, purpose, focus, goals, timing, value, vision of the march

· Includes discussions about *why* we should have the march in the first place (i.e., its *cause*): What is the purpose? What is the value?

· Includes tensions between radicals/separatists and mainstream/assimilationists

· Includes disagreements over unspecified "ideological differences"

· Includes debates about whether we are like heterosexuals or different

· For 2000: includes discussion that this is an "ill-conceived" march

50. Single-issue versus coalition: is the conflict a result of whether the march should address exclusively gay concerns or embrace a coalition-type politics? ($K = .895$, $p < .001$)

51. Subgroup representation: is the conflict a result of different subgroups feeling excluded? ($K = .887$, $p < .001$)

- Bisexuals (K = 1.00, p < .001)
- Economic class (K = .655, p < .001)
- Gender (e.g., lesbians/women's issues) (K = 1.00, p < .001)
- Lifestyle (e.g., leather, NAMBLA) (K = 1.00, p < .001)
- Political factions (e.g., radicals, conservatives, moderates, Republicans, Democrats, grassroots) (K = 1.00, p < .001)
- People with AIDS (PWAs) (K = 1.00, p < .001)
- Race (e.g., "third world" gays, all races/ethnicities) (K = 1.00, p < .001)
- Regions (e.g., the "Hinterlands," urban gays) (K = .875, p < .001)
- Transgender (e.g., transpeople, transsexuals, transgender, cross-dressers) (K = .788, p < .001)
- Youth (e.g., "age of consent") (K = .788, p < .001)
- Other (e.g., religion) (K = 1.00, p < .001)

52. Other: are there other sources of infighting?

Notes

Chapter One

1. For more on the *Crisis*, see (Morris and Ghaziani 2005). DuBois quotes from (DuBois 1903).
2. For more on the ERA, see (Critchlow 2005); (Mansbridge 1986).
3. (Mankiller, Mink et al. 1998); (Bunch 1994; Jay 1999).
4. For more on cultural and categorical reconfiguration, see (Rich 1980). For more on the Radicalesbians, see (Radicalesbians 1970).
5. (Taylor and Rupp 1993:41).
6. (Echols 1983:53).
7. (Echols 1983:34; Echols 1989).
8. For advocates of creative disunity, see (Lorde 1984:66–71; see also Ryan 1989).
9. (McAdam 1982:189).
10. (Meier and Rudwick 1973:311).
11. For more information on these and other leadership debates, see (McAdam 1982; Morris 1984).
12. (White and Langer 1999:537).
13. (Penelope 1992).
14. Belafonte Won't Back Down from Powell Slave Reference. Reported by CNN, October 16, 2002. See http://archives.cnn.com/2002/US/10/15/belafonte. powell/ (accessed April 26, 2006).
15. For more on "Homocons," see (Goldstein 2002).
16. (White and Langer 1999:537–38).
17. An "ideology" can be defined as "symbolic meanings" (Barber 2002:221), "sets of statements" (Wuthnow 1987:147), "ideas and expectations and presuppositions" (Schudson 1989:155), or "a set of interconnected beliefs and their associated attitudes . . . [with] an explicit evaluative and implicit behavioral component" (Fine and Sandstrom 1993:24).

18. (Polletta 2002).

19. Here I allude to research on oppositional consciousness, or the "subjective roots of social protest" (Mansbridge and Morris 2001).

20. (Epstein 1999:76).

21. (Seidman 1993; Warner 1993; Adam 1995; Gamson 1995; Gamson 1997; Kirsch 2000; Engel 2001; Armstrong 2002; Goldstein 2002; Goldstein 2003; Ghaziani 2005; Robinson 2005).

22. Unity, Diversity, Insipidity, by Paul Varnell. *Windy City Times,* July 2, 1998:15.

23. (Armstrong 2002:110).

24. For tricky infighting as a staple of American politics, see (Polletta 2002:1). For lesbian/gay movement fragmentation, see (Kirsch 2000:115).

25. Many social movement theorists have challenged the divide between strategy and identity, with the latter considered expressive and the former material (Cohen 1985). Few scholars these days maintain that distinction. My intention here is not to resurrect an old and sometimes artificial divide but to integrate these two central concepts, as each has something valuable in itself to offer analysis.

26. Unless otherwise indicated, all quotes in this section are taken from (Epstein 1999).

27. Quintessential identity movement quote from (Melucci 1989; Bernstein 1997:532; Armstrong 2002).

28. False universalism quote from (Stein 1997:15).

29. See (Cohen 1999) for a similar study in African American communities.

30. "Community Infighting" Number One Gay Problem. *Windy City Times* May 2, 1991:8.

31. (Seidman 1997).

32. Our Fractal Subculture, by Jon Henri Damski. *Windy City Times* March 25, 1993:15.

33. (Barber 2002:3); see also (Klinkner and Smith 1999; Smith 2000).

34. Ibid.

35. For more on mobilizing consensus, see (Klandermans 1988). For more on linking local communities, see (Taylor and Whittier 1992:112).

36. Why a Signer of the Ad Hoc Call Is Marching in the MMOW, by Jim Fouratt. *Windy City Times,* April 6, 2000:13.

37. (Weber 1949:26–27); (Park and Burgess 1921:578); (Simmel 1955:13, 17); (Coser 1956:80); (Ross 1920:164–65, emphasis in original).

38. (Coser 1956:21–23); (Parsons 1945; Parsons 1949).

39. (Coser 1956:71); (Simmel 1955:48–49).

40. Countermovements and countermobilization efforts are "a particular kind of protest movement which is a response to the social change advocated by an initial movement." These reactionary "anti" movements are "a conscious,

collective, organized attempt to resist or to reverse social change" (McCarthy and Zald 1977; Mottl 1980:620; Zald and Useem 1987; Barrow 1990; Meyer and Staggenborg 1996; Andrews 2002). Notable examples include STOP ERA, the pro-life movement (as a countermovement to the pro-choice, abortion movement), the Ku Klux Klan (a white supremacist countermovement that reacted to the civil rights movement), and the Christian Right (which initially grew as a countermovement in reaction to the lesbian/gay movement). Movement-countermovement interactions comprise archetypical us-versus-them dynamics and are outside the scope of the present study's focus on infighting.

41. A more precise definition of factionalism is "conflict that develops between groups, belonging to the same organization, who formerly held common beliefs but who experience a growing divergence in their views and interests" (Firey 1948; Zald and Ash 1966; Stern, Tarrow et al. 1971; Zald and McCarthy 1980; Miller 1983; Mushaben 1989; Balser 1997:200).

42. (Marx and Engels 1978:480–81).

43. For a fuller consideration of the classical tradition of infighting, see (Zald and Ash 1966; McCarthy and Zald 1977); (Von Eschen, Kirk et al. 1969; Stern, Tarrow et al. 1971; Gamson 1975; Piven and Cloward 1977); (c.f., Oberschall 1973; McCarthy and Zald 1977; Gitlin 1980; Jenkins 1983; Morris 1984; Jenkins and Eckert 1986).

44. (Gamson 1975:99–100, 101).

45. Taken from p. 100–102. Some may be inclined to elevate Gamson's conclusions since his is an "equal probability" or "representative sample" of 53 challenging groups in the U.S. that represent a "universe" of "all those challenging groups that surfaced in American society between 1800 and 1945" (which amounts to a total of between five and six hundred such groups) (p. 19, 22). Although this itself has produced some debate, it is notable that factionalism occurred in 43 percent of the groups in his sample. Of these, 16 organizations experienced splits. Given these numbers, it is unclear whether Gamson has the necessary statistical power for such conclusions.

46. (Rupp and Taylor 1987).

47. (Mushaben 1989; Walsh and Cable 1989).

48. (Gerlach and Hine 1970:64).

49. (Benford 1993:694, 698).

50. (Balser 1997).

51. (McAdam 1982:189–90).

52. (Mushaben 1989:269).

53. Some scholars suggest that the question of origins—why do movements form?—is the sine qua non of research (Morris and Herring 1987). It is thus not surprising that the study of infighting also shifted to questions of origins.

54. On racist attitudes and beliefs, see (Meier and Rudwick 1976; Moraga and Anzaldua 1981; Fantasia 1988); on sexist attitudes and beliefs, see (Robnett

1997; Chesler 2001; Armstrong 2002); on other social divisions, see (Morris 1984:11; Gamson 1995; Gamson 1997; Cohen 1999; Cohen 2000; Gamson 2000; Waite 2001; Goldstein 2002; Robinson 2005); on coordination and reconciliation problems and multiple oppressions, see (Stockdill 2001; Stockdill 2003); on generations and cohorts, see (Klandermans 1994; Whittier 1997); on economic aggregation problems, see (Oliver 1993); on failure to mobilize consensus, see (Klandermans 1988; Mushaben 1989); on tactics and strategy disputes, see (McAdam 1982; Carson [1981] 1995); and on participatory democracy and other issues related to decision-making, see (Miller 1983; Polletta 2002; Wilde 2004).

55. On movement culture and identity, see (Melucci 1985; Downey 1986; Melucci 1988; Feldman 1990; Morris and Mueller 1992; Larana, Johnston et al. 1994; Johnston and Klandermans 1995; Lichterman 1995; Melucci 1995; Bernstein 1997; Jasper 1997; Polletta 1997; Wood 1999; Stryker, Owens et al. 2000; Mansbridge and Morris 2001; Polletta and Jasper 2001); on values, visions, and viewpoints, including concerns of ideological purity, see (Echols 1983; Echols 1989; Ryan 1989; Taylor and Rupp 1993); on frames, frame alignment, frame disputes, and other cultural resources, see (Snow and Benford 1988; Snow and Benford 1992; Benford 1993; Hunt and Benford 1994; Hunt, Benford et al. 1994; Binder 2002).

56. (Gamson 1975:72); (McAdam 1982:58).

57. Despite some assertions to move "beyond identity" by regressing to the related concepts of "identification," "self-understanding," "self-representation," and "social location," identity retains its analytic utility among activists, academics, and laypeople. I argue the directive should not be for renouncement but methodological rigor. For more on moving "beyond identity," see (Brubaker and Cooper 2000) and (Calhoun 1994) for defense of its analytic utility. Definition of identity cited from (Johnston, Larana et al. 1994:15). For catness and netness, see (White 1965; Tilly 1978:62–63; White 1992; Melucci 1995). For we-ness, see (Taylor and Whittier 1992). For categorical commonality and relational connectedness, see (Brubaker and Cooper 2000:20).

58. A March Proponent, by Joe Murray. *Windy City Times,* May 14, 1998:12.

59. Tyler to LGNY, by Robin Tyler. *Windy City Times,* October 28, 1999:13.

60. (Jehn 1995:257–58). See Coding Manual for operational details.

61. For morality versus civil liberties, see (Loftus 2001). For equal protection versus sex, see (Yang 1997). For more on the calculus itself, see (Epstein 1999:74). For more on black communities and cultural battles, see (Gamson 1997; Cohen 2000:385).

62. Lavender Fascists, Homocons, and Other Cannibals, by Richard Rouilard. *Advocate,* August 13, 1992:6.

63. Swidler (2001:19).

64. (Hebdige 1979:79).

65. (Swidler 2001:19). I think of infighting as belonging to a family of related processes. As such, my intention is not to suggest that the literature is wrong per se, but instead to open up new research possibilities by critically differentiating the public expression of internal dissent from organizational splits and/or dissolution. My cases allow me to isolate under-theorized, meaning-making processes, which I use to appraise how infighting enables culture to work in some unexpected ways. For a more complete discussion of these and other methodological concerns, please refer to the Methods Appendix A.

66. (Fine 1979:733). See the conclusion for a detailed discussion of this argument.

67. See (Arnold [1869] 1949) for the best that has been thought and known and (Tylor [1871] 1958) for that complex whole.

68. (Griswold 1994:4).

69. For more on matters of culture being blocked due to a persisting divide between the social (material) and the cultural (non-material), see (Friedland and Mohr 2004:6; Bonnell and Hunt 1999). For more on culture's new prestige, see (Kaufman 2004:353). For more on efforts to isolate culture's autonomy from social structure, see (Sewell 1999; Alexander 2003). For more on culture remaining a diffused mist today, see (Swidler 1995:38, 39).

Chapter Two

1. For more on these views, see (D'Emilio 1983).

2. For more on the 1960s and 1970s in American life, see (Gitlin 1980; Gitlin 1995).

3. Many scholars have endeavored to document this long history of political activism and resistance. A non-exhaustive list of notable monographs includes (Humphreys 1972; D'Emilio 1983; D'Emilio and Freedman 1988; Duberman, Vicinus et al. 1989; Berube 1990; Duberman 1993; Kennedy and Davis 1993; Chauncey 1994; Adam 1995; Kaiser 1997; Loughery 1998; Clendinen and Nagourney 1999; Armstrong 2002; Marcus 2002; Carter 2004).

4. For more on the Stonewall Inn riots, see (Armstrong 2002; Carter 2004); (Berube 1990:271); (Duberman 1993:xvii); (Kaiser 1997:206); (Adam 1995:81); (D'Emilio 1983:232). For a critical perspective on why this particular riot is commemorated over comparable others, see (Armstrong and Crage 2006).

5. Before this moment in history, and inspired by women's culture, "coming out" was part of campy gay argot that "used to refer to the ritual of a debutante's being formally introduced to, or 'coming out' into, the society of her cultural peers. . . . A gay man's coming out originally referred to his being formally presented to the largest collective manifestation of prewar gay society, the enormous drag balls that were patterned on the debutante and masquer-

ade balls of the dominant culture." Gay liberation activists of the late 1960s and 1970s "deliberately changed the meaning of the term" (Armstrong 2002:16, 61, 67–68).

6. (Armstrong 2002:105).

7. (Johnson 2004).

8. (Armstrong 2002:108).

9. Ibid:107–10.

10. Ibid:140, 143.

11. Ibid:144.

12. Ibid:145.

13. Ibid:147, 150.

14. For more on single- versus multi-issue strategies, see (Epstein 1987; Fuss 1989; Armstrong 2002:152). For more on "unity through diversity," see (Armstrong 2002:153).

15. For more on this argument of shifting political logics, see (Armstrong 2002:113).

16. For more on the notion of compulsory heterosexuality, see (Rich 1980).

17. For more on gay ghettos, see (Escoffier 1998); (Berube 1990). For more on eroticized topographies, see (Bell and Valentine 1995:1).

18. For more on geographic insularity, see (Futrell and Simi 2004 for review). For more on oppositional consciousness, see (Mansbridge and Morris 2001).

19. (Shenk and Silberman 1994:308); See also: http://www.algonet.se/~iguana/ DRAKE/tonyreifpostscript.html, accessed May 24, 2006.

20. (Witt, Thomas et al. 1995:7)

21. For more on the Kinsey Report, see (Kinsey, Pomeroy et al. 1948:638). For more on Harry Hay, see (Timmons 1990:134). The term "Mattachine" references medieval dancers who appeared wearing masks in public, a metaphor with which gay people were able to widely relate.

22. This discussion draws from the following: http://jasewells.com/gayi-cons/; http://www.glbtq.com/arts/rainbow_flag.html; and the Alyson Almanac (see http://www.cs.cmu.edu/afs/cs.cmu.edu/user/scotts/bulgarians/rainbow-flag .html).

23. See also (Vezeris 1995:435).

24. (http://thecastro.net/bryant.html, accessed August 12, 2004); see also (Armstrong 2002:127).

25. (Tin 2007).

26. Quoted in (Kaiser 1997:269–70). See (Adam 1995:112) for more on Bryant-related protests.

27. (Armstrong 2002:127–28).

28. (http://journalism.berkeley.edu/projects/prop22/runkleb.html, accessed August 12, 2004).

29. Advocate Archives: 20 Years Ago—Briggs Initiative Defeated—Failed

1978 California Referendum Banning Gays from Public School Jobs, by Don Romseburg. *Advocate* June 9, 1998.

30. Although Harvey Milk was the first openly gay person to be elected as a city supervisor in San Francisco, Elaine Noble was the first openly gay person *ever* to be elected to office at the state level in 1974 (Massachusetts).

31. (Cloud 1999).

32. Personal interview with Ray Hill. November 1, 2003.

33. (Adam 1995:114); (Clendinen and Nagourney 1999:403).

34. (Adam 1995:114); (Shilts 1982); See also http://thecastro.net/milk/white-night.html (accessed May 25, 2006).

35. See http://www.rotten.com/library/bio/crime/assassins/dan-white/; http://www.mistersf.com/notorious/notwhiteindex.htm (accessed May 25, 2006); and (Epstein 1984).

36. Museum Opens Downtown with Look at "Saint Harvey": Exhibitions Explore History of Slain Supervisor, Rainbow Flag, by Ray Delgado. *San Francisco Chronicle,* June 6, 2003.

37. A Stonewall Nation (unauthored editorial). *Gay Community News,* June 23, 1979:4.

38. March on Washington (unauthored editorial). *Gay Community News,* October 13, 1979:4.

39. See (Piven and Cloward 1977:3–4) on necessary cognitions and (McAdam 1982:110, 180) on the will to act.

40. Quoted in (Kaiser 1997:235).

41. For more on the 1952 *DSM,* see (Clendinen and Nagourney 1990:200). For more on the APA as a key target, see (Marcus 2002:145). For more on the politics of diagnosis, see (Bayer 1987).

42. For Auschwitz quote, see (Clendinen and Nagourney 1990:201). For Lahusen quote, see (Marcus 2002:146).

43. (Clendinen and Nagourney 1999:199).

44. For more on the tripartite system of domination (in the civil rights movement), see (Morris 1984:1).

45. (Marcus 2002:146, 122).

46. For more on federal and state-level bills, see (Clendinen and Nagourney 1999:240; Suffredini 2005:20–21).

47. (Clendinen and Nagourney 1999:240).

48. (Murray 1996:401–2).

49. Stop the film and *Celluloid Closet* quotes from (Russo 1987). Remaining quotes from (Gross 2001:65).

Chapter Three

1. An Idea Whose Time Has Come: A March on the Nation's Capitol, Fall 1979. Personal Papers of Steve Ault:3, 5. See also "Lesbian Feminist Liberation Opposes the Inclusion of the Equal Rights Amendment as a Major Demand in a National March on Washington for Lesbian and Gay Rights." The memo states, "This march has the potential . . . to unify our efforts to build a movement." Folder: March on Washington, 1979. Box: Paula Lichtenberg Papers, Box 2. GLBT Historical Society of Northern California.

2. Why the March? *Modern Times* dated "Today, 1979":3. Folder: Modern Times 14: March on Washington—1979. Box: Ephemera Collection, Recurring Events, Parades and Marches on Washington. GLBT Historical Society of Northern California.

3. An Idea Whose Time Has Come: A March on the Nation's Capitol, Fall 1979. Personal Papers of Steve Ault:3, 5.

4. (Armstrong 2002:41).

5. Personal Papers of Robin Tyler Productions Inc.

6. (Armstrong 2002:130).

7. National March on Washington for Lesbian and Gay Rights, September 10, 1979. In the folder titled "March on Washington (1979)." The ONE Institute and Archives.

8. All information from the 1973 meeting in Urbana-Champaign comes from the David Aiken papers, titled "March on Washington," November 12, 1973, courtesy of the Rainbow History Project.

9. National Gay Convention Planned. Newspaper article dated November 1973. Source unknown. Personal papers of Jeff Graubart.

10. P. 2 of a letter signed by James P. Zais. Personal Papers of Jeff Graubart.

11. Personal papers of Jeff Graubart.

12. National Gay Convention Planned. Newspaper article dated November 1973. Personal papers of Jeff Graubart.

13. Washington Gays Not Happy about "Mass March" Plans, by David L. Aiken. *Advocate,* December 5, 1973:19.

14. Letter to the National Gay Mobilizing Committee from the Washington Area Gay Community Council, dated November 4, 1973. Personal papers of Jeff Graubart.

15. Letter to the National Gay Mobilizing Committee from the Mattachine Society of Washington, dated July 19, 1973, signed by Franklin E. Kameny. Personal papers of Jeff Graubart.

16. Washington Gays Not Happy about "Mass March" Plans, by David L. Aiken. *Advocate,* December 5, 1973:19.

17. Information on the Minneapolis-based Committee for the March on Wash-

ington comes from: 1) reports in Boston's *Gay Community News,* November 1978–March 1979, and 2) the personal papers of Joyce Hunter.

18. An Idea Whose Time Has Come: A March On the Nation's Capitol, Fall 1979. Personal Papers of Steve Ault.

19. The March on Washington 1979. Report compiled by Joyce Hunter. Personal papers of Joyce Hunter.

20. Ibid.

21. An Idea Whose Time Has Come:4.

22. Human Rights and Foreign Policy (1977). Jimmy Carter, Public Papers of the Presidents of the United States: Jimmy Carter, vol.1 (1977):954. Accessible online: http://usinfo.state.gov/usa/infousa/facts/democrac/55.htm.

23. For more on comparisons with the civil rights movement in this particular regard, see (Layton 2000).

24. Proposal circulated by the Committee for the March on Washington on Interim Steering Committee letterhead. Special Collections, Gerber/Hart Library. See also "An Idea Whose Time Has Come":5.

25. Undated press release authored by Dennis Walen:1. Special Collections, Gerber/Hart Library.

26. Information on the dissolution of the Minneapolis-based ISC comes from the *Gay Community News,* November 25, 1978. Article titled, Committee Dissolves Itself: Planned March on Washington Is in Trouble, by John Graczak:1.

27. Letter to the National Gay Mobilizing Committee from the Washington Area Gay Community Council, dated November 4, 1973. Personal papers of Jeff Graubart.

28. Information compiled from the personal papers of Joyce Hunter.

29. Long, Long Road to Washington:12. Official program of the 1979 March on Washington.

30. 100,000 March in Washington, by Rick Hillegas. *Gay Community News,* October 27, 1979:9.

31. National March on Washington for Lesbian and Gay Rights, September 10, 1979. In the folder titled "March on Washington (1979)." The ONE Institute and Archives.

32. (Rosenberg, Scagliotti et al. 1984).

33. Impressions of the National March, by Allen Young. *Gay Community News* October 15, 1979. See photograph by Susan Fleischmann on p. 15.

34. Personal papers of Joyce Hunter. See also *Gay Community News,* March 10, 1979:1.

35. A copy of the questionnaire was obtained from Gerber/Hart Library. See also "Discussions Continue on Conference for March on Washington," *Gay Community News,* February 10, 1979:1.

36. Plans Move Ahead for October March on Washington, *Gay Community News,* March 10, 1979:1.

37. 1979 & 1987 March Notes, on p. 8 of the official program of the 1987 National March on Washington for Lesbian and Gay Rights. Primary source materials from Gerber/Hart. See also letter dated March 3, 1979, to: National Board of Dignity, INC, from: John Chester. Ephemera Collection, Gerber/Hart Library.

38. Ibid.

39. We Still Might March to DC, *GayLife,* February 2, 1979:2.

40. Letter from the Coalition for Lesbian and Gay Rights to the Committee for the March on Washington, dated November 4, 1978. Personal Papers of Steve Ault.

41. Untitled letter, "Dear Supporters of Lesbian and Gay Rights," September 10, 1919. Folder: March on Washington (1979). The ONE Institute and Archives.

42. Gays Mark Riot That Sparked Movement. *The Washington Post,* June 25, 1979. Folder: 1979 March on Washington Box: Robert Starkey/Robert Villacari, Box 1 of 2. GLBT Historical Society of Northern California.

43. For more on the state of national organizations in the 1970s, see (D'Emilio 2005).

44. Board Acts on D.C. March. *It's Time: Newsletter of the National Gay Task Force,* May 1979, 6(4):1.

45. Mid-Atlantic Regional Follow-Up/National March on Washington for Lesbian and Gay Rights * October 14, 1979/Coinciding with the National Third World Lesbian and Gay Conference * October 12–15, 1979, Minutes from the Follow-up Meeting, June 16, 1979, Baltimore, Md. Folder: 1979 March on Washington. Box: Robert Starkey/Robert Villacari, Box 1 of 2. GLBT Historical Society of Northern California.

46. D.C. March Plans Undecided, *GayLife,* March 2, 1979:17.

47. Plans Move Ahead for October March on Washington. *Gay Community News,* March 10, 1979:1.

48. National March on Washington for Lesbian and Gay Rights: Organizer's Handbook. Gerber/Hart Library.

49. Letter from Sharon Ayling, dated September 19, 1979, re: "October 14 National March on Washington for Lesbian & Gay Rights." Folder: March on Washington 1979. Box: 1987 March on Washington, National Committee—Record, Box 2. GLBT Historical Society of Northern California, San Francisco, Calif.

50. Plans Move Ahead for October March on Washington. *Gay Community News,* March 10, 1979:1.

51. (Armstrong 2002:141, 148).

52. Sisters . . . We Need You in Washington . . . Oct. 14. Folder: March on

Washington 1979. Box: 1987 March on Washington, National Committee Record, Box 2. GLBT Historical Society of Northern California.

53. Meeting minutes of the Philadelphia Conference. Personal Papers of Eric Rofes.

54. Meeting minutes of the Philadelphia Conference.

55. March on Washington, D.C. Political Committee Report. Dated December 10, 1978. Folder: March on Washington, 1979. Box: Paula Lichtenberg Papers, Box 2. GLBT Historical Society of Northern California.

56. Meeting minutes of the Philadelphia Conference.

57. The March on Washington 1979. Personal papers of Joyce Hunter.

58. At the rally, Milk alluded to the Statue of Liberty: "On the Statue of Liberty it says: 'Give me your tired, your poor, your huddled masses yearning to breathe free . . .' No matter how hard you try, you cannot chip those words off the base of the Statue of Liberty." He concluded his speech with an assertion Alpert ultimately used on the logo: "Rights are not won on paper: They are won only by those who make their voices heard." Untitled document with a picture of the Liberty Logo at the header. Folder: 1979 March on Washington. Box: Robert Starkey/Robert Villacari, Box 1 of 2. GLBT Historical Society of Northern California.

59. Bay Area Conference of the National March on Washington for Lesbian and Gay Rights. Cover letter for March 7, 1979, General Meeting. Folder: March on Washington, 1979, Miscellaneous, Paula Lichtenberg Papers, #89-1. Box: Paula Lichtenberg Papers, Box 2. GLBT Historical Society of Northern California.

60. A Monumental March Marks a Big Moment in Gay History. *Advocate*, November 29, 1979:7.

61. National Conference Plans March. *Gay Community News*, July 21, 1979:1.

62. The March on Washington 1979. Personal papers of Joyce Hunter.

63. Personal Interview and Papers of Paul Boneberg.

64. All remaining evidence from the Houston Conference come from: "National Conference Plans March." *Gay Community News*, July 21, 1979:1.

65. Transpeople Caucus: Motion for Consideration. Folder: March on Washington 1979. Box: 1987 March on Washington, National Committee Record, Box 2. GLBT Historical Society of Northern California.

66. October 14 National March on Washington for Lesbian and Gay Rights. Letter dated September 19, 1979, from Sharon Ayling. Folder: March on Washington 1979. Box: 1987 March on Washington, National Committee Record, Box 2. GLBT Historical Society of Northern California.

67. Further Reflections on Houston, by Lee Stone. *Gay Community News*, July 28, 1979:12.

68. Nomenclature, by Bunny LaRue. *Gay Community News*, October 20, 1979:5.

69. Further Reflections on Houston, by Lee Stone. *Gay Community News,* July 28, 1979:12.

70. (Thompson 1999:217).

71. Welcome to the March, by Alan Young. P. 3 of the official program of the 1979 National March on Washington for Lesbian and Gay Rights. Courtesy of the Rainbow History Project and Gerber/Hart Library.

72. (Thompson 1994:187; Ghaziani 2005).

73. Stonewall to Washington, by Nancy Walker. *Gay Community News,* October 27, 1979:16.

74. Personal, joint interview with Steve Ault and Joyce Hunter. January 3, 2004.

75. Long, Long Road to Washington, by Jim Kepner. Official program:13.

76. Stonewall to Washington, by Nancy Walker. *Gay Community News,* October 27, 1979:16.

77. Mixed Feelings about Gay March, by Louis Freedberg and Christopher Heredia. *San Francisco Chronicle,* April 10, 2000:A2.

78. For more on ideological purity in the women's movement, see (Echols 1983; Echols 1989; Ryan 1989; Taylor and Rupp 1993). For a similar argument on audience calculations in the Michigan Women's Music Festival and in NAMBLA debates, see (Gamson 1997).

79. 25th Anniversary of the March on Washington—Thoughts and Reflections. Press release, Thursday, October 14, 2004. http://www.thetaskforce.org/media/release.cfm?print = 1&releaseID = 745 (accessed December 7, 2004).

80. Mixed Feelings about Gay March, by Louis Freedberg and Christopher Heredia. *San Francisco Chronicle,* April 10, 2000:A2. Quoted in Armstrong (2002:130). For scholarly comments, see (Andriote 1999:14; Armstrong 2002:131).

81. Further Reflections on Houston, by Lee Stone. *Gay Community News,* July 28, 1979:12.

82. Stonewall to Washington, by Nancy Walker. *Gay Community News,* October 27, 1979:16.

83. Washington is Scene of National March. *Gay Community News,* October 20, 1979:1.

84. Stonewall to Washington, by Nancy Walker. *Gay Community News,* October 27, 1979:17.

85. Stonewall to Washington, by Nancy Walker. *Gay Community News,* October 27, 1979:17.

86. Further Reflections on Houston, by Lee Stone. *Gay Community News,* July 28, 1979:12.

87. Third World Conference Meets, by Jil Clark. *Gay Community News,* October 27, 1979:1, 9.

Chapter Four

1. (Armstrong 2002:81).

2. Pulling Through in a Big Way, by Steve Greenberg. *Washington Blade,* October 11, 1987.

3. See (Turner 2000) for more on reconfiguring gay life. Vaid quote from (Vaid 1994:xi).

4. (Meyer 2002:14).

5. March on Washington, by Dave Walter. *Advocate,* August 18, 1987:11.

6. Civil Disobedience: Are We Entering a New Militant Stage in the Struggle for Gay Rights? by Mark Vandervelden. *Advocate,* September 29, 1987:48.

7. (Vaid 1994:xi).

8. March on Washington, by Dave Walter. *Advocate,* August 18, 1987:11.

9. Civil Disobedience: Are We Entering a New Militant Stage in the Struggle for Gay Rights? by Mark Vandervelden. *Advocate,* September 29, 1987:48.

10. Outbreak of a Rare Cancer Baffles Doctors. *CBS,* December 5, 1981.

11. (Jones and Dawson 2000). See also the Gay Men's Health Crisis: http://www.gmhc.org/about/timeline.html and http://www.bbc.co.uk/bbcthree/news/7oclocknews/features/aids_day_011204.shtml (accessed January 12, 2005).

12. (Shilts 1987).

13. See Kaiser Family Foundation Web site, accessed December 12, 2004.

14. Altman, Lawrence K. 1981 (July 3). Rare Cancer Seen in 41 Homosexual Men. *New York Times:*A20.

15. Karposi's Sarcoma and *Pneumocystis Carinii* Pneumonia Among Homosexual Men—New York City and California. Centers for Disease Control and Prevention. July 4, 1981; 30:305–8.

16. (Shilts 1987: 138).

17. Ibid.

18. (Schlager 1998:17).

19. Current Trends Update on Acquired Immune Deficiency Syndrome (AIDS)—United States. *Morbidity and Mortality Weekly Report* 31(37):507–8, 513–14 (September 24, 1982). See also http://www.cdc.gov/mmwr/preview/mmwrhtml/00001163.htm (accessed January 12, 2005); http://www.aegis.com/topics/timeline/default.asp (accessed January 12, 2005); and http://www.gmhc.org/about/timeline.html (accessed January 12, 2005).

20. See the Kaiser Family Foundation Web site, accessed December 14, 2004.

21. http://www.gmhc.org/about/timeline.html.

22. (Shilts 1987:290).

23. Patrick Buchanan, Nature's Retribution, *Washington Times,* May 27, 1983.

24. For more on this point, see (Blumenfeld 1992).

25. (Buckley 1986).

26. (Krauthammer 1983:20).

27. For more on this point, see (Padgug 1989:296).

28. See A National March Proposed for '87, *Washington Blade*, September 5, 1986.

29. (Shilts 1987; quoted in Kaiser 1997:289).

30. (Schlager 1998:17).

31. (Kaiser 1997:285).

32. (Jones and Dawson 2000:188).

33. The March on Washington, by Peter Freiberg. *Advocate*, November 10, 1987:11, 24.

34. For gay history books and Reagan, see (Marcus 2002:331). For angry activist chants, see (Jones and Dawson 2000:188). For viruses and social identity boundaries, see (Armstrong 2002:173).

35. Prejudice and discrimination as concrete quote from (Turner 2000:22). Resurgence of overall hostility quote from (Turner 2000:27). Conspiracy of silence quote from (Adam 1995). Information on the *New York Times* from (Kaiser 1997:287).

36. For more on the Moral Majority, see (Kaiser 1997:273) and (Shilts 1987:44).

37. Mixner quote from (Scagliotti, Baus et al. 1999). For more on the relationship between AIDS and coming out, see (Engel 2001) and (Adam 1995). For more on refocusing the cultural content, see (Morris 1984:96).

38. Philly Meeting Calls for National March. *Advocate*, April 5, 1979:7.

39. March on Washington (unauthored editorial). *Gay Community News*, October 13, 1979:4.

40. For more on disease ownership and organizational growth, see (Armstrong 2002:162). She argues that San Francisco, although not the only site of such organizational growth, is a typical case for major urban centers in the United States. According to Armstrong (2002:213n5), "It is through understanding what happened in San Francisco, and other major urban areas, that the birth of a national gay movement can be understood." As an example of specific types of organizational growth, see (Ghaziani and Cook 2005).

41. See the Kaiser Family Foundation Web site, accessed December 14, 2004, for more on the GMHC. McFarlane quote from (Engel 2001:48).

42. For more on the AIDS Industry, see (Adam 1995). For more on AIDS social movements, see (Gamson 1989; Clendinen and Nagourney 1999; Armstrong 2002; Gould 2002).

43. (Greenberg Unpublished Paper); See www.actupny.org (accessed January 20, 2005).

44. (Crimp and Rolston 1990; Crimp 1996).

45. (Jones and Dawson 2000:xv, 259–60).

46. For more on conflict and integration, see (Bain 1939:499). For common bonds, see (Coser 1956:90). For cooperation, see (Horowitz 1962).

47. Quote from (Cruikshank 1992:183). For more on gay male and lesbian solidarity around AIDS, see (Cruikshank 1992; Schartz 1993:232; Armstrong 2002:147).

48. (Seidman 1994:172).

49. (Kramer 1978; quoted in Kaiser 1997:290–91).

50. For more on this point, see (Epstein 1996).

51. (Murray 1996:116).

52. (Armstrong 2002:160; Shilts 1987:305).

53. No science to support and out of the tubs quotes from (Murray 1996:110, 114). Likelihood of contraction quote from (Shilts 1987:305). Information on the *New York Times Magazine* article from (Kaiser 1997:308).

54. Bathhouses and gay male sexual culture quote from (Armstrong 2002:160). Sex as a revolutionary act and sex as devoid of intimacy quote from (Shilts 1987:19, 24). Kramer quote from (Marcus 2002:247). Gay trust quote from (Armstrong 2002:160).

55. (Shilts 1987:19); see also (Kaiser 1997:289) for bathhouse quote.

56. Murder and suicide quotes from (Murray 1996:111; Shilts 1987:437). Flouting quote from (Shilts 1987:588).

57. For more on AIDS impact, see (Armstrong 2002:168). Historian quote from Kaiser (1997:279).

58. It is important to note that this line of reasoning suggests that the lesbian and gay movement was immature in the 1970s and before. For a discussion and rebuttal of this line of thinking, see (Armstrong 2002, chapter 8). See also (Murray 1996:197; Armstrong 2002:168); Kaiser 1997:300) for more on the specific quotes used in this section. For more on the idea of a real community, see (Bellah, Madsen et al. 1985:153–54; see also Murray 1996:197).

59. Crucial engine and second-class citizenship quotes from (Murdoch and Price 2001:276, 344). For more on the implications of the case (blurring lines, conflating principles), see (Engel 2001:117). Unless otherwise indicated, all details on the narrative of the case are taken from (Murdoch and Price 2001:277–84).

60. *Bowers v. Hardwick* remained in effect until 2003, when it was reversed and remanded in a ruling of 6–3 by the *Lawrence v. Texas* case in 2002, a major case in which Justice Kennedy, who delivered the opinion of the court, concluded, "*Bowers* was not correct when it was decided, and it is not correct today. It ought not to remain a binding precedent. *Bowers v. Hardwick* should be and now is overruled." See (*Lawrence v. Texas* 2003).

61. (Engel 2001:117).

62. (Sterba 1994).

63. All excerpts taken from (*Bowers v. Hardwick* 1986).

64. (Kaiser 1997:319–20).

65. With the exception of the *Advocate,* quotes from (Clendinen and Nagourney 1999:537–38). *Advocate* quote from: Civil Disobedience, by Mark Vandervelden. *Advocate,* September 29, 1987:48.

66. We Too, Have a Dream! Newsletter from the Southern California Regional Support Network of the National March on Washington for Lesbian and Gay Rights. Folder: Atlanta Meeting May 2–3, 1987. Box 2. GLBT Historical Society of Northern California.

67. Civil Disobedience. *Advocate,* September 29, 1987:48.

68. (Clendinen and Nagourney 1999:538).

69. Ibid.

70. Primary source material flier from Gerber/Hart Library.

Chapter Five

1. See (Lang and Lang 1961:495) for originating spark, (Fine 1979:742) for triggering event, and (Smelser 1963:16–17) for precipitating factor. Information gathered from 1) "1979 & 1987 March Notes," p. 8–9 of the march program, Gerber/Hart, and 2) "Call to Action for a New March on Washington for Lesbian and Gay Rights," the ONE Institute. Box: March on Washington 1987 (#103–151), Folder: National March on Washington 1985–1987, Book 1.

2. Letter from the March on Washington Committee Inc., dated 8/22/86, signed by Steve Ault. ONE Institute. Box: March on Washington 1987 (#103–151), Folder: National March on Washington 1985–1987, Book 1.

3. Civil Disobedience, by Mark Vandervelden. *Advocate,* September 29, 1987:48..

4. For a National March on Washington—Some Preliminary Considerations. The ONE Institute. Box: March on Washington 1987 (#103–151), Folder: National March on Washington 1985–1987, Book 1.

5. See 1) Call to Action for a New March on Washington for Lesbian and Gay Rights and 2) March on Washington Committee, letter dated 7/31/86 and signed by Gwendolyn Rogers and Steve Ault. The ONE Institute. Box: March on Washington 1987 (#103–151), Folder: National March on Washington 1985–1987, Book 1.

6. For Love and For Life, We're Not Going Back. Undated letter, signed by The March on Washington Committee. The ONE Institute. Box: March on Washington 1987 (#103–151), Folder: National March on Washington 1985–1987, Book 1.

7. (Olson 1965).

8. Organizers are alluding to a decision made in the summer of 1986 in which the Justice Department ruled that employers have the right to fire people with AIDS, or those perceived to have AIDS. This ruling was made despite over-

whelming scientific and medical evidence that HIV is spread through sexual encounters. See "For Love and For Life, We're Not Going Back," The ONE Institute. Box: March on Washington 1987 (#103–151), Folder: National March on Washington 1985–1987, Book 1.

9. Besides Raising Gay/Lesbian Issues, a March on Washington Will Strengthen Our Movement. The ONE Institute. Box: March on Washington 1987 (#103–151), Folder: National March on Washington 1985–1987, Book 1.

10. For more on the politics of numbers, see (Alonso and Starr 1987; Hacking 1990; Porter 1995).

11. March on Washington, by Dave Walter. *Advocate,* August 18, 1987:11.

12. (Layton 2000:9).

13. When Reagan came to power in 1981, foreign policy attention toward Nicaragua and other Central American countries intensified due to concerns about the proliferation of communism in third world countries. Such fears were generated by the Sandinista Revolution (i.e., on behalf of all people whose property had been unlawfully confiscated under land reform in the 1980s), which, according to Reagan, stood as "the threat of a good example," due to its potential success and hence viability of communism. The Reagan administration accused Nicaragua, in particular, of shipping arms from Soviet-bloc countries to Salvadoran rebels who fought against a U.S.-backed regime. Some believe this manifest explanation concealed the truth of U.S. intervention, namely, the opportunity to emphasize international U.S. hegemony, especially after its failure in Vietnam (see Walker 1987).

14. For more on the idea of resonance for cultural effectiveness, see (Schudson 1989).

15. (Armstrong 2002:149–50).

16. For a National March on Washington—Some Preliminary Considerations. The ONE Institute. Box: March on Washington 1987 (#103–151), Folder: National March on Washington 1985–1987, Book 1.

17. On this point, see also (Ghaziani 2005).

18. For more on oppositional consciousness, see (Mansbridge and Morris 2001). For more on framing, see (Snow, Rochford et al. 1986). For more on optimism and political efficacy, see (McAdam 1982). For more on committing to the movement, see (Polletta 2002).

19. For more on issues of local organizational development, see (Minkoff 1993; Andrews 1997).

20. Plans for Nat'l March Begin amidst NY-DC Turf Battle, by Peg Byron. *Washington Blade,* November 21, 1986:1. Bitter Debate Opens Nat'l March Planning, by Bob Lederer. *Gay Community News,* December 7–13, 1986:1.

21. March on Washington Planning Conference. The ONE Institute. Box: March on Washington 1987 (#103–151), Folder: National Conference; March on Washington; New York City; Nov. 14–16, 1986.

22. March on Washington 1987, by Peg Byron. *Washington Blade,* November 21, 1986:1, 7.

23. See (Habermas 1989:244) for political public sphere arguments.

24. See (Jehn 1995) for more on how openness norms affect group performance.

25. Call Issues for March on Washington in '87. Organizing conference in NYC this November. Press release dated 8/22/86. Courtesy of the ONE Institute. Box: March on Washington 1987 (#103–151), Folder: National March on Washington 1985–1987, Book 1.

26. Visually, lesbian and gay marches on Washington look very much like the annual Gay Pride Parades. Because of this resemblance and to prevent confusion, organizers wanted to be explicit about the political focus of the event (unlike Pride, which explicitly self-defines as a *non*-political event. See Armstrong 2002).

27. All information on date and physical structure from: "Proceedings of the Organizing Conference for the March on Washington for Lesbian and Gay Rights, November 15, 1986." Box: March on Washington 1987 (#103–151). Folder: National Conference; March on Washington; New York City; November 14–16, 1986. The ONE Institute.

28. Unless otherwise noted, all information on the organizing structure compiled from: "Organizing Kit." Folder: National March on Washington, October 11, 1987, Book 2. Box: March on Washington 1987 (Temporary Collection Number: 103–151). The ONE Institute.

29. March on Washington 1987, *Washington Blade,* November 21, 1986:1, 7.

30. Pulling Through in a Big Way, by Steve Greenberg. *Washington Blade,* October 11, 1987:7.

31. Plans for Nat'l March Begin amidst NY-DC Turf Battle, *Washington Blade,* November 21, 1986:7. The Gay Rights National Lobby was defunct by the 1987 march and so played no role in its organizing.

32. Plans for Nat'l March Begin amidst NY-DC Turf Battle, *Washington Blade,* November 21, 1986:1.

33. For synergy, see (Morris 1984; Morris 1993; McAdam [1982] 1999). For variable see (Andrews 2002:111–12).

34. March on Washington, by Dave Walter. *Advocate,* August 18, 1987:11.

35. For more on this idea of "identity fields," see (Hunt, Benford et al. 1994).

36. Pulling Through in a Big Way, by Steve Greenberg. *Washington Blade,* October 11, 1987:7.

37. Plans for Nat'l March Begin amidst NY-DC Turf Battle, *Washington Blade,* November 21, 1986:1.

38. Bitter Debate Opens Nat'l March Planning, *Gay Community News,* December 7–13, 1986:1, 3.

39. Ibid. See also: Building a Successful March on Washington. A Working

Paper for the New York March on Washington Conference, by Lavender Left. Primary source materials from the ephemera files of Gerber/Hart.

40. The March: Room for Local, "Non-Gay" Issues? by Bob Lederer. *Gay Community News,* January 4–10, 1987:3.

41. (Cohen 2000:399, 402).

42. National March on Washington for Lesbian and Gay Rights, October 11, 1987:34 (official program). Primary source material, Gerber/Hart Library.

43. Notes from the People of Color Caucus at the National Conference for the March on Washington November 14–16, 1986. Signed by Jaime Credle. Folder: "1987 L & G March/Jan. L.A. Meeting." Box: "1987 March on Washington National Committee Record, Box 1." GLBT Historical Society of Northern California.

44. Ibid.

45. The March: Room for Local, "Non-Gay" Issues? by Bob Lederer. *Gay Community News,* January 4–10, 1987:3.

46. March on Washington Committee Censures So. Cal. Organizers, Charges Racism, by Mark Vandervelden. *Advocate,* September 15, 1987:16.

47. For more on this, see (Gitlin 1980; Breines 1989; Diggins 1992; Polletta 2002).

48. List of March Demands Is a Lampoon of Itself, by Rick Rosendall. *Washington Blade,* October 9, 1987:B-15.

49. March on Washington, by Dave Walter. *Advocate,* August 18, 1987:11.

50. (Dougan and Lipsman 1984:177).

51. A Call to Bisexuals, by Lucy Friedland and Liz Nania. *Washington Blade,* September 25, 1987:B-13.

52. (Armstrong 2002:145).

53. (Gamson 1997:180).

54. See also (Hutchins 1996).

55. Information on the West Hollywood Conference from the March on Washington for Lesbian & Gay Rights Steering Committee Meeting [Minutes] January 17 & 18, 1987 City of West Hollywood. Folder: 1987 L & G March/Jan. L.A. Meeting. Box: 1987 March on Washington National Committee Record, Box 1. GLBT Historical Society of Northern California, San Francisco, Calif.

56. Thousands Expected at Historic D.C. Gay March, by Johanna Stoyva. *Windy City Times,* March 5, 1987:1.

57. Notes from the People of Color Caucus at the National Conference for the March on Washington November 14–16, 1986. Folder: 1987 L & G March/Jan. L.A. Meeting. Box: 1987 March on Washington National Committee—Record. Box 1. GLBT Historical Society of Northern California, San Francisco, Calif.

58. Ibid.

59. Unless otherwise noted, information on the Atlanta Conference from the conference meeting minutes. March on Washington for Lesbian & Gay

Rights, National Steering Committee Meeting, May 2 & 3, 1987, Atlanta, Minutes. Folder: Atlanta Meeting May 2–3, 1987. Box 2. GLBT Historical Society of Northern California.

60. March Coordinator Hired, by Robert Blizard. *Washington Blade,* March 27, 1987:9.

61. We're Off and Running for the Big March, by Chris Bull. *Gay Community News,* May 24–31, 1987:3.

62. This Is Our Stage: The March on Washington, by Stephanie Poggi. *Gay Community News,* August 2–8, 1987:3.

63. Jesse Jackson Will Address National March Rally, by Lou Chibbaro Jr. *Washington Blade,* September 25, 1987:1, 13.

64. (Gamson 1994).

65. For more on theories of cultural reception, see (Jauss 1982:20–45; Radway 1984; Griswold 1987:10; Griswold 1987; Shively 1992; Beisel 1993).

66. Letter addressed to the Reverend Jesse Jackson, dated June 5, 1986, and signed by Steven Ault. Folder: Rev. Jesse Jackson. Box: 103–258. Box 3. ONE Institute and Archives.

67. In 1984, Jesse Jackson founded the National Rainbow Coalition, "a national social justice organization . . . devoted to political empowerment, education, and changing public policy." According to Jackson, "The American Dream is one big tent of many cultures, races and religions. Under that tent, everybody is assured equal protection under the law, equal opportunity, equal access and a fair share. Our struggle demands that we open closed doors, extend the tent and even the playing field." According to the mission statement of the organization, "We're working to move the nation and the world toward social, racial, and economic justice. From our national headquarters in Chicago and a bureau in Washington, D.C., we're uniting people of diverse ethnic, religious, economic, and political backgrounds to make America's promise of 'liberty and justice for all' a reality." Jackson's organization did not include lesbians and gay men. (See the organization's Web sites: http://www.rainbowpush.org/founder/ and http://www.rainbowpush.org/about/index.html, accessed March 4, 2005.)

68. We're Off and Running for the Big March. *Gay Community News,* May 24–31, 1987:3.

69. This Is Our Stage: The March on Washington. *Gay Community News,* August 2–8, 1987:3.

70. DC Goes Gay! by Chris Bull. *Gay Community News,* October 18–24, 1987:3.

71. Ibid.:6.

72. Unless otherwise noted, information on sponsorship derived from: National March on Washington for Lesbian and Gay Rights, October 11, 1987 [official program]. Gerber/Hart Library:39–42.

73. March on Washington for Lesbian & Gay Rights, National Steering Com-

mittee Meeting, May 2 & 3, 1987, Atlanta, Minutes. Folder: Atlanta Meeting May 2–3, 1987. Box 2. GLBT Historical Society.

74. "A Day for the Country" Provides "A Time to Shine." *Bay Area Reporter,* August 27, 1987:37.

75. The March on Washington, by Peter Freiberg. *Advocate,* November 10, 1987:19.

76. From Gold Trim to Simple Sheets, "AIDS Quilt" Is Growing, by Lou Chibbaro Jr. *The Washington Blade,* September 4, 1987:3.

77. http://www.savethemall.org/moments/quilt.html (accessed March 6, 2005).

78. Unless otherwise noted, all information on the civil disobedience action comes from: Civil Disobedience: Are We Entering a New Militant Stage in the Struggle for Gay Rights? by Mark Vandervelden. *Advocate,* September 29, 1987:45–69.

79. October March to Include Mass Weddings, Arrests, by Lou Chibbaro Jr. *The Washington Blade,* March 13, 1987:4.

80.Over 50 Lesbian and Gay Activists Meet to Plan March on Washington Non-violent Civil Disobedience Action. Press release, dated July 10, 1987. Folder: Miscellaneous. Box: 1987 March on Washington National Committee–Record. Box 1. GLBT Historical Society of Northern California.

81. Civil Disobedience at the Supreme Court, by Rick Harding. *Advocate,* November 10, 1987:26.

82. March on Washington, by Dave Walter. *Advocate,* August 18, 1987:12, 20.

83. Philadelphia MOW Committee Letter. Dated April 10, 1987, and signed by Walter L. Wheeler. Folder: Atlanta Meeting May 2–3, 1987. Box 2. GLBT Historical Society of Northern California, San Francisco, Calif.

84. Thousands Expected at Historic D.C. Gay March, by Johanna Stoyva. *Windy City Times,* March 5, 1987:1.

85. Letter addressed to the National March on Washington Steering Committee, dated January 15, 1987, and signed by Walter L. Wheeler. Folder: National March on Washington 1985–1987. Book One. Box: March on Washington 1987 (#103–151). ONE Institute and Archives, Los Angles, Calif.

86. The March on Washington, by Peter Freiberg. *Advocate,* November 10, 1987:28.

87. Letter written to the March on Washington National Steering Committee on the letterhead of the United Methodist Church of West Hollywood, and signed by Miriam Stump, Chair of the Religious Committee. Folder: National March on Washington 1985–1987. Book 1. Box: March on Washington 1987 (#103–151). ONE Institute.

88. We're Off and Running for the Big March, by Chris Bull. *Gay Community News,* May 24–31, 1987:3.

89. This Is Our Stage: The March on Washington, by Stephanie Poggi. *Gay Community News,* August 2–8, 1987:11.

90. On Lesbian and Gay Weddings and the Urge to Smash Blenders, by Positively Revolting Affinity Group. *Gay Community News,* September 20–26, 1987:5.

91. (McAdam 1982:164–5; McAdam 1983).

92. On Lesbian and Gay Weddings and the Urge to Smash Blenders, by Positively Revolting Affinity Group. *Gay Community News,* September 20–26, 1987:5.

93. The March on Washington, by Peter Freiberg. *Advocate,* November 10, 1987:28.

94. A Gay Affair: The Wedding Comes Off, amid Criticism, but to the Delight of Thousands, by Michael C. Botkin. *Gay Community News,* October 18–24, 1987:16.

95. (D'Emilio 2005:34).

96. See a flier titled "National Coming Out Day." Box: March on Washington 1987 (#103–151). The ONE Institute and Archives.

97. Personal interview, January 5, 2004.

98. This insight from the march confirms a forgotten sociological insight. See (Firey 1948:22).

99. In a recent study of the movement, sociologist Elizabeth Armstrong (2002) notes that "Harvey Milk called for a gay march on Washington in 1979. The idea of a gay march on Washington had been circulating through political circles *since the spring of 1978.*" (p. 130, emphasis added). Armstrong makes no note of the 1973 meeting.

100. For Love and For Life, We're Not Going Back. *Advocate* Editorial, August 18, 1987:19.

101. The March: What Will We Get for the Investment? by Larry J. Uhrig. *The Washington Blade,* October 9, 1987:B-15, B-17.

102. Ibid.

103. For more on identity work, see (Snow and Anderson 1987; Snow and McAdam 2000).

Chapter Six

1. D'Emilio quote from the back cover of (D'Emilio 2002).

2. Washington—by Way of Stonewall. *New York Times,* April 27, 1993:A20.

3. See CLAGS Web site: http://web.gc.cuny.edu/clags/history.htm (accessed May 25, 2005).

4. (Walters 2001:76).

5. I borrow the terms *identity-building* and *identity-blurring* from (Gamson 1995).

6. For more on religion and broadcasting, see (Capsuto 2000:1). Russo quote from (Capsuto 2000:9).

7. For more on the idea of *Geist,* see (Hegel 1807).

8. Illinois State Senator quote from (Gross 2001:117n7). For more on ignoring the 1979 march, see (Gross 2001:50). For more on the *Times* and signaling the start of a new era, see (Gross 2001:119).

9. For more on gay visibility in the mainstream media, see (Russo 1987; Ringer 1994; Capsuto 2000; Gross 2001; Walters 2001). For more on the rise of the gay press, see (Streitmatter 1995).

10. Gay was in from (Gross 2001:239). Loughery quote from (Loughery 1998:441). For more on imagined communities, see (Anderson 1983).

11. (Gross 2001:123).

12. John D'Emilio quote from (D'Emilio 2002:87). See also (Marcus 2002:245–246).

13. Frank quote from: Barney Frank's Story. *Newsweek* September 25, 1989. For more on Studds, see (Scagliotti, Baus et al. 1999). Rosen quote from same source. For more on openly gay elected officials by 1992, see A Record of Gay— and Pain. *Newsweek,* September 14, 1992:39.

14. The March's Legacy: Mainstreaming the Movement, by David Olson. *Windy City Times* May 6, 1993:4.

15. Our Time Has Come, by David Olson. *Windy City Times.* April 29, 1993:21.

16. D.C. March: "Historic" Coalition Forged, by David Olson. *Windy City Times.* March 4, 1993:1.

17. Marching Is Not Enough. *Windy City Times* editorial. May 6, 1993:13.

18. The March's Legacy: Mainstreaming the Movement, by David Olson. *Windy City Times* May 6, 1993:4.

19. Savior quote from (Kaiser 1997:331). Gay moment quote from (D'Emilio 2000:478).

20. Outsider status quote from (D'Emilio 2002:139). Clinton quote from (Rimmerman 2000:43).

21. (Rimmerman 2000:43–4).

22. For more on the Clinton election victory, see (Kaiser 1997:333; Marcus 2002). Vaid quote from (Kaiser 1997:334). Cautiously optimistic quote from (Marcus 2002:345).

23. For more on gay rights as a major dividing line, see (Kaiser 1997:331). Political pit bull and the poor homosexuals quotes from (Kaiser 1997:332). Buchanan's culture war quote from (Kaiser 1997:332).

24. Culture war as a household expression quote from (DiMaggio 2003:81). For more on the concept of culture war and surrounding debates, see (Hunter 1991; Gitlin 1995; DiMaggio, Evans et al. 1996; DiMaggio 2003). Additional Bu-

chanan and Family Rights quotes from (McGarry and Wasserman 1998:246). Virginia Beach quote from: Gays Under Fire. *Newsweek,* September 14, 1992:36–37.

25. (Kaiser 1997:332–333).

26. Gays Under Fire. *Newsweek,* September 14, 1992:36.

27. Homosexuality and Politics: A Newsweek Poll. *Newsweek,* September 25, 1989:19.

28. Data from the New York Times/CBS poll from (Kaiser 1997:333). Sociological study results from (Loftus 2001).

29. For more on this point, see (Loughery 1998:439).

30. See the Kaiser Family Foundation's Timeline of Key Milestones: http://www.kff.org/hivaids/aidstimeline/timeline.cfm?showyear = all (accessed December 14, 2002).

31. See the NIA Plan of the African American AIDS Policy and Training Institute's Chronology of Selected Events. http://www.blackaids.org/niaplan/niaexec_chronology.htm (accessed June 21, 2005).

32. Information on the AIDS timelines taken from the Kaiser Family Foundation: http://www.kff.org/hivaids/aidstimeline/timeline.cfm?showyear = all (accessed December 14, 2002).

33. AIDS field quote from (Armstrong 2002:156). Gay people of color organizations quote from (D'Emilio 1992:262). For more on their leadership in AIDS service organizations, see (McGarry and Wasserman 1998). For more on the institutionalization of the fight against AIDS, see (Marcus 2002:246).

34. For a review of the military debate, see (Berube 1990; Shilts 1993; Schlager 1998; Gross and Woods 1999:163–164; McFeeley 2000). *Newsweek* (1947) story from: Homosexuals in Uniform. *Newsweek,* June 9, 1947:54. *Time* (1975) story from: *Time,* September 8, 1975.

35. (Kaiser 1997:335).

36. Schindler diary quote from A Grisly Murder Mystery. *Newsweek,* February 1, 1993, p. 57. For more on Clinton opposition, see (Schlager 1998). For more on Aspin, see (Marcus 2002:358). Mixner quote from (Scagliotti, Baus et al. 1999).

37. See http://www.glbtq.com/social-sciences/dont_ask.html (accessed May 25, 2005).

38. See the Servicemembers Legal Defense Network: http://www.sldn.org (accessed June 1, 2005).

39. See the Servicemembers Legal Defense Network: www.sldn.org. I intend this discussion of Don't Ask, Don't Tell not as an argument that the policy has been more detrimental than the previous one, per se, but instead to frame the military debate in general as central for 1993 march organizing.

40. (Marcus 2002:360).

41. "Abnormal" quote from Gays Under Fire. *Newsweek,* September 14, 1992:36. For more on the details of Oregon, see (Schlager 1998:23).

42. Trial description quotes from (Keen and Goldberg 2000:ix). For more on *Romer* as described in this section, see (McGarry and Wasserman 1998:246). See also chapter 7.

43. See (Schlager 1998).

44. (Keen and Goldberg 2000:133).

45. The equal rights versus special rights debate presents a fascinating perspectives on sexuality and the law. For an excellent consideration of this topic, see (Keen and Goldberg 2000, especially chapter 6).

46. Born or Bred? *Newsweek,* February 24, 1992:46, 48.

47. Hardly monolithic quote from (Diaz 1999:215). Curable quote from (Keen and Goldberg 2000:44). D'Emilio quote from (D'Emilio 2002:163).

48. (D'Emilio 2002:159).

49. For more on queer politics and queer theory, see (Foucault 1978; Butler 1990; Sedgwick 1990; Warner 1993; Epstein 1994; Cohen 1996; Seidman 1996; Seidman 1997; Kirsch 2000; Turner 2000; Blasius 2001; Gamson and Moon 2004). Tenets of queer theory from (Stein and Plummer 1994:181–182). Quotes on cultural politics from (Blasius 1994:129; Epstein 1999).

50. (Gamson 1995:395, 402).

51. (Seidman 1993:133).

52. For more on Queer Nation, see (Berube and Escoffier 1991; Duggan 1992; Berlant and Freeman 1993; Browning 1993; Patton 1993; Browning 1996). Armstrong quote from (Armstrong 2002:182). Identity quote from (Berube and Escoffier 1991:14).

53. (Armstrong 2002:110 [emphasis in original]).

54. This is not to say that the meanings of *queer,* as a keyword, were entirely supplanted or subsumed under the phrase *gay and lesbian.* For a discussion on the operations of keywords, see Ghaziani and Ventresca (2005). For more on border skirmishes, see (Stein 1992; Taylor and Whittier 1992; Gamson 1995; Gamson 1997). For more on the domestication of the queer challenge, see (Armstrong 2002:176, 183).

55. For more on this, see (Epstein 1999).

56. For more on binary and biphobic discourse, see (Queen 1999). For more on spaces to be open, see (Hutchins and Kaahumanu 1991; Hutchins 1996).

57. (Hutchins 1996:247).

58. (Wilson 1999:108).

59. Some Groups Feel Left Out of Gay Rally. *Chicago Tribune,* April 25, 1993.

60. Ka'ahumanu quote from (Hutchins 1996:249 [emphasis in original]).

61. (Brown 1998:4).

62. For more on transactivists being met with confusion and resistance, see (Frye 2000; Namaste 2000). Source for information on *transgender* as a term from http://usilgbt.org/index.php?categoryid=35. For more on transgression, see (Dahir May 25, 1999).

63. For more on the politics of drag, see (Rupp and Taylor 2003).

64. For more on *gender queer*, see (Nestle, Howell et al. 2002).

65. Wilchins quote from (Dahir May 25, 1999). Frye workshop title from (Frye 2000:452). For more on gay, bi-, and transphobia, see (Califia 2003).

66. For more on Stonewall, see (Duberman 1993; Feinberg 1996; Carter 2004; Armstrong 2006).

67. (Dahir May 25, 1999).

68. (Dahir May 25, 1999).

69. A Record of Gain—and Pain. *Newsweek,* September 14, 1992:39.

70. Common ground agenda and diversity as source of strength quotes from (McGarry and Wasserman 1998:251). Vaid quote from (McGarry and Wasserman 1998:251).

Chapter Seven

1. Why Another March? October 1992. Folder: March on Washington (1993). Box: Ephemera Collection, Recurring Events, Parades & Marches on Washington. GLBT Historical Society.

2. Unless otherwise noted, all information about the invitation from: Letter from Urvashi Vaid, NGLTF, to Grassroots Activists and National Organization Representatives dated January 24, 1991, and Re: Next March on Washington for Lesbian and Gay Rights. Folder: March on Washington 1993 III. The ONE Institute.

3. Creating Change is the annual conference of the National Gay and Lesbian Task Force. Its Web site says, "Creating Change is for you if you are: (i) An activist and organizer in your community, campus, or workplace; (ii) A board member, staff member, or leader in a LGBT organization, community center, or foundation; (iii) An elected or appointed official; (iv) An advocate for our communities; (v) A change agent for justice, freedom, & equality for all." See http://www.thetaskforce.org/ourprojects/cc/index.cfm (accessed July 2, 2005).

4. Another March? by Lou Chibbaro Jr. *The Washington Blade,* March 15, 1991:1.

5. 1993 Lesbian & Gay National March on Washington: Update Newsletter. Folder: March on Washington 1993 III. The ONE Institute.

6. Unless otherwise noted, all information from the Initiating Meeting compiled from: Report on March 9, 1991 Meeting Concerns: A March on Washington. Folder: March on Washington 1993 III. The ONE Institute.

7. March 9, 1991 Agenda. Folder: March on Washington 1993 III. The ONE Institute and Archives.

8. Another March?:17.

9. Another March?:17. See also Report on March 9, 1991 Meeting Concerns: A March on Washington.

10. Press Release: Planning Meeting Called for National March on Washington for Lesbian and Gay Rights. Dated April 5, 1991. Folder: March on Washington 1993 III. The ONE Institute and Archives.

11. Media Release: Gays and Lesbians Organize National March on Washington for April, 1993. Dated June 17, 1991. Folder: March on Washington 1993 III. The ONE Institute and Archives.

12. March on Washington for Lesbian and Gay Rights, National Planning Meeting, May 11–12, 1991, Washington, D.C. Folder: March on Washington 1993 III. The ONE Institute and Archives.

13. National Lesbian and Gay March Set for '93, by Cliff O'Neill. *Windy City Times,* May 23, 1991:6.

14. For more on habitual routines, see (Gersick and Hackman 1990; Hermanowicz and Morgan 1999).

15. National Lesbian and Gay March Set for '93:6.

16. Next March on D.C. Planned for April 1993, by Lou Chibbaro Jr. *The Washington Blade,* May 17, 1991:1.

17. National Lesbian and Gay March Set for '93:6.

18. 1993 Lesbian & Gay National March on Washington: Update Newsletter. Folder: March on Washington 1993 III. The ONE Institute.

19. National Organizers to Meet in LA this January to "Hammer Out the Officials" for the 1993 March on Washington. Undated News Release. Folder: March on Washington 1993 III. The ONE Institute and Archives.

20. National Lesbian and Gay March Set for '93:6.

21. Next March on D.C. Planned for April 1993:9.

22. National Lesbian and Gay March Set for '93:6.

23. Lesbian and Gay March on Washington Misscheduled, letter to the editor by Michael Marholz. *Windy City Times,* December 12, 1991:12.

24. National Lesbian and Gay March Set for '93:6.

25. Cultural sociologists are sometimes accused of merely describing or deconstructing some text (like a newspaper article) or some practice (like an organizational decision) but not demonstrating the mechanism through which culture structures action (Archer 1996). The cultural template is one corrective example of how to address this charge.

26. For more on periods of political quiescence, see (Taylor 1989; Staggenborg 1995; Polletta 2002:9).

27. For originating spark, see (Lang and Lang 1961:495); for triggering event, see (Fine 1979:742); for precipitating factor, see (Smelser 1963:16–17).

28. Extra!!! Extra!!! Extra!!! Gay/Lesbian March on Washington '93 Update. Memo from the National Leather Association dated September 13, 1991. Folder: March on Washington 1993 III. The ONE Institute. See also Organizing Structure and By-laws. Personal Papers of Billy Hileman. See also March on Washington Planning Meeting Set. *Windy City Times,* July 18, 1991:9. See also Chicago Hosts Meeting for 1993 March on D.C. *Windy City Times,* August 1, 1991:15. Additional evidence in this section comes from a personal interview with Billy Hileman, July 7, 2005.

29. Unless otherwise noted, information on the organizing structure from: Operational Proposal for the 1993 National March on Washington for Lesbian and Gay Rights. Proposal accepted at the Chicago 3–4, 1991, meeting. Including amendments and subsequent ICC changes (in header). Personal papers of Billy Hileman.

30. Building a Successful March on Washington. A Working Paper for the New York March on Washington Conference, submitted by Lavender Left. Primary source materials (for the 1987 march on Washington) from an ephemera file of the Gerber/Hart Library.

31. Half the Organizers of 1993 March on D.C. to Be People of Color, by Lou Chibbaro Jr. *Washington Blade,* August 9, 1991:1, 6.

32. Date Set for '93 March on D.C., by David O'Connor. *Windy City Times,* August 22, 1991:7.

33. Date Set for '93 March on D.C.

34. Half the Organizers of 1993 March on D.C. to Be People of Color:6.

35. Personal letter from Billy Hileman, dated July 8, 2005 (emphasis in original).

36. Ibid.

37. Date Set for '93 March on D.C.

38. National Lesbian and Gay March Structure Undemocratic, by Jeff Richards. *Windy City Times,* December 12, 1991:12.

39. 1993 March: Goals into Quotas, by Rick Rosendall. *Washington Blade,* September 6, 1991:30.

40. For an excellent review of affirmative action debates, see (Skrentny 1996).

41. Unless otherwise noted, information on Los Angeles from: 1993 March on Washington National Steering Committee Meeting, Los Angeles, Calif., January 18–19, 1992, Meeting Summary. Personal Papers of Billy Hileman.

42. First March on Washington Meeting Proves Contentious, by Bruce Mirken. *Windy City Times,* January 30, 1992:4.

43. For more on the concept of cultural scripts, see (Sahlins 1981; Sahlins 1985).

44. For more on the concept of path dependence, see (see Levitt and March 1988).

45. First March on Washington Meeting Proves Contentious. For more on the carnival spirit, see (Bakhtin 1984:49). For more on the social functions of laughter, see (Irving and Young 2002).

46. First March on Washington Meeting Proves Contentious:4.

47. First March on Washington Meeting Proves Contentious:4.

48. National March Adds the Word 'Bi' to Official Title. *Washington Blade,* January 31, 1992.

49. Major Mistake, by Dave Reyman. *Washington Blade,* February 14, 1992:31.

50. Fed Up, by B. G. Johnson. *Washington Blade,* February 21, 1992:31.

51. Expand Definition, by Loraine Hutchins. *Washington Blade,* February 28, 1992:31.

52. Same Struggle, by Debra R. Kolodny. *Washington Blade,* February 28, 1992:31.

53. Transgender people were still fighting an uphill battle. Although delegates were more educated about transgenderism (compared to 1979), knowledge harmed advocacy efforts due to recognized distinctions between sexual and gender identities. I explore this issue more in my discussion of the platform.

54. Variety of Meetings, Events Shows Community's Diversity, by David Olson. *Windy City Times,* April 29, 1993:4.

55. A Disaster in the Making (unauthored editorial). *Windy City Times.* December 10, 1992:13.

56. National Steering Committee Meeting, Dallas, Tex., Meeting Notes. Personal papers of Billy Hileman.

57. Letter from Urvashi Vaid to Alan Rueckgauer and the MOW Committee, July 22, 1991. Personal papers of Billy Hileman.

58. The 1993 March on Washington for Lesbian, Gay, and Bi Equal Rights and Liberation, Update. Letter dated March 7, 1992, signed by Billy Hileman. Personal papers of Billy Hileman.

59. Dallas meeting notes:7.

60. New March Platform Garners Criticism, by Lou Chibbaro Jr. *Washington Blade,* May 22, 1992:1, 25.

61. D.C. March Committee Says It Can't Endorse Dallas Platform, by Lou Chibbaro Jr. *Washington Blade,* May 29, 1992:11. See also D.C. March Committee Urges Platform Rescission, *Windy City Times,* June 18, 1992:10.

62. Political Correctness Endangers March on Washington, by Franklin E. Kameny. *Windy City Times,* December 3, 1992:19.

63. A Clear Majority, by Jarmila Dokladalova. *Washington Blade,* May 29, 1992:33.

64. Ibid.

65. What Are We Marching For? by Paul Varnell. *Windy City Times,* June 4, 1992:14.

66. 1993 March on Washington Finalizes Agenda, Executive Committee Meets to Complete Platform Planks and Items. Press release dated June 9, 1992. Folder: March on Washington–April 1993 IV, the ONE Institute and Archives.

67. March Leaders Modify Controversial Platform, by Lou Chibbaro Jr. *Windy City Times,* June 25, 1992:8.

68. June 9, 1992, press release.

69. Going with the Community's Flow, by Joseph Schuman. *Windy City Times,* February 4, 1993:12 (emphasis in original).

70. March Leaders Modify Controversial Platform.

71. A Disaster in the Making (unauthored editorial). *Windy City Times,* December 10, 1992:13.

72. Setting the Record Straight, by Scott Barea. *Windy City Times,* October 8, 1992:13.

73. Political Correctness Endangers March on Washington.

74. A Disaster in the Making (unauthored editorial). *Windy City Times,* December 10, 1992:13.

75. . . . But Don't Risk the Movement (unauthored editorial). *Windy City Times,* March 25, 1993:13.

76. Information on the third NSC meeting in Denver from: 3rd National Steering Committee Meeting, October 3–4, 1992, Denver, Colorado meeting minutes. Personal Papers of Billy Hileman.

77. Gays to March on Washington in 2000. *New York Blade,* February 6, 1998. Personal papers of Ann DeGroot.

78. Information on the fourth NSC meeting in D.C. from: "4th National Steering Committee, Dupont Plaza Hotel, Washington, D.C." meeting minutes. Notes taken by Mandy Carter, February 6, 1993. Personal Papers of Billy Hileman, Pittsburgh, Penn. D.C. delegates made other decisions in addition to including transgender persons in the platform. Most notably, delegates decided on the line-up of the march, placing Colorado as the first state. Here again we see the impact of the sociopolitical context on internal movement functions, as the movement had boycotted Colorado (see chapter 7).

79. Transgendered People at the March on Washington. The March on Washington for Lesbian, Gay, and Bi Equal Rights and Liberation Newsletter:13. GLBT Historical Society of Northern California, San Francisco, Calif.

80. The logic Princess was using to urge inclusion was the same that others used as grounds for exclusion. This was a march on Washington for *gay* rights, for sexual orientation. Transgenderism is about *gender identity*, not sexual identity, and so transactivists should consider organizing their own march.

81. A Disaster in the Making (unauthored editorial). *Windy City Times,* December 10, 1992:13.

82. . . . But Don't Risk the Movement (unauthored editorial). *Windy City Times,* March 25, 1993:13.

83. Activists Debate Transgender Issues, by David Olson. *Windy City Times,* February 4, 1993:4.

84. Transgendered People at the March on Washington. The March on Washington for Lesbian, Gay, and Bi Equal Rights and Liberation Newsletter:13. GLBT Historical Society of Northern California, San Francisco, Calif.

85. Community Unites around D.C. March, by David Olson. *Windy City Times,* February 4, 1993:4.

86. Going with the Community's Flow, by Joseph Schuman. *Windy City Times,* February 4, 1993:12 (emphasis in original).

87. D.C. March: "Historic" Coalition Forged, by David Olson. *Windy City Times,* March 4, 1993:1.

88. Support the March . . . (unauthored editorial). *Windy City Times,* March 25, 1993:13.

89. The March's Legacy: Mainstreaming the Movement, by David Olson. *Windy City Times,* May 6, 1993:4.

90. Our Time Has Come, by David Olson. *Windy City Times,* April 29, 1993:21.

91. The March's Legacy: Mainstreaming the Movement.

92. Our Time Has Come:21.

93. Ibid.

94. Personal Interview with Derek Charles Livingston, December 6, 2003.

95. Destruction from Within (unauthored editorial). *Windy City Times,* September 16, 1993:13.

96. The March: Now, More Than Ever, by Derek Charles Livingston. *Windy City Times,* January 7, 1993:12.

97. Going with the Community's Flow, by Joseph Schuman. *Windy City Times,* February 4, 1993:12.

98. The 1993 March: Harvey Milk Would Have Loved It! by Richard L. Andrews, M.D. *Windy City Times,* April 22, 1993:12.

99. 'Our Time Has Come.

100. The March's Legacy: Mainstreaming the Movement.

101. Lessons from the March, by Barbara A. Warner. *Windy City Times,* May 27, 1993:12.

Chapter Eight

1. Past, Present, Future, by Judy Wieder. *Advocate,* April 30, 2000:9.

2. Marching On, by Lisa Neff. *Advocate,* June 22, 1999:40.

3. Gays, Lesbians, and the Media: The Slow Road to Acceptance.

4. See Back in the Day: Coming Out with Ellen by Malindo Lo, April 2005. http://www.afterellen.com/column/2005/4/backintheday.html (accessed December 23, 2005).

5. Gays, Lesbians, and the Media: The Slow Road to Acceptance, by Barbara Raab. *USA Today,* July 1996.

6. America Sees Shades of Gay: A Once-Invisible Group Finds the Spotlight, by Jess Cagle. *Entertainment Weekly,* September 8, 1995:22.

7. Gays, Lesbians, and the Media: The Slow Road to Acceptance.

8. *Entertainment Weekly,* October 6, 2000.

9. Ibid.:27–28.

10. For an excellent treatment of blackface, see (Lott 1995).

11. Reference to Amanda Bearse, see http://www.afterellen.com/People/amandabearse.html (accessed December 22, 2005); to Melissa Etheridge, see http://www.afterellen.com/column/2005/2/backintheday.html (accessed December 23, 2005); see also America Sees Shades of Gay:28; for Elton John, see http://www.nndb.com/people/528/000022462/ (accessed December 22, 2005); for George Michael, see http://www.glbtq.com/arts/michael_g.html (accessed December 28, 2005); for Lea DeLaria, see http://www.glbtq.com/arts/delaria_l.html (accessed December 22, 2005); and for RuPaul, see http://www.glbtq.com/arts/rupaul.html (accessed December 23, 2005).

12. Worthy to headline quote from (Walters 2001:81). Fictional TV character quote from (Capsuto 2000:378). Klein quote from (Gross 2001:157–58).

13. *Ellen* phenomenon quote from (Walter 2001:82). Defining moment quote from (Walters 2001:95). *Ellen* controversy quote from (Capsuto 2000:379, 388). Lo quote from http://www.afterellen.com/column/2005/2/backintheday.html (accessed December 23, 2005).

14. (Gross 2001:179).

15. All quotes in this section from (Walters 2001:13, 108).

16. America Sees Shades of Gay:27, 29, 31.

17. (Gross 2001:14).

18. America Sees Shades of Gay:20, 22, 24.

19. (Chasin 2000:34).

20. (Chasin 2000:xv, xvii).

21. Gay Today: How the Battle for Acceptance has Moved to Schools, Churches, Marriage, and the Workplace. *Newsweek,* March 20, 2000.

22. Capital Gains and Losses: A State by State Review of Gay, Lesbian, Bisexual, Transgender, and HIV/AIDS-Related Legislation, 1996. National Gay and Lesbian Task Force.

23. (D'Emilio 2002:88).

24. No ENDA in Sight—Employment Non-discrimination Act of 1996. *Advocate,* May 13, 1997.

25. (Schlager 1998:89–90).

26. See http://www.civilrights.org/issues/enda/care.html and http://www.afge.org/Documents/2004_IP_14_ENDA.pdf (accessed January 17, 2006).

27. See http://www.religioustolerance.org/hom_empl2.htm (accessed January 17, 2006).

28. See Nationwide Support for ENDA, Human Rights Campaign Web site (www.hrc.org).

29. See http://www.religioustolerance.org/hom_empl4.htm (accessed January 17, 2006).

30. Ibid.

31. See the Human Rights Campaign: www.hrc.org.

32. Ten Years of "Don't Ask, Don't Tell": A Disservice to the Nation. Publication of the Servicemembers Legal Defense Network:23.

33. Ten Years of "Don't Ask, Don't Tell": A Disservice to the Nation:16.

34. See Historical Timeline of Don't Ask, Don't Tell, Don't Pursue, Don't Harass from the Servicemembers Legal Defense Network: www.sldn.org.

35. (Marcus 2002:359).

36. (Schlager 1998:261).

37. Joe Zuniga was another prominent figure who challenged DA, DT. Celebrated as the Sixth U.S. Army Soldier of the Year in 1992 and Persian Gulf War veteran, Zuniga publicly came out on the main rally stage of the 1993 march, only to be discharged one month later. Instead of appealing his case like Cammermeyer, Zuniga wrote an autobiography, *Soldier of the Year: The Story of a Gay American Patriot* (1994), in which he seethed against DA, DT as a "sellout to homophobes and bigots."

38. Shattering disappointment quote from (Rimmerman 1996:119). Bawer quote from (Bawer 1993:117). Clinton comment from (Marcus 2002:360).

39. (Schlager 1998:269–70).

40. See http://auschwitz.dk/Allen.htm (accessed January 6, 2005). See also *Unsafe Haven, The New Republic* June 21, 1993.

41. (Rimmerman 1996:120).

42. (Keen and Goldberg 2000:ix, 3).

43. Special rights quote from (Keen and Goldberg 2000:133). Halting religious right quote from (McGarry and Wasserman 1998:246). Kennedy quote from: *Roy Romer, Governor of Colorado v. Richard G. Evans,* 517 U.S. 620 (1996), No. 94–1039. May 20, 1996.

44. See also (Leonard 2000).

45. See (Sullivan 1997; Chauncey 2004; Hull 2006) for reviews of the same-sex marriage debate. Quote from (Sullivan 1997:4–6).

46. Ruling that roiled the land quote from (Sullivan 1997:104). Court decree from: *Baehr v. Lewin (Ninia Baehr, Genora Dancel, Tammy Rodrigues, Antionette Pregil, Pat Lagon, and Joseph Melillo, Plantiffs-Apellants, v. John C. Lewin, Director of the Department of Health, State of Hawaii, Defendant-Apellee),* Hawaii Supreme Court, 74 Haw. 645, 852 P.2d 44. Decided May 5, 1993.

47. (Chambers 2000:292–93).

48. Ibid.

49. (Sullivan 1997:204–9).

50. Capital Gains and Losses: A State by State Review of Gay, Lesbian, Bisexual, Transgender, and HIV/AIDS-Related Legislation, 1996:i.

51. Capital Gains and Losses: A State by State Review of Gay, Lesbian, Bisexual, Transgender, and HIV/AIDS-Related Legislation, 1997:1.

52. Capital Gains and Losses: A State by State Review of Gay, Lesbian, Bisexual, Transgender, and HIV/AIDS-Related Legislation, 1996:ii.

53. (Chambers 2000:296).

54. *Stan Baker et al. v. State of Vermont et al.,* Vermont Supreme Court, 98–032. Decided December 20, 1999.

55. Information in this section from (Chambers 2000:298–99).

56. Power of the word quote from (Chambers 2000:303); for more on the word *marriage,* see (Chauncey 2004:129); for more on keywords, see (Williams 1976) and (Ghaziani and Ventresca 2005). For more on the Toronto campaign, see http://www.samesexmarriage.ca/advocacy/psa.htm (accessed January 17, 2005).

57. Capital Gains and Losses: A State by State Review of Gay, Lesbian, Bisexual, Transgender, and HIV/AIDS-Related Legislation, 1997:1.

58. For more on gay families, see (Polikoff 2000).

59. (D'Emilio 2006:10 [emphasis in original]).

60. Holy War quote from The Holy War on Gays, by Robert Dreyfuss. *Rolling Stone* magazine, March 18, 1999:38–41. See also: www.pflagdetroit.org/Holy_War_onGays.htm (accessed May 20, 2005). Culture War quote from (Diamond 1995:1). 1992 fund-raiser quote from: The Ex-Gay Movement and the Christian Right: A Shared Agenda. A document by the Political Research Associates. See www.publiceye.org/equality/x-gay/X-Gay-05.html (accessed May 20, 2005).

61. See www.religioustolerance.org/hom_0078.htm and www.stopdrlaura.com/home.htm (both accessed January 19, 2006).

62. Ibid.

63. Dr. Laura, Be Quiet! by Katha Pollitt. *The Nation,* April 27, 2000 (posted/printed in the May 15, 2000, issue). See http://www.thenation.com/doc/20000515/pollitt (accessed January 19, 2006).

64. Dr. Laura, Talk Radio Celebrity: She Apologizes After Antagonizing the Gay Community. *Newsweek,* March 20, 2000:52.

65. See article by Surina Khan, http://www.publiceye.org/equality/x-gay/X-Gay-03.html (accessed January 20, 2006).

66. Taken from NARTH's Web site: www.narth.com (accessed January 20, 2006).

67. From the PFOX organizational Web site: www.pfox.org (accessed January 20, 2006).

68. The Ex-Gay Movement and the Christian Right: A Shared Agenda. See www.publiceye.org/equality/x-gay/X-Gay-05.html (accessed January 20, 2006).

69. For more on the anti-violence movement, see (Herek and Berrill 1992; Jenness 1995; Jenness 1999; Wertheimer 2000). For more on support and passage of the Hate Crimes Statistics Act, see (Wertheimer 2000:272).

70. See http://www.courttv.com/archive/trials/mckinney/100899_ctv.html and http://www.cnn.com/US/9904/05/gay.attack.trial.03/index.html (accessed January 25, 2006).

71. See http://www.courttv.com/archive/trials/mckinney/100899_ctv.html (accessed January 25, 2006).

72. See http://www.geocities.com/WestHollywood/Stonewall/2878/ (accessed January 25, 2006) for a collection of media reports on the beatings and the trial.

73. The New Gay Struggle, by Richard Lacayo. *Time,* October 26, 1998:33–36.

74. The Crucifixion of Matthew Shepard, by Melanie Thernstrom. *Vanity Fair,* March 1999. See http://www.geocities.com/WestHollywood/Stonewall/2878/vf1 .html (accessed January 25, 2006).

75. Capital Gains and Losses: A State by State Review of Gay, Lesbian, Bisexual, Transgender, and HIV/AIDS-Related Legislation:7.

76. The New Gay Struggle.

77. Suspect Pleads Guilty in Beating Death of Gay College Student. Reported by CNN, April 5, 1999.

78. See (Schlager 1998:177–81) and Kaiser Family Foundation's Global HIV/ AIDS Epidemic: A Timeline of Key Milestones: www.kff.org/hivaids/aidstime-line/timeline.cfm?showyear = all (accessed December 14, 2004).

79. The End of AIDS? *Newsweek,* December 2, 1996.

80. Source: Food and Drug Administration (FDA): www.fda.gov/oashi/aids/ virals.html (accessed June 16, 2003). One major challenge that emerged in light of protease inhibitors was a wave of gay men who had prematurely retired onto AIDS disability who, in the late 1990s amid unexpected health, were now confronted with the challenge of returning to work. For more on this, see (Ghaziani 2004).

81. Neutralized quote from (Armstrong 2002:178). Thin politics quote from (Seidman 1993:135). Domestication quote from (Armstrong 2002:183). For more on identity movements, see (Gamson 1995).

82. Neutralized quote from (Armstrong 2002:182). For more on the international bisexual movement, see (Hutchins 1996). For more on the *Bisexual Resource Guide,* see (Armstrong 2002).

83. For more on the politics of social erasure, see (Frye 2000; Namaste 2005:1). Categories of queers quote from (Frye 2000:453 [emphasis in original]). For more on NGLTF, see Transgender Equality: A Handbook for Activists and

Policymakers, by Paisley Currah and Shannon Minter. A publication of the Policy Institute of the National Gay and Lesbian Task Force:iv.

84. Transgender Equality: A Handbook for Activists and Policymakers:15.

85. D'Emilio quote from (Gamson 2000:20). Gamson quote from (Gamson 2000:20). For more on mobilizing structures, see (McCarthy and Zald 1977; Jenkins 1983; Morris 1984; Morris and Herring 1987).

86. For more on role played by organizations versus an organizational movement, see (Gamson 2000:20) and (Rimmerman 2000:58).

87. From How Did the MCC Begin? See www.mccchurch.org (accessed February 1, 2006).

88. Information in this section from (Perry and Swicegood 1990; Schlager 1998:51).

89. (Smith and Haider-Markel 2002).

90. (D'Emilio 2000:469).

91. See http://www.thetaskforce.org/ourprojects/cc/index.cfm (accessed January 31, 2006).

92. See NGLTF's Web site: www.thetaskforce.org (accessed January 26, 2005).

93. See (Armstrong 2002:145) for a similar argument with respect to lesbians.

94. (D'Emilio 2000:472).

95. See www.spiritus-temporis.com/human-rights-campaign/controversies.html (accessed February 1, 2006).

96. HRC Press Release, dated Wednesday, October 21, 1998.

97. The D'Amato Factor, by Charles Kaiser. *Advocate,* July 18, 2000.

98. A Painful Coming of Age: Human Rights Campaign Angers Gay Voters in New York, by David Kirby. *Advocate,* December 8, 1998.

99. Rebuilding the Gay Movement, by Doug Ireland. *The Nation,* July 12, 1999.

100. The D'Amato Factor, by Charles Kaiser. *Advocate,* July 18, 2000. National Conference Creates Controversy Among Activists. See http://www.mountainpridemedia.org/oitm/issues/1998/dec98/cchange.htm (accessed February 1, 2006).

101. A Painful Coming of Age, by David Kirby. *Advocate,* December 8, 1998.

102. A Painful Coming of Age, by David Kirby. *Advocate,* December 8, 1998.

103. When Did Gays Get So Straight? How Queer Culture Lost Its Edge. *New York* magazine, September 30, 1996:24–31.

104. (Vaid 1995:302, 306, 373).

105. Ibid.

106. Maupin quote from back cover of (Vaid 1995). Vaid quote from inside flap of (Vaid 1995).

Chapter Nine

1. A Gay Rights Rally Over Gains and Goals, by Robin Toner. *New York Times*, May 1, 2000:A14.

2. (Gamson 2000:16).

3. March Shows Gays Taking Different Roads, by Phuong Ly. *Washington Post*, March 29, 2000:B01.

4. Millennium March: Gay Rally Bares Deep Divisions, by Marc Sandalow. *San Francisco Chronicle*, April 29, 2000.

5. A Gay Rights Rally Over Gains and Goals, by Robin Toner. *New York Times*, May 1, 2000:A14.

6. Quoted in (Gamson 2000:18).

7. When the Saints Go Marchin' In, by Ann Rostow. *Girlfriends*, February 2000:30.

8. Praise Be Our Leaders: Does the Millennium March Herald a Brave New Age for the Gay Movement? *The Guide* (Boston), April 2000 edition.

9. Why We Should All Sit This One Out and Why We Aren't Marching. Ad Hoc Committee for an Open Process press releases, April 5, 2000.

10. A Gay Rights Rally Over Gains and Goals.

11. GLBT Activists Urge Millennium March Organizers to Put the March on Hold, by Michael C. Bradbury. *Seattle Gay News*, January 27, 2000.

12. Boycott the MMOW. Press release from the Ad Hoc Committee for an Open Process, March 9, 2000. See also, Illinois Groups Boycott March, by Lisa Neff. *Chicago Free Press*, March 8, 2000.

13. Marching to Nowhere. *Bay Area Reporter* staff editorial. April 14, 2000.

14. Ibid.

15. MMOWin' Over Millennium March Madness, by Wade Hyde. *Texas Triangle*, January 28, 2000.

16. What March? by Eric Resnick. *Gay People's Chronicle* (Cleveland, Ohio), March 3, 2000.

17. Millennium What? by Matthew McQuilkin. *Seattle Gay News*, February 4, 2000.

18. March Shows Gays Taking Different Roads, by Phuong Ly. *Washington Post*, March 29, 2000:B01.

19. Praise Be Our Leaders: Does the Millennium March Herald a Brave New Age for the Gay Movement? *The Guide* (Boston), April 2000 edition.

20. An Open Letter to the Lesbian, Gay, Bisexual, and Transgender Com-

munity, written and locally circulated by Queer to the Left, a Chicago-based group. Dated March 9, 2000. Letter signed by Chicago Democratic Socialists of America, Queer Commission; Chicago Metro Area Gay Youth Coalition (C-MAGYC); Coalition for Positive Sexuality; Equality Illinois; Homocore Chicago; Hysterical Women; It's Time Illinois; Khuli Zuban; Queer to the Left; Transsexual Menace Chicago; Women in the Director's Chair.

21. (Gamson 2000:20).

22. Her words, quoted in (Gamson 2000:18).

23. Boycott the MMOW. Press release from the Ad Hoc Committee for an Open Process, March 9, 2000.

24. Cease Fire! by Richard Goldstein. *Advocate,* February 15, 2000:36–40.

25. Top 5 Reasons to Skip MMOW, by Billy Hileman. *Windy City Times,* April 27, 2000:12–13.

26. Personal interview with Billy Hileman, December 12, 2003.

27. Personal interview with Robin Tyler, December 3, 2003.

28. Work Robin Tyler Has Done on March, dated June 14, 1998. Personal papers of Robin Tyler.

29. Personal Interview with Robin Tyler.

30. Ibid.

31. Millennium March: The Call. *Gay Community News,* Spring 1998:19.

32. Whose Faith? by Alisa Solomon. *Village Voice,* June 30, 1998:78.

33. An Open Letter to the Lesbian, Gay, Bisexual, and Transgender Community. Signed by: Chicago Democratic Socialists of America, Queer Commission; Chicago Metro Area Gay Youth Coalition (C-MAGYC); Coalition for Positive Sexuality; Equality Illinois; Homocore Chicago; Hysterical Women; It's Time Illinois; Khuli Zaban; Queer to the Left; Transsexual Menace Chicago; and Women in the Director's Chair. *Windy City Times,* March 9, 2000:10.

34. Marching On, by Lisa Neff. *Advocate,* June 22, 1999:42.

35. Ibid.

36. March Madness, by Chris Bull. *Advocate,* March 31, 1998:24.

37. National March Put on "Pause": HRC Agrees to Open Discussion on Feasibility of March in 2000, by Lisa Keen and Lou Chibbaro Jr. *Washington Blade,* February 13, 1998:1, 20. See also: March Is Put on "Pause": HRC Agrees to Open up a Discussion with Other Groups, by Lisa Keen and Lou Chibbaro Jr., *New York Blade,* February 13, 1998; A March Divided? by Lisa Neff, *Windy City Times,* February 26, 1998:1, 16; and Tough Choice, by Lisa Neff, *Windy City Times,* April 29, 1999:4.

38. A March Divided?

39. Ibid.

40. Letter to the Editor, signed by Joan M. Garry, Brian K. Bond, Lorri L. Jean, Kevin M. Cathcart, and Jubi Headley. *Gay Community News,* v23, n4, 1998:20–21.

41. News Release from the Human Rights Campaign, dated March 5, 1998. *Gay Community News*, v23, n4, 1998:22–23.

42. Ibid.

43. Ibid.

44. (Cohen 1999:117–8).

45. See http://thinkexist.com/quotations/dissent/ (accessed March 25, 2007).

46. (Gamson 2000:16).

47. Forum Organizes "Town Meetings" on 2000 March, by Rhonda Smith. *Washington Blade*, April 17, 1998:21.

48. The Discussion of the Decade? by Billy Hileman. *Windy City Times*, April 30, 1998:12.

49. Black Forum Organizes Discussions on the March, by Rhonda Smith. *Washington Blade*, April 17, 1998:27.

50. A March Critic, by Barbara Smith. *Windy City Times*, May 14, 1998:12.

51. Forum Organizes "Town Meetings" on 2000 March.

52. The Defense, by Nicole Ramirez-Murray. *Gay Community News*, Spring 1998, v 23, n4:26.

53. National, State Gay Marches Set, by Lisa Neff. *Windy City Times*, May 7, 1998:1.

54. March Moves Forward on Misguided Course, by Nadine Smith. *The Washington Blade*, April 17, 1998:33.

55. Millennium March—Who Decides? by Billy Hileman. *Gay Community News*, v23, n4, 1998:34–36.

56. March On (unauthored editorial). *Windy City Times*, March 19, 1998:13.

57. With the Millennium March behind Them, Gays and Lesbians Take Its Message to Their Hometowns, by Chris Bull. *Advocate*, June 6, 2000:24.

58. March Madness, by Chris Bull. *Advocate*, March 31, 1998:26.

59. Ibid:25.

60. The March: A Producer's Perspective, by Robin Tyler. *Windy City Times*, March 19, 1998:12.

61. March to Nowhere, by Paul Varnell. *Windy City Times*, June 18, 1998:15.

62. A March Divided?

63. Marching On, by Lisa Neff. *Advocate*, June 22, 1999:42.

64. The View from the Hill, by Chris Bull. *Advocate*, April 30, 2000:16.

65. A Song for Unsung Heroes, by Jonathan Capehart. *Advocate*, July 4, 2000:88.

66. March Madness: Political Infighting Raises Questions about the Worthiness of a Millennium March on Washington, by Chris Bull. *Advocate*, March 31, 1998:26.

67. Backward March: Why Are Gays Protesting a Gay Rights March? *The New Republic*, April 17, 2000:24.

68. Queer Atheists Raise Objections to Millennium March.

69. Momentum Builds Behind 2000 March.

70. Queer Atheists Raise Objections to Millennium March, by Tom Klein. *Bay Area Reporter,* July 30, 1998:6.

71. Momentum Builds Behind 2000 March, by C. Barillas. The Data Lounge, Tuesday, February 10, 1998. See www.datalounge.com/datalounge/news/record. html?record = 2736 (accessed October 20, 2003).

72. (Chasin 2000:218, 219).

73. Gays to March on Washington in 2000: Organizers Say "Millennium March" Will Bring Themes of "Families" and "Faith" to the Forefront, by Lou Chibbaro Jr. *New York Blade,* February 6, 1998.

74. Whose Faith? The Next Gay March on Washington Could Be a Boon to the Christian Right, by Alisa Solomon. *Village Voice,* June 30, 1998:78.

75. Troy Perry Responds to the Ad Hoc Committee on Millennium March, News Release dated September 23, 1998. From the personal papers of Reverend Troy Perry.

76. (Chasin 2000: 217–8).

77. Millennium March, Assessing Part II, by Michelangelo Signorile. May 11, 2000. See http://boards.gay.com/boards?13@174.Q7wGaqdxM3F^1@.ee6b860 (accessed May 11, 2000).

78. Unless otherwise noted, all information on the D.C. invitation-only meeting from Minutes, dated June 9, 1998. From the personal papers of Ann DeGroot.

79. March to Nowhere, by Paul Varnell. *Windy City Times,* June 18, 1998:15. For details on the meeting itself, see Activists Reject Offer to Join Panel, by Rhonda Smith. *The Washington Blade,* June 12, 1998:18.

80. March to Nowhere.

81. Open Door Policy. From the personal papers of Ann DeGroot.

82. See Activists Reject Offer to Join Panel, by Rhonda Smith. *Washington Blade,* June 12, 1998:18.

83. Introduction to the Millennium March Leadership Council. From the personal papers of Ann DeGroot.

84. Associate Producer (job description). From the personal papers of Ann DeGroot.

85. Draft Synopsis of MMOW Staff Job Descriptions. From the personal papers of Ann DeGroot.

86. Ad Hoc Committee for an Open Process: Who We Are. Folder: March on Washington 2000. The ONE Institute and Archives.

87. Millennium March Malaise Moves Forward, by Tony Peregrin. *Windy City Times,* December 23, 1999:4.

88. Activists Reject Offer to Join Panel, by Rhonda Smith. *Washington Blade* June 12, 1998:18. See also Activists Call for an Open Process Regarding Decision-making on National Events. *Gay Community News* v23, n4, 1998:42–43.

89. The Call for an Open Process. Personal papers of Bill Dobbs; and Eclipsing a Grassroots Movement, by Leslie Cagan. *Gay Community News* 1998, 24(1):18–23.

90. The Call for an Open Process.

91. Eclipsing a Grassroots Movement.

92. (Chasin 2000:217).

93. For more on this benefit of participatory democracy, see (Polletta 2002:8).

94. The Call for an Open Process..

95. See Poll Results. *Gay Community News,* spring 1998 (vol. 23, n4):31.

96. Ibid.

97. For more on the digital divide, see (DiMaggio, Hargittai et al. 2001; Norris 2001; Wellman and Haythornthwaite 2002).

98. Powerful Gay Media: Is "The Advocate" Getting Savvy or Selling Out? by Cynthia Cotts. *Village Voice,* April 1, 2000. From the personal papers of Bill Dobbs.

99. For more on questions of validity in non-experimental designs, see (Shadish, Cook et al. 2002).

100. Activists Reject Offer to Join Panel.

101. Eclipsing a Grassroots Movement.

102. Millennium March Staggers On: Plans for Event Crippled by Further Internal Dissension, by Tony Peregrin. *Windy City Times,* October 14, 1999:4.

103. Millennium March on Washington Under Fire: 300 Notables Challenge Top-down Process in Ad. Ad Hoc Committee For An Open Process Press Release. See http://gaytoday.badpuppy.com/garchive/events/092298ev.htm (accessed October 2, 2003).

104. See *Gay Community News* 24(1), 1998:24–25 for reprint.

105. Copies of personal e-mail correspondences from the papers of Ann DeGroot.

106. Millennium March on Washington for Equality, 2000: Separating Facts from Fiction. HRC Fax Transmission from Don Temples dated October 2, 1998. From the personal papers of Reverend Troy Perry.

107. An Open Letter to the Lesbian, Gay, Bisexual, and Transgender Community, written and locally circulated by Queer to the Left, a Chicago-based group. Dated March 9, 2000. Letter signed by Chicago Democratic Socialists of America, Queer Commission; Chicago Metro Area Gay Youth Coalition (C-MAGYC); Coalition for Positive Sexuality; Equality Illinois; Homocore Chicago; Hysterical Women; It's Time Illinois; Khuli Zuban; Queer to the Left; Transsexual Menace Chicago; Women in the Director's Chair.

108. Personal interview with Donna Redwing, February 28, 2004.

109. MMOW Board Resolutions. Resolution No. 1 concerns racial justice,

resolution No. 7 concerns gender equality, and resolution No. 8 concerns "visible gender variance." From the personal papers of Ann DeGroot.

110. March Leaders to Poll Gays Nationwide on Issues. *Windy City Times,* January 21, 1999:10.

111. Marching On, by Lisa Neff. *Advocate,* June 22, 1999:42.

112. (Gamson 2000:16).

113. MMOW Response Lukewarm in Chicago, by Tony Peregrin. *Windy City Times,* March 9, 2000:1, 6.

114. AHC letter and memo dated January 24, 2000, and signed by Steve Ault, Mandy Carter, Billy Hileman, and Diana Onley-Campbell. Personal papers of Ann DeGroot.

115. Putting It Together, by John Gallagher. *Advocate,* February 29, 2000:30.

116. Putting It Together:29.

117. March Unites Gay Masses, by Karen Hawkins and Tony Peregrin. *Windy City Times,* May 4, 2000:1, 6.

118. Millennium March Was Success for Some, Failure for Others. *Windy City Times,* May 18, 2000:13.

119. Marching Forward. *Chicago Free Press,* May 10, 2000:12.

120. March Leaders to Poll Gays Nationwide on Issues.

121. Put Event on Hold, *Washington Blade* letter to the editor. October 29, 1999:36.

122. Millennium March Leaders to Poll "Thousands" of Gays. *Washington Blade,* January 15, 1999.

123. Personal interview with Robin Tyler, December 3, 2003.

124. An Open Letter to the Lesbian, Gay, Bisexual and Transgender Community. *Windy City Times,* March 9, 2000:10.

125. Personal, joint interview with Steve Ault and Joyce Hunter, January 3, 2004.

126. AHC letter and memo dated January 24, 2000, and signed by Steve Ault, Mandy Carter, Billy Hileman, and Diana Onley-Campbell. Personal papers of Ann DeGroot.

127. Let You're your Voice Set the Agenda of the Millennium March. From the personal papers of Ann DeGroot.

128. Put Event on Hold.

129. AHC letter and memo dated January 24, 2000, and signed by Steve Ault, Mandy Carter, Billy Hileman, and Diana Onley-Campbell. Personal papers of Ann DeGroot.

130. Millennium March Leaders to Poll "Thousands" of Gays.

131. Who Would You Like to See Perform or Speak at the Rally? From the personal papers of Ann DeGroot, Minneapolis, Minn. See also: Master Work Plan:29, from the personal papers of Troy Perry.

132. The Board did not release information on how it elected its cochairs. The four cochairs for the Millennium March were Duane Cramer, Ann DeGroot, Nicole Ramirez-Murray, and Donna Redwing. After all the restructurings, the final composition of the board included Ingrid Duran, Michael Armentrout, Irene Monroe, Butch McKay, David Medina, Dana Rivers, Reverend Troy Perry, Deborah Oakley-Melvin, Margaret Conway, Dennis Gorg Jr., Michael Williams, Kirsten Kingdom, Bridget Bane, Charles Ching, Rabbi Jane Litman, Nick Metcalf, and Elizabeth Toledo.

133. See Activists Reject Offer to Join Panel, by Rhonda Smith. *Washington Blade,* June 12, 1998:18.

134. Lobel Leaves March Board, by Peter Freiberg. *Washington Blade,* April 30, 1999:1, 25.

135. Ibid.

136. Put Event on Hold.

137. Millennium March Staggers On, by Tony Peregrin. *Windy City Times,* October 14, 1999:4.

138. March Board Restructures, by Peter Freiberg. *Washington Blade,* October 15, 1999:1, 24.

139. Millennium March Staggers On.

140. March Board Restructures.

141. Time Marches On, by Peter Freiberg. *Washington Blade,* November 26, 1999:19.

142. March Board Restructures.

143. MMOW Organizer Resigns, by Rhonda Smith. *Washington Blade,* February 25, 2000:1, 19.

144. Millennium March Staggers On.

145. Too Much Anger, by Frank Asher. *Washington Blade,* November 19, 1999:37.

146. Put Event on Hold.

147. Clarifying Terms, by Ann DeGroot. *Windy City Times,* December 2, 1999:13.

148. Counting the Masses, by Lisa Keen. *Washington Blade,* May 5, 2000:1.

149. Marching Forward. *Chicago Free Press* editorial. May 10, 2000:12.

150. Monumental Millennium March. *Windy City Times,* May 4, 2000:6.

151. Millennium March: Gay Rally Bares Deep Divisions. *San Francisco Chronicle* April 29, 2000.

152. Personal Interview with Elizabeth Birch, November 21, 2003.

153. Personal papers of Ann DeGroot.

154. Personal Interview, Billy Hileman, December 12, 2003.

155. MMOW Is Not the 4th Gay-rights March, by Billy Hileman. Dated April 5, 2000, source indiscernible. Personal papers of Bill Dobbs.

156. Monumental Millennium March.

157. Waving the Rainbow Flag, by Will O'Bryan. *Washington Blade,* May 5, 2000:25.

158. Ibid.

159. Boycott the MMOW. Dated March 9, 2000, and signed by Henry Moses. Author's personal papers. See also: http://www.millenniummarch.com/pressrlo102.shtml (accessed April 6, 2000).

160. Why We Aren't Marching. Folder: March on Washington 2000. The ONE Institute and Archives. See also: Why We Should All Sit This One Out and Why We Aren't Marching. Author's personal papers. See also: www.foranopenprocess.org/sit-this-out-f.html (accessed May 11, 2000) and www.foranopenprocess.org/why-we-are-f.html (accessed May 11, 2000).

161. MMOW: Is This a Gay March? Or a Gay Market? Queer to the Left Press Release. Personal Papers of Bill Dobbs.

162. Year in Review: Movement or Market? by Bob Roehr, *Windy City Times,* January 3, 2001:10.

163. Waving the Rainbow Flag.

164. Militant Marketing March, by Karla Solheim. *Mother Jones,* April 25, 2000. See www.motherjones.com/reality_check/mmow.html (accessed October 2, 2003).

165. March Organizes Release Projections, by Rhonda Smith. *Washington Blade,* January 28, 2000:26.

166. An Open Letter to the Lesbian, Gay, Bisexual, and Transgender Community, by Queer to the Left. Dated March 9, 2000. *Windy City Times.*

167. Top 5 Reasons to Skip MMOW, by Billy Hileman. *Windy City Times,* April 27, 2000:12.

168. The Millennium Party's Over, by Michelangelo Signorile. The *Advocate,* January 16, 2001:30.

169. Waving the Rainbow Flag.

170. Where Did All the Money Go? by John Gallagher. The *Advocate,* June 20, 2000:28.

171. Year in Review: Movement or Market?

172. The Millennium Party's Over.

173. March of the Missing Money, by Toney Peregrin. *Windy City Times,* May 18, 2000:1.

174. All Over Except the Counting, by John Gallagher. The *Advocate,* January 16, 2001:64.

175. Personal Interview with John D'Emilio, December 29, 2003.

176. Successes of MMOW Signals Changes, by Hastings Wyman. *Windy City Times,* May 11, 2000:13.

177. (Armstrong 2002).

178. We're Here! We're Queer! Let's Get Coffee! *New York Magazine,* September 30, 1996:24–31.

179. (Vaid 1995).

Chapter Ten

1. (Epstein 1999:31–2).

2. Activists sometimes refer to this as the "gay state of the union." See The View from the Hill, by Chris Bull. *Advocate,* April 30, 2000:13.

3. Because infighting serves as evidence against the inevitability of actions, framings, self-definitions, etc., it mimics the function of a counterfactual in experimental and quasi-experimental designs.

4. (Gamson 2000:20).

5. (Wittgenstein 1953:66).

6. (Gamson 2000:17, 20).

7. Ibid:17.

8. Cease Fire! by Richard Goldstein. *Advocate,* February 15, 2000:39.

9. (Hamilton 2002:279).

10. The Longing of the Age of Aquarius, by Judy Wieder. *Advocate,* January 18, 2000:7.

11. The View from the Hill, by Chris Bull. *Advocate,* April 30, 2000,:14.

12. Why Can't We Talk This Out? By Billy Hileman. *Windy City Times,* January 13, 2000:8–9.

13. Honest Answers, by Nicole Murray-Ramirez. *Windy City Times,* June 10, 1999:12.

14. E-mail correspondence with Thomas Scott Tucker, March 7, 2005.

15. Different Times, Different Marches: Numbers Grow, Missions Shift, History Gets Made, by Bill Roundy. *Washington Blade,* April 28, 2000:1; The Odyssey: 1979–2000: Four Decades, Four Marches, by Lisa Neff. *Free Press,* April 26, 2000:1.

16. As I state in Appendix A, I assess evidence for this claim by tracking the statistical distribution of why activists decided to march and their primary sources of dissent during a given march. To do this, I examined Pearson's chi-square and adjusted standardized residual statistics. I use chi-square to determine if there is a relationship between an idea and a march—that is, to assess the aggregate distribution of particular ideas across the four marches. Does a debate surface across marches in different frequencies in a way that is patterned or just due to chance? Adjusted standardized residual values, on the other had, are similar to normally distributed z-scores and, when greater than the absolute value of 1.96, are significant at $p < .05$. A positive value suggests an idea is over-

prevalent *within a march* vis-à-vis other possible discussion topics from what we would expect if it were talked about equally with other ideas (i.e., an assumption of statistical independence). A negative value does the reverse. The advantage of this statistic over a standardized residual is that it allows for cross-category comparisons.

17. See Appendixes A and B for detailed information on the coding and analysis.

18. (Lapham 2004:14).

19. (Bollinger 1998).

20. (Hamilton 2002:1).

21. (Lapham 2004:1).

22. (Breines 1989:6).

23. A Transformational Movement, by Kerry Lobel. *Windy City Times,* May 7, 1998:12.

24. Eating Our Own. *Advocate,* August 13, 1992:38.

25. Cease Fire!

26. Eating Our Own. *Advocate,* August 13, 1992; Pride and Prejudice, by Niles Merton. *Advocate,* February 9, 1993:6; Why I Hated the March on Washington, published by QUASH. Undated (but referencing the 1993 Washington march); Shredding the Rainbow, by William J. Mann. *Frontiers,* May 28, 1999:63; The Longing of the Age of Aquarius, by Judy Wieder. *Advocate,* January 18, 2000:7; Cease Fire! by Richard Goldstein. *Advocate,* February 15, 2000:36.

27. (Campbell 1966; Shadish, Cook et al. 2002).

28. For specifics on labor organizing, see p. 30; for SNCC, see p. 90, 102; for the New Left, see p. 133; for women's liberation, see p. 151; for faith-based organizing, see p. 185, in (Polletta 2002).

29. For an excellent biography on Rustin, see (D'Emilio 2003).

30. For more on practical politics, see p. 117; for more on Coxey, see p. 18; for more on suffrage, see p. 63; for more on Randolph's 1941 march, see p. 114 and p. 125; for more on the 1963 civil rights march, see pp. 145–46, in (Barber 2002).

31. Making this move requires a leap of imagination and the important caveat that a responsible answer cannot fully be provided outside the context of empirical support. The examples provided here are for illustration purposes only, not definitive suggestions of limitless generalizability.

32. See, for example, Republican Infighting Gets Real, by Andrew Taylor. *The Huffington Post,* January 14, 2006; Republican Infighting Before the Midterm Elections, by David Shuster, MSNBC, posted September 20, 2006; GOP Infighting on Detainees Intensifies, by Peter Baker. *Washington Post,* September 16, 2006. This also suggests that using *infighting* as the primary term to conceptually organize this study is not limited to the lesbian and gay movement. This strategy is consistent with counsel in cultural sociology to use the terms that actors deploy to describe themselves (Griswold 1987; Hunter 1991:46).

33. Rebuff for Bush on Terror Trials in Senate Test, by Kate Zernike. *New York Times,* September 15, 2006.

34. An Unexpected Collision over Detainees, by Carl Hulse. *New York Times,* September 15, 2006.

35. (Moody and White 2003).

36. (Bourdieu 2001).

37. (Sewell 1999:40, 41–42, 44–46).

38. Williams quote from (Williams 1976:87). As a disclaimer, prominent culture theorist Michael Schudson (1989) points out that asking how culture "works" may be a question some find "bizarre, one that by the asking reveals a fundamental misunderstanding." However, if scholars conceive of culture as the "symbolic dimension of human activity" and link it to organizational aspects of social life, as I do in the present study, "then the question of what work culture does and how it does it is not self-evidently foolish. Indeed, it can then be understood as a key question in sociology" (Schudson 1989:153). I proceed with this assumption.

39. (Marx and Engels 1978:172).

40. Ethos quote from (Weber 1930:166). Switchmen quote from (Weber 1946:280).

41. (Durkheim 1912).

42. See (Swidler 1995; Swidler 2001) for excellent reviews of these and other approaches.

43. Fine offered his solution in response to national-level research on American culture and its associated values. His intention was to narrow the unit of analysis and provide behavioral concretization. See (Fine 1996; Fine 1998; Fine 2001).

44. For more on imagined communities, see (Anderson 1983).

45. (Wuthnow 1987; Wuthnow 1989). For more on ideological fields, see (1987:149). For more on language and ideologies, see (1987:147).

46. (Swidler 1986; Swidler 2001). See also (Ghaziani and Ventresca 2005) for review. For more on her identity model, see (2001:87).

47. (Becker 1998).

48. (Polletta 2002; Wilde 2004).

49. See also (Downey 1986; Lichterman 1995; Williams 1995; Wood 1999; Armstrong 2002; Hallett 2003).

50. (Schudson 1989).

51. (Swidler 1995; Friedland and Mohr 2004).

52. For more on institutional retention, see (Schudson 1989:171). For details on worker infighting, see (Marx and Engles 1978:481). Sorry reputation and movement collapse quotes from (Gamson 1975:101). For details on Gitlin's New Left arguments, see (Gitlin 1980, especially 239). Ideological postures quotes from (Gamson 1975:100).

Appendix A

1. (Wuthnow, Hunter et al. 1984; Mohr 1998).

2. For the imperative, see (Williams 1981). For endogenous explanation, see (Kaufman 2004). For the search for underlying patterns, see (Wuthnow, Hunter et al. 1984:255; Wuthnow 1987; Ghaziani 2004:278; Ghaziani and Ventresca 2005:533). For more on the tripartite model, see (Mukerji and Schudson 1991; Gamson 1994; Gamson 1998:227).

3. Gerber/Hart did not have records for the *Bay Area Reporter* for the first march. I therefore substituted *Bay Windows* and the *Sentinel,* two other local San Francisco papers, for just the first march.

4. *GCN* started in 1973 as a "forum to organize the progressive voice in the gay community." It was originally a local, Boston-based publication. In 1978, they went national in scope and distribution. They experienced financial troubles in the late 1980s and 1990s and eventually switched from weekly to bimonthly after temporarily ceasing publication. Gerber/Hart's records for *GCN* are incomplete after the second march. I therefore did not include *GCN* in the sample for the third and fourth marches. See http://www.lib.neu.edu/archives/collect/findaids/m64find.htm.

5. Gerber/Hart did not have records for the *Washington Blade* for the first march.

6. The *Windy City Times* did not begin circulation until 1985. Prior to that, Chicago's local gay newspaper was *GayLife.* Founded by Grant L. Ford, *GayLife* was the first biweekly newspaper in Chicago for the lesbian and gay community. *GayLife* went defunct in the mid-1980s. Its lifespan covered eleven volumes (volume 1, number 1 was published June 20, 1975; volume 11, number 32—the last issue—was published January 30, 1986 [see http://www.lib.uchicago.edu/e/su/gaylesb/glgi-gen.html]). For the second through the fourth marches, I used the weekly *Windy City Times,* which to this day is operative and remains Chicago's oldest LGBT newspaper.

7. For more on maximum variation, see (Patton 1987:52; Shadish, Cook et al. 2002; Babbie 2004; List 2004).

8. See (Fuller 2003) for a similar approach.

9. (Neuendorf 2002:141); (Cohen 1960).

10. Standard measure quote from (Kolbe and Burnett 1991:248). For more on Cohen's Kappa, including relevant formulas and comparisons in situations of more than two coders, see (Lombard, Snyder-Duch et al. 2005).

11. (Streitmatter 1995:117).

12. Gay Community News: 30 Years Later, by Scott A. Giordano. *Bay Windows,* January 16, 2003.

13. This framing is motivated by (Geertz 1973:12).

14. (Ortiz, Myers et al. 2005:397).

15. For more on these and other biases in newspaper data, see (Gurr 1972:34; McAdam 1982:235).

16. (McAdam 1982:236).

17. For a detailed assessment of this debate, see (McCarthy, McPhail et al. 1996; Oliver and Myers 1999; Oliver and Maney 2000; Smith, McCarthy et al. 2001; Earl, Soule et al. 2003; Earl, Martin et al. 2004).

18. (Ortiz, Myers et al. 2005:397, 407, 411–12).

19. (Ortiz, Myers et al. 2005:412).

20. Gays and the Media, by Peter Friberg. *The Washington Blade* April 23, 1993:53.

21. Editors Respond at Mainstream Newspaper Forum. *Windy City Times,* September 9, 1993:7.

22. Talking to Each Other, by Eric K. Browning. *Gay Community News,* July 28, 1979:4.

23. IRB Project No. 0979–008.

24. For more on these and related issues, see (Cherry and Rodgers 1979); (Loftus and Marburger 1983); (Golden 1992); (Coughlin 1990).

Works Cited

Adam, B. D. (1995). *The Rise of the Gay and Lesbian Movement.* New York: Twayne Publishers.

Adam, B. D., J. W. Duyvendak, and A. Krouwel (1999). *The Global Emergence of Gay and Lesbian Politics.* Philadelphia: Temple University Press.

Alexander, J. C. (2003). *The Meanings of Social Life.* New York: Oxford University Press.

Alonso, W. and P. Starr, eds. (1987). *The Politics of Numbers.* New York: Sage.

Anderson, B. (1983). *Imagined Communities.* New York: Verso.

Andrews, K. (1997). The Impacts of Social Movements on the Political Process: The Civil Rights Movement and Black Electoral Politics in Mississippi. *American Sociological Review* 62: 800–819.

Andrews, K. (2002). Creating Social Change: Lessons from the Civil Rights Movement. In *Social Movements: Identity, Culture, and the State,* eds. D. S. Meyer, N. Whittier, and B. Robnett. New York: Oxford University Press: 105–117.

Andrews, K. (2002). Movement-Countermovement Dynamics and the Emergence of New Institutions: The Case of "White Flight" Schools in Mississippi. *Social Forces* 80(3): 911–36.

Andriote, J.-M. (1999). *Victory Deferred: How AIDS Changed Gay Life in America.* Chicago: The University of Chicago Press.

Archer, M. S. (1996). *Culture and Agency.* New York: Cambridge University Press.

Armstrong, E. A. (2002). *Forging Gay Identities: Organizing Sexuality in San Francisco, 1950–1994.* Chicago: The University of Chicago Press.

Armstrong, E. A. and S. M. Crage (2006). Movements and Memory: The Making of the Stonewall Myth. *American Sociological Review* 71: 724–51.

Arnold, M. ([1869] 1949). Culture and Anarchy. In *The Portable Matthew Arnold,* ed. L. Trilling. New York: Viking.

Babbie, E. (2004). *The Practice of Social Research.* Belmont, Calif.: Wadsworth/ Thomson Learning.

Bain, R. (1939). Cultural Integration and Social Conflict. *American Journal of Sociology* 44(4): 499–509.

Bakhtin, M. M. (1984). *Rabelais and His World.* Bloomington, Ind.: Indiana University Press.

Balser, D. B. (1997). The Impact of Environmental Factors on Factionalism and Schism in Social Movement Organizations. *Social Forces* 76(1): 199–228.

Barber, L. G. (2002). *Marching on Washington: The Forging of an American Political Tradition.* Berkeley: University of California Press.

Barrow, C. W. (1990). Counter-Movement within the Labor Movement: Workers' Education and the American Federation of Labor, 1900–1937. *The Social Science Journal* 27(4): 395–417.

Bawer, B. (1993). *A Place at the Table: The Individual in American Society.* New York: Poseidon Press.

Bayer, R. (1987). *Homosexuality and American Psychiatry: The Politics of Diagnosis.* Princeton, N.J.: Princeton University Press.

Becker, P. E. (1998). Making Inclusive Communities: Congregations and the "Problem" of Race. *Social Problems* 45: 451–72.

Beisel, N. (1993). Morals versus Art: Censorship, the Politics of Interpretation, and the Victorian Nude. *American Sociological Review* 58: 145–62.

Bell, D. and G. Valentine, eds. (1995). *Mapping Desire: Geographies of Sexualities.* New York: Routledge.

Bellah, R. N., R. Madsen, et al. (1985). *Habits of the Heart.* Berkeley: Universty of California Press.

Benford, R. D. (1993). Frame Disputes within the Nuclear Disarmament Movement. *Social Forces* 71(3): 677–701.

Berlant, L. and E. Freeman (1993). Queer Nationality. In *Fear of a Queer Planet,* ed. M. Warner. Minneapolis, University of Minnesota Press: 193–229.

Bernstein, M. (1997). Celebration and Suppression: The Strategic Uses of Identity by the Lesbian and Gay Movement. *American Journal of Sociology* 103(3): 531–65.

Berube, A. (1990). *Coming Out Under Fire: The History of Gay Men and Women in World War Two.* New York: Penguin Books.

Berube, A. and J. Escoffier (1991). Queer/Nation. *Out/Look: National Lesbian and Gay Quarterly* 11(Winter): 12–23.

Binder, A. J. (2002). *Contentious Curricula: Afrocentrism and Creationism in American Public Schools.* Princeton, N.J.: Princeton University Press.

Blasius, M. (1994). *Gay and Lesbian Politics: Sexuality and the Emergence of a New Ethic.* Philadelphia: Temple University Press.

Blasius, M., ed. (2001). *Sexual Identities, Queer Politics.* Princeton, N.J.: Princeton University Press.

Blumenfeld, W. J., ed. (1992). *Homophobia: How We All Pay the Price*. Boston: Beacon Press.

Bollinger, L. C. (1998). *The Tolerant Society*. New York: Oxford University Press.

Bonnell, Victoria E., and Lynn Hunt, eds. (1999). *Beyond the Cultural Turn: New Directions in the Study of Society and Culture*. Berkeley: University of California Press.

Bourdieu, P. (2001). *Sociology Is a Martial Art (La Sociologie Est un Sport de Combat)*, video. Directed by P. Carles. Éditions Montparnasse.

Bowers v. Hardwick, 478 U.S. 186 (Supreme Court 1986).

Breines, W. (1989). *Community and Organization in the New Left, 1962–1968: The Great Refusal*. New Brunswick, N.J.: Rutgers University Press.

Brown, K. (1998). *20th Century TransHistory and Experience: Biographies and Essays*: www.transhistory.net.

Browning, F. (1993). *The Culture of Desire*. New York: Vintage.

Browning, F. (1996). *A Queer Geography*. New York: Noonday Press.

Brubaker, R. and F. Cooper (2000). Beyond Identity. *Theory and Society* 29: 1–47.

Buckley, W. F., op-ed. Crucial Steps in Combating the AIDS Epidemic: Identify All Carriers. *New York Times*, March 18, 1986, A27.

Bunch, C. (1994). Learning from Lesbian Separatism. In *Lavender Culture*, eds. K. Jay and A. Young. New York: New York University Press: 433–44.

Butler, J. (1990). *Gender Trouble: Feminism and the Subversion of Identity*. New York: Routledge.

Calhoun, C., ed. (1994). *Social Theory and the Politics of Identity*. Oxford: Blackwell.

Califia, P. (2003). *Sex Changes: The Politics of Transgenderism*. San Francisco: Cleis Press.

Campbell, D. T. The Principle of Proximal Similarity in the Application of Science. Thesis, Department of Sociology, Northwestern University, 1966.

Capsuto, S. (2000). *Alternate Channels: The Uncensored Story of Gay and Lesbian Images on Radio and Television*. New York: Ballantine Books.

Carson, C. ([1981] 1995). *In Struggle: SNCC and the Black Awakening of the 1960s*. Cambridge, Mass.: Harvard University Press.

Carter, D. (2004). *Stonewall: The Riots That Sparked the Gay Revolution*. New York: St. Martin's Press.

Chambers, D. L. (2000). Couples: Marriage, Civil Union, and Domestic Partnership. In *Creating Change: Sexuality, Public Policy, and Civil Rights*, eds. J. D'Emilio, R. H. Turner and U. Vaid. New York: St. Martin's Press: 281–304.

Chasin, A. (2000). *Selling Out: The Gay and Lesbian Movement Goes to Market*. New York: Palgrave.

Chauncey, G. (1994). *Gay New York: Gender, Urban Culture, and the Making of the Gay Male World, 1890–1940.* New York: BasicBooks.

Chauncey, G. (2004). *Why Marriage? The History Shaping Today's Debate Over Gay Equality.* New York: Basic Books.

Cherry, N. and B. Rodgers (1979). Using a Longitudinal Study to Assess the Quality of Retrospective Data. In *The Recall Method in Social Surveys,* eds. L. Moss and H. Goldstein. Hove, Sussex: University of London Institute of Education.

Chesler, P. (2001). *Woman's Inhumanity to Woman.* New York: Nation Books.

Clendinen, D. and A. Nagourney (1999). *Out for Good: The Struggle to Build a Gay Rights Movement in America.* New York: Simon and Schuster.

Cloud, J. (1999). Harvey Milk. *Time.* June 14: http://www.time.com/time/time100/ heroes/profile/milk01.html.

Cohen, C. J. (1996). Punks, Bulldaggers, and Welfare Queens: The Radical Potential of Queer Politics? *GLQ: Journal of Lesbian and Gay Studies* 3: 4, 437–65.

Cohen, C. J. (1999). *The Boundaries of Blackness: AIDS and the Breakdown of Black Politics.* Chicago: The University of Chicago Press.

Cohen, C. J. (1999). What Is This Movement Doing to My Politics? *Social Text* 17(4): 111–18.

Cohen, C. J. (2000). Contested Membership: Black Gay Identities and the Politics of AIDS. In *Creating Change: Sexuality, Public Policy, and Civil Rights,* eds. J. D'Emilio, W. B. Turner and U. Vaid. New York: St. Martin's Press: 382–406.

Cohen, J. (1960). A Coefficient of Agreement for Nominal Scales. *Educational and Psychological Measurement* 20: 37–46.

Cohen, J. L. (1985). Strategy or Identity: New Theoretical Paradigms and Contemporary Social Movements. *Social Research* 52(4): 663–716.

Coser, L. (1956). *The Functions of Social Conflict.* New York: The Free Press.

Coughlin, S. S. (1990). Recall Bias in Epidemiologic Studies. *Journal of Clinical Epidemiology* 43: 87–91.

Crimp, D., ed. (1996). *AIDS: Cultural Analysis, Cultural Activism.* Cambridge, Mass.: MIT Press.

Crimp, D. and A. Rolston (1990). *AIDS Demographics.* Seattle: Bay Press.

Critchlow, D. T. (2005). *Phyllis Schlafly and Grassroots Conservatism : A Woman's Crusade.* Princeton, N.J.: Princeton University Press.

Cruikshank, M. (1992). *The Gay and Lesbian Liberation Movement.* New York: Routledge.

Dahir, M. (1999). Whose Movement Is It? *The Advocate.* May 25: http://findarticles.com/P/articles/mi_m1589/is_1999_May_25/ai_54775067.

D'Emilio, J. (1983). *Sexual Politics, Sexual Communities: The Making of a Ho-*

mosexual Minority in the United States, 1940–1970. Chicago: The University of Chicago Press.

D'Emilio, J. (1992). *Making Trouble: Essays on Gay History, Politics, and the University.* New York: Routledge.

D'Emilio, J. (2000). Organizational Tales: Interpreting the NGLTF Story. In *Creating Change: Sexuality, Public Policy, and Civil Rights,* eds. J. D'Emilio, R. H. Turner and U. Vaid. New York: St. Martin's Press: 469–86.

D'Emilio, J. (2002). *The World Turned: Essays on Gay History, Politics, and Culture.* Durham, N.C.: Duke University Press.

D'Emilio, J. (2003). *Lost Prophet: The Life and Times of Bayard Rustin.* New York: Free Press.

D'Emilio, J. (2005). The 1979 March's Place in History. *The Gay and Lesbian Review* 12(2): 33–34.

D'Emilio, J. (2006). The Marriage Fight Is Setting Us Back. *The Gay and Lesbian Review* 13(6): 10–11.

D'Emilio, J. and E. B. Freedman (1988). *Intimate Matters: A History of Sexuaity in America.* New York: Harper & Row Publishers.

Diamond, S. (1995). *Roads to Dominion: Right-Wing Movements and Political Power in the United States.* New York: The Guilford Press.

Diaz, K. (1999). Are Gay Men Born That Way? In *The Columbia Reader on Lesbians and Gay Men in Media, Society, and Politics,* eds. L. Gross and J. D. Woods. New York: Columbia University Press: 211–17.

Diggins, J. P. (1992). *The Rise and Fall of the American Left.* New York and London: W. W. Norton & Company.

DiMaggio, P. (2003). The Myth of the Culture War. In *The Fractious Nation? Unity and Division in Contemporary American Life,* ed. S. Steinlight. Berkeley: University of California Press: 79–97.

DiMaggio, P., J. Evans, et al. (1996). Have Americans' Social Attitudes Become More Polarized? *American Journal of Sociology* 102: 690–755.

DiMaggio, P., E. Hargittai, et al. (2001). Social Implications of the Internet. *Annual Review of Sociology* 27: 307–36.

Dougan, C. and S. Lipsman (1984). *A Nation Divided: The War at Home, 1945–1972.* Boston: Boston Publishing Company.

Downey, G. L. (1986). Ideology and the Clamshell Identity: Organizational Dilemmas in the Anti-Nuclear Power Movement. *Social Problems* 33(5): 357–73.

Duberman, M. (1993). *Stonewall.* New York: Penguin Books.

Duberman, M. B., M. Vicinus, et al., eds. (1989). *Hidden from History: Reclaiming the Gay and Lesbian Past.* New York: NAL Books.

DuBois, W. E. B. (1903). *The Souls of Black Folk.* Chicago, A. C. McClurg & Company.

Duggan, L. (1992). Making It Perfectly Queer. *Socialist Review* 22: 11–32.

Durkheim, E. (1912). *The Elementary Forms of Religious Life.* New York: The Free Press.

Earl, J., A. Martin, et al. (2004). The Use of Newspaper Data in the Study of Collective Action. *Annual Review of Sociology* 30: 65–80.

Earl, J., S. A. Soule, et al. (2003). Protest Under Fire? Explaining the Policing of Protest. *American Sociological Review* 68(4): 581–606.

Echols, A. (1983). Cultural Feminism: Feminist Capitalism and the Anti-Pornography Movement. *Social Text* 7 (Spring-Summer): 34–53.

Echols, A. (1989). *Daring to Be Bad. Radical Feminism in America 1967–1975.* Minneapolis: University of Minnesota Press.

Engel, S. M. (2001). *The Unfinished Revolution: Social Movement Theory and the Gay and Lesbian Movement.* Cambridge, UK: Cambridge University Press.

Epstein, R. (1984). *The Times of Harvey Milk.* Black Sand Productions.

Epstein, S. (1987). Gay Politics, Ethnic Identity: The Limits of Social Constructionism. *Socialist Review* 93/94: 9–54.

Epstein, S. (1994). A Queer Encounter: Sociology and the Study of Sexuality. *Sociological Theory* 12(2): 188–201.

Epstein, S. (1996). *Impure Science: AIDS, Activism, and the Politics of Knowledge.* Berkeley: University of California Press.

Epstein, S. (1999). Gay and Lesbian Movements in the United States: Dilemmas of Identity, Diversity, and Political Strategy. In *The Global Emergence of Gay and Lesbian Politics,* eds. B. D. Adam, J. W. Duyvendak, and A. Krouwel: 30–90. Philadelphia: Temple University Press.

Escoffier, J. (1998). *American Homo: Community and Perversity.* Berkeley: University of California Press.

Fantasia, R. (1988). *Cultures of Solidarity: Consciousness, Action, and Contemporary American Workers.* Berkeley: University of California Press.

Feinberg, L. (1996). *Transgender Warriors: Making History from Joan of Arc to Dennis Rodman.* Boston: Beacon Press.

Feldman, S. P. (1990). Stories as Cultural Creativity: On the Relation between Symbolism and Politics in Organizational Change. *Human Relations* 43: 809–28.

Fine, G. A. (1979). Small Groups and Cultural Creation: The Idioculture of Little League Baseball Teams. *American Sociological Review* 44: 733–45.

Fine, G. A. (1996). *Kitchens: The Culture of Restaurant Work.* Chicago: The University of Chicago Press.

Fine, G. A. (1998). *Morel Tales: The Culture of Mushrooming.* Cambridge, Mass.: Harvard University Press.

Fine, G. A. (2001). *Gifted Tongues: High School Debate and Adolescent Culture.* Princteon, N.J.: Princeton University Press.

Fine, G. A., and K. Sandstrom (1993). Ideology in Action: A Pragmatic Approach to a Contested Concept. *Sociological Theory* 11: 21–38.

Firey, W. (1948). Informal Organization and the Theory of Schism. *American Sociological Review* 13(1): 15–24.

Foucault, M. (1978). *The History of Sexuality.* New York: Vintage Books.

Friedland, Roger, and John W. Mohr (2004). The Cultural Turn in American Sociology. In *Matters of Culture: Cultural Sociology in Practice,* eds. Roger Friedland and John W. Mohr. Cambridge, UK: Cambridge University Press: 1–70.

Frye, P. R. (2000). Facing Discrimination, Organizing for Freedom: The Transgender Community. In *Creating Change: Sexuality, Public Policy, and Civil Rights,* eds. J. D'Emilio, W. B. Turner, and U. Vaid. New York: St. Martin's Press: 451–68.

Fuller, S. (2003). Creating and Contesting Boundaries: Exploring the Dynamics of Conflict and Classification. *Sociological Forum* 18(1): 3–30.

Fuss, D. (1989). *Essentially Speaking: Feminism, Nature, and Difference.* New York: Routledge.

Futrell, R. and P. Simi (2004). Free Spaces, Collective Identity, and the Persistence of U.S. White Power Activism. *Social Problems* 51(1): 16–42.

Gamson, J. (1989). Silence, Death, and the Invisible Enemy: AIDS Activism and Social Movement "Newness." *Social Problems* 36: 351–67.

Gamson, J. (1994). *Claims to Fame: Celebrity in Contemporary America.* Berkeley: University of California Press.

Gamson, J. (1995). Must Identity Movements Self-Destruct? A Queer Dilemma. *Social Problems* 42(3): 390–407.

Gamson, J. (1997). Messages of Exclusion: Gender, Movements, and Symbolic Boundaries. *Gender & Society* 11(2): 178–99.

Gamson, J. (1998). *Freaks Talk Back: Tabloid Talk Shows and Sexual Nonconformity.* Chicago: The University of Chicago Press.

Gamson, J. (2000). Whose Millennium March? *The Nation* 270(15): 16–20.

Gamson, J. and D. Moon (2004). The Sociology of Sexualities: Queer and Beyond. *Annual Review of Sociology* 30: 47–64.

Gamson, W. A. (1975). *The Strategy of Social Protest.* Belmont, Calif.: Wadsworth Publishing Company.

Geertz, C. (1973). *The Interpretation of Cultures.* New York: Basic Books.

Gerlach, L. and V. Hine (1970). *People, Power, Change: Movements of Social Transformation.* Indianapolis, Ind.: Bobbs-Merril.

Gersick, C. J. and J. R. Hackman (1990). Habitual Routines in Task-Performing Groups. *Organizational Behavior & Human Decision Processes* 47(1): 65–97.

Ghaziani, A. (2004). Anticipatory and Actualized Identities: A Cultural Analysis of the Transition from AIDS Disability to Work. *The Sociological Quarterly* 45(2): 273–301.

Ghaziani, A. (2005). Breakthrough: The 1979 National March. *The Gay and Lesbian Review* 12(2): 31–32.

Ghaziani, A. and T. D. Cook (2005). Reducing HIV Infections at Circuit Parties: From Description to Explanation and Principles of Intervention Design. *Journal of the International Association of Physicians in AIDS Care* 4(2): 32–46.

Ghaziani, A. and M. J. Ventresca (2005). Keywords and Cultural Change: Frame Analysis of Business Model Public Talk, 1975–2000. *Sociological Forum* 20(4): 523–59.

Gitlin, T. (1980). *The Whole World Is Watching.* Berkeley: University of California Press.

Gitlin, T. (1995). *The Twilight of Common Dreams: Why America Is Wracked by Culture Wars.* New York: Metropolitan Books.

Golden, B. (1992). The Past Is the Past—Or Is It? The Use of Retrospective Accounts as Indicators of Past Strategy. *Academy of Management Journal* 35: 848–60.

Goldstein, R. (2002). *The Attack Queers: Liberal Society and the Gay Right.* London and New York: Verso.

Goldstein, R. (2003). *Homocons: The Rise of the Gay Right.* New York: Verso.

Gould, D. B. (2002). Life during Wartime: Emotions and the Development of ACT UP. *Mobilization* 7(2): 177–200.

Greenberg, J. (Unpublished Paper). ACT UP Explained. www.actupny.org/documents/greenbergAU.html.

Griswold, W. (1987). The Fabrication of Meaning: Literary Interpretation in the United States, Great Britain, and the West Indies. *American Journal of Sociology* 92(5): 1077–1117.

Griswold, W. (1987). A Methodological Framework for the Sociology of Culture. *Sociological Methodology* 17: 1–35.

Griswold, W. (1994). *Cultures and Societies in a Changing World.* Thousand Oaks, Calif.: Pine Forge Press.

Gross, L. (2001). *Up From Invisibility: Lesbians, Gay Men, and the Media in America.* New York: Columbia University Press.

Gross, L. and J. D. Woods, eds. (1999). *The Columbia Reader on Lesbians and Gay Men in Media, Society, and Politics.* New York: Columbia University Press.

Gurr, T. (1972). The Calculus of Civil Conflict. *Journal of Social Issues* 28(1): 27–47.

Habermas, J. (1989). *The Structural Transformation of the Pubilc Sphere.* Cambridge, Mass.: MIT Press.

Hacking, I. (1990). *The Taming of Chance.* New York and Cambridge, UK: Cambridge University Press.

Hallett, T. (2003). Symbolic Power and Organizational Culture. *Sociological Theory* 21: 128–49.

Hamilton, N. A. (2002). *Rebels and Renegades: A Chronology of Social and Political Dissent in the United States.* New York: Routledge.

Hebdige, D. (1979). *Subculture: The Meaning of Style.* London and New York: Routledge.

Hegel, G. W. F. (1807). *The Phenomenology of Mind.* London: George Allen and Unwin.

Herek, G. M. and K. T. Berrill, eds. (1992). *Hate Crimes: Confronting Violence Against Lesbians and Gay Men.* New York: Sage.

Hermanowicz, J. C. and H. P. Morgan (1999). Ritualizing the Routine: Collective Identity Affirmation. *Sociological Forum* 14(2): 197–214.

Horowitz, I. L. (1962). Consensus, Conflict, and Cooperation: A Sociological Inventory. *Social Forces* 41(2): 177–88.

Hull, K. E. (2006). *Same-Sex Marriage: The Cultural Politics of Love and Law.* Cambridge, UK: Cambridge University Press.

Humphreys, L. (1972). *Out of the Closets: The Sociology of Homosexual Liberation.* Englewood Cliffs, N.J.: Prentice-Hall.

Hunt, S. A. and R. D. Benford (1994). Identity Talk in the Peace and Justice Movement. *Journal of Contemporary Ethnography* 22(4): 488–517.

Hunt, S. A., R. D. Benford, et al. (1994). Identity Fields: Framing Processes and the Social Construction of Movement Identities. In *New Social Movements: From Ideology to Identity,* eds. E. Larana, H. Johnston, and J. R. Gusfield. Philadelphia: Temple University Press: 185–208.

Hunter, J. D. (1991). *Culture Wars: The Struggle to Define America.* New York: BasicBooks.

Hutchins, L. (1996). Bisexuality: Politics and Community. In *Bisexuality: The Psychology and Politics of an Invisible Minority,* ed. B. A. Firestein. Thousand Oaks, Calif.: Sage: 240–59.

Hutchins, L. and L. Kaahumanu, eds. (1991). *Bi Any Other Name.* Boston: Alyson.

Irving, A. and T. Young (2002). Paradigm for Pluralism: Mikhail Bakhtin and Social Work Practice. *Social Work* 47(1): 19–29.

Jasper, J. M. (1997). *The Art of Moral Protest: Culture, Biography, and Creativity in Social Movements.* Chicago: The University of Chicago Press.

Jauss, H. R. (1982). *Toward an Aesthetic of Reception.* Minneapolis: University of Minnesota Press.

Jay, K. (1999). *Tales of the Lavender Menace.* New York: Basic Books.

Jehn, K. A. (1995). A Multimethod Examination of the Benefits and Detriments of Intragroup Conflict. *Administrative Science Quarterly* 40: 256–82.

Jenkins, C. J. (1983). Resource Mobilization Theory and the Study of Social Movements. *Annual Review of Sociology* 9: 527–53.

Jenkins, C. J. and C. M. Eckert (1986). Channeling Black Insurgency: Elite Patronage and Professional Social Movement Organizations in the Development of the Black Movement. *American Sociological Review* 51(6): 812–29.

Jenness, V. (1995). Social Movement Growth, Domain Expansion, and Framing Processes: The Gay/Lesbian Movement and Violence against Gays and Lesbians as a Social Problem. *Social Problems* 42(1): 145–70.

Jenness, V. (1999). Managing Differences and Making Legislation: Social Movements and the Racialization, Sexualization, and Gendering of Federal Hate Crime Law in the U.S., 1985–1998. *Social Problems* 46(4): 548–71.

Johnson, R. (2004). Gay Pride History, Rainbow Flag and 2004 Events Calendar. http://gaylife.about.com/cs/4/a/gaypridedates.htm.

Johnston, H. and B. Klandermans, eds. (1995). *Social Movements and Culture.* Social Movements, Protest, and Contention. Minneapolis: University of Minnesota Press.

Johnston, H., E. Larana, et al. (1994). Identities, Grievances, and New Social Movements. In *New Social Movements: From Ideology to Identity,* eds. E. Larana, H. Johnston, and J. R. Gusfield. Philadelphia: Temple University Press: 3–35.

Jones, C. and J. Dawson (2000). *Stitching a Revolution: The Making of an Activist.* New York: HarperSanFrancisco.

Kaiser, C. (1997). *The Gay Metropolis: The Landmark History of Gay Life in America Since World War II.* New York: Harcourt Brace & Company.

Kaufman, J. (2004). Endogenous Explanation in the Sociology of Culture. *Annual Review of Sociology* 30: 335–57.

Keen, L. and S. B. Goldberg (2000). *Strangers to the Law: Gay People on Trial.* Ann Arbor, Mich.: University of Michigan Press.

Kennedy, E. L. and M. D. Davis (1993). *Boots of Leather, Slippers of Gold: The History of a Lesbian Community.* New York: Penguin Books.

Kinsey, A. C., W. B. Pomeroy, et al. (1948). *Sexual Behavior in the Human Male.* Philadelphia: W.B. Saunders.

Kirsch, M. H. (2000). *Queer Theory and Social Change.* New York: Routledge.

Klandermans, B. (1988). The Formation and Mobilization of Consensus. *International Social Movement Research* 1: 173–96.

Klandermans, B. (1994). Transient Identities? Membership Patterns in the Dutch Peace Movement. In *New Social Movements: From Ideology to Identity,* eds. E. Larana, H. Johnston, and J. R. Gusfield. Philadelphia: Temple University Press: 168–84.

Klinkner, P. A. and R. M. Smith (1999). *The Unsteady March: The Rise and Decline of Racial Equality in America.* Chicago: The University of Chicago Press.

Kolbe, R. H. and M. S. Burnett (1991). Content-Analysis Research: An Examination of Applications with Directives for Improving Research Reliability and Objectivity. *Journal of Consumer Research* 18(2): 243–50.

Kramer, L. (1978). *Faggots*. New York: Grove Press.

Krauthammer, C. (1983). The Politics of a Plague. *The New Republic* March 27: 18–21.

Lang, K. and G. E. Lang (1961). *Collective Dynamics*. New York: Thomas Y. Crowell Company.

Lapham, L. H. (2004). *Gag Rule: On the Suppression of Dissent and the Stifling of Democracy*. New York: The Penguin Press.

Larana, E., H. Johnston, et al., eds. (1994). *New Social Movements: From Ideology to Identity*. Philadelphia: Temple University Press.

Lawrence v. Texas, 539 U.S. 558 (Supreme Court 2003).

Layton, A. S. (2000). *International Politics and Civil Rights Policies in the United States, 1941–1960*. Cambridge, UK: Cambridge University Press.

Leonard, A. S. (2000). From *Bowers v. Hardwick* to *Romer v. Evans*: Lesbian and Gay Rights in the U.S. Supreme Court. In *Creating Change: Sexuality, Public Policy, and Civil Rights,* eds. J. D'Emilio, R. H. Turner, and U. Vaid. New York: St. Martin's Press: 57–77.

Levitt, B. and J. G. March (1988). Organizational learning. *Annual Review of Sociology* 14: 319–40.

Lichterman, P. (1995). Piecing Together a Multicultural Community: Cultural Differences in Community Building among Grassroots Environments. *Social Problems* 42: 513–34.

List, D. (2004). Maximum Variation Sampling for Surveys and Consensus Groups: www.audiencedialogue.org/maxvar.html. Adelaide, Australia: Audience Dialogue.

Loftus, E. L. and W. Marburger (1983). Since the Eruption of Mount St. Helen's, Has Anyone Beaten You Up? Improving the Accuracy of Retrospective Reports with Landmark Events. *Memory and Cognition* 11: 114–20.

Loftus, J. (2001). America's Liberalization in Attitudes Toward Homosexuality, 1973–1998. *American Sociological Review* 66: 762–82.

Lombard, M., J. Snyder-Duch, et al. (2005). Practical Resources for Assessing and Reporting Intercoder Reliability in Content Analysis Research Projects. http://www.temple.edu/mmc/reliability/#What%20is%20intercoder%20reliability. (accessed 2006).

Lorde, A. (1984). *Sister Outsider: Essays and Speeches*. Trumansburg, N.Y.: Crossing Press.

Lott, E. (1995). *Love and Theft: Blackface Minstrelsy and the American Working Class*. New York: Oxford University Press.

Loughery, J. (1998). *The Other Side of Silence: Men's Lives and Gay Identities: A Twentieth-Century History*. New York: Henry Holt and Company Inc.

Mankiller, W., G. Mink, et al., eds. (1998). *The Reader's Companion to U.S. Women's History.* New York: Houghton Mifflin Company.

Mansbridge, J. (1986). *Why We Lost the ERA.* Chicago: The University of Chicago Press.

Mansbridge, J. and A. Morris, eds. (2001). *Oppositional Consciousness: The Subjective Roots of Social Protest.* Chicago: The University of Chicago Press.

Marcus, E. (2002). *Making Gay History: The Half-Century Fight for Lesbian and Gay Equal Rights.* New York: HarperCollins.

Marx, K. and F. Engels (1978). The German Ideology. In *The Marx-Engels Reader,* ed. R. C. Tucker. New York: W. W. Norton and Company: 146–200.

Marx, K. and F. Engels (1978). Manifesto of the Communist Party. In *The Marx-Engels Reader,* ed. R. C. Tucker. New York and London: W. W. Norton and Company: 469–500.

McAdam, D. (1982). *Political Process and the Development of Black Insurgency, 1930–1970.* Chicago and London: The University of Chicago Press.

McAdam, D. (1983). Tactical Innovation and the Pace of Insurgency. *American Sociological Review* 48: 735–54.

McCarthy, J. D., C. McPhail, et al. (1996). Images of Protest: Dimensions of Selection Bias in Media Coverage of Washington Demonstrations, 1982 and 1991. *American Sociological Review* 61: 478–99.

McCarthy, J. D. and M. N. Zald (1977). Resource Mobilization and Social Movements: A Partial Theory. *American Journal of Sociology* 82: 1212–41.

McFeeley, T. (2000). Getting it Straight: A Review of the Gays in the Military Debate. In *Creating Change: Sexuality, Public Policy, and Civil Rights,* eds. J. D'Emilio, W. B. Turner, and U. Vaid. New York: St. Martin's Press: 236–50.

McGarry, M. and F. Wasserman (1998). *Becoming Visible: An Illustrated History of Lesbian and Gay Life in Twentieth-Century America.* New York: Penguin Studio.

Meier, A. and E. Rudwick (1973). *CORE: A Study in the Civil Rights Movement, 1942–1968.* New York: Oxford University Press.

Meier, A. and E. Rudwick (1976). Attorneys Black and White: A Case Study of Race Relations within the NAACP. *The Journal of American History* 62(4 [March]): 913–46.

Melucci, A. (1985). The Symbolic Challenge of Contemporary Movements. *Social Research* 52: 789–816.

Melucci, A. (1988). Getting Involved: Identity and Mobilization in Social Movements. *International Social Movement Research* 1: 329–48.

Melucci, A. (1989). *Nomads of the Present: Social Movements and Individual Needs in Contemporary Society.* Philadelphia: Temple University Press.

Melucci, A. (1995). The Process of Collective Identity. In *Social Movements and Culture,* eds. H. Johnston and B. Klandermans. Minneapolis: University of Minnesota Press: 41–63.

Meyer, D. and S. Staggenborg (1996). Movements, Countermovements, and the Structure of Political Opportunity. *American Journal of Sociology* 101: 1628–60.

Meyer, D. S. (2002). Opportunities and Identities: Bridge-Building in the Study of Social Movements. In *Social Movements: Identity, Culture, and the State*, eds. D. S. Meyer, N. Whittier, and B. Robnett. New York: Oxford University Press: 3–21.

Miller, F. D. (1983). The End of SDS and the Emergence of Weatherman: Demise through Success. *Social Movements of the Sixties and Seventies*. J. Freeman. New York: Longman: 279–97.

Minkoff, D. (1993). The Organization of Survival: Women's and Racial-Ethnic Voluntarist and Activist Organizations. *Social Forces* 71: 887–908.

Mohr, J. W. (1998). Measuring Meaning Structures. *Annual Review of Sociology* 24: 345–70.

Moody, J. and D. R. White (2003). Structural Cohesion and Embeddedness: A Hierarchical Concept of Social Groups. *American Sociological Review* 68(1): 103–27.

Moraga, C. and G. Anzaldua, eds. (1981). *This Bridge Called My Back: Writings By Radical Women of Color*. New York: Kitchen Table: Women of Color Press.

Morris, A. (1984). *The Origins of the Civil Rights Movement: Black Communities Organizing for Change*. New York: Free Press.

Morris, A. (1993). Birmingham Confrontation Reconsidered. *American Sociological Review* 58: 621–36.

Morris, A. and A. Ghaziani (2005). DuBoisian Sociology: A Watershed of Professional and Public Sociology. *Souls* 7(3–4): 47–54.

Morris, A. and C. Herring (1987). Theory and Research in Social Movements: A Critical Review. *Annual Review of Political Science* 2: 137–98.

Morris, A. D. and C. M. Mueller, eds. (1992). *Frontiers in Social Movement Theory*. New Haven, Conn.: Yale University Press.

Mottl, T. L. (1980). The Analysis of Countermovements. *Social Problems* 27(5): 620–35.

Mukerji, C. and M. Schudson (1991). Introduction: Rethinking Popular Culture. *Rethinking Popular Culture*. M. Schudson. Berkeley: University of California Press: 1–61.

Murdoch, J. and D. Price (2001). *Courting Justice: Gay Men and Lesbians v. the Supreme Court*. New York: Basic Books.

Murray, R. (1996). *Images in the Dark: An Encyclopedia of Gay and Lesbian Film and Video*. New York: Plume.

Murray, S. O. (1996). *American Gay*. Chicago: The University of Chicago Press.

Mushaben, J. M. (1989). The Struggle Within: Conflict, Consensus, and Decision Making among National Coordinators and Grass-Roots Organizers in the

West German Peace Movement. *International Social Movement Research* 2: 267–98.

Namaste, V. K. (2000). *Invisible Lives: The Erasure of Transsexual and Trans-gendered People.* Chicago: The University of Chicago Press.

Namaste, V. K. (2005). *Sex Change, Social Change: Reflections on Identity, Institutions, and Imperialism.* Toronto, Ontario: Women's Press.

Nestle, J., C. Howell, et al., eds. (2002). *Gender Queer: Voices from Beyond the Sexual Binary.* New York: Alyson Books.

Neuendorf, K. A. (2002). *The Content Analysis Guidebook.* Thousand Oaks, Calif.: Sage.

Norris, P. (2001). *Digital Divide : Civic Engagement, Information Poverty, and the Internet Worldwide.* New York: Cambridge University Press.

Oberschall, A. (1973). *Social Conflict and Social Movements.* Englewood Cliffs, N.J.: Prentice Hall.

Oliver, P. E. (1993). Formal Models of Collective Action. *Annual Review of Sociology* 19: 271–300.

Oliver, P. E. and G. M. Maney (2000). Political Processes and Local Newspaper Coverage of Protest Events: From Selection Bias to Triadic Interactions. *American Journal of Sociology* 106(2): 463–505.

Oliver, P. E. and D. J. Myers (1999). How Events Enter the Public Sphere: Conflict, Location, and Sponsorship in Local Newspaper Coverage of Public Events. *American Journal of Sociology* 105(1): 38–87.

Olson, M. Jr. (1965). *The Logic of Collective Action.* Cambridge, Mass.: Harvard University Press.

Ortiz, D. G., D. J. Myers, et al. (2005). Where Do We Stand with Newspaper Data. *Mobilization* 10(3): 397–419.

Padgug, R. A. (1989). Gay Villain, Gay Hero: Homosexuality and the Social Construction of AIDS. In *Passion and Power: Sexuality in History,* eds. K. Peiss and C. Simmons. Philadelphia: Temple University Press: 293–313.

Park, R. E. and E. W. Burgess (1921). *Introduction to the Science of Society.* Chicago: The University of Chicago Press.

Parsons, T. (1945). Racial and Religious Differences as Factors in Group Tension. *Approaches to National Unity.* L. Bryson, L. Finkelstein, and R. M. MacIver. New York: Harper Brothers: 182–99.

Parsons, T. (1949). *The Structure of Social Action.* Glencoe, Ill.: Free Press.

Patton, C. (1993). Tremble, Hetero Swine! In *Fear of a Queer Planet,* ed. M. Warner. Minneapolis: University of Minnesota Press: 143–77.

Patton, M. Q. (1987). *How to Use Qualitative Methods in Evaluation.* Newbury Park, Calif.: Sage.

Penelope, J. (1992). *Call Me Lesbian: Lesbian Lives, Lesbian Theory.* Freedom, Calif.: Crossing Press.

Perry, T. D. and T. L. P. Swicegood (1990). *Don't Be Afraid Anymore: The Story of Reverend Troy Perry and the Metropolitan Community Churches.* New York: St. Martin's Press.

Piven, F. F. and R. Cloward (1977). *Poor People's Movements: Why They Succeed, How They Fail.* New York: Vintage.

Polikoff, N. D. (2000). Raising Children: Lesbian and Gay Parents Face the Public and the Courts. In *Creating Change: Sexuality, Public Policy, and Civil Rights,* eds. J. D'Emilio, R. H. Turner, and U. Vaid. New York: St. Martin's Press: 305–35.

Polletta, F. (1997). Culture and Its Discontents: Recent Theorizing on the Cultural Dimensions of Protest. *Sociological Inquiry* 67(4): 431–50.

Polletta, F. (2002). *Freedom Is An Endless Meeting: Democracy in American Social Movements.* Chicago: The University of Chicago Press.

Polletta, F. and J. M. Jasper (2001). Collective Identity and Social Movements. *Annual Review of Sociology* 27: 283–305.

Porter, T. M. (1995). *Trust in Numbers: The Pursuit of Objectivity in Science and Public Life.* Princeton, N.J.: Princeton University Press.

Queen, C. (1999). Strangers at Home: Bisexuals in the Queer Movement. In *The Columbia Reader on Lesbians and Gay Men in Media, Society, & Politics,* eds. L. Gross and J. D. Woods. New York: Columbia University Press: 105–8.

Radicalesbians (1970). *The Woman-Identified Woman.* Pittsburgh: KNOW Inc.

Radway, J. A. (1984). *Reading the Romance: Women, Patriarch, and Popular Literature.* Chapel Hill, N.C.: University of North Carolina Press.

Rich, A. (1980). Compulsory Heterosexuality and Lesbian Existence. *Signs: Journal of Women in Culture and Society* 5(Summer): 631–60.

Rimmerman, C. A., ed. (1996). *Gay Rights, Military Wrongs: Political Perspectives on Lesbians and Gays in the Military.* New York: Garland.

Rimmerman, C. A. (2000). Beyond Political Mainstreaming: Reflections on Lesbian and Gay Organizations and the Grassroots. In *The Politics of Gay Rights,* eds. C. A. Rimmerman, K. D. Wald, and C. Wilcox. Chicago: The University of Chicago Press: 54–78.

Rimmerman, C. A. (2000). A Friend in the White House? Reflections on the Clinton Presidency. In *Creating Change: Sexuality, Public Policy, and Civil Rights,* eds. J. D'Emilio, W. B. Turner, and U. Vaid. New York: St. Martin's Press: 43–56.

Ringer, R. J., ed. (1994). *Queer Words, Queer Images: Communication and the Construction of Homosexuality.* New York: New York University Press.

Robinson, P. (2005). *Queer Wars: The New Gay Right and Its Critics.* Chicago: The University of Chicago Press.

Robnett, B. (1997). *How Long? How Long? African-American Women in the Struggle for Civil Rights.* New York: Oxford University Press.

Rosenberg, R., J. Scagliotti, et al. (1984). *Before Stonewall.* Directed by G. Schiller. New York: First Run Features.

Ross, E. A. (1920). *The Principles of Society*. New York: The Century Company.

Runkle, Patrick. Prop 22 Causes Ballot Box Deja Vu. http://journalism.berkeley.edu/projects/prop22/runkleb.html (accessed August 12, 2004).

Rupp, L. J. and V. Taylor (1987). *Survival in the Doldrums: The American Women's Rights Movement, 1945 to the 1960s*. New York: Oxford University Press.

Rupp, L. J. and V. Taylor (2003). *Drag Queens at the 801 Cabaret*. Chicago: The University of Chicago Press.

Russo, V. (1987). *The Celluloid Closet: Homosexuality in the Movies*. New York: Perennial.

Ryan, B. (1989). Ideological Purity and Feminism: The U.S. Women's Movement from 1966 to 1975. *Gender & Society* 3: 239–57.

Sahlins, M. (1981). *Historical Metaphors and Mythical Realities: Structure in the Early History of the Sandwich Islands Kingdom*. Ann Arbor, Mich.: University of Michigan Press.

Sahlins, M. (1985). *Islands of History*. Chicago: The University of Chicago Press.

Scagliotti, J., J. Baus, et al. (1999). *After Stonewall*. Directed by J. Scagliotti. New York: First Run Features.

Schartz, R. L. (1993). New Alliances, Strange Bedfellows: Lesbians, Gay Men, and AIDS. In *Sisters, Sexperts, Queers: Beyond the Lesbian Nation*, ed. A. Stein. New York: Penguin: 230–44.

Schlager, N., ed. (1998). *Gay and Lesbian Almanac*. Detroit and New York: St. James Press.

Schudson, M. (1989). How Culture Works: Perspectives from Media Studies on the Efficacy of Symbols. *Theory and Society* 18(2): 153–80.

Sedgwick, E. K. (1990). *Epistemology of the Closet*. Berkeley: University of California Press.

Seidman, S. (1993). Identity and Politics in a "Postmodern" Gay Culture: Some Historical and Conceptual Notes. In *Fear of a Queer Planet: Queer Politics and Social Theory*, ed. M. Warner. Minneapolis and London: University of Minnesota Press: 105–42.

Seidman, S. (1994). Symposium: Queer Theory/Sociology: A Dialogue. *Sociological Theory* 12: 166–77.

Seidman, S., ed. (1996). *Queer Theory/Sociology*. Oxford, UK: Blackwell Publishers.

Seidman, S. (1997). *Difference Troubles*. Cambridge, UK: Cambridge University Press.

Sewell, W. H. Jr. (1999). The Concept(s) of Culture. In *Beyond the Cultural Turn: New Directions in the Study of Society and Culture*, ed. L. Hunt. Berkeley: University of California Press: 35–61.

Shadish, W. R., T. D. Cook, et al. (2002). *Experimental and Quasi-Experimental*

Designs for Generalized Causal Inference. New York: Houghton Mifflin Company.

Shenk, D. and S. L. Silberman (1994). *Skeleton Key.* New York: Doubleday.

Shilts, R. (1982). *The Mayor of Castro Street: The Life and Times of Harvey Milk.* New York: St. Martin's Press.

Shilts, R. (1987). *And the Band Played On: Politics, People, and the AIDS Epidemic.* New York: St. Martin's Press.

Shilts, R. (1993). *Conduct Unbecoming: Lesbians and Gays in the U.S. Military.* New York: St. Martin's Press.

Shively, J. (1992). Cowboys and Indians: Perceptions of Western Films Among American Indians and Anglos. *American Sociological Review* 57: 725–34.

Simmel, G. (1955). *Conflict and the Web of Group-Affiliations.* New York: Free Press.

Skrentny, J. D. (1996). *The Ironies of Affirmative Action: Politics, Culture, and Justice in America.* Chicago: The University of Chicago Press.

Smelser, N. J. (1963). *Theory of Collective Behavior.* New York: Free Press.

Smith, J., J. D. McCarthy, et al. (2001). From Protest to Agenda Building: Description Bias in Media Coverage of Protest Events in Washington, D.C. *Social Forces* 79(4): 1397–1423.

Smith, N. (2000). Three Marches, Many Lessons. In *Creating Change: Sexuality, Public Policy, and Civil Rights,* eds. J. D'Emilio, W. B. Turner, and U. Vaid. New York: St. Martin's Press: 438–50.

Smith, R. A. and D. P. Haider-Markel (2002). *Gay and Lesbian Americans and Political Participation.* Santa Barbara, Calif.: ABC-CLIO.

Snow, D. A. and L. Anderson (1987). Identity Work among the Homeless: The Verbal Construction and Avowal of Personal Identities. *American Journal of Sociology* 92: 1336–71.

Snow, D. A. and R. D. Benford (1988). Ideology, Frame Resonance, and Participant Mobilzation. *International Social Movement Research* 1: 197–217.

Snow, D. A. and R. D. Benford (1992). Master Frames and Cycles of Protest. In *Frontiers in Social Movement Theory,* eds. A. Morris and C. M. Mueller. New Haven, Conn.: Yale University Press: 133–55.

Snow, D. A. and D. McAdam (2000). Identity Work Processes in the Context of Social Movements: Clarifying the Identity/Movement Nexus. In *Self, Identity, and Social Movements,* eds. S. Stryker, T. J. Owens, and R. W. White. Minneapolis: University of Minnesota Press: 41–67.

Snow, D. A., E. B. Rochford Jr., et al. (1986). Frame Alignment Processes, Micromobilization, and Movement Participation. *American Sociological Review* 51(4): 464–81.

Staggenborg, S. (1995). Can Feminist Organizations Be Effective? In *Feminist Organizations: Harvest of the New Women's Movement,* eds. M. M. Ferree and P. Y. Martin. Philadelphia: Temple University Press: 339–55.

Stein, A. (1992). Sisters and Queers: The Decentering of Lesbian Feminism. *Socialist Review* 22: 33–55.

Stein, A. (1997). *Sex and Sensibility: Stories of a Lesbian Generation.* Berkeley, Calif.: University of California Press.

Stein, A. and K. Plummer (1994). "I Can't Even Think Straight": "Queer" Theory and the Missing Sexual Revolution in Sociology. *Sociological Theory* 12: 178–87.

Sterba, J. P. (1994). *Morality in Practice.* Belmont: Wadsworth Publishing Company.

Stern, A. J., S. Tarrow, et al. (1971). Factions and Opinion Groups in European Mass Parties. Some Evidence from a Study of Italian Socialist Activists. *Comparative Politics* 3(4): 529–59.

Stockdill, B. C. (2001). Forging a Multidimensional Oppositional Consciousness: Lessons from Community-Based AIDS Activism. In *Oppositional Consciousness: The Subjective Roots of Social Protest,* eds. J. Mansbridge and A. Morris. Chicago: The University of Chicago Press: 204–37.

Stockdill, B. C. (2003). *Activism Against AIDS: At the Intersections of Sexuality, Race, Gender, and Class.* Boulder, Colo.: Lynne Rienner.

Streitmatter, R. (1995). *Unspeakable: The Rise of the Gay and Lesbian Press in America.* Boston, Mass.: Faber and Faber.

Stryker, S., T. J. Owens, et al., eds. (2000). *Self, Identity, and Social Movements.* Minneapolis: University of Minnesota Press.

Suffredini, K. S. (2005). What a Difference a Decade Makes: Lesbian, Gay, Bisexual and Transgender Nondiscrimination Law and Policy in the United States. *The Diversity Factor* 13(1): 18–24.

Sullivan, A., ed. (1997). *Same-Sex Marriage: Pro and Con, A Reader.* New York: Vintage Books.

Swidler, A. (1986). Culture in Action: Symbols and Strategies. *American Sociological Review* 51: 273–86.

Swidler, A. (1995). Cultural power and social movements. *Social Movements and Culture.* B. Klandermans. Minneapolis, University of Minnesota Press: 25–40.

Swidler, A. (2001). *Talk of Love: How Culture Matters.* Chicago: University of Chicago Press.

Taylor, V. (1989). Social Movement Continuity: The Women's Movement in Abeyance. *American Sociological Review* 54: 761–75.

Taylor, V. and L. J. Rupp (1993). Women's Culture and Lesbian Feminist Activism: A Reconsideration of Cultural Feminism. *Signs: Journal of Women in Culture and Society* 19: 33–61.

Taylor, V. and N. E. Whittier (1992). Collective Identity in Social Movement Communities. In *Frontiers in Social Movement Theory,* eds. A. D. Morris and C. McClurg. New Haven, Conn.: Yale University Press: 104–29.

Thompson, L. (1999). *Making the Team: A Guide for Managers.* Englewood Cliffs, New Jersey: Prentice Hall.

Thompson, M., ed. (1994). *Long Road to Freedom: The Advocate History of the Gay and Lesbian Movement.* New York: St. Martin's Press.

Tilly, C. (1978). *From Mobilization to Revolution.* Reading, Mass.: Addison-Wesley.

Timmons, S. (1990). *The Trouble with Harry Hay: Founder of the Modern Gay Movement.* Boston, Mass.: Alyson Publications.

Tin, L-G. (2007). *Dictionary of Homophobia: A Global History of Gay and Lesbian Experience.* Vancouver, B.C.: Arsenal Pulp Press.

Turner, W. B. (2000). *A Genealogy of Queer Theory.* Philadelphia: Temple University Press.

Turner, W. B. (2000). Mirror Images: Lesbian/Gay Civil Rights in the Carter and Reagan Administrations. In *Creating Change: Sexuality, Public Policy, and Civil Rights,* eds. J. D'Emilio, W. B. Turner, and U. Vaid. New York: St. Martin's Press: 3–28.

Tylor, E. B. ([1871] 1958). *Primitive Culture: Researches into the Development of Mythology, Philosophy, Religion, Art, and Custom.* Gloucester, Mass.: Smith.

Uncle Donald's Castro Street. Save Our Children: Anita Bryant's 1977 Anti-Gay Campaign. http://thecastro.net/bryant.html (accessed August 12, 2004).

Vaid, U. (1994), foreword to*My American History: Lesbian and Gay Life During the Reagan/Bush Years,* by S. Schulman. New York: Routledge: xi–xiii.

Vaid, U. (1995). *Virtual Equality: The Mainstreaming of Gay and Lesbian Liberation.* New York: Anchor Books.

Vezeris, S. (1995). History of the Rainbow Flag. In *Out in All Directions: The Almanac of Gay and Lesbian America,* eds. L. Witt, S. Thomas, and E. Marcus. New York: Warner Books: 435.

Von Eschen, D., J. Kirk, et al. (1969). The Disintegration of the Negro Non-Violent Movement. *Journal of Peace Research* 6(3): 215–34.

Waite, L. G. (2001). Divided Consciousness: The Impact of Black Elite Consciousness on the 1966 Chicago Freedom Movement. In *Oppositional Consciousness: The Subjective Roots of Social Protest,* eds. J. Mansbridge and A. Morris. Chicago and London: The University of Chicago Press: 170–203.

Walker, T. W., Ed. (1987). *Reagan versus the Sandinistas.* Boulder, Colo.: Westview Press.

Walsh, E. and S. Cable (1989). Realities, Images, and Management Dilemmas in Social Movement Organizations: The Three Mile Island Experience. *International Social Movement Research* 2: 199–211.

Walters, S. D. (2001). *All the Rage: The Story of Gay Visibility in America.* Chicago: The University of Chicago Press.

Warner, M., ed. (1993). *Fear of a Queer Planet: Queer Politics and Social Theory.* Minneapolis: University of Minnesota Press.

Weber, M. (1930). *The Protestant Ethic and the Spirit of Capitalism*. London and New York: Routledge.

Weber, M. (1946). The Social Psychology of the World Religions. In *From Max Weber: Essays in Sociology*, ed. C. W. Mills. New York: Oxford University Press: 267–301.

Weber, M. (1949). *The Methodology of the Social Sciences*. Glencoe, Ill.: Free Press.

Wellman, B. and C. Haythornthwaite, eds. (2002). *The Internet in Everyday Life*. Malden, Mass: Blackwell.

Wertheimer, D. M. (2000). The Emergence of a Gay and Lesbian Antiviolence Movement. In *Creating Change: Sexuality, Public Policy, and Civil Rights*, eds. J. D'Emilio, R. H. Turner, and U. Vaid. New York: St. Martin's Press: 261–78.

White, H. C. Notes on the Constituents of Social Structure. Thesis, department of sociology, Harvard University, 1965.

White, H. C. (1992). *Identity and Control: A Structural Theory of Social Action*. Princteon, N.J.: Princeton University Press.

White, J. B. and E. J. Langer (1999). Horizontal Hostility: Relations Between Similar Minority Groups. *Journal of Social Issues* 55(3): 537–59.

Whittier, N. (1997). Political Generations, Micro-Cohorts, and the Transformation of Social Movements. *American Sociological Review* 62: 760–78.

Wilde, M. J. (2004). How Culture Mattered at Vatican II: Collegiality Trumps Authority in the Council's Social Movement Organizations. *American Sociological Review* 69: 576–602.

Williams, R. (1976). *Keywords: A Vocabulary of Culture and Society*. New York: Oxford University Press.

Williams, R. (1981). *The Sociology of Culture*. New York: Schocken Books.

Williams, R. H. (1995). Constructing the Public Good: Social Movements and Cultural Resources. *Social Problems* 42(1): 124–44.

Wilson, A. (1999). Just Add Water: Searching for the Bisexual Politic. In *The Columbia Reader on Lesbians and Gay Men in Media, Society, & Politics*, eds. L. Gross and J. D. Woods. New York: Columbia University Press: 108–12.

Witt, L., S. Thomas, et al., eds. (1995). *Out in All Directions: The Almanac of Gay and Lesbian America*. New York: Warner Books.

Wittgenstein, L. (1953). *Philosophical Investigations*. Oxford, UK: Blackwell.

Wood, R. L. (1999). Religious Culture and Political Action. *Sociological Theory* 17(3): 307–32.

Wuthnow, R. (1987). *Meaning and Moral Order: Explorations in Cultural Analysis*. Berkeley, Calif.: University of California Press.

Wuthnow, R. (1989). *Communities of Discourse: Ideology and Social Structure in the Reformation, the Enlightenment, and European Socialism*. Cambridge, Mass.: Harvard University Press.

Wuthnow, R., J. D. Hunter, et al. (1984). *Cultural Analysis: The Work of Peter L. Berger, Mary Douglas, Michel Foucault, and Jurgen Habermas.* Boston, Mass.: Routledge & Kegan Paul.

Yang, A. S. (1997). Trends: Attitudes toward Homosexuality. *Public Opinion Quarterly* 61(3): 477–507.

Zald, M. N. and R. Ash (1966). Social Movement Organizations: Growth, Decline, and Change. *Social Forces* 44: 327–40.

Zald, M. N. and J. D. McCarthy (1980). Social Movement Industries: Competition and Cooperation among Movement Organizations. *Research in Social Movements, Conflict, and Change* 3: 1–20.

Zald, M. N. and M. Useem (1987). Movement and Countermovement Interaction: Mobilization, Tactics, and State Involvement. *Social Movements in an Organizational Society.* M. N. Zald and J. D. McCarthy. New Brunswick, N.J.: Transaction: 247–71.

Index